MENTAL HEALTH IN

CHILDREN

840772

GENETICS, FAMILY

AND COMMUNITY STUDIES

MENTAL HEALTH IN CHILDREN
VOLUMES I, II AND III

Details of Volume I
Library of Congress Catalog Card No.   74-27252
International Standard Book Number   0-9600290-7-9

MENTAL HEALTH IN CHILDREN

EDITED BY

D. V. SIVA SANKAR

VOLUME I

CONTRIBUTING AUTHORS

Harry J. Aponte, Christopher Bagley, Harvey A. Barocas, Brian Bell, Dorothy F. Berezin, Ruth D. Bruun, Christo Christozov, Donald Cohen, Armando R. Favazza, Richard Frank, John H. Fryer, Rachel Gittelman-Klein, Paul N. Graffagnino, Myron A. Hofer, Leonard Hollander, Adelaide S. Hulse, Marvin S. Hurvich, Ricahrd L. Jenkins, Francis P. Kehoe, Judith Klotz, Narottam Lal, Erica Loutsch, Saranoff A. Mednick, Julien Mendlewicz, James Minard, Elaine Mura, Bernard L. Pacella, Bertram Pepper, Abdul C. Raman, Fini Schulsinger, Brij B. Sethi, Arthur K. Shapiro, Don Shapiro, Elaine Shapiro, James H. Shore, D. V. Siva Sankar, James R. Stabenau, Robert J. F. Stepney, John S. Strauss, Richard D. Sweet, Peter H. Venables, Hilmar Wagner and Norman F. Watt.

PJD PUBLICATIONS LIMITED

WESTBURY, N.Y. 11590

PREFACE

My original training is in the field of biochemistry, but I have been involved for the past many years in the clinical, demographic, psychopharmacological and other subdisciplines of mental health. I entered the fascinating field of the biochemistry of mental health under the tutelage of Dr. Lauretta Bender, with the ambition ($\bar{a}$ *la* Pauling) of attempting to describe schizophrenia as a monogenic disorder. I have not been successful, nor would I think that anyone can ever show that *"schizophrenia"* is a unitary disease. It is the total effect of a behavior equilibrium delicately balanced on the psychobiological and sociodynamic events of morphogenesis, of maturation and of life patterns and the psychobiologically defined abilities to cope with the daily stresses and anxieties. One could certainly be rehabilitated to handle these, even by behavior modification or transcendental meditation, if the involvement of the biological components is not deep.

Seven years ago, in the Epilogue to my previous book, *"Schizophrenia - Current Concepts and Research"*, I wished that the next seven years may be fat ones for the areas of mental health. Since 1968, a lot of new events have happened in the handling of mental disease. Some for good and some not so good. The spirit of "anti-intellectualism" is partly in vogue now, and again the benefits of science and technology are being taken for granted. This is partly because the plethora of technological modifications of human living are engendering confusion as to the basic human relations. The family unit has become more nuclear, but again Man may be rediscovering that the most important object of man's study is Man himself. Our politics are more jumbled up, our Presidents are being torn down to subhuman indignities and even the right of parents as guardians of children is being questioned under the concept of pediatric rights. This book is partly conceived against such a background and is partly the fulfilment of a Conference sponsored by the Eastern Psychiatric Research Association in 1974.

I would have certainly not been able to bring forth these three volumes and the one on *"Psychopharmacology of Childhood"* without the kind patience and help from the many contributors. Writing or editing a book, one may not realize it, puts a considerable amount of stress on the author or editor's family life, and one can only thank heavens for little girls that become such wonderful wives as mine did.

Autumn, 1975   D. V. Siva Sankar

New York   Editor

TABLE OF CONTENTS

MENTAL HEALTH IN CHILDREN, Volume I
Edited By D. V. Siva Sankar
Copyright © 1975 by
PJD Publications Ltd., Westbury, N.Y.

MULTITHEMIC ETIOLOGY [MTE]

AND PROFILE BASED THERAPY [PBT]

IN MENTAL DISEASE

D. V. Siva Sankar
Queens Children's Psychiatric Center
Bellerose, N. Y. 11426

Mental health is a matter of comprehensive psychobiology. The word, 'Schizophrenia(s)' is both a fortunate and an unfortunate choice - fortunate because it brought forth in a single word-expression the *"in toto"* problems of mental health; unfortunate because it stylzed, rigorized and formalized a disease of immense diversity into what could often be mistaken for a single entity. Thus "schizophrenia" may be a myth, but the fact of mental disease is very real in our modern heterogeneous cultures and nuclear families, so excellently illustrated by the American culture. Culture, incidentally, is contagious because behavior is patterned after imitating and "imprinting". Humanity has a right to *freedom from anxiety* amongst other freedoms and our cultures threaten this hardly recognized and hardly popular freedom.

Then came biochemistry, the science that was thrust into leadership because of its achievements in other fields. Leadership should be given a leading hand; but "machine minds" will always yield a "stupid answer" in response to a "stupid question". However, the most important answer that basic sciences have yielded in the fields of mental health, is that *mental health or its aberrations are not singular simplifiable entities* like malaria or syphilis, but multitudinous in etiology, multitudinous in course of disease and again multitudinous in prognosis. This painful answer was not pleasing enough to the powers to be, basic sciences were relegated to the second or third row, and politics of science administration took over. I would like to maintain my theories in this plethora of crossing inroads and outroads of the principles and practices of mental health, even at the risk of being "unpolitical".

I have previously suggested (1) that most living organisms can be subdivided into four groups in their reactions to environmental stresses and anxieties:

(1).　Those that can handle every day stresses and anxieties without significant psychosomatic dysfunction.

(2).　Those that manifest psychosomatic problems of a somatic nature in response to stress and anxiety. These responses include gastrointestinal, cardiac, respiratory, urogenital, sexual and other "maladies".

(3).　Those that manifest psychiatric aberrations not necessarily accompanied by somatic aberrations. These would include even a "psychiatric" or "nervous" breakdown. These are in the truest sense of the word, "pseudopsychopathic". The prognosis is good. Psychotherapy with or without pharmacotherapy will be beneficial depending on the intensity of the psychobiological response to the anxiety and the defences and compensations built up for self-protection. This group suffers from a "Biodynamic Inequilibrium".

(4).　The fourth group consists of those that have a deeper involvement of biological dysfunction in the generation and lack of resistance to psychiatric disease. These are the hardest to treat. They do not benefit from psychotherapy. Pharmacotherapy is at best supportive. Rehabilitation to a functional level is the goal of treatment.

In all the above discussion, there are three factors involved: (a). The biological component (b). The developmental, psychological components and (c). The environmental, cultural, socio-economic components. A simple, transient involvement of the environmental stresses is most readily amenable to therapy. Blessed is the Psychiatric Facility that can screen their admissions and admit only these, because their success rate will be high. The deeper the biological component, the more resistant is the dysfunction to therapeutic modalities. It is then no longer a matter of "biodynamic inequilibrium" but of congenital, biologically defined psychopathology. The biological etiology, of course, is necessarily of a "multi-themic" nature.

Equations of a "sort of" mathematical nature were also developed (1). Stress in the environment is seen as the initial event (Bender called this the "precipitating crisis"). This event can cause or result in (1) Reaction or response (2) Anxiety and (3) Compensation through psychobiological channels. In other words, the following quotients may be defined:

The Response Quotient dR/dS

The Anxiety Quotient dA/dS

The Compensation Quotient dC/dS

The Anxiety Content Quotient dA/dR

The Compensation Content Quotient dC/dR

dC/dt, dR/dt and dA/dt are (reactivity) rate quotients with respect to time t.

Dr. Zubin has since then used the words "coping" and "vulnerability" in lieu of some of the above Quotients. Vulnerability is dependent on the quotients that define the content of anxiety (A) and compensation (C) in the given response to a stimulus (S). It is possible that the response quotient in two given individuals may be comparable, but the content of anxiety and compensatory defences may widely differ. Again, there is one unique situation, where a person may generate anxiety in response to either a "true" or "false" internal psychobiological event, as opposed to an environmental, external stimulus. This is often the case in cases where the mental disease is compounded by "paranoia" or "hallucinations". Some illustrative applications of these equations were also presented in the previous paper (1).

Further, besides the general (G) factors that may be common to most of the patients (example, lackadaisical toilet habits, or metabolic "waywardness") there may be involved special (S) factors peculiar to each person, in the overall definition of psychopathology.

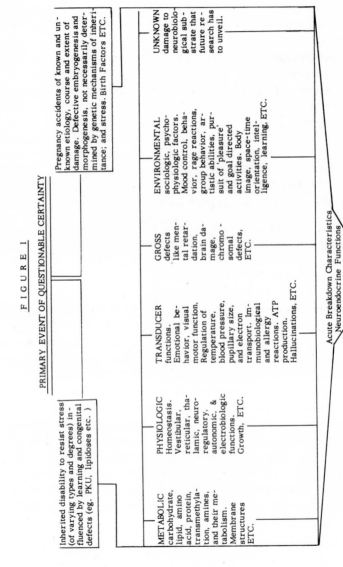

F I G U R E I

PRIMARY EVENT OF QUESTIONABLE CERTAINTY

TABLE I

Possible etiological types of schizophrenia*

I. Overt biological disease:
Leading primarily to psychobiological dysfunction
Leading secondarily to psychobiological dysfunction

II. Subclinical abnormalities
Ordinary stress leads to psychiatric dysfunction
Abnormal stress leads to psychiatric dysfunction

III. Genetic abnormalities

IV. Defective embryogenesis

---

*Genetic predisposition on a polygenic basis is tacitly assumed in all these cases.

Final equilibrium in personality is a delicate balance depending on a multitude of variables mentioned above. In other words, the most important contribution of basic research to psychopathology is the demonstration that mental disease is not a unitary disease. The nature, scope and prognosis are also very widely divergent. We need to consider each case on its own "entirety" and not try to have unitary and universal treatment goals.

The picture of mental health in children is all the more complicated by developmental stages that the children go through during these precious years. From development of behavior and of emotional patterns to having their teeth knocked out by "Johnny" in the environment, the hostility to existing life patterns etc. are all so very important in the final picture of the "happy, healthy" adult. The requirement for security, again the freedom to learn how to face danger, without falling prey to it, the appropriate venting of irritations and frustrations, all these complicate the picture of mental health in children ever so much.

Then we come to the question of "treatment" and "treatment goals". In as much as the dysfunction is multithemic, the therapy can never be singular in its modality. All available treatment programs smack of the four or five blindmen trying to figure out what was an elephant. The complete treatment goal depends on the *profile of the total personality* in terms of the four factors enumerated at the very onset. These are the biological, psychological, sociological and personal (S) factors. In other words, what we need is a "PROFILE BASED THERAPY", which is given the abbreviation PBT.

Each adult or child must be evaluated in terms of a complex profile. In as much as the average cost per mental patient has often skyrocketed to about $8,000.00 per patient in recent times, it is certainly worth the expenditure to do special chemistries, genetics, psychological test batteries, socio-dynamic analyses etc. These should be formulated for a general population and the patient's profile compared to these. Even without waiting for somebody to develop profiles and norma for general population, each patient should have a treatment goal based on a comprehensive establishment of a profile. Therapy should be based on this and may include behavior modification, psychiatric support, pharmacotherapy etc. On the other hand, where the prognosis is poor (as it is in many cases of infantile autism), different treatment centers in less expensive areas of the country should be maintained. Even autistic children have special abilities and these should be taken advantage of and put to work in a vocational type environment.

Many psychiatric centers are financed by government agencies at various levels. Most governmental institutions are fettered or are subject to special situations where the overall output is not comparable to that from institutions run on a profit basis. If there is an operational loss, the government simply taxes the people more. Unfortunately, the government is the only agency that we can turn to, in our fight for a right to psychiatric or somatic health. The government is the only agency that is endowed to care for the sick, the weak and the elderly. Alas, this is where all the turmoil starts and never seems to end. We are Republicans, Democrats, cronies and whatever, but rarely are we genuinely humans.

REFERENCES

1. D.V. Siva Sankar: In *"Schizophrenia: Current Concepts and Research."* PJD Publications, Westbury, N.Y. (1969).

MENTAL HEALTH IN CHILDREN, Volume I
Edited By D. V. Siva Sankar

UNTANGLING THE ANTECEDENTS OF SCHIZOPHRENIC BEHAVIORS [1]

John S. Strauss
University of Rochester Medical School
Rochester, N. Y. 14642

Many variables appear to play a role as causal antecedents of schizophrenic behaviors. There is little information, however, to clarify the relative importance of these variables or their interactions. For this reason, only a very incomplete and fragmented picture of causality in this disorder is available.

A major source of this problem has been the apparent complexitites of the cause-effect relationships involved. These complexities arise from several sources. First, schizophrenic behaviors appear to be caused by combinations of antecedent conditions. No variable by itself appears to play a preponderant causal role. Schizophrenia, in this sense, may be different, for example, from certain infectious diseases where a few antecedent variables appear to be necessary and sufficient to account for most occurrences.

---

1   This research was carried out in the Department of Psychiatry of the University of Rochester Medical School and was supported by National Institute of Mental Health Grant #MH-22836-01.

A second complexity arises from the sequential, rather than simultaneous, occurrence of the antecedent conditions to schizophrenia. Many of the antecedents of adult schizophrenia date from childhood experiences which are themselves preceded by important perinatal factors, preceded in turn by gestational and genetic variables. This sequential order suggests that the earlier antecedents influence those occurring later so that no assumptions of independence among the antecedents can be made.

A third complicating factor in understanding the causes of schizophrenia arises from problems determining which antecedents have particular roles. Some studies, for example, have suggested that the characteristic of schizophrenia that determines genetic transmission is severity - irrespective of the type of symptoms involved (1). Other studies imply that chronicity may be the major characteristic important in genetic transmission (2), while others imply that symptom type (3) or personality abnormalities such as interpersonal withdrawal (4) may be the most important traits genetically. The possible importance of any one of these characteristics individually implies that each must be evaluated and analyzed in studies of antecedents. Combining them indistinguishably, for example into a diagnostic category, before they can be further validated could mean losing much predictive power and the opportunity to isolate the most crucial variables.

Finally, tracing causal processes in schizophrenia is further complicated by the possiblity that this "disorder" may actually represent many different disorders or even independent traits or behaviors. Behaviors supposedly schizophrenic occur in a wide range of situations. They can occur individually or in various combinations (5). They can even occur in other conditions such as manic depressive disorder (6).

The likelihood that there are complex causal relationships between antecedents and resulting behaviors is certainly not unique to schizophrenia. Complex causation of behavior is common, even in subhuman species. This fact was emphasized by Blumental (7), noting that even the lowly plankton, *Daphnia magna*, is so complex that to predict whether its dance will be mostly horizontal or vertical, the interaction of several variables, temperature, type of lighting, hunger, and presence of food, must be considered. For this organism, when the ambient light is above a certain wave length the direction of dance is primarily horizontal. If the temperature is below a certain level, however, the response to short wave lengths disappears; while if the animals are hungry, the response to longer wave lengths is eliminated. If food is added to a group of hungry *Daphnia*, all movement will be primarily in the vertical direction regardless of the wave length of ambient light. If causality is so complex for the dance of *Daphnia magna*, it is not surprising that many interacting variables may also be involved in a causally complex way with the various schizophrenic behaviors.

Delineating complex causal systems requires the use of special techniques since, as pointed out (7), it is practically impossible to discover by intuition alone the relationships even in a system for only four variables. Nor does attending to one variable while controlling or randomizing others provide a solution, since that approach cannot provide an accurate picture of the overall process involved. It seems likely, therefore, that the causes of schizophrenic behaviors can only be understood through the use of methodology adequate to untangle the complex relationships between the schizophrenic behaviors and the major antecedents by obtaining an overview of their interactions.

Although there is increasing interest in developing such an approach (3, 8-10), it has been extremely difficult to progress towards this goal. This difficulty has been caused primarily by the problems of obtaining data on a large number of antecedent and behavior variables, and problems analyzing their combined effects and interactions. This report is an attempt to suggest an approach for overcoming these problems. The approach consists of four steps: operational definition of the schizophrenic behaviors to be studied; selection of a moderate number of the most promising antecedent variables; collection of reliable data in dimensional form; and use of both proven and exploratory methods for multivariate data analysis.

1. *Operational Definition of the Schizophrenic Behaviors*

The first step in obtaining an overview of the realtion-ships among the antecedent variables and schizophrenic behaviors is to describe clearly the behaviors themselves since these will be the criteria to which the antecedents must relate. Since the diagnosis of schizophrenia, if used without careful description of the component behaviors, is too unreliable for most research or clinical purposes (11), the behavioral criteria used for the diagnosis must be opera-tionally defined.

One way to achieve such a definition is to use opera-tional criteria that are commonly accepted by a consensus of diagnosticians from many backgrounds. Such a set of con-sensus diagnostic criteria has been described elsewhere (12). Another approach for selecting behavioral criteria of schizo-phrenia is to use those clinical features of schizophrenia for which there is evidence of external validity such as a link to genetic or prognostic findings.

These two approaches can be combined by selecting, wherever possible, criterion behaviors that are both widely accepted diagnostically and also have demonstrated external validity. In order to apply this combined approach, criteria can be derived from reports of clinical usage, genetic studies and prognostic studies (3, 5, 13). These reports suggest that four behavior variables (Table 1) might be particularly important as diagnostic criteria. They are: 1) *Positive symptoms* (14). These include so-called active or high energy symptoms such as certain delusions and hallucinations. This group of symptoms is comprised of the most widely used diagnostic criteria for schizophrenia although they may have less prognostic and genetic validity than was once assumed. 2) *Negative symptoms* (14). These include withdrawal and blunting of affect, signs which are commonly used to esta-blish the diagnosis of schizophrenia. These behaviors also appear to have prognostic validity (15). Their genetic valid-ity has not been determined. 3) *Severity.* Although this variable needs to be carefully defined, severity in some sense appears to be genetically as well as clinically important (16). 4) *Course of Disorder.* Ths parameter is considered by some as a major diagnostic criterion (17), by others as a criterion for defining important subtypes of schizophrenia (18), and by others as important genetically (3).

2. *Selection of the Most Promising Antecedent Variables*
The second step in obtaining an overview is to evaluate which variables, according to evidence currently available,

TABLE I

SOME CHARACTERISTICS OF SCHIZOPHRENIC BEHAVIORS

Variables	Examples
1. Positive Symptoms	Delusions, hallucinations
2. Negative Symptoms	Blunted affect, withdrawal
3. Severity	Amount of disability or symptomatology
4. Course of Disorder	Chronic, remittant, recovered

are the most likely antecedents of the schizophrenic behaviors. This selection is important because enough variables must be considered to obtain an overview, but inclusion of too many will make results impossible to interpret.

TABLE II

POSSIBLE ANTECEDENTS OF SCHIZOPHRENIC
BEHAVIORS

Variables	Types of Characteristics
1. Genetic	family member "phenotypes": severity, type, and course of psychopathology, personality type, communication deviance
2. Gestational and Perinatal	complications of pregnancy, birthweight
3. Psychophysiological	autonomic characteristics, perceptual styles
4. Early Development	mothering patterns, family pathology, family communication
5. Early Personality	schizoid, antisocial
6. Later Stresses	leaving home, death in family
7. Treatment Given	long-term institutionalization

Seven possible antecedent variables appear to be of particular importance (Table 2). 1) *Genetic background.* Investigations have demonstrated the importance although not the specific nature of the contribution of genetic antecedents to schizophrenia(1,2,3,19). 2) *Gestational and perinatal factors.* Others (8, 20) have suggested that such factors as birth weight and complications of pregnancy may be important antecedents of schizophrenia. 3) *Psychophysiological characteristics.* Certain types of autonomic activity and patterns of stimulus processing have been suggested as predisposing characteristics of schizophrenia (21, 22). They may also be the genetically transmitted characteristics that serve as the predisposing factors to schizophrenia. 4) *Early developmental experiences.* Parental communication deviance (23) may have an impact on the developing pre-schizophrenic child inhibiting his ability to deal with the world cognitively and affectively. Thought content (24, 25) in terms of type of delusion may often be transmitted through communications from the schizophrenic parent to the pre-schizophrenic child. 5) *"Premorbid" personality characteristics.* Schizoid and antisocial characteristics in children have been found to occur frequently as antecedents of schizophrenic behaviors (26, 27, 28). Some of these personality patterns have also been shown to have an inherited component and thus may represent a genetic link (29). 6) *Precipitating events.* Stresses such as a death in the family or leaving home often occur in an individual's life just prior to the appearance of schizophrenic behaviors (30). These stresses may serve as precipitants contributing to the emergence of the schizophrenic behaviors. 7) *Treatment factors.* Institutionalization (31) even when carried out in a family setting (32) appears to be a major contributor to the apathy, withdrawal, and flatness of affect often considered as characteristic of schizophrenia.

3.   *Collection of Reliable and Dimensional Data.*
The third step for obtaining an overview of the antecedents to schizophrenic behaviors is in the process of data collection. Variables should be reliably and dimensionally defined. The difficulty in applying these principles to studies

of psychopathology has arisen from the problem of translating the often vague but basic clinical data of psychiatric signs, symptoms, and histories to reliable, quantifiable measures. Recently methods have been developed for operationalizing the clinical data of psychiatry through the use of semi-structured interviews (33, 34). These techniques have made it possible to collect reliable data while approximating the type of information used by mental health workers for evaluation and decision making. These methods also have the important characteristic of providing data in a form that facilitates using a variety of alternative techniques for data analysis to explore the effect of different methods for combining variables (35, 36).

Besides promoting reliability, data collection techniques for evaluating causes of schizophrenia should use dimensionally defined variables wherever possible. The need for dimensionally defined data stems from two sources. Such data, describing for example degree for thought disorder or degree of perceptual distortion rather than presence/absence dichotomies, permit accurate ratings that fit the wide range of characteristics found in patients (37, 38). Another advantage of dimensional data is that they permit the use of analytic techniques to evaluate many variables simultaneously without the need to increase the sample size geometrically, as would be required for dichotomized data. Although preferable for these reasons, dimensionalized data also require certain precautions (39).

4.   Methods of Data Analysis.

The fourth step to obtain an overview of the antecedents to schizophrenic behaviors is to use a number of different techniques for multivariate data analysis. The use of many techiques is necessary because any one of several alternative approaches might reveal most accurately the particular kinds of roles and interactions involved. The use of mulivariate procedures is essential because the interactions of the schizophrenic criterion behaviors and the antecedents can only be determined if the identity of the variables is maintained constant during the data analysis procedures. Assumptions that all criterion behaviors can be usefully combined, for example, to indicate simply presence or absence of schizophrenia is unjustified. As described earlier, the occurrence and effects of the different variables are often quite independent. Mixing them without first using the multivariate techniques now available to analyze roles and interactions could obscure the major causal relationships.

The reason for evaluating the many variables both singly and in combination can be shown further by a visual representation. Figure 1 depicts some relationships among the variables that might be most relevant to a clinician; the schizophrenic criteria behaviors and two antecedent sets, Genetic and Personality factors.

One approach suggested by this Figure is the desirability of evaluating the relative importance of the six "index" parent characteristics as possible antecedents of each of the six "index" offspring characteristics, as for example the description of identical delusions in parents and their children (16, 25). Another approach implied by this Figure is to evaluate the interaction of the six variables in the "index" parent as they relate to offspring behavior, investigating whether several variables interact to cause a particular behavior as in the interacting causes for the "dance" of *Daphnia magna*.

In order to analyze the relationships among independent and criterion variables, multivariate analysis of variance, multiple regression analysis, discriminant function analysis, and canonical correlation can be used to evaluate the cumulative contributions of a number of independent variables to a criterion, or for assigning membership to a group (39, 40). For example, a child's score on degree of schizoidness, his level of autonomic reactivity, and the degree of communication deviance in his family could all be analyzed with multiple regression analysis to determine their degree of correlation, both singly and in combination, with level of withdrawal at follow-up. Using discriminant function techniques, these variables could be analyzed to determine their role in predicting whether the child will be

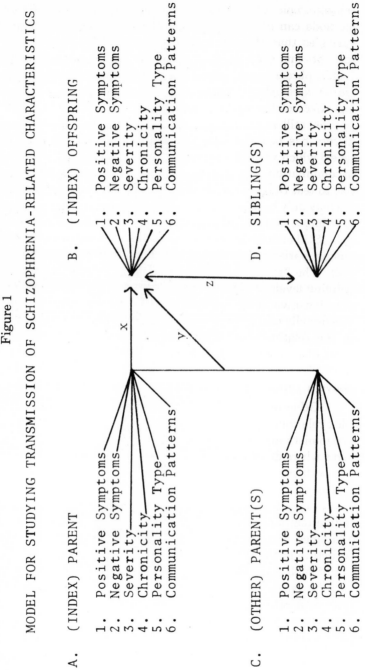

Figure 1

MODEL FOR STUDYING TRANSMISSION OF SCHIZOPHRENIA-RELATED CHARACTERISTICS

A. (INDEX) PARENT

1. Positive Symptoms
2. Negative Symptoms
3. Severity
4. Chronicity
5. Personality Type
6. Communication Patterns

B. (INDEX) OFFSPRING

1. Positive Symptoms
2. Negative Symptoms
3. Severity
4. Chronicity
5. Personality Type
6. Communication Patterns

C. (OTHER) PARENT(S)

1. Positive Symptoms
2. Negative Symptoms
3. Severity
4. Chronicity
5. Personality Type
6. Communication Patterns

D. SIBLING(S)

1. Positive Symptoms
2. Negative Symptoms
3. Severity
4. Chronicity
5. Personality Type
6. Communication Patterns

schizophrenic or non-schizophrenic as an adult.   These methods can also be used to isolate suppressor variables, variables that obscure important correlations between anecedents and schizophrenic behaviors, as for example if the "schizophrenogenic" effect, genetic or psychological, of one parent were being "suppressed" or concealed by a contrasting effect of the other parent.

A still more sophisticated approach to complex predictors has been recently developed which can be used to reveal which variables serve as predictors only if they occur in combination (41). This method would be useful, for example, to test the hypothesis (3) that schizoid behavior early in life may only be a predictor of schizophrenia if the individual also has a genetic predisposition for that disorder.

Still another approach to determining the relationships among variables in clinical problems has been suggested (42). The "stratification" technique provides a method for defining levels or "strata" at which a given variable or combination of variables predicts a given outcome. This method is especially useful for non-linear relationships as for example in the relationship between blood pressure and coronary heart disease where a broad range of blood pressures has no predictive utility, but where the predictive relationship above a certain level increases progressively.

Other more exploratory techniques for analyzing complex relationships among variables have been developed by economists and sociologists dealing with multivariate systems where determination of causes, interactions and effects are both complex and crucial. Two techniques for this kind of analysis are structural equations (43) and recursive equations (44). Structural equations are sets of equations that define relationships within a system. The equations can be combined and compared in an attempt to approximate the structure of the whole system. A psychiatric example of a set of such equations might be: 1) very sick mother plus healthy father plus no environmental stresses equals child with moderate withdrawal; 2) very sick mother plus healthy father plus many environmental stresses equals child with severe withdrawal; 3) very sick mother plus very sick father with no environmental stresses equals child with severe withdrawal.

The use of recursive equations ("path analysis") is another means for defining the interactions among antecedents and schizophrenic behaviors. These equations are of special interest because they provide models for describing and evaluating causal chains. Through the use of partial correlations they describe how much a variable, 'A', helps predict 'B', how much 'B' in turn helps predict 'C' and how 'A' and 'B' together predict 'C'. They could be used, for example, to describe how a given genetic background lessens the error in predicting shizoid personality in childhood; how knowing the presence of schizoid personality in childhood lessens the error in predicting schizophrenic behaviors in adolescence; and how the two antecedents in combination operate to predict schizophrenic behaviors.

Finally, equations reflecting certain concepts of systems analysis need to be used for determining antecedents to schizophrenia. Systems concepts have been increasingly applied to analyzing mental health problems (10, 45), but equations defining these concepts have not. These equations have long been used, however, to understand the relationships within systems that exist in physical and social sciences. The use of such an equation to describe a simple system in physics, for example, is Boyle's law which describes the reciprocal and direct relationships among pressure, temperature, and volume of a gas. An analogous equation for describing systems in schizophrenia has often been implied in family studies when it is said that if a schizophrenic adolescent in a family were to improve, a parent or sibling would be come more pathological to take his place. Many relationships of this type can be operationally stated as general principles and then tested.

Although these various data analysis techniques have important limitations, their application to the study of the antecedents of schizophrenic behaviors is particularly appropriate. They can serve at the very least to help record hypotheses clearly so that they can be tested. Beyond this, they may also help to reveal more precisely the roles and interactions of the most crucial variables.

Application

The need for these techniques at each of the four steps can be readily demonstrated with data already published to suggest ways for modifying studies currently in progress and for constructing future studies. The need for the first step, defining and regularly recording criterion behaviors of schizophrenia (e.g., positive symptoms, negative symptoms, severity, and course) is most apparent in genetic studies. These investigations, which are among the most carefully controlled and documented in schizophrenia research, have provided strong evidence for significant heritability. However, most studies suggest that only certain components of schizophrenia, not an entire syndrome, are found in the "schizophrenic" relatives of schizophrenics. Because of the absence of regularly collected data on the four variables, however, it has not yet been possible to determine which of the characteristics singly or in combination are genetically most important.

The need for the second step, selection of a moderate number of predictor variables, is also shown by genetic studies. Again, the great care with which these studies have been carried out makes it apprent that failure to collect data routinely on certain antecedents, e.g., the major clinical characteristics of parents, has made it difficult to determine which parental characteristics are most related to the development of schizophrenia in offspring.

The importance of the third step, collection of data that are operationally, reliably, and dimensionally defined, can also be demonstrated on results available from genetic studies. The concept of a "schizophrenia spectrum" (4) to account for genetic transmission, may help to explain many perplexing findings. However, until the spectrum is defined in terms of operational dimensions, this concept cannot be replicated or tested in other contexts.

The fourth step, use of a variety of multivariate data analysis techniques, could help clarify the nature of many key relationships. For example, data have been reported in one excellent study (16) describing developmental and clinical characteristics for a series of twins, some of whom were concordant and others discordant for schizophrenia. It might be possible with these data to use discriminant function techniques to determine whether certain characteristics of the index schizophrenic twin would predict degree of concordance for schizophrenia and thus provide clues to the most crucial variables involved.

Another study in which similar multivariate techniques might be applicable (3) is that comparing the ability of different diagnostic methods to predict concordance for schizophrenia among twins. In this sophisticated study, the investigators determined which diagnosticians were most able to predict the characteristics of a twin whose co-twin would be concordantly schizophrenic. If the additional step were made to operationalize the criteria used by the diagnosticians, e.g., by rating characteristics of the twins diagnosed schizophrenic by each and then carrying out a discriminant function analysis, an operational description might be generated describing the diagnostic criteria that are most powerful for predicting twin concordance. These criteria would provide an operational basis for understanding the key variables determining concordance in order to get beyond the more limited impressions derived from attempting to understand the diagnosticians' general orientation.

Conclusion

There are many possible antecedents of the various schizophrenic behaviors. To determine the causal relationships involved, an overview of their roles and interactions must be obtained through the use of the techniques of data collection and analysis described here.

The author expresses his appreciation to Drs. Dean Harper and Howard Iker for their helpful suggestions.

REFERENCES

1. Kringlen, E. Hereditary and social factors in schizophrenic twins. An epidemiological clinical study. In *The Origins of Schizophrenia.* Edited by Romano, J. Proceedings of the first Rochester International Conference on Schizophrenia, March 29-31, 1967, Excerpta Medica Foundation.

2. Heston, L. L. and Denney, D. Interactions between early life experience and biological factors in schizophrenia. In *The Transmission of Schizophrenia.* Edited by Rosenthal, D. and Kety, S. Pergamon Press, New York, (1968).

3. Gottesman, I. I. and Shields, J. *Schizophrenia and Genetics: A Twin Study Vantage Point.* Academic Press, New, York, (1972).

4. Kety, S., Rosenthal, D., Wender, P. H. and Schulsinger, F. The types and prevalence of mental illness in the biological and adoptive families of adopted schizophrenics. In *The Transmission of Schizophrenia.* Edited by Rosenthal, D. and Kety, S. Pergamon Press, New York, (1968).

5. Strauss, J. S., Carpenter, W. T. and Bartko, J. J. Speculations on the processes that underlie schizophrenic symptoms. *Schizophrenia Bull.* In press.

6. Carpenter, W. T., Strauss, J. S. and Muleh, S. *Arch. Gen. Psychiat. 28,* 847, (1973).

7. Blumenthal, M. D. Research strategy in schizophrenia. In *Schizophrenia: Current Concepts and Research.* Edited by Sankar, D. V. S. PJD Publications Ltd, (1969).

8. Sameroff, A. J. and Zax, M. *J. Nerv. Ment. Dis. 157,* 191 (1973).

9. Sameroff, A. J. and Zax, M. *Amer. J. Orthopsychiat. 43,* 744, (1973).

10. Wynne, L. Family communication and the potential for becoming schizophrenic and/or human. Fortyfirst series of the Thomas William Salmon Lectures presented at the New York Academy of Medicine, (1973).

11. Kendell, R. E., Cooper, J. E., Gourlay, A. J., Copeland, J. R. M. and Gurland, B. J. *Arch. Gen. Psychiat.* 25, 123, (1971).

12. Carpenter, W. T., Strauss, J. S. and Bartko, J. J. *Science* 182, 1275, (1973).

13. Carpenter, W. T., Strauss, J. S. and Bartko, J. J. The use of signs and symptoms for the identification of schizophrenic patients. *Schizophrenia Bull.* In press.

14. Jackson, H. *J. Ment. Sci.* 33, 25, (1887).

15. Astrup, C. and Noreik, K. *Functional Psychoses: Diagnostic and Prognostic Models.* Charles C. Thomas, Springfield, (1966).

16. Kringlen, E. *Heredity and Environment in the Functional Psychoses. Vol. I. An Epidemiological Clinical Twin Study. Vol. II. Case Histories.* Universitetsforlaget, Oslo, (1968).

17. Feighner, J. P., Robins, E., Guze, S. B., Woodruff, R. A., Winokur, G. and Munoz, R. *Arch. Gen. Psychiat.* 26, 57, (1972).

18. Snezhnevsky, A. V. The symptomatology, clinical forms and nosology of schizophrenia. In *Modern Perspectives in World Psychiatry*. Edited by Howells, J. G. Oliver and Boyd, London, (1968).

19. Rosenthal, D., Wender, P. H., Kety, S. S., Schulsinger, F., Welner, J. and Ostergaard, L. Schizophrenics' offspring reared in adoptive homes. In *The Transmission of Schizophrenia*. Edited by Rosenthal, D. and Kety, S. Pergamon Press, New York, (1968).

20. Pollin, W. and Stabenau, J. R. Biological, psychological and historical differences in a series of monozygotic twins discordant for schizophrenia. In *The Transmission of Schizophrenia*. Edited by Rosenthal, D. and Kety, S. Pergamon Press, New York, (1968).

21. Mednick, S. A. and Schulsinger, F. Some premorbid characteristics related to breakdown in children with schizophrenic mothers. In *The Transmission of Schizophrenia*. Edited by Rosenthal, D. and Kety, S. Pergamon Press, New York, (1968).

22. Silverman, J. *J. Cons. Psychol. 28*, 385, (1964).
23. Wynne, L. and Singer, M. *Arch. Gen. Psychiat. 9*, 191, (1963).
24. Lidz, T., Fleck, S., Alanen, Y. and Cornelison, A. *Psychiatry 26*, 1, (1963).
25. Anthony, E. J. *J. Psychiat. Res 6, Suppl 1*, 293, (1968).
26. Bleuler, M. and Angst, J. *The Origin of Schizophrenia.* Heinz Huber Publishers, 1971.
27. O'Neal, P. and Robins, L. N. *Amer. J. Psychiat. 115*, 385, (1958).
28. Watt, N. F. *J. Nerv. Ment. Dis. 155*, 42, (1972).
29. Gottesman, I. I. *Psychol. Monogr 77*, 1, (1963).
30. Birley, J. L. T. and Brown, G. W. *Brit. J. Psychiat. 116*, 327, (1970).
31. Wing, J. K. *Brit. J. Soc. Clin. Psychol. 1*, 38, (1962).
32. Gruenberg, E. M. *Lancet, 721*, (1969).
33. Cooper, J. E., Kendell, R. E., Gurland, B. J., Sharpe, L., Copeland, J. R. M. and Simon, R. *Psychiatric Diagnosis in New York and London: A Comparative Study of Mental Hospital Admissions.* Maudsley Monograph #20, Oxford University Press, London, (1972).
34. World Health Organizations. *The International Pilot Study of Schizophrenia.* WHO Press, Geneva, (1973).
35. Strauss, J. S. and Carpenter, W. T. *Arch. Gen. Psychiat. 27*, 739, (1972).
36. Strauss, J. S. and Carpenter, W. T. *Arch. Gen. Psychiat. 31*, 37, (1974).
37. Strauss, J. S. *Arch. Gen. Psychiat. 29*, 445, (1973).
38. Strauss, J. S. *Arch. Gen. Psychiat. 31*, 581, (1969).
39. Maxwell, A. E. *Brit. J. Psychiat. 121*, 19, (1972).
40. Bartko, J. J., Strauss, J. S. and Carpenter, W. T. Expanded perspectives for describing and comparing schizophrenic patients. *Schizophrenia Bull.* In press.
41. Koplyay, C. D., Gott, C. and Elton, J. Automatic Interaction Director Version 4 (AID-4) Reference Manual. Computational Sciences Division of the Air Force Human Resources Laboratory. Lackland, Texas, (1973).
42. Feinstein, A. R. *Clin. Pharmacol. Ther. 13*, 608, (1972).

43. Goldberger, A. S. and Duncan, O. D. *Structural Equation Models in Social Sciences.* Seminar Press, New York, (1973).
44. Blalock, H. M. Jr. *Causal Inferences in Non-Experimental Research.* The University of North Carolina Press, Chapel Hill, (1961).
45. Bertalanffy, L. General system theory and psychiatry. *American Hand Book of Psychiatry* Vol. III. Edited by Arieti, S. Basic Books, New York, (1966).

SOME GENETIC AND FAMILY STUDIES IN AUTISM AND CHILDHOOD SCHIZOPHRENIA

James R. Stabenau
University of Connecticut Health Center
School of Medicine

INTRODUCTION

In order to conduct research on the effectiveness of treatment methods specific for a given psychotic child, as in other medical sciences, one must create diagnostic syndromes of signs and symptoms of behavior and then utilize differential diagnosis to arrive at a rational treatment method as specific as possible for that condition in that individual.

Psychosis "in infancy, childhood, and adolescence comprises a group of related and overlapping syndromes characterized by withdrawal, regression, and disassociation. Diagnostic criteria include 1) withdrawal from the environment, 2) disturbance of thought and speech, 3) inappropriate affect (and behavior), 4) alteration in mobility, 5) disorientation, 6) preoccupation, 7) retardation, 8) disintegration of body image, 9) resistance to change, and 10) anxiety." (1).

DATA

In order to discuss genetic and family studies of Early
Infantile Autism (E.I.A.) and Childhood Schizophrenia (C.S.),
a brief historical review of the developmental observations of
child behavior and the subsequent diagnostic categories that
emerged may be helpful.

I.   HISTORY OF CLINICAL CONCEPTS

As seen in the diagnostic listings in Table I, the early
19th century consideration of aberrant child behavior was considered as a variant of "mental retardation or deficiency".
Kraepelin,however,in his careful diagnostic studies noted "Dementia Precox" (D.P.) in the childhood histories of 3.5% of his
adult D.P. cases(2). Later,DeSanctis and Heller characterized
the psychotic changes in their syndromes as occurring in the
child at about 3 years of age or older(3,4). Later studies reinfor-
ced this as a "critical period" in childhood and psychotic decom-
pensation. By 1919 White (Brill and Jeliffe) and others noted
"Psychosis in Childhood" and related it to the family life style
(5).   In 1933 Potter began to describe prepubescent "Schizophrenia in children" with a set of diagnostic criteria similar to
adult schizophrenia (6). Kanner established a set of criteria for
a new syndrome "Early Infantile Autism" with or without
known organic deficit (Table I) (7). Bender by 1947 was
using the term "Childhood Schizophrenia" observing, as
Corberi did in 1932, that schizophrenia in all its manifestations
may appear early in childhood (8, 2). Bender and later Fish,
noted that infants with a syndrome of neurologic abnormality
called the "floppy baby" were at high risk to develop childhood
schizophrenia (9). Margaret Mahler introduced a "regressive
psychosis" occuring about age 3-4 seemingly which centered
around separation from the mother. She labelled the syndrome
"Symbiotic Psychosis" (10). Kallmann studied the "Preadolescent Schizophrenic" in twins and their siblings finding in both
groups the peak age of breakdown was about 14 and 15 years of
age (11).   Asperger (1944) introduced the term "Autistic
Psychopathy" and Rank (1949) espoused the concept of the
"Atypical Child" (12, 13).

II. SOME CLINICAL DIFFERENCES BETWEEN EARLY INFANTILE AUTISM (E.I.A.) AND CHILDHOOD SCHIZOPHRENIA (C.S.).

There appears to be a need to consider in some depth the differences between Early Infantile Autism (E.I.A.) a rare but seemingly distinct entity, and Childhood Schizophrenia (C.S.) which as a diagnosis has been used to embrace the less clear childhood psychoses, in order to decide if they are separate diagnostic entities or not.

E.I.A. as noted is rare, about 4.5 cases in 10,000 live births (.045%) (14). Some investigators feel "nuclear" E.I.A. occurs before two years of age, and "Childhood Schizophrenia" appears most frequently with onset after age eight. Cases with onset and regression between three and eight years may be a heterogenous group of organic and/or socially degenerative psychoses (15).

a.   Sex Ratio

One of the most striking findings is the over representation of boys in the E.I.A. category as high as 4.8:1, M:F although C.S. too has a higher incidence in boys, about 2.5:1 (16, 11). Other conditions relying on an intact central nervous system such as "subnormality" and "aphasias" and speech and language disorders (5:1) also favor boys (17-20). A review of such sex ratios is found on Table II. The "normal" ratio of live births in America over the whole population is about 1.22:1, M:F.

A consistant (9 studies) *overrepresentation of males* in E.I.A. has been documented with a range from 2.1:1 to 4.8:1 with the mode being 3.6:1 (14, 16, 21-27). The lower ratios are from the epidemologic studies (less sampling bias) and the higher ratios from the families and parents of hospitalized children.

Spence examined full siblings, maternal and paternal siblings, and the first cousins of his population of 43 males and 9 females with E.I.A. (Four families had two males affected and one family, a child of each sex). This is an unusual finding! There was no sex ratio effect in Spence's study in the full sibling categories. "For the siblings of the mother, deviation both for families of

male and female probands is significantly toward the
same sex sibling as the effected child. For the paternal
siblings there were significantly more of them male if
the proband was female and more, but not significantly
so, females if the proband was male." Most striking,
however, is that for the children of the paternal siblings,
"although the father siblings do not show any significant deviation of sex ratio M:F themselves, when the
proband is male, they have an extremely higher proportion of males among their offspring" (p<.001) (Table
II) (16). Shearer, Davidson, and Finch report *no* males
were born to 14 schizophrenic women who had onset of
symptoms within one month of conception" (28).
Mothers in Spence's sample (100 consecutive children
seen at the University of California Neuropsychiatric
Institute Clinic in the ten years prior to his report) had
a rate of 11.7% miscarriages or abortions. Only one
fetus sex was identified and that was male. One might
conclude an *increased susceptability for E.I.A. through
the males* and not a female loss or female wastage of
females. This would incriminate the Y chromosome, but
other autosomes would also have to play a part in
accounting for the 20% female portion of the E.I.A. sample!

B.   *Twin Reports*

In E.I.A. monozygotic or identical twins concordant
rates, where complete data is available, indicate all but
one of the 15 monozygotic pairs (a female pair, case #15)
had been concordant for E.I.A. (29-39) (Detailed account
on Table III). That monozygotic female pair, case #15,
Kamp, (40) has a possible neurologic source for discordance, i.e. production by adverse environment at age one
month when placed out from the family possibly producing a "phenocopy" of autism in one of that monozygotic pair (personal communication Kamp, 1965).
The review of twins on Table III shows that of the 15
monozygotic twin pairs reported, 14 pairs are concordant, 6 known male and 3 female pairs and one female
pair discordant for E.I.A. For the 5 dizygotic twin pairs

all appear discordant, 4 known to be male. (24,39,41, 42, 61) Case 13 reported by Ward is described in his report as dizygotic and concordant, however, our experience with "schizophrenic adult twins", if they were indistinguishable and mistaken often by their parents or others when young, as was in the case no. 13, invariably they turned out monozygotic on blood determination (43). Case # 13 has been considered here as monozygotic concordant.   Later "environmental" factors affect weight, dress, posture, and behavior which may lead an observer using similarity methods at that time to lean toward dizygoticity. Only a blood test would truly help in this case # 13 and some of the others, of course.

Keeler briefly notes that he "has seen E.I.A. develop in a child adopted after 10 days of birth to a warm and loving family" (22).   More cross fostering natural "experiments" would aid in understanding etiological factors immensely but this is impractical due to the rare frequency of the E.I.A. (Table VI section on genetics provides some details of such adoptee studies of schizophrenics). Kallmann found preadolescent twins have a rate of schizophrenia of 71% (12 of 17 pairs) in monozygotic twin pairs where both developed schizophrenia before the age of 15 while only 17% of dizygotic twins were concordant, (6 of 35 pairs) (Table IV) (11). He also found in contrast to the absense of schizophrenia in E.I.A. parents a rate of 7.0% in parents of childhood schizophrenics. Siblings of twins had a rate of schizophrenia of 15.6% with the breakdown occuring most often at ages 14-15 years, (Table V), while E.I.A. siblings rate for E.I.A. reaches about 2% (by pooled reported samples) (37). This is low but higher than that of the general population, .045%.

C.   *Chromosomal Studies*

Chromosomal karyotypes have been done on three separate groups of E.I.A. subjects. The x and y and autosomal chromosomes all have been found to be "normal" in all studies, (27, 41, 44). There is one minor exception.

TABLE I

HISTORY OF DIAGNOSTIC CATEGORIES FOR "PSYCHOSIS" IN CHILDHOOD

Year *	Author	Diagnostic Title	Major Characteristics
1790 (2)	Itard		Attempted to train defective feral child
1896 (2)	Witmer	"Mental Deficiency" caused by CNS defects	Congenital defects linked with "retardation".
1899 (2)	Kraepelin	Dementia Precox (D.P.)	He noted 3.5% of adult cases began in childhood.
1905 (3)	DeSanctis	Dementia Praecocissma	Children 3-10 yrs. old seen with D.P.
1905 (4)	Heller	Dementia Infantilis	Six children with mental deterioration without neurological signs, age of onset 3-4 yrs, "deteriorization" in nine months.
1919 (5)	White	Psychosis in Childhood	Felt heredity had role but especially child's early experience with parents with similar defects might account for the emergence of the disturbance.
1932 (2)	Corberi	Felt Dementia Praccocissima a form of D.P.	He distinguished these children from those with organic brain disease such as Juvenile Paresis, Tuberous sclerosis and cerebral lipoidoses.
1933 (6)	Potter	Schizophrenia in Children	6 cases with onset before 10, elaborated diagnostic criteria for children, limiting it to prepubescence.

1943 (7)	Kanner	Early Infantile Autism	1) Lacked plastic molding in parents arms. Distant from humans. 2) Failure to use language for communication. 3) Obsessive desire for maintainance of sameness. 4) Fascination for objects handled with fine motor skill. Onset usually about age 1 yr., before 2 yr., mainly males. Absent family history for psychosis.
1944 (12)	Asperger	Autistic Psychopathy	Onset in third yr., walks late, speaks early, lives in own world, good social progress, "a personality trait"? Psychosis.
1947 (8)	Bender	Childhood Schizophrenia	Felt "floppy baby", with "neurologic" signs, high risk for schizophrenia as an "organic" child.
1949 (13)	Rank	Atypical child	The concept became so broad, the diagnostic label was not too helpful in treatment or research. However, emotional deprivation of such children & emotional disturbance of mothers noted.
1952 (10)	Mahler	Symbiotic Psychosis	Noted child 1) had close attachment to mother 2) developed language 3) at age of separation (age 3 or 4) onset of severe psychotic regression and panic. Often hallucinations & delusions. Presence of family history of psychosis.
1956 (11)	Kallmann	Preadolescent	As in symbiotic psychosis, higher incidence in males, family history of psychosis and all symptoms of "adult (older than 15 yrs.) Schizophrenics" although younger than 15 yrs.

*Year and reference (in brackets).

TABLE II
SEX RATIO IN EARLY INFANTILE AUTISM (E.I.A.), INDEX AND FAMILY

Early Infantile Autism	Index*
Spence (1973) (16)	4.8:1
Rutter (1967) (21)	4.3:1
Kanner (1957) (22)	4.1:1
Rutt (1971) (23)	3.8:1
Creak (1960) (24)	3.6:1
Treffert (1970) (25)	3.4:1
Wing (1967) (14)	2.8:1

Sex Ratio M:F
Family of E.I.A. Index (Spence, 1973) (16)

Index	Full Siblings	Mat. Siblings	Pat. Siblings	Cousins (1st) Mat. (M:F)	Pat. (M:F)
Male	1:1	4.5:1	1:1	1:1	1.7:1
Female	1:1	4.2:1	5.7:1	1:1	1:1

1.3:1 For "Extended Family"

Kolvin   (1970)(26)   2.5:1

Wolraich   (1970)(27)   2.1:1

Adolescent and Childhood Schizophrenia*

Kallmann (1956)(11)   2.5:1
(twins & singletons)

Other Conditions*

Mongolism
   Drillien (1961)(18)   1.3:1
Subnormal Children
   Wing (1966)(17)   1.7:1
Aphasia and Specific
   Language Disorders
Ingram & Orton (19,20)   5:1

*Senior Author listed only, see references.

TABLE III

REPORTED CASES OF EARLY INFANTILE AUTISM (E.I.A.) IN TWINS

Case	Author+	Year	Zygosity* Method	Diag- nosis**Sex	Age of Onset	Age When Studied	Symptomalogy
1.	Sherwin (29)	1953	MZ Sim.	CC M	9 mo.-1 yr.	3½ yrs.	Unresponsive to adults, banging heads, no speech.
2.	Bakwin (30)	1954	MZ Bld.#	CC M	1 yr.	23 mos.	Did not speak, play together or with other children, ignored parents.
3.	Lehman (31)	1957	MZ Sim.	CC M	?	5 yrs.	? Did not develop speech and play together.
4.	Chapman (32)	1957	MZ Sim.	CC F	?	2 yrs. and 11 mos.	Listless, apathetic, not respond to speech.
5.	Bruch (33)	1959	MZ Sim.	CC M	?	5 yrs.	"They behaved in a way des- cribed by Kanner", no speech.
6.	Ornitz (34)	1965	MZ Sim.	CC M	?	?	"Classical examples of the syndrome of E. I. Autism.
7.	Keeler (42)	1958	MZ Sim.	CC M	?	?	Retrolental Fibroplasia plus E.I.A. "Inclusion of pairs such as these in which the psychosis

No.	Reference	Year	Zygosity					Notes
8.	Polan (36)	1959	MZ Sim.	CC	?	?	?	"was probably due to a physical disorder would confuse the genetic issue" (37) Rutter.
9.	Chapman (35)	1960	MZ Sim.	CC	?	?	?	"Is slightly atypical in that there was not the degree of aloneness or insistence on sameness". (37) Rutter. ? According to Rimland (1964) (35)
10.	Chapman (35)	1960	MZ Sim.	CC	?	?	?	? According to Rimland (1964) (35).
11.	Lovaas (37)	1965	MZ Sim.	CC	?	?	?	According to Rutter (1967) (37).
12.	Brown (39)	1963	MZ Sim.	CC	?	?	?	According to personal communication to Vaillant (1963) (39). ? Abnormal EEG.
13.	Ward (38)	1962	MZ ++ Sim.	CC	F 15 mos.		3 yrs.	++Due to early misidentification, this reviewer felt monozygosity should be considered. "After 1 yr. called autistic". Due to 10lb. wt. difference the twins were easily distinguishable. No bloods were compared.

Table III continued....

								Question of E.I.A.
14.	Vaillant (39)++	1963	MZ Sim.	CC	F	2 mos.	4 yrs.	++Author in review was impressed with organicity, "mannerisms and athetoid movement" and retardation,? Organic.
15.	Kamp (40)	1964	MZ Bld.#	DC	F	10 mos.	3 yrs.	"Not identical with E.I.A. described by Kanner", withdrawal on on approach, no speech, "psychotic isolation". Index was separated from co-twin and family and at one mo. was thought to have been "beaten" according to father.
16.	Creak (24)	1960	DZ ?	DC	M	?	?	Discordant "non-identical twin, last of a sibship of 5".
17.	Böök (41)	1963	DZ (Op. Sex)	DC	M	1 yr.	?	"Rocking, no speech, withdrawn from other people."
18.	Vaillant (39)	1963	DZ Sim.?	DC	M	less than 2 yrs.	11	"No use of language or feeding of self (co-twin retarded).
19.	Keeler (42)	1957	DZ Sim?	DC	?	?	?	"I have observed this disorder (E.I.A.) in one of non-identical twins". (cited by Kanner, Eisenberg, 1957) (22).

| 20. | Stabenau (61) | 1973 | DZ | Sim | DC | M | 1 yr. | 3 yrs. | "Kanner's signs", no speech developed. |

*Determined by either similarity, finger prints, or #blood grouping (MZ=monozygotic or identical; DZ=dizygotic or fraternal)

**E.I.A. according to Kanner's criteria (CC meaning concordant for E.I.A.; DC meaning discordant (only one ill).

+Senior author only, see references.

TABLE IV

TWIN STUDY OF CHILDHOOD PSYCHOSIS (AFTER KALLMANN, 1956) (11)

Case	Author	Year	Zygosity by Similarity Method	Diagnosis % CC	Diagnosis CC	Diagnosis DC	Sex	Studied	Symptomotology
1-17	Kallmann	1956	MZ	71	12	5		3-15 yrs of age	Author Diagnosed Cases
18-35	Kallmann	1956	DZ	17	6	29	Total 37M 15F	i.e. between age of onset and hospitalization	Author Diagnosed Cases

TABLE V

"SCHIZOPHRENIC" DIAGNOSIS IN PARENTS AND SIBLINGS OF PROBAND SCHIZOPHRENIC ADOLESCENT AND CHILDHOOD TWINS

Relationship		Schizophrenia Diagnosis		Schizoid Diagnosis	% Schizophrenia
		M	F		
Parents	< 45 yrs	> 45 yrs			7.0
N = 254	170	84			
		9	9	46	
Siblings	5-14 yrs.				
N = 118	Total 16 (Probable)			13	15.6

(AFTER KALLMANN 1956) (11)

In one of ten E.I.A. families examined by Judd and Mandell, the father and the E.I.A. subject had a large elongated y chromosome (44). Although no visable chromosomal aberrations have been noted, it is possible that genetic subunits or DNA and RNA combinations are not normal in the E.I.A. subject or perhaps in his parents. Mongolism, one must remember, was first postulated as a genetic chromosomal abnormality when it was observed that monzygotic twins were almost uniformly concordant i.e. both twins had Downs Syndrome (D.S.) (45). Later the technique was available to examine the chromosomes singly and in pairs under high power magnification and trisomy 21 was found in all Down Syndrome patients and some variations of this in their parents.

D.   *Parental, Environmental, Symptomatologic and Other Clinical Differences.*

Other comparisons of clinical differences between E.I.A. and C.S. are outlined in Table VI. Some of these are lower in I.Q. in E.I.A. and "normal" range I.Q. in C.S. probands. Early failure to use language to communicate in E.I.A. and the appearance of auditory hallucination in C.S. and Symbiotic psychosis aid clinical differentiation. The later is included by many investigators of C.S. because of the similarity of symptoms i.e. the regression from "normal functioning" accompanied by anxiety and panic at separation (13). Parents of E.I.A. children are found in a higher social class, have significantly more education, higher I.Q.'s and professional occupations. In E.I.A.'s almost all pairs of monozygotic (one egg or identical twins), mostly males, both developed the E.I.A. syndrome if one became ill, while only one pair of female monozygotic twins are apparently discordant (Table III). Parents of E.I.A. children are said to never exhibit autism and siblings of E.I.A. probands rarely (2%) have E.I.A., while for C.S. probands there appear approximately 8-12% parents and siblings who develop schizophrenic symptoms in their lifetime (37, 11). There will be more discussion of these data in tabular comparisons (Table VI).

The *higher social class* or higher I.Q. and education or professionalism especially in the fathers of E.I.A. cases has been a consistent finding since 1943, (Table VI). The possibility of superior global intelligence in the parents genetically shifted in the proband to abnormal "special intelligence" is an intriguing hypothesis.

Other factors such as "ordinal position, neonatal factors, relationship to the child, I.Q., symptomatology, and follow-up studies are also found on Table VI.

Discussion

The evidence seems to indicate a genetic and sex linked etiology in E.I.A. A review of some data and speculation on a variety of possible etiologic variables associated with, but not definitely causally linked with autism is given on Table VII. Those included are: extreme introversion; social withdrawal; a type of schizophrenia; a psychogenic disorder; a deprivation syndrome; a type of subnormality; a neurologic abnormality; a cognitive-language disorder; and a genetic disorder.

The data seems to support a genetically determined cognitive-language disorder in E.I.A. Others in their extensive work with E.I.A. have concluded some of the following statements:

1) Wing states of E.I.A. "The high M:F ratio; the greater likely-hood of having parental compliance; the higher proportion of offspring with physical abnormalities; (particularly speech disorder), suggest organic etiology" (14).

2) Koupernik states "Autism cannot be explained either in elementary and quantitative neurologic terms or in purely psychoanalytical ones. It is an example of a complex disorder which to my mind has a biological basis but whose essential consequence is a severe disease of relationship" (60).

3) Rutter and Bartak conclude in their extensive review article entitled "Causes of Infantile Autism: Some Considerations From Recent Research": "Experimental,

TABLE VI

CLINICAL DIFFERENCES BETWEEN EARLY INFANTILE AUTISM AND CHILDHOOD PSYCHOSIS
(INCLUDING SYMBIOTIC PSYCHOSIS)

Variables	Early Infantile Autism (E.I.A.)	Childhood Schizophrenia (C.S.)
Rate	4/10,000 live births (.045%) (14)	3.5% of adult schizophrenics were Childhood Schizophrenics (2) (.035%)
Age of Onset	0-1, especially before 2 yrs. (7)	After 2 yrs. especially ages 3-5 Mahler (10).
Sex Ratio	In 9 extensive studies range 2.1:1 M:F to 4.8:1. Mode 3.6:1 (See Table II)	2.5:1 (Kallmann). 1:1 in adult schizophrenia (Kallmann) (11).
Ordinal Position	Varies from 1st born over representation (Kanner, Rutter) to no evidence (Lotter). Wing found in large families, late in birth order for E.I.A. (22,37, 46,14)	Reports of excess in 1st & last born for adult schizophrenia. There seems to be question of cultural and family size on this observation.
I.Q. Probands	Wing found of 15 nuclear E.I.A. 5 had I.Q. > 55. (14)	Preschizophrenic school children I.Q. lower than siblings & matched controls (Albee) but in "normal" range. (47)

Neonatal Factors	Lotter & Wing found no excess. Low birth weight ($<$ 5½ lb.) in E.I.A. (46,14)	A significant correlation of childhood schizophrenia with prematurity and natal injury (Passamanick). Low birth weight in twins with adult schizophrenia (Stabenau) (53) (43).
Major Symptoms	Kanner--lack of moulding; failure to use language for communication; obsessive desire for sameness. (22) Kolvin suspected only 2 of 47 E.I.A. of hallucinations. Both had speech (26). Mahler--E.I.A. child reacts to people as inanimate objects. (10) (See Table 1)	Kolvin "Auditory hallucinations are basic: Bodily and visual hallucinations follow. C.S. has strong maternal attachment and trouble separating. (26).
Organicity	Lobascher--56 to 84% of 25 autistic children had organic CNS disease (48). Kolvin--Early onset autistics 25 of 46 (54%) had some of 4 organic features. (26)	Goldfarb has demonstrated a group of childhood schizophrenics with organicity and a group "free" of organic deficits. (49). Kolvin--10 of 32 or 31% of late onset C. S. had similar organicity factors (26).
Family Characteristics Social Class	Kanner, Creak & Ini, Rutter & Lockyer, Lotter & Wing all demonstrate in large controlled samples of E.I.A., excess of parents professional or in class I & II. (22,24,21,46,17)	Demeyer--Autistic and childhood schizophrenics (N=33) No social class difference between parents and parents of subnormal children (N=30) (50). Wing--11/16 parents of C.S. in class III-V. (i.e. low) (14).

Table VI continued....

Occupation Lotter--found 17 E.I.A. versus 22 handicapped children--no difference in fathers occupation. (46).

I.Q. Parents Lotter--found higher I.Q. level in parents of E.I.A. than handicapped. (46).

Education Lotter--father's education significantly higher. (46). Ritvo--148 E.I.A. versus 74 other neurologic diseases; found no significant difference in parents education, income or social class. (51).
Gibson--In parents of 60 E.I.A. versus 75 brain-injured controls, found significantly higher education level in E.I.A. (52).
Wing--32% of nuclear E.I.A. parents versus 2% of nonautistic were "professionals". (14).

Maternal Age Lotter, Ritvo--found no difference in maternal age between autism or handicapped controls or neurologic controls. (mean mid 20's) (46, 51).

Relationship to Child	Kanner--(N=100+) described parents of autistic children as obsessive, cold, with limited genuine interest in people and showing emotional frigidity. (22). Creak & Ini--in a large study did not substantiate this (24). Same studies, in fact, found parents of autistic children stimulated their children more than the parents of "normals".	Demeyer--Parents of 33 autistic and chronic schizophrenic children. Found parents of control 30 subnormal infants reacted coldest and were least stimulating. (50). Bender--believes C.S. produces pathological problems and effects in the parents of such children. (8). Gianascol's review of C.S.--found no support for the concept of a "schizophrenogenic mother" (2).
Genetic Factors	Lotter--noted 5 parents of 32 pairs, with an autistic child, who were hospitalized for psychiatric diagnosis, only one of 22 control parents had a pschiatric diagnosis (possible schizophrenia (46). Kolvin--1 of his 47 E.I.A. parents had schizophrenic-affective disorder (26). Keeler--reported that E.I.A. developed in a child adopted at 10 days after birth to warm loving parents (22).	Kolvin--in 32 C.S. couples, evidence of schizophrenia in 6 (13%) (26). Kallmann--found schizophrenia in 7-8% of parents of C.S. schizophrenic twins (11). Gianascol--in a series of 203 C.S. 12% had one, and occasionally, two, parents unequivocally psychotic (2). Kety, Rosenthal, Wender's and Heston's studies demonstrated that 9% of children, born to biologic parents with schizophrenia and placed in adoptee homes, soon after birth, developed schizophrenia in childhood and adulthood while none of the control adoptees developed schizophrenia (54).

Table VI continued...

Chromosomal Study	Wolraich--11 E.I.A. with the exception of one xxx were all chromosomally normal (27). Judd and Mandell, Book, et al. also found no chromosomal abnormalities in blood cells, mucosa and cultured skin biopsies (44,41).	
Twin Studies	As in singletons, twin pairs are almost entirely *male*. And for those reported as "identical", in *almost all cases, both twins were concordant for autism*. *No clear fraternal case has been concordant.*	Kallmann found 71% of 17 pairs identical twins, both ill with schizophrenia before the age of 15, while only 17% of fraternal twins were concordant. (11)
Follow-up	Kanner--absence of remission or relapses, of 11 cases only 2 (who had speech) now "functional", rest institutionalized in hospitals or homes. (55)	Frequent remissions with quick relapses. About 30% recover; most become adult schizophrenics.

reference in brackets

clinical and longitudinal studies of infantile autism are reviewed and the evidence with respect to different views of the causation of the condition are considered. Several independent investigations have shown the presence of the severe, extensive defect in language comprehension, in control functions associated with lanuage, and with the processing of symbolic or sequence information. Circumstantial evidence suggests that this cognitive defect constitutes the primary handicap in autism, the social and behavioral abnormalities arising as secondary consequences. It remains uncertain whether the cognitive-language defect is a sufficient cause for autism or whether some inter-action with particular personality attributes or family environment is necessary. A basic cause of the cognitive defect is unknown, although the high rate of fits in intellectually retarded children suggests the presence of some kind of brain disorder.

Among the intelligent autistic children, there is less evidence for structural brain pathology; it remains possible then in some cases autism may arise on the basis of some maturational disorder or genetically determined condition." (57).

SUMMARY

From this incomplete review directed mainly at genetic and family factors in E.I.A. and Childhood Schizophrenia: the possibility that in the non-organic E.I.A. child an etiology may mostly represent a genetic disorder with central nervous system mechanisms related to perceptual and cognitive-language malfunctions exists. Separate organic syndromes may overlay a basic C.N.S. neuronal defect. The childhood psychosis after age 2 differs in the phenomenon of regression from "normal" seemingly more as a response to stressful environment and may be psychogenically understandable. The higher intellectual endowment of E.I.A. parents may predispose to E.I.A. in a child if there is a shift genetically in the genotype controlling the central nervous system global intelligence to a more "specific" intellectual dysfunction of the central nervous sys-

TABLE VII

PROPOSED ETIOLOGIES FOR EARLY INFANTILE AUTISM (AFTER RUTTER, 1968) (56)

Etiologic Variable	Suggestive or Supportive Data
Extreme Introversion	Ounsted & Hutt 1966-70, noted gaze aversion and introversion associated with high arousal in social institutions. This has not altogether been supported. (56).
Social Withdrawal	Social withdrawal and avoidance of speech.
A Type of Schizophrenia	Against this is a high male sex difference; higher social class; lack of family history of schizophrenia; absence of hallucinations and delusions.
A Psychogenic Disorder	Lack of Support for absence of warmth in parents. Recent studies demonstrating no parental differences between E.I.A., "normal", and subnormal children. Also child may have pathogenic effect on parent.
A Deprevation Syndrome	There has been a lack of supporting evidence of a history of depriving experiences. Social isolation may be an effect not a cause of the child's illness.

A Type of Subnormality	1/4 of E.I.A. show normal I.Q.. Defects don't seem to be global intelligence, but more specifically a language defect. (Lockyer & Rutter 1970) (56)
Neurologic Abnormality	In follow-up of seemingly "deficit free" E.I.A. children develop neurologic impairments, often gross seizures. The multiplicity of organic defects appears against a single causation.
A Cognitive-Language Disorder	"Retardation of speech and language are almost universal in E.I.A. with notable lack of response to sounds. E.I.A. is poor in ability to transfer information from one sensory modality to another in the child's meaning of the spoken word and in his use of gesture". (Rutter & Bartak) (57). There may also appear a developmental aphasia. Demeyer, Ornitz and Martin all have suggested variations in disordered sensory motor integration. (50,58,59)
A Genetic Disorder	A rate of E.I.A. in siblings of 2% is low, but above general population .045%. Normal chromosomal profiles exist. However, almost all MZ twins are concordant for E.I.A. (See Table 4). Thus, with the high 4:1 M:F sex ratios a genetic causation is quite likely.

tem and which may appear phenotypically as E.I.A. The over-representation of E.I.A. in males and overrepresentation by males in other conditions such as aphasias involving cognitive and language functions, suggests that genetic link may be primarly through a gene on a sex chromosome. Recent psycho-physiologic studies of the vestibular apparatus which involves sensory and motor coordination and other areas of central nervous system pathophysiology have been increasingly promising leads that one or more sections of the central nervous system may be involved in E.I.A. (58, 59).

This rare, pathetic and intransigent behavior pattern of E.I.A. beginning so early in life may be carefully and scientifically studied along the genetic, CNS cognitive-language and neurophysiologic functioning directions and may provide some leads as to molecular, cellular, system, and "inter-personal relational" capacity and function and lead to a clearer notion of "normal" brain function and behavior and critical factors in other severe psychopathologies.

REFERENCES

1. Chan, J. C., Fras, I., Wilson, Jr. R., and Moeller, H.G. *Amer. J. Dis. Child. 121*, 538, (1971).

2. Gianascol, A. *Psychodynamic approaches to childhood schizophrenia: A review in clinical studies in childhood psychoses.* Edited by Szurek, S. and Berlin, I. Brunner-Mazel, New York, (1973).

3. De Sanctis, S. *Folia Neuro-Biologica 2*, 9, (1908).

4. Heller, T. *Uber dementia infantilis z. kinderforsch, 37*, 661, (1930). (Hulse, W. C. Trans. About dementia infantilis. *J. Nerv. Ment. Dis. 119*, 471, (1954).

5. White, W. *The Mental Hygiene of Childhood.* Little, Brown. Boston (1919).

6. Potter, H. W. *Amer. J. Psychiat. 89*, 1253, (1933).

7. Kanner, L. *J. Pediat.* *25*, 211, (1944).

8. Bender, L. *Amer. J. Orthopsychiat.* *17*, 40, (1947).

9. Fish, B., Shapiro, W. *et al.* The prediction of schizophrenia in infancy: II. A ten-year follow-up report of prediction made at one month of age, in *Psychopathology of Schizophrenia,* Edited by Hoch, P. and Zubin, J. Grune and Stratton Inc., (1966).

10. Mahler, M. *Psychoanal. Study Child.* 7, 286, (1952).

11. Kallmann, F. *Amer. J. Psychiat.* *112*, 599, (1956).

12. Asperger, H. *Archiv. fur psychiatric and nervenkrankenheiten 117*, 76, (1944).

13. Rank, B. *Amer. J. Orthopsychiat.* *19*, 130, (1949).

14. Wing, J., O'Connor, N. and Lotter, V. *Brit. Med. J. 3*, 389, (1967).

15. Rutter, M. *J. Autism Child Schizophrenia 2*, 315, (1972).

16. Spence, M., Simmons, J., Brown, N. *et al. Amer. J. Mental Defic. 77*, 405, (1973).

17. Wing, J. *Early childhood autism: clinical, educational and social aspects.* Pergamon Press Inc., N.Y. (1966).

18. Drillien, C. *Arch. Dis. Child. 41*, 528, (1966).

19. Ingram, T., and Reid, J. *Arch. Dis. Child. 31*, 161, (1956).

20. Orton, S. *Reading, Writing and Speech Problems in Children.* Chapman and Hall Ltd., London, (1937).

21. Rutter, M. and Lockyer, L. *Brit J. Psychiat. 113*,1169, (1967).

22. Kanner, L. and Eisenberg, L. Early infantile autism 1943-1955, in *Child Psychiatry, Psychiatric Research Reports No. 7*, American Psychiatric Association, April (1957).

23. Rutt, C. and Offord, D. *J. Nerv. Ment. Dis.* *152*, 324, (1971).

24. Creak, M. and Ini, S. *J. Child Psychol, Psychiat.* *1*, 156 (1960).

25. Treffert, D.A. *Arch. Gen. Psychiat.* *22*, 431, (1970).

26. Kolvin, I. *Psychoses in childhood-- a comparative study* In *Infantile Autism; Concepts; Characteristics and Treatment*, Edited by Rutter, M. Churchill, London, (1971).

27. Wolraich, M. *N. Engl. J. Med.* *283*, 1231, (1970).

28. Shearer, M., Davidson, R., and Finch, S. *J. Psychiat.Res.* *5*, 349, (1967).

29. Sherwin, A., *Am. J. Psychiat.* *109*, 823, (1953).

30. Bakwin, H. *J. Pediat.* *45*, 492, (1954).

31. Lehman, E., Haber, J., and Lesser, S. *J. Nerv. Ment. Dis.* *125*, 351, (1957).

32. Chapman, A. *AMA Arch. Neurol.Psychiat.* *78*, 621, (1957).

33. Bruch, H. *Acta Psychiat, Neurol. Scand. Suppl.* *130, 34*, 15, (1959).

34. Ornitz, E., Ritvo, E., and Walter, R. *Arch. gen. Psychiat.* *12*, 77, (1965).

35. Rimland B: *Infantile Autism.* Appelton, Centry, Crofts, N.Y. (1964).

36. Polan, C., and Spencer, B. *W. Virg. med. J. 55*,198, (1959).

37. Rutter, M. Psychotic disorders in early childhood, in *Recent Developments in Schizophrenia: A Symposium.* Edited by Coppen A, Royal Medicio Psychological Association, London, pp 133-158, (1967).

38. Ward, T., Hoddinott, B. *Can. Psychiat. Ass. J. 7*, 191, (1962).

39. Vaillant, G. *Arch. Gen. Psychiat. 9*, 163, (1963).

40. Kamp, L. *Psychiat. Neurol. Neurochir. 67*, 143, (1964).

41. Böök, J., Nichtern, S., and Gruenberg, E. *Acta. Psychiat. Scand. 39*, 309, (1963).

42. Keeler, W. Autistic patterns and defective communication in blind children with retrolental fibroplasia, in *Psychopathology of Communication.* Edited by Hoch, P., and Zubin, S. Grune and Stratton, N.Y., pp 64-83, (1958).

43. Stabenau, J., and Pollin, W. *Arch. Gen. Psych. 17*, 723, (1967).

44. Judd, L., and Mandell, A. *Arch. Gen. Psychiat. 18*, 450 (1968).

45. Jacobs, P., Baike, A. and Court Brown, W. *Lancet 1*, 710, (1959).

46. Lotter, B. *Soc. Psychiat. 1*, 163, (1967).

47. Lane, E., and Albee, G. *J. Abnorm. Soc. Psychol.68*,193, (1964).

48. Lobascher, M., Kingerlee, P. and Gubbay, S. *Brit. J. Psychiat. 117*, 525, (1970).

49. Goldfarb, W. *Childhood Schizophrenia.* Harvard Univ. Press, N. Y. (1967).

50. DeMeyer, M. *et al. J. Autism and Child. Schizophrenia 2*, 49, (1972).

51. Ritvo, E., *et al. J. Autism and Child. Schizophrenia 1*, 297, (1971).

52. Gibson, D. *The Can. Psychologist 9*, 36, (1968).

53. Pasamanick, B., and Knobloch, H. *J. Psychol. 56*, 73, (1963).

54. Wender, P. *Am. J. Orthopsychiat. 37*, 447, (1969).

55. Kanner, L. *Childhood Psychosis: Initial Studies and New Insights.* Halstead Press, Wiley, N.Y. (1973).

56. Rutter, M. *Concepts of autism,* in *Aspects of Autism.* Edited by Mittler, P., British Psycholgoical Society, London, (1968).

57. Rutter, M., and Bartak, L. *J. Autism Child Schizophrenia 1*, 20, (1971).

58. Ornitz, E. Childhood autism: a disorder of sensorimotor integration, in *Infantile Autism: Concepts, Characteristics and Treatment.* Edited by Rutter, M. Churchill, London, (1971).

59. Martin J. Sensory disorder in the autistic child and its implications for treatments. In *Infantile Autism: Concepts, Characteristics and Treatment.* Edited by Rutter, M. Churchill, London, (1971).

60. Koupernick, C. A pathogenic approach to infantile autism, in *Infantile Autism: Concepts, Characteristics and Treatment.* Edited by Rutter, M. Churchill, London, (1971).

61. Stabenau, J. Observed case, (1973).

MENTAL HEALTH IN CHILDREN, Volume I
Edited By D. V. Siva Sankar
Copyright © 1975 by
PJD Publications Ltd., Westbury, N.Y.

PREVENTIVE MENTAL HEALTH PROGRAMS FOR AMERICAN INDIAN YOUTH-- SUCCESS AND FAILURE

James H. Shore
University of Oregon Medical School
Portland, Oregon 97201

This paper describes two preventive mental health programs for American Indian youth. The purpose of this report is threefold:

1. to describe an Indian reservation and an Indian boarding school program, both of which utilize a systematic case finding approach for early detection and intervention,
2. to outline the preventive implications of this approach and
3. to describe the success and failure of community psychiatrists who have worked to develop programs for American Indian children.

In 1969 a new mental health program for the Portland Area Indian Health Service was begun with consultation services to the tribal councils of the Pacific Northwest, including the states of Washington, Oregon, and Idaho. The mental health consultants sought the viewpoint of each tribal government concerning their mental health priorities. The response of the tribal councils was clear and enlightening in their concern for Indian youth. "Our most valuable possession is our children. Many are being lost through the process of foster home placement outside of their own Indian community. Others suffer from the effects of school drop-out. The children leave home; the family breaks down; and it is impossible to reverse the process or repair the damage." Concern about the process of foster home placement and school drop-out was expressed by all Northwest tribal leaders. These concerns were given a high priority in the development of their new mental health program. Indian leaders felt that significant efforts in prevention must begin with the young people. They requested assistance in changing the process that contributed to family breakdown, the loss of Indian identity by those raised in non-Indian communities, and the subsequent loss of Indian youth.

The Indian Whipper Man Custom

There was an old Indian custom among the plateau tribes of the Pacific Northwest that exemplified community responsibility for child care. The tradition concerned an individual called the Whipper Man who was outside of the immediate family. The Whipper Man was a highly respected person. Respect was shown him by elders and the young. However, this respect had to be earned. He was chosen by tribal leaders and relatives, based on the development of character beyond reproach. The Whipper Man functioned in the role of disciplinarian. He disciptlined youngsters if they were disrespectful to elders. The discipline was administered in a very positive sense, and was understood by young and old. The whip he used hung over the door or on the wall and was the omnipresent symbol reminding the children that "the Whip Man might be coming"(1).

In July, 1973, an Indian interpreter was asked to explain the development of a tribal child care program to a general council meeting of a Northwest plateau tribe. The interpreter explained that the new child care program was like going back to the old ways, when there was a Whipper Man not connected with the immediate family, who came and discussed and disciplined the children. The child care center was seen as taking up the Whipper Man's role in the village as a non-family participant in child rearing practices with community sanction. The general council, an open community meeting, voted overwhelmingly to approve the budget requested for the child care program. In this example, a new mental health program, developed within and supported by the Indian community, was seen as being compatible with ancient Indian tradition and part of a culture in which extended family contacts and community responsibilities for child rearing were as important as the immediate responsibilities of the nuclear family (1).

A Tribal Group Home (1)

The tribal group home developed by this Pacific Northwest plateau tribe has demonstrated the impact of community sponsorship on the effectiveness of an Indian child care program. The tribe opened the children's group home following two years of intensive planning. Development of this service had taken place under the sponsorship of the tribal council with mental health consultation from the Indian Health Service and support from several agencies including the National Institutes of Mental Health. A child neglect committtee of community participants had been functioning for several years with official tribal council endorsement. This committtee had established a precedent for community initiative in making decisions for the placement of Indian children. At the time that the group home opened there were 219 Indian children under the age of 18 who were not living with their natural parents. These children were part of a total tribal youth population of approximately 800 under 18 years of age. The children in placement represented one out of four of the total youth population. Of those in placement, one out of three (n=74) were in foster care placement with the state children's service agency; one out of five (n=47) were in boarding schools; a few in tribal foster homes. The remainder were in other off-reservation placements. In 1971 and 1972 the number of new placements in foster homes was 40 and 30 respectively. Children were most often removed from their families because of complaints of neglect or abandonment. It is noteworthy that child abuse or battered child syndrome was virtually unknown.

The group home was designed to provide short-term shelter care, long term placement, counseling, and minor medical treatment for Indian children ranging from one to eighteen years. The tribal child care services were developed to include outreach family counseling in addition to residential care. Staff for the group home and the outreach family counseling program were 90 percent Indian. Most Indian staff members came from the local community. In the first twelve months of operation 246 Indian children from 135 separate families were placed in the residential center. This involved 20 percent of all reservation families. In age the children ranged from two and one half weeks to 19 years. Problems related to excessive drinking by the parents accounted for the majority of placements although child behavior difficulties such as juvenile delinquency and runaway reaction were also represented. Four children were placed in the center for care of a major medical problem.

Through clinical experience on American Indian reservations, I have often encountered a sense of hopelessness and despair when working with Indian parents about problems of alcohol misuse and child neglect. Following placement of the children, Indian parents often withdraw, become depressed, and begin or resume intensive drinking. The non-Indian outsider usually misinterprets this process as evidence of emotional instability and further lack of concern for the children. A more correct interpretation for the parents' perspective is their sense of helplessness and isolation. They feel manipulated and controlled by the dominant non-Indian society, a culturally alien force.

An essential step in the program's development was the creation of a community resource where Indian children could be adequately cared for in close proximity to their parents. The outreach program by Indian counselors was a further attempt to keep parents involved. The decision to place Indian children was made by the Indian community through tribal courts. The impact of placement was minimized by clearly stating a policy of returning children to their families within the shortest possible period of time. Although some children continue to need off-reservation placement in individualized treatment plans, the initial success of the program was highlighted by a dramatic reduction of off-reservation referrals.

From the opening of the children's group home in January of 1973 through the first twelve months of operation, only one Indian child was placed off-reservation in a non-Indian foster home. This child was previously under the custody of the state courts and remained under their jurisdiction for the off-reservation placement. Many additional Indian families received out-patient services before placement was indicated. The majority of children referred to the group home were returned to their parents who received out-patient follow-up, while some children were placed in reservation-sponsored foster homes.

An Indian Boarding School Program

Since referral to an Indian boarding school is another method of responding to the pressure of Indian youth in crisis, it is no surprise that boarding school adjustment is significantly affected by alcohol abuse. Of the 47 students referred to boarding school from this Pacific Northwest plateau tribe in 1972, one out of two (n=28) were enrolled because of excessive drinking problems by a parent. There were 12 student dropouts in this group. Seven of these students dropped out or were dismissed because of their own alcohol involvement at school. This example of referral practice from one tribe illustrates the selection procedure that operates for many, but not all, Indian children who are referred to boarding school. If this referral mechanism functions for a particular boarding school, it significantly affects student adjustment.

During the 1969-1970 and 1970-1971 school years, a dropout epidemic occurred at the Indian boarding school serving the states of the Pacific Northwest. In a mental health consultation project with the boarding school staff and the school Indian advisory board, associates and myself conducted a retrospective dropout evaluation (2). The project was designed to match all student dropouts with a student group who remained in school for the entire year. There were several goals in conducting this dropout survey:

1. to describe the student group who dropped out in their preschool adjustment, reasons for referral to boarding school, health adjustment, academic achievement, and in-school behavior;

2. to compare the characteristics of the dropout population to a student group who stayed in school;

3. to determine if factors could be identified which differentiated the dropouts from the stayers;

4. to search for demographic, academic, and behavioral criteria which could serve as a predictive index for morbidity in boarding school dropout; and

5. to utilize these findings in the development of a preventive school mental health program which would utilize a systematic case finding approach for early detection of school maladjustment.

The Indian Boarding School

This Indian boarding school is the only one of its type sponsored by the Bureau of Indian Affairs in the Pacific Northwest. The school campus is on the site of the original institution which began in 1880. During the 1969-1970 school year, the school had an enrollment of 860 Indian students. This Indian school was in a transitional phase, moving toward an acceptance of a larger percentage of students from the Pacific Northwest. Since the 1968-1969 school year the student body had changed from 87 percent Alaskan and 13 percent Navajo to a composition of 64 percent Alaskan native and Alaskan Indian, 35 percent Northwest Indian, and one percent Navajo Indian students. This diverse population does not represent all Alaskan, Navajo, or Northwest students who attend Bureau of Indian Affairs boarding schools, since many students may be assigned to a school in another geographic area. The students range in age from 14 to 23 years and attend grades 9 through 12. Alaskan and Navajo boarding school student referrals most frequently were made on the basis of geographic isolation and a lack of public school facilities in the local community.   All Northwest reservation communities are situated close to public schools which serve the majority of Northwest Indian students. Referral of a Northwest Indian student to boarding school is often made on the bais of disorganizing social or interpersonal factors.

It is important to emphasize the diversity of the student body in this and other Indian boarding schools. Indian students are referred from different tribes and from different regions of the country. In some cases Indian boarding school is the student's last source of help, following dropout from a local public school, involvement with the juvenile court, or an unstable home environment. In other instances Indian parents will encourage their children to apply to boarding school to maintain cultural identity in an all-Indian setting.

The Dropout Epidemic

The student body and school staff had experienced increased stress over a four year period as a result of this change in student population. The stresses were manifested by an eight-fold increase in the dropout rate between the 1967-68 and the 1970-71 school years. From the school year 1967-68 until 1970-71 the dropout rate rose from three to twenty-six percent of the student body. In the 1969-70 school year, 74 percent of the disciplinary dropouts and 58 percent of the administrative dropouts came from the Northwest student group. This is significant when the dropout group is compared to the total student body representation of that time: 64 percent Alaskan and 35 percent Northwest Indian students. This trend continued in the 1970-71 school year with 78 percent of the disciplinary dropouts and 54 percent of the administrative dropouts coming from the Northwest student group.

In the summer of 1970 a systematic inquiry was conducted evaluating 263 student records from the dropout and non-dropout groups. Three items in the students' background are significantly related to a subsequent boarding school dropout. These were:

1. a history of institutional or foster home care prior to school referral,
2. a history of wardship status for the Northwest student group, and
3. the level of grade point average and achievement scores prior to boarding school admission.

Alcohol abuse among boarding school students frequently related to school dismissal, particularly if associated with an arrest or physical violence. Suicide attempts were inversely related to dropout potential. This behavior seemed to represent an effective way of requesting help. Since this pattern of boarding school dropout can be shown to be significantly associated with a permanent school dropout pattern, it seemed important to use this data as a basic yardstick in predicting a student's dropout potential and in developing an appropritate program for dropout prevention.

Several distinct programs were initiated simultaneously that were intended to affect the 1971-1972 school year.

1. First, results of the dropout survey were shared with the Indian school board and school administration.

2. Plans were started to recruit additional counseling staff, emphasizing early contact with identified high-risk students.

3. A special training program was initiated for dormitory aides to increase their skills in coping with student behavior adjustment problems in the residential settings. Dismissal from boarding school was often related to maladjustment in the dorm and conflict or confrontation with dorm staff. Students were rarely dismissed for scholastic reasons.

4. An alcohol abuse counseling and education project was proposed with grant application submitted to NIMH. This pilot project was designed to function with Indian school board sponsorship, an all-Indian counseling staff, and groups of student volunteers. The student government would actively participate in policy setting and recruitment of student volunteers. The program was approved and funded in the summer of 1971.

5. A new superintendent was appointed as administrator for the boarding school. This event was obviously not planned or influenced by this consultation and appeared to be coincidental in occurring with four projects mentioned above. However, his appointment was highly significant. It led to a clarification of school policy and improvement in the consistency of administrative decision making.

In the 1971-1972 school year the dropout rate was lowered from 26 percent to 19 percent of the total student body. This change meant that 50 additional students remained in school as compared to the previous school year. And yet, this apparent success was clouded by mixed results. The school has undergone an annual change in admission policy, first including, then excluding the high-risk students. In fact, when high-risk students are identified, an overwhelmed administration can use this data to exclude these students from admission in an effort to have fewer behavior problems on campus. The new superintendent departed after eighteen months. After the fall of 1971 high-risk students did not receive special services. The student alcohol counseling project has continued to function, contacting many students. At the beginning of the 1973-1974 school year the dropout rate was reported to be on the increase once again.

Factors Influencing Success and Failure

What are the significant factors which have influenced success and failure in the mental health consultation to these two programs for American Indian youth?

The successful consultations involved the development of clinical services, based on a thorough understanding of the psychiatric epidemiology, and aggressive administrative planning to direct those services towards earlier stages of intervention. The Indian tribe and Indian school board were involved in the planning and sponsorship. Both the tribal group home and school alcohol counseling project are currently operating successfully.

However, mental health consultation at the Indian boarding school met with mixed results. The factors influencing failure merit special consideration. First, the consultants entered an institutional setting that is not usually interested in a mental health approach and where educational goals are often limited to the classroom. I was confronted with the sentiment, "We are here to teach kids, not treat them." There is a potential conflict between the problem-oriented perspective of the clinical model and the desire of Indian people to emphasize the importance of Indian culture in their educational institutions. Although identifying a particular behavior problem may bring needed services for Indian youth, it may also emphasize a stereotype of Indian youngsters and actually

reinforce a negative self-image.   The consultation efforts at
the boarding school were in response to a dropout epidemic,
a crisis of major proportion.   The crisis provided a reason for
alarm and collaboration.   However, the momentum was lost in
subsequent school years.   And finally, development of a mental
health school program was often overwhelmed and bypassed by
the bigger issues, e.g., the transfer of school authority to
greater Indian control and federal funding for a new physical
plant.

Discussion

     Hammerschlag (3) has stated that the more Indian
boarding schools accept the charge of dealing with "problem"
children, the more they de-emphasize the real need for these
problems to be dealt with elsewhere, by parents and by the
tribes themselves at home.   While this may be theoretically
correct, it is not practical.   Too often the response of American
psychiatry has been to call for the disbanding of Indian
boarding schools, a position that is not supported by American
Indians.   And too often the special needs of Indian students
with behavior adjustment problems remain unattended.
     That history repeats itself is no new discovery.   In 1963
at the same Northwest boarding school a technique was
validated for identifying emotionally disturbed students (4).
The goal then, as in the more recent consultation, was to
identify high-risk students and to initiate a program designed
for early intervention.   The technique involved use of the
Cornell Medical Index Health Questionnaire.   The results were
published in the American Journal of Psychiatry in June of
1964.   Indian students were not screened for special services
following the publication of that report.
     Bergman and Goldstein (5) have recently reported on
the development of a model dorm project at a Navajo boarding
school in the American Southwest.   In 1969, as a strategy for
promoting change, one school dormitory housing two hundred
children for five to eleven years of age was taken as a model and
sufficient funds were found to increase the dorm staff.   The
ratio of children to house parents became twelve to one,
compared to a usual ratio of eighty to one and even as high as
two hundred to one.   House parents were given intensive

in-service training in child care. The house parents were all Navajo and Navajo-speaking. Life in the dormitory became warmer and less regimented. The model dorm and a matched control dorm at another school were evaluated throughout the first three years of operation. Results clearly indicated that in areas such as intellectual, emotional, and physical development, children of the model dormitory were significantly superior to those of the control dorm. In the fall of 1973 the Navajo model dorm project was closing for lack of funds.

REFERENCES

1. Shore, J.H., and Nicholls, W.W., Indian Children and Tribal Group Homes: New Interpretations of the Whipper Man. *Am. J. Psychiat. 132*:454-456, April 1975.

2. Shore, J.H., Levy, J., Foster, A. and VonFumetti, B. Dropout Epidemic at an Indian Boarding School. Mental Health Office Report, Portland Area Indian Health Service, (1971).

3. Hammerschlag, C.A., Clayton, P.A., and Berg, D. *Amer. J. Psychiat. 130*, 1098, (1973).

4. Nelson, L.G., Tadlock, L.D., Dawes, J.W., Hipple, J.L., and Jetmalani, N.B. *Amer. J. Psychiat., 120*,1155, (1964).

5. Bergman, R.L., and Goldstein, G.S., The Model Dorm: Changing Indian Boarding Schools, presented at the annual meeting of the American Psychiatric Association, Honolulu, Hawaii, May 7-11, (1973).

MENTAL HEALTH IN CHILDREN, Volume I
Edited By D. V. Siva Sankar
Copyright © 1975 by
PJD Publications Ltd., Westbury, N.Y.

BEHAVIOUR DISORDERS IN ETHNIC MINORITY CHILDREN: A REVIEW OF BRITISH EVIDENCE

Christopher Bagley
University of Surrey
Guildford
Surrey, U. K.

It is fairly clear that the prevalence of behavioral pathology is greater in migrants than in geographically stable populations, and that this is due to a combination of selection factors (e.g. being unstable or mentally ill before migrating) and stress factors (e.g. poor material conditions and stresses of cultural re-adaptation) in the new environment (1, 2, 3). The same problems apply to internal migrants, who have higher rates of mental illness than non-migrants (4). All of the above studies have been of adults, and give us only indirect clues to the likely behavioural outcome in children of migrants. The effect of parental mental illness on children is complex, depending on the sex and ages of children, and the type of interactions involved (5). Internal migration *per se* does not seem to have adverse effects on the mental health of children; a more important variable seems to be the anxieties of parents concerning such moves (6). An English ecological study has in fact shown that a variety of types of pathology (crime, mental illness, juvenile delinquency, and child welfare problems) occur together in in-migrant areas characterized by poor quality housing (7).

The position of post-war migrants to Britain is socio-
logically complex. Of special interest is the position of post-war
migrants from the former Commonwealth territories of the
Carribbean, Africa and Asia. These migrants, including their
children, are clearly identifiable ethnic minorities in terms of
language, skin colour or dress. They have also been used as
scapegoats for some of the chronic economic and social
problems which beset British society (8, 9).

The number of "black" immigrants in Britain is not
large-about 1.38 million, or approximately three per cent of the
total population (10). However, since these migrants are young
and often have larger families than average, the proportion of
black children in the school population is somewhat higher.
Since the migrants have settled in areas of available employment and housing, they are disproportionately represented in
the conurbations of London, Birmingham and Yorkshire.
Because of racial discrimination in both employment (which
limits income available to spend on housing) and in housing
itself (denial of access to the subsidised public housing occupied
by nearly a third of the British population) Commonwealth
immigrants have perforce settled in the most depressed city
areas.   For children this means attending schools whose
buildings are old, poorly equipped, ill-served by teachers, and
attended by lower class white children whose attitude to
education is itself one born of alienation (11).

Because of the problems of low income and the high cost
of housing, many West Indian mothers with young children
work long hours. In a recent London study (12) of mothers
with children of school age, four-fifths of West Indian mothers
were in employment, compared with a half of English mothers
with children in the same schools. While their mothers work,
pre-school children are placed with "daily minders" (nursery
school places are extremely scarce, and are usually allocated to
children of one-parent families; about a fifth of West Indian
households fall into this category).

The reports of conditions in the homes of these minders
(13) have drawn a picture of as many as ten children kept in
one room during the whole day in conditions of "Dickensian
squalor", and given the minimum of cognitive stimulation and
emotional care. Jackson estimates that at least half of West
Indian under-fives are so "minded". The mothers of these

children have, after work, little time or energy to interact with their children in ways which are conducive to normal intellectual or emotional growth. This supposition has been corroborated by clinical investigation of 100 West Indian mothers in London (14). Many of the mothers in this study were working in order to maintain mortgage payments on poor quality housing; many seemed to be clinically depressed; and many had children with various behaviour problems. In 13 of the children studied a curious self-denigration syndrome was observed, which transcended the observed tendency of black children in Britain to disparage their ethnic identity (15, 16). The 13 pre-school children in Stroud and Moody's series had developed aggressive tendencies towards children darker than themselves, and regarded themselves as actually being pale or white.

Another syndrome was observed by Prince (17) in a study from the same London hospital-that of "pseudo-autism". Twenty-three West Indian children were observed who had many of the features of autism - aloofness, withdrawal, apathy, loss of speech, and non-response to stimuli. However, the condition seemed to be distinguished from true autism by social background factors. Twenty of the mothers were seriously depressed, and 14 of them were working; 17 of the children had been separated from their mothers for long periods, and the majority had been "daily minded".

Another London study by Pollack (18) of 104 English and 107 immigrant three-year-olds in a London general practice has confirmed the depressing picture painted by the other workers. Two-thirds of the mothers of the 75 West Indian children in Pollack's study were working long hours; 95 per cent of West Indian children had never had a holiday compared with 38 per cent of English children; 88 per cent of West Indian children had not been on a family outing in the previous four weeks compared with 20 per cent of English children. The family income and housing conditions of the West Indian families were significantly poorer than those of their English counterparts. The homes of the West Indian children were frequently heated by unguarded paraffin stoves, and no less than 60 per cent of the West Indian children had suffered burns, compared with 35 per cent of English children. Significantly more black children had suffered eczema, asthma, or

bronchitis (corroborating the earlier finding of work by Hood
et al.(19). Forty-eight of the 75 West Indian children had at
some stage been 'minded', and four-fifths had experienced more
than one minder; 11 had been through the hands of four or more
minders. According to Pollack's criteria, only 55 per cent of
West Indian mothers, compared with 92 per cent of English
mothers, were able to give their children "adequate mothering". Most alarming of all, the West Indian children had
significantly lower scores than their English counterparts on
scores measuring linguistic, adaptive, and personal-social
skills. Pollack concluded: "...it is unusual for there to be any
one person to make the average West Indian child in this study
feel particularly needed and loved. He is not made to feel that
he is a human being in his own right, precious to his parents,
and with all the dignity which a human being possesses. Due
to the meagreness of contact between him and his parents, he is
deprived of many of the advantages which a greater degree of
personal contact can offer. As a result he develops a weak
sense of his own identity " (20). It is interesting to note in this
context that a sample of West Indian school children in Britain
have significantly lower scores than a matched control group
of English children on the Coopersmith self esteem scale. This
is in contrast to the American data reported by Coopersmith
(21) which indicate that black children in America do not have
a poorer self esteem than whites; nor indeed do they now
disparage their ethnic self identity as they did in earlier
years (22).

In the British school system a disproportionate number
of black West Indian children are taken in their early school
years from normal classrooms and assigned to schools for the
"educationally subnormal" (23); very often this allocation is
based on behavioural rather than intellectual criteria (24). The
wide range of environmental factors which depress achievement
in black children are also ignored in such decisions (25).

A number of clinical studies of psychiatric disorder in
West Indian children have been carried out. Graham and
Meadows (26) investigated fifty-five West Indian children, and
matched English-born controls, referred to the Brixton Child
Guidance Clinic over a three-year period. Twenty-nine of the
subjects were boys (mean age 9.1) and twenty-six were girls
(mean age 9.6 years). The West Indian children represented 9.5

per cent of the clinic population. No control group of *normal* West Indian children was studied.

The West Indian group contained proportionately more girls than the clinic population as a whole, and this sex difference was taken into account in selecting clinic controls. No differences between West Indian children and controls were found with respect to domestic circumstances (including absence of parents from home). However, significantly more of the West Indian girls than controls had experienced earlier maternal separation, and both West Indian girls and boys had experienced significantly more paternal separation than controls. The study and control children were not matched for diagnosis, and a comparison of symptom patterns indicated that significantly more of both West Indian boys and girls were disobedient in the school setting. The West Indian girls were significantly less anxious than the control girls. The authors of this study concluded that "...there is felt to be a clear cause for concern in the frequent and sometimes traumatic separations that the current immigration pattern imposes on West Indian family life".

Walker (27) reported that some 12 per cent of children seen at a psychiatric clinic in a West London hospital were from the West Indies. Thirty-seven West Indian children and controls were studied, and the author reported that material circumstances in the homes of the West Indian families were much poorer than in the homes of the English-born control children. A high rate of separation from one or both parents was found in the children of West Indian origin. The author, by means of an investigation of home circumstances, suggests that many of the simpler psychological difficulties encountered in the West Indian children were traceable to abnormal family conditions, including over-crowding, daily minding and fostering, and separation from a parent.

It should be borne in mind that in studies such as those of Graham and Meadows, and of Walker, differences in circumstances between disturbed immigrant and native children are not sufficient grounds for inferring a causal relationship between social background and symptoms. The investigation of a normal West Indian control group is necessary before such inferences can be drawn. For example, there is epidemiological evidence of a high rate of mental illness (especially schizophrenia) in West Indian immigrants in Britain (28, 29). A detailed study of West Indian schizophrenics, English schizophrenic controls and normal West Indian controls (30) showed that the West Indian schizophrenics had significantly poorer material circumstances than the English patients, even when age and occupational class were controlled. However, there was no difference in material circumstances between the West Indian patients and the similarly matched West Indian normals.

A school-based study by Wight and Norris (31) in Birmingham compared scores on the Bristol Social Adjustment Guide for 220 West Indian children and 102 English children aged between 5 and 13 years. At the infant level (5-7 years) West Indian children were described as significantly more restless, hostile to adults, anxious for the approval of other children, while at the same time expressing hostility to them, and significantly more depressed than English children. At the junior level (8-9 years) the West Indian were significantly more restless, hostile to adults, hostile to other children and unconcerned for adult approval. At the secondary level (12-13 years) West Indian children were significantly more hostile to adults.

However, compared with English children of this age they showed significantly fewer 'physical defects' and 'ailment possibly psychosomatic or aggravated strain'. There was a definite trend in the data for the behavioural differences between West Indian and English children to be greater the younger the child. The difficulties in social adjustment were both severer and more numerous in the younger West Indian children.

A comparison was made between West Indian children 'newly arrived' and those 'born here'. No significant differences were recorded for the infant and junior groups, but for the secondary group 'hostility to other children' was significant at the one per cent level, the newly arrived showing much more hostility than those born in England.

Nicol (32) studied 204 West Indian children attending a south London child guidance clinic in the decade 1960-69. Of these, ninety-three were born in Britain and 111 had migrated from the west Indies. Referrals for 1967 were specially studied, and it was found that while the unusual number of girls was apparent in the clinic population born in the West Indies, the population of West Indian children born in England contained no such excess of girls. A comparison of the two groups indicated that anti-social disorder was much commoner in children born in the West Indies than in black children born in England; these anti-social disorders were associated with separation experiences in boys, but not in girls. Material factors (overcrowding, of social class, large families) did not differ between the two populations.

Bhatnager (33) constructed a scale to measure "adjustment" in secondary school children in London. The term 'adjustment' covered social relations, feelings of personal satisfaction, good self-concept, and freedom from anxiety. A sample of 174 West Indian boys and girls, and 200 English children were studied. The West Indian children had a mean adjustment score of 41.94 and the English children a score of 60.33, indicating markedly and significantly better "adjustment" in the English pupils. West Indian girls were found to be significantly more anxious than West Indian boys. Apart from this no other significant sex differences emerged, and adjustment appeared to be related to variables other than sex. Adjustment was *not* found to increase the longer West Indian children had been in the school system. However, immigrant children whose families were on visiting terms with English families were better adjusted than others.

Taken as a whole, "immigrant" children seem to have no greater prevalence of behaviour disturbances in the school setting than indigenous children. (34) This seems to be, however, because of the extremely quiescent behaviour of Asian children in the class room. Haynes (35) found that the Indian pupils she studied were considerably more stable and favourable in their attitudes to education than English children. A similar finding is reported by Herman (36) who collected data on behavior disturbance in 2,587 girls in a large number of junior and secondary schools in the London area. The "best behaved" group were Japanese and Chinese girls, followed by girls of Indian and Pakistani origin (including those from Kenya). This group was closely followed in good behaviour by the British girls. Immigrant girls from Europe and Ireland were badly behaved, and the "worst behaved" group (according to the norms of an English observer) were girls from the West Indies and Africa.

A study (37) of seven-year-olds (112 English and 74 West Indian) in five multiracial schools in the London area indicated a higher prevalence of behaviour disorder in black children, as indicated by the Rutter questionnaire for teachers. (38) Children of British parents had a mean score of 5.41 on this scale, compared with the mean 8.39 for West Indian children, a highly significant difference. An investigation of background factors based on parental interviews found that separation from one or more parent for a period of six months or more was related to behaviour disturbance in the group as a whole, although material factors such as overcrowding bore no such relationship.

Thirty-seven per cent of the West Indian children had experienced separation from a parent for six months or more (mainly through being left in the West Indies with a relative, or because of father absence in England) compared with 13 per cent of English children. When the effect of parental separation was controlled for, the difference in mean scores between the two ethnic groups became smaller, but nevertheless a significant difference remained, indicating more behaviour disturbance (as observed by teachers) in West Indian children. A principal components analysis of the 27 items making up the Rutter scale indicated four important factors. The first three represented "acting out behaviour and hyperactivity", (restless, destructive, irritable, disobedient, poor concentration); "nervousness" (school refusal, nail-biting, worries, miserable, pains and aches); and "anti-social behaviour" (lying, stealing, fighting, solitary). On all of these three components being West Indian did not load significantly, although separation from parents loaded significantly on the third, "anti-social behaviour" syndrome. The fourth factor, which had significant loadings on being West Indian and being female, represented children who tended to be worried, miserable, and often absent from school. Such children also tended to have had prolonged absence from a parent.

Another study in London schools (39) based on random sampling in infant, junior and junior high schools studied 58 black West Indian children and a similar number of English controls. Tape recorded interviews (by both black and white researchers) were conducted, and it was found that some 40 per cent of black children wanted white physical characteristics, compared with 12 per cent of white children preferring some black characteristics. Teachers were asked to rate the school behaviour of the study children (without knowledge of other ratings) and it was found that black children who rejected their ethnic identity were to a significant extent seen as behaviour problems by their teachers. It was concluded that "alienation" was a factor(in addition to the previously identified factor of separation from a parent) which could account for the increased prevalence of behaviour disorders in black children in London schools.

The largest study in this field is that carried out by Rutter and his colleagues (40, 41, 42) who surveyed by means of Rutter's questionnaire for teachers some 2,000 English and West Indian ten-year-olds in local authority schools in a London Borough. Of the 1,689 English children, 24.5 per cent of boys had deviant scores according to previously established cut-off points, (43) and 13.2 per cent of girls were disturbed at this level, giving a combined proportion for the sexes of 19.1 per cent. In the 354 West Indian children, 48.8 per cent of boys and 34.1 per cent of girls were "deviant", giving a combined rate of deviance in West Indian boys and girls of 41.2 per cent. The differences between the West Indian and the English children were highly significant.

The notions of "deviance" implies that the behaviour involved only a small proportion of the population; but in this London sample, 19 per cent of English children and 41 per cent of West Indian children have been termed "deviant". The reason for this apparent anomaly is that the norms for the Rutter scale were established in the Isle of Wight, a stable rural-urban community on a small island a few miles off the coast of southern England. Children with high scores (qualifying as "deviant") on the teachers' questionnaire had scores in the Isle of Wight study which were similar to those of children attending child guidance clinics for treatment of conventionally defined child psychiatric disorder. Clearly the prevalence of behaviour disorders in the inner city area studied (which, even among the white children contains migrants from Ireland, Scotland and other parts of England) is much higher than in the stable and largely non-migrant community of the Isle of Wight.

An examination of item responses to the Rutter questionnaire showed that West Indian boys had significantly higher "deviant" scores than English boys on the following items: restlessness; being squirmy or fidgety; unable to settle; fighting; disobedient; resentful or aggressive; bullying; destructive; lying; stealing; unresponsiveness; irritable; and absent for trivial reasons. Items discriminating to a significant extent (at the one per cent level) between West Indian and English girls were: restlessness; squirmy or fidgety; unable to settle; fighting; disobedient; resentful or aggressive; bullying; destructive; lying; stealing; unresponsive; disliked by others; solitary; irritable; miserable or unhappy. In both West Indian boys and girls, then, the higher rate of deviance was accounted for by items in the acting out and aggressive domains of behaviour.

In order to check on the validity of the teachers' ratings of behaviour, and to assess potential factors in the aetiology of these disorders, special groups were selected for study. These consisted of a randomly selected control group of 58 West Indian children; a random sample of 60 West Indian children with a score of nine or more on the teachers' scale, and subscores, which indicated a conduct disorder (i.e. and acting out, or aggressive disorder); a randomly selected control group of 106 English children (selected without regard to the presence or absence of deviant behavior); and a random sample of 159 English children with conduct disorder.

Detailed interviews with the parents of these children were carried out using the methods standardized by Rutter and Brown. (44, 45) Interviewers were unaware of teachers' ratings of the children, so that interviewers were not biased by such information. Black and white interviewers were employed for interviewing black families, but few differences in response to interviewers from the two ethnic groups were detected.

The parents were asked about their children's behaviour, a standardized approach of known reliability being used to assess psychiatric disorder. The interviews revealed a markedly different picture from that indicated by the teacher ratings. Only 28 per cent of West Indian boys and 39 per cent of girls of West Indian parents were "deviant" on both the parental and teacher ratings. The estimated prevalence of psychiatric disorder as judged from the parental interviews was 62/354 or 17.5 per cent in West Indian children, and 422/1689 or 25% in English children. The black children are thus *less* likely than their English peers to manifest disturbed behavior at home.

A further check on the teacher ratings was made by a further series of interviews (again, of a standardized and previously validated nature) with the teachers in study. These interviews were carried out by workers who were unaware both of the teachers' original ratings, and of the results of parental interview. These interviews indicated a better concordance with the original teacher ratings, 69% of West Indian children and 65% of English children who were deviant on the screening questionnaire having psychiatric disorder according to the interviews. The total estimated prevalence of psychiatric disorder in West Indian children, based on the teacher interviews, was 135/354 or 38.2%, compared with 466/1689 or 27.6% in English children. It appears then that the disturbed behaviour of West Indian children is focused in the school, and not in the home.

Examination of a wide range of data from the interviews with parents in the special sub-groups revealed only two clearly distinguishing factors between deviant and non-deviant West Indian children: the former were much less likely (47 per cent versus 16 per cent) to be living with both natural parents; and there was a dearth of father-child communication for the deviant West Indian children compared with the non-deviant (42 per cent versus 12 per cent). These factors alone cannot explain the difference in the prevalence of deviance in the school setting between West Indian and English children (material factors such as overcrowding were not significantly related to disorder) and clearly some further aetiological factors have to be identified. I have hypothesized (46) that the alienating experiences of black children in the British schools could be responsible for this deviance, which is in the nature of a disorganised or individualistic "revolt". It is of note that studies with a population of black 15-year-olds in British schools have indicated that radical criticism of a racially exploitive social structure, and adherence to radical black values was not associated with aggressive attitudes towards their white peers. (47) This is in accord with the study cited above (46) which indicated that children with a strong sense of their own ethnic identity did not tend to act out in aggressive ways in the classroom. From a curiculum point of view there are obvious advantages in fostering the growth of black studies in British multiracial schools in order to give black children mature and magnanimous pride in being black, and having an Afro-Carribbean heritage.

It is possible that the low rates of deviance observed in Asian children in Britain are due to the strengths which such children have in terms of family cohesiveness, language, religion, and cultural tradition.* It is of interest in this context that Milner's English study (48) found that Asian children were much less likely than West Indian children to identify themselves with the physical characteristics of white children, or to reject their own ethnic identity. It is also of note that the social and economic status of Asian parents, and the educational achievement of their children is actually higher than that of the host population. (49, 50)

Studies of the adaptation of teenagers from ethnic minorities are few, largely because of the pattern of migration. Bottoms (53) has argued that children of migrants, born and socialized in British culture will have much higher expectations than their parents and will not readily accept systems of racial discrimination and may in fact turn to delinquency. Dondy (54) suggests that significant numbers of young black teenagers leaving London schools prefer to remain unemployed rather than take the inferior jobs assigned to them.

I have argued (55) that consciousness of such alienation should in time lead to a maturity of group consciousness in which young blacks engage in political activity to combat racism, rather than engaging in individual acts of revolt which are likely to be self-destructive, but there is not much evidence of such a phenomenon at the present time. In a Birmingham study, White (56) found that the proportion of black teenagers

---

* But cf. Kurokawa's study of Mennonite children (51) which indicated that acculturation from a "stable, well-integrated and highly structured social system" could lead to manifestation of psychological aymptoms. The position of some Indian and Pakistani children in Britain may be analogous (52).

(aged 14-19) in a series of attempted suicides was twice as high as in the community as a whole. The significant aetiological factors identified were a history of early separation from parents, crises in personal relationships, and a history of behaviour difficulties at school. In a London study of "black suicide" we found that the two successful suicides were black teenagers aged 14 and 15. (57) These were the only completed adolescent suicides in a series of 210 patients of all ages and races admitted to hospital for emergency treatment.

CONCLUSIONS

The conclusions from this survey are as follows:

1. Commonwealth immigrants to Britain, especially those from the Carribbean, are faced with a variety of stresses which tend to disorganise the family life and depress the possibilities for adequate child rearing. This takes its toll on the physical and mental health of pre-school black children, although accurate epidemiological surveys of the full extent of these conditions are lacking.

2. In school, black children are perceived as behaving badly by their teachers, and also as underachieving. Clinical studies have indicated a differential pattern of disturbance in West Indian girls. The epidemiological basis of the prevalence of behaviour disorders in 10-year-old West Indian boys and girls is well established, and they are significantly more likely than their white peers to manifest conduct disorders in the classroom. The aetiology of these disturbances is complex, and the following factors have been tentatively identified: separation from parents early in life; lack of adequate family life during the early years of childhood; sense of personal disparagement, lack of ethnic consciousness, and poor self-esteem; and a sense of personal alienation at the various observable facts of racism in British culture.

3. No particular problems seem to be associated with Asian children in Britain. This is probably due to the cultural cohesiveness of the Asian community, and its generally higher social status.

4. In the future, the manifestation of "deviance" in adolescent blacks, no longer immigrants in the literal sense, will probably take two forms-delinquency and mental illness of an individualized form (similar to that observed in adult blacks (58)) and of a greater prevalence than in white teenagers; and secondly,

an organized and more constructive integration of black teenagers in various kinds of group "deviance" or political activism. In contrast to the integrative processes of black activism, acculturation may give rise to some behavioral deviance in Asian teenagers.

REFERENCES

1. Bagley, C. *Race, 9,* 343, (1968).

2. Bagley, C. *J. Biosocial. Sci. 3,* 461, (1971).

3. Bagley, C.   The built environment as an influence on personality and social behaviour . In: *Psychology and the Built Environment,* D. Canter and T.Lee, eds., The Architectural Press, London, (1974).

4. Malzberg, B. International migration and mental disease among the white population of New York State 1960-61. *Internat. J. Soc. Psychiat.,13,* 184, (1967).

5. Rutter, M. *Children of Sick Parents,* Oxford University Press, London, (1966).

6. Barrett, C. and Noble, H. *J. Marriage and Family,35,* 181, (1973).

7. Bagley, C., Jacobson, S., and Palmer, C. *Psychol. Med. 3,* 177, (1973).

8. Deakin, N. *Colour, Citizenship and British Society.* Panther Books, London, (1970).

9. Bagley, C. *Social Structure and Prejudice in Five English Boroughs,* Institute of Race Relations, London, (1970).

10. Lomas, J. *The Coloured Population of Great Britain,* Runnymede Trust, London, (1974).

11. Little, A. "The background of underachievement in immigrant children in London", In *Race and Education Across Cultures,* G. Verma and C. Bagley, eds., heinemann Educational Books, London, (1975).

12. Rutter, M., Yule, B., Morton, J., and Bagley, C. *Child Psychol. Psychiat. 15,* 241-261, (1974).

13. Jackson B. Childminders. *New Society,* November 29, 521-424, (1973).

14. Stroud, C. and Moody, V. *Maternal and Child Care, 3,* 487, (1967).

15. Milner, D. *Europ. J. soc. Psychol. 3,* 281, (1973).

16. Bagley, C. and Coard, B. "Cultural knowledge and rejection of ethnic self-identity in West Indian children in London" In: *Race and Education Across Cultures,* G. Verma and C. Bagley, eds. Heinemann Educational Books, London, (1975).

17. Prince, G. *Maternal and Child Care, 3,* 483, (1967).

18. Pollack, M.: *Today's Three-year-olds in London.* Heinemann Medical Books, London, (1972).

19. Hood, C., Oppe, T., Bless, I. and Apte, E. *Children of West Indian Immigrants.* Institute of Race Relations, London, (1970).

20. Pollack, *op. cit.,* pp. 142-143.

21. Coopersmith, S. Self-concept, race and education In: *Race andEducation Across Cultures,* G. Verma and C. Bagley, eds. Heinemann Educational Books, London, (1975).

22. Fox, D. and Jordan, V. Racial preference and identification of black American, Chinese and white children. *Genetic Psychology Monographs, 88,* 229, (1973).

23. Townsend, B. *Immigrant Pupils in England.* National Foundation for Educational Research, London, (1971).

24. I.L.E.A. *Children with Special Difficulties,* Report No.2 of the Schools Sub-Committee. Inner London Education Authority, London, (1972).

25. Coard, B. *How the West Indian child is made educationally subnormal by the British school system.* New Beacon Books, London, (1971).

26. Graham, P. and Meadows, C. *J. Child Psychol. Psychiat.,* **8,** 105, (1967).

27. Walker, A. *Cultural variants and psychological illness in West Indian and British children.* Paper given to 2nd Annual Race Relations Conference of the Royal Anthropological Society, London, (1968).

28. Bagley, C. *Race, 9,* 343, (1968).

29. Bagley, C. *J. Biosoc. Sci. 3,* 449, (1971).

30. Bagley, C. *Inernatl. J. soc. Psychiat. 17,* 292, (1971).

31. Wight, J. and Morris, R. *Teaching english to West Indian children.* Evans-Methuen Schools Council Working Paper 29, London, (1970).

32. Nicol, A. *J. Child Psychol. Psychiat. 12,* 233, (1971).

33. Bhatnagar, J. *Immigrants at School.* Cornmarket Press, London, (1970).

34. Department of Education and Science. *The education of Immigrants.* Education survey 13. Her Majesty's Stationery Office, London, (1971).

35. Haynes, J. *Educational Assessment of Immigrant Pupils.* National Foundation for Educational research, London, (1971).

36. Herman, D. *Times Educational Supplement,* May 5, 8, (1972).

37. Bagley, C. *Research in Education,* *8,* 47, (1972).

38. Rutter, M. *J. Child Psychol. Psychiat. 8,* 1, (1967).

39. Bagley, C. and Coard, B. "Cultural knowledge and rejection of ethnic identity in West Indian children in London" In: *Race and Education Across Cultures.* G. Verma AND C. Bagley, eds, Heinemann Educational Books, London, (1975).

40. Rutter, M., Yule, W., Berger, M., Yule, B., Morton, J. and Bagley, C. *J. Child Psychol. Psychiat. 15,* 241-262, (1974).

41. Yule, W., Berger, M., and Rutter, M. *J. Child Psychol. Psychiat.,* in press, (1975).

42. Rutter, M., Yule, B., Morton, J., and Bagley, C. *J. Child Psychol. Psychiat.,* in press, (1975).

43. Rutter, M., Tizard, J. and Whitmore, K. *Education, Health and Behaviour.* Longmans, London, (1971).

44. Rutter, M. and Brown, G. *Soc. Psychiat., 1,* 38, (1966).

45. Brown, G. and Rutter, M. *Human Relations, 19,* 241, (1966).

46. Bagley, C. The background of deviance in black children in London. In:*Race and Education Across Cultures.* G. Verma and C. Bagley, eds. Heinemann Educational Books, London, New York, (1974).

47. Bagley, C. and Verma, G. Interethnic attitudes and behaviour in British multiracial schools. In: *Race and Education Across Cultures.* G. Verma and C. Bagley, eds. Heinemann Educational Books, London, (1974).

48. Milner, D. *Europ. J. Soc. Psychol., 3,* 281, (1973).

49. Deakin, N.: *Colour, Citizenship and British Society.* Panther Books, London, (1970).

50. Durojaie, S. *Educational Research,* June, 179, (1971).

51. Kurakowa, M. *Child Development,* 40, 689, (1969).

52. Bagley, C. *Race, 11,* 65, (1969).

53. Bottoms, A. *Race, 8,* 357, (1967).

54. Dondy, F. *Race Today, 6,* 44, (1974).

55. Bagley, C. *International MigrationReview, 5,* 18, (1971).

56. White, H. Self-poisoning in adolescents. *Brit. J. Psychiat., 123,* 113, (1973).

57. Bagley, C. and Greer, S. *J. Soc. Psychol., 86,* 175, (1973).

58. Bagley, C. The social aetiology of schizophrenia in immigrant groups. *Internat. J. Soc. Psychiat., 17,* 292, (1971).

MENTAL HEALTH IN CHILDREN, Volume I
Edited By D. V. Siva Sankar
Copyright © 1975 by
PJD Publications Ltd., Westbury, N.Y.

THE EARLY DETECTION
AND PREVENTION OF MENTAL ILLNESS:
THE MAURITIUS PROJECT

Fini Schulsinger, Sarnoff A. Mednick and Brian Bell
Psykologisk Institut, Copenhagen, Denmark
Peter H. Venables
University of York, England
Abdul C. Raman
Brown Sequard Hospital, Beau Bassin, Mauritius

The work described in this preliminary report was supported by
grants from the Medical Research Council of Great Britain,
the Danish International Development Agency, and the World
Health Organization. We are indebted to the Government of
Mauritius and the Ministry of Health for their active support
and encouragement. Ramesh Cheeneebash, Rashid Nabee and
Miss P. Saccaram assisted in the data collection. Mr. Regis
Rose provided invaluable liaison between the project and
various governmental departments.

It has been traditionally acknowledged in medicine that primary prevention consummates the triad: etiology, therapy, and prevention. This has been the case in spite of the fact that the order has been quite different in several important instances; for example, both in smallpox and tuberculosis.

Considering the enormous, but frequently frustrated efforts which have been made in the search for causes of schizophrenia, one should not be too eager to reject the possibility of finding methods for primary prevention of this scourge - or its partial amelioration - before the etiology (or etiologies) have been established.

From the experimental point of view, etiological research into serious mental illness has a number of severe drawbacks, as was pointed out in a methodological paper by Mednick and McNeil (1968). First, the large differences in the development of brain between the primate and human species excludes the possibility of interpreting the results from behavioural animal research as pertinent to psychiatric illness. Secondly, it is neither feasible nor desirable to expose children experimentally to the kind of traumas which have been hypothesized as possible etiological factors in schizophrenia, whether it be a cold and rejecting mother or the ablation of the adrenal glands, etc.

Since possible preventive methods would most likely be of a protective or beneficial nature, responsible ways of trying out their effect in experimental settings would be a more feasible approach. However, one major problem is to determine the kinds of preventive intervention one might use. Can the results from current or previous research guide us in the right directions? A second major difficulty derives from the selection of potential subjects for preventive research.

No matter what kind of intervention procedure one might consider, the economic difficulties with regard to manpower and facilities would force one to try out such an approach on those limited groups with a particular high risk for schizophrenia. We can all agree that beneficial social and medical procedures ought to be available for every child in the world. But, when we look at a world where the rich get richer and the poor get poorer, it seems obvious that beneficial interventions in limited and well-defined risk groups would be a more realistic task than waiting for general improvements in medical care.

This leads us to the question of early detection. Can we, well before the age of risk, detect with satisfactory reliability those individuals who will eventually become schizophrenic or seriously mentally deviant? If this is possible we can define the target groups for preventive experimentation. Furthermore, the characteristics of such a high-risk group and its life circumstances would probably indicate various guidelines for the selection of preventive procedures.

So far, all this has been rather simple and obvious; but is this approach realistic or is it just fancy? In other words, can we indeed identify some important risk characteristics?

The most established risk factor in schizophrenia is that of heredity: additionally, we know for certain that environmental factors must also be of great importance (Mednick, Schulsinger, Higgins and Bell, 1974). Were it otherwise, the concordance rate for monozygotic twins with regard to schizophrenia would be 100% and not approximately 40% as was found in the more recent and well performed twin studies of Gottesman and Shields (1973) and of Kringlen (1967). From those studies of monozygotic twins who are discordant for schizophrenia (Pollin and Stabenau, 1968) we know that both perinatal complications (which might encompass early childhood CNS infections) and a certain hostile attitude towards the child on the part of the most psychologically deviant parent are potential environmental factors.

Mednick and Schulsinger (1968) began in 1962 a longitudinal study of 207 children with severely schizophrenic mothers and 104 matched low-risk controls. In 1967, 20 of these genetically defined high-risk subjects had suffered mental breakdowns of various kinds, and the authors were then able to look back in order to determine the ways in which these 20 subjects differed in 1962 from comparable subjects who did not subsequently break down.

As was originally hypothesized by Mednick (1958), certain psychophysiological variables discriminated very well between the breakdown subjects and their matched non-breakdown controls from the original high-risk group. The best discriminator was a fast recovery time (from a mild stressor to the ANS). In addition, the breakdown group was characterized by faster latencies of response, poor extinction of the conditioned electrodermal response (EDR), and greater reactivity, i.e. higher response amplitudes. All these variables, except poor extinction, were to a lesser degree characteristic of the total high-risk group when compared with the low-risk control group. Besides these ANS characteristics, Mednick and Schulsinger (1973) also found certain environmental factors to be precursors of breakdown. These were perinatal complications, early parental separation and severe social disruptions during the mother's pregnancy: (the latter finding has been reported by Birgitte Mednick, 1973). Some of these environmental factors worked in addition to the genetic factors while others had an interactive effect. The fast recovery time seemed to be especially associated with genetic predisposition. A recent study with twins completed in our laboratory in Copenhagen provides further indication of the genetic loading in relation to recovery parameters (Bell, Gottesman, Mednick and Sergeant, 1974). It can be added that further indication of the relevance of a fast recovery rate for schizophrenia has been established in research with a variety of schizophrenic patients (Ax and Bamford, 1970; Gruzelier and Venables, 1972).

In spite of the general simplicity of doing prospective studies of genetically defined high-risk groups, Mednick and Schulsinger's 1962 study was the first of its kind with regard to serious mental illness. As such, it provoked a certain amount of interest, and following a WHO Technical Conference on Neurophysiology in Psychiatry held in 1968 it was recommended as a useful model for comparative research in different countries. This was partially due to the fact that the physiological parameters were considered to be relatively independent from cultural influences.

In 1968 the small island country of Mauritius became an independent nation, and subsequently a member of the UN and WHO. On this occasion the chief psychiatrist in Mauritius, Dr. A.C. Raman, suggested that WHO should initiate a program of mental health research in Mauritius in order to stimulate this aspect of the country's health service. WHO then asked Schulsinger to visit Mauritius in 1969 in order to find out whether a replication of Mednick and Schulsinger's high-risk project in Copenhagen would be possible on the island.

Mauritius is a densely populated country with about 900,000 inhabitants occupying an area of approximately 2,400 square kilometers. The population is composed of Hindus and Tamils (51%), Moslems (16%), Creoles (29%), and Chinese (4%). The economy is poor and is based mainly on a single crop (sugar cane). The annual per capita income in 1969 was about US $220. In spite of this, the infrastructure is quite advanced. Perinatal care is of a relatively high standard. Some 90% of the children attend elementary school for several years. Emigration is limited. Infections and parasitic disorders are relatively well under control. Mild malnutrition (hypoproteinemia) is common but pronounced kwashiorkor or marasmus is rare.

There is approximately one psychiatric hospital bed per 1,000 inhabitants, a ratio which is far higher than in other developing countries. The climate is sub-tropical to tropical. Foreigners manage well with French or English, since both are official languages. The indigenous population speak a variety of "patois". In some rural areas Hindi is the major language.

In 1969 we were very preoccupied with our substantial findings that certain ANS variables were precursors of mental breakdown. We considered it justified in a new project to hypothesize that it was possible to select high-risk subjects with regard to serious mental breakdown on a psychophysiological basis, paying no attention to heredity or other factors. We then proposed to WHO that instead of a replication of the Copenhagen Study we should launch a prospective study on a population of 3 year-old children. We would then select on a psychophysiological basis a subgroup for subsequent intensive observation and preventive intervention based on our experience gained from the Copenhagen project.

WHO agreed to the extent that they would sponsor the project except for the funding which was to be provided by the Psykologisk Institut in Copenhagen. Not every agency was interested in supporting an adventurous project in a country about which they had heard very little. In our search for financial support we met colleagues from related fields, who became very interested in the project. Peter Venables wanted to take responsibility for the psychophysiological aspects of the study with Brian Bell as his assistant. (The initial psychophysiological aspects of the project were subsequently supported by the Medical Research Council of Great Britain). Brian Sutton-Smith, from the Department of Child Development at Teachers College, Columbia University, was interested in running the psychological assessment of the childrens' development. Turan Itil and George Ulett offered assistance in order to obtain EEG examinations of the Mauritian children. Finally, the psychiatrists at the Brown-Sequard Hospital in Mauritius offered their help as pediatric examiners of the children. The Mauritian Government through the Minister of Health, Sir Harold Walter, and the assistant secretary, M.A. Desiré, gave a lot of practical assistance with regard to transportation and other services. They also secured the necessary official backing and promoted the public relation aspects of the study. The project is now run by a charitable organization, the Joint Child Health Project, which is under the auspices of both the Ministry of Health in Mauritius and WHO. The main funding, so far, has come from the Danish Government through its branch for assistance to developing countries (DANIDA) which alone supports the establishment and running expenses for two kindergartens each catering for 50 children on the condition that the project takes responsibility for the education and training of the first 14 nursery school teachers in Mauritius. The kindergartens and the training program is run by two Danish kingergarten experts, Steen Møller and Bodil Birket-Smith. Thus, if nothing else happens, Mauritius will have two modern kindergartens with well trained staff when our project is completed.

METHOD

The psychophysiological research started during August 1972 in its own building in the town of Quatre Bornes in Mauritius. The facility comprised a neurophysiology laboratory with a 4-channel Grass polygraph. Two channels for skin conductance and skin potential, one channel for EKG, and 2 channels for EEG which were recorded on magnetic tape. The psychophysiology was scored manually by Mauritian assistants. There was a psychological test room, a waiting room equipped with a play area where observations of the childrens' natural behavior could take place, an office, a kitchen and two staff rooms used for pediatric examinations and data preparation. The psychlogical assessments were performed by an American student, Miss Athena Chiriacka, from Columbia University and local assistants. The EEGs were recorded by Mr. Leigh Bagley, a chief EEG technician from the Missouri Institute of Psychiatry in St. Louis. Two Mauritians worked as assistants in the physiology laboratory.

SAMPLE AND PROCEDURE

It was our original intention to examine all children in the two neighbouring municipalities, Quatre Bornes and Vacoas, who on the day of examination would be between three and three and one quarter years old - a total of approximately 2000 children. The Central Statistical Office of Mauritius had information showing that these municipalities were representative for Mauritius with regard to the distribution of ethnic groups and rural/urban residents.

For practical reasons concerned with staffing arrangements we terminated the examinations during July 1973 with child number 1800, leaving very few potential subjects unexamined. The schedule permitted us to study a maximum of ten children per day, but usually there were about eight who came to the laboratory each day. They were picked up at home as a morning group and an afternoon group, and returned to their homes some four hours later.

The testing program comprised:

1) A field examination consisting of a parent's interview and judgements about the health and living conditions of the family - carried out by a young Mauritian field worker trained briefly by Schulsinger.
2) Psychological observations in the play - and waiting room.
3) A psychological assessment within a Piagetian framework.
4) A psychophysiological test made during a conditioning experiment comparable with our 1962 high-risk project in Copenhagen.
5) An electroencephalography examination.
6) A brief pediatric examination with a focus on nutritional symptoms. Laboratory analyses for haemoglobin percentage and the presence of sugar and protein were made with urine and blood samples.

7) A collection of obstetrical information from midwife and hospital records; this was possible for approximately 60% of the children.

In this report we shall consider some preliminary data from the psychophysiology test and from three of the other data sources: the parent interview, the pediatric examination, and the obstetrical investigation.

The primary purpose of the project was to examine on a battery of tests a sample of three year-old children and on the results of the physiology test we planned to select our subgroups which we characterized as "high" and "low" risk. The criterion for selection was that of fast ANS recovery, and in this instance we determined upon the half-time recovery of the skin conductance response as the principal index*.

RESULTS

Psychophysiological selection.

Each child who was examined at the laboratory provided a physiological record from the conditioning experiment. The following parameters were measured:

1. Skin Conductance (SC)
2. Skin Potential (SP).
3. Electrocardiogram (EKG).

The stimulus tape used during the experiment consisted of a series of tones and included 6 "orienting" trials and 18 "conditioning" trials. The physiological parameters were monitored continuously during the presentation of the tape, which lasted approximately 20 minutes.

Ultimately, we will extract from each record data relevant to both tonic and phasic activity on all three measures. For the purposes of selection we confined ourselves essentially to electrodermal parameters, essentially that of responsivity. Mednick and Schulsinger's 1962 study concerned itself with this metric, and data handling problems encountered during the summer of 1973 forced us to assign highest priority to processing the skin conductance and potential data. Thus, only a part of the data derived from the electrocardiogram had been processed for computer analysis when we began our

---

*A detailed report of the selection procedure is in preparation.

selection procedure in the fall of 1973. The entire data-set for the 1800 subjects will amount to a total of some 130,000 computer cards which, when complete, will be entered upon magnetic tape files. The collation and handling of the data is being carried out by the Medical Research Council Computer Services Unit in London. This organization provided the facilities for the selection procedure.

In order to carry out the selection we decided to abstract data from the three measures. The first task was to select out those children who were characterized as "electrodermal responders"; this procedure provided us with two groups, "responders" and "non-responders". The second phase of the selection produced a sample of children whose electrodermal records indicated that they were typically "short-recoverers" and "high amplitude responders" with reference to skin conductance activity. By this point in the selection process, we now had three groups from which we selected the children who would be placed in the kindergartens and those who would remain in the community. The final stage of selection was carried out on a random choice basis within an ethnic group and place of residence framework. We had determined that each school would cater for 50 children, of whom approximately three-quarters were to be "high-risk" children (short-recoverers and extremely low responders). The remainder of the children in the school were considered to be the "low-risk" group (medium recoverers and medium amplitude responders). This distribution was repeated in the community groups. As far as was possible, we attempted to have an equal balance between males and females. The final make-up of the four groups is given in Table 1. We have attempted to replicate within each group the ethnic distribution seen in the island.

It is likely that we will have to make some modifications to the final make-up of the groups*-some of the children selected in the fall of 1973 were not able to attend the school

---

*Since this report was written various problems with organization on the island, particularly with regard to the school in Quatre Bornes, have necessitated changes to be made in the selection for this area. Supplementary information relating to the Quatre Bornes groups will be available shortly.

TABLE I

Distribution of the selected children into groups

	QUATRE BORNES SCHOOL			VACOAS SCHOOL		
	short recovery	non responders	low risk	short recovery	non responders	low risk
Hindu	9	3	5	12	5	7
Tamil	2	0	3	2	0	1
Moslem	5	1	3	9	2	5
General population (Creole)	12	2	5	3	1	3
Group Total	28	6	16	26	8	16

School total=50   School total=50

	QUATRE BORNES COMMUNITY			VACOAS COMMUNITY		
	short recovery	non responders	low risk	short recovery	non responders	low risk
Hindu	8	2	7	12	5	7
Tamil	3	0	3	2	0	1
Moslem	3	1	1	9	2	5
General population (creole)	14	3	5	3	1	3
Group Total	28	6	16	26	8	16

Table II

Adverse items from the Parent Interview protocol

Item	Short Recovery N = 108	Non Responder N = 28	Low Risk N = 64
1. Mother's occupational status: none, part-time labourer, agricultural worker	80	26	53
2. Father's occupational status: as in item 1.	48	15	26
3. Mother's schooling: less than 2 years	24	10	16
4. Father's schooling: less than 2 years	27	8	15
5. Mother's judgement of child's a) physical development -below average	6	3	6
b) intellectual development -below average	7	3	5
c) health -below average, often ill	22	3	13

Table II continued.

6.	More than 4 persons per room	61	17	39
7.	Number of rooms: only one room	18	6	15
8.	Appearance of house: poor	7	1	2
9.	Medical information reported by parent: a) serious illness during pregnancy	15	8	10
	b) delivery problems	6	1	2
	c) serious illness in childhood	27	6	18
10.	Behaviour problems: a) awkward in running or walking	1	1	0
	b) destructive	1	0	1
	c) poor speech	3	1	2

Table III

Adverse items from the Obstetric Information protocol

Item	Short Recovery N = 108	Non Responder N = 28	Low Risk N = 64
PREGNANCY			
1. Anemia: second lowest Hb% less than 70%			
a) second trimester	6	0	3
b) third trimester	21	8	20
2. Albuminuria: with hospital treatment	2	1	1
3. Blood pressure: with hospital treatment for hypertension	2	0	0
4. Fits: with hospital treatment	0	0	0
5. Bleeding PV	0	1	1
DELIVERY			
6. Dyne delivery	13	3	8
7. Pregnancy number: more than 8	4	0	2
8. Fetal presentation: breech or foot	0	0	0
9. Premature rupture of membrane by more than one hour	1	1	1
10. Fetal distress found more than once	0	0	0
POST DELIVERY			
11. Child born blue	0	0	0
12. Premature	1	0	1
13. Birth weight less than 5½ pounds	2	0	2

Table IV
Adverse items from the Pediatric Examination

Item	Short Recovery N = 108	Non Responders N = 28	Low Risk N = 64
SKIN			
1. Edema:			
a) facial	3	1	1
b) extremities	0	1	0
2. Folds	1	1	3
3. Scabies	17	6	12
4. Purulent lesions	8	0	3
MOUTH			
5. Angular stomatitis	7	3	3
6. Caries	32	7	24
HAIR			
7. Sparse	4	2	4
8. Easily pulled out	28	7	20
9. Reddish color	6	1	4
OTHER			
10. Skeletal deformity	0	0	0
11. Throat infection	5	3	0
12. Enlarged liver	2	1	0
13. Hb gram% : less than 70%	39	14	32
14. Sugar	3	3	2
15. Albumin	4	0	3

to which they were assigned. For example, we found that one of the children we had originally selected had died in the period since testing. So far we have had only two refusals from parents when they were invited to send their child to the kindergarten. At first sight it appears that problems of non-cooperation, etc. will not be extensive in the community groups; however, we are now extending our original psychophysiological testing program to include a retest on two occasions during 1974 of all the selected children. Thus, community group children who refuse to be retested will be substituted by those who are available for retest. In addition to the retest program we are currently obtaining recordings from samples aged 5, 10, 15, 20 and 25 years. This part of the project (under Peter Venables' direction) is being carried out by Ramesh Cheeneebash, a young Mauritian who was trained in psychophysiological techniques during the testing in 1972-1973.

Our major concern following the end of the testing program was to complete the selection outlined previously. We have, however, completed an initial analysis which deals with data derived from the parent interview, pediatric examination, obstetric and laboratory behaviour protocols of the selected children. The purpose of this exercise was to find out, whether the "physiological risk" was associated with perinatal complications, malnutrition and bad social conditions. The possible relation of a psychiatric family history will be reported in a subsequent paper.

The Parent Interview.

This comprised 55 items which dealt with the occupational status of the parents, their educational history, and the living accomodation of the family. It also included items about siblingship, etc. We looked at a number of items and determined for each what we considered to be an adverse response. For example, it was decided that within the Mauritian context that employment as a part-time labourer or a job as an agricultural worker could be regarded an adverse condition; similarly, when the household was limited to accomodation of only one room this was noted as an adverse situation. The results from this analysis are given in Table 2. Items from the protocol are expressed as the "adverse" item. It can be readily seen, taking into account the varying numbers involved, that there is little difference between the groups.

The large numbers of families who enter under the low occupational status items tends to reflect the general employment situation in Mauritius where the majority of the population are engaged in work connected with the sugar industry. The secondary process industries such as refining, employ only a small number of workers. Most of the labour derives from the harvesting and cultivation of the cane.

The Obstetric Information Questionnaire.

The items on this questionnaire were completed from ante-natal and delivery cards maintained by the local health authorities. Information was available for 60.5% of the children in the selected groups. Details were not available for the remainder either because no official record was traceable or because a number of the children had been delivered by an unofficial midwife (termed "dyne" in Creole patois).

Items on the obstetric questionnaire encompassed information about anemia and albuminuria during pregnancy, the fetal presentation and weight at birth. Table 3 shows the presence of adverse conditions in the three groups. Again, we are unable to point to any appreciable differences between the three groups.

The Pediatric Examination.

The pediatric examination was carried out by a group of Mauritian doctors. Our interest was essentially to obtain information which related to the nutritional state of the child. Particular emphasis was given to items concerning malnutrition and the presence of worm infestation. We used as indicators of these states those symptoms commonly noted in the tropical environment; for example, whether facial edema was present, skin folds, angular stomatitis, and condition of the hair and its pigmentation status. Laboratory determination of blood and urine samples provided information on haemoglobin values, and the occurrence of sugar and albumin. The results of the pediatric examination are given in Table 4. Taking those items which indicate nutritional status (haemoglobin percentage, hair condition, etc.) we can conclude that in all three groups the percentage of children who appear to some extent as being undernourished is about 25%. Some 30% of the children in all groups evidence caries to a significant degree. (Both chldren and adults can be readily observed in all areas of the island eating sticks of sugar cane at all times of the day.)

Comparison of the three groups indicates once again no large differences.

The Laboratory Behaviour Questionnaire.

The laboratory behaviour questionnaire was mainly completed before the psychophysiological recording was made for each child. It was largely intended as a checklist on which the ambient temperature and humidity of the laboratory together with other technical details concerning apparatus performance could be noted. Additionally, we included items covering the child's reaction to the testing and methodological points concerning the placement of electrodes, etc. We have abstracted those items which deal specifically with the child's response to the testing situation - his reaction in terms of whether he cried or not, the extent of his distress, the amount of movement made during the test, and whether he was friendly and cooperative to the laboratory staff. The adverse items are shown in Table 5.

In contrast to the data provided in the previous tables it is apparent that there are a number of differences between the various groups. The data obtained under item 1 - whether the child cried or did not cry during testing - were cast into a 2 x 3 contingency table and a significant chi-square of 13.78 ,(2 df) $p < .01$ was found. The short recovery group includes a much larger number of children who either cried uncontrollably or cried quietly *but* continuously than the other groups. Taking only the "short recovery" and "low risk" groups for comparison results in a chi-square of 6.07, (1 df) $p < 0.25$. When we turn to the second item - reaction to testing - a significant difference is again found between the groups (chi-square $= 12.67$ (2 df) $p < .01$). Here, we note that the non-responder group is appreciately more passive in the testing situation, whereas the "short recovery" group evidenced a greater amount of fear and anxiety. Again, comparison between the "short recovery" and "low risk" groups yields a significant chi-square of 4.84, (1df) $p < .05$. Comparison of the three groups on the item dealing with activity in the testing situation also results in a significant chi-square of 8.86, (2df) $p < .025$; the non-responder group showed a

higher frequency of children who were judged as hypoactive.
There is no significant difference between the short recovery
and low-risk group (chi-square is not significant). The item
concerning sociability failed to indicate any differences between
the three groups. In short, the items taken from the laboratory
behaviour questionnaire indicate that overall the short recovery

Table V

Adverse items from the Laboratory Behaviour protocol

Item	Short Recovery N = 108	Non Responders N = 28	Low Risk N = 64
1. Child cries uncontrollably, or quietly through *entire* session	34	1	10
2. Reaction to test: a) frightened and anxious	57	6	25
b) passive	41	21	37
3. Sociability in the laboratory: unresponsive	23	5	14
4. Activity in the testing situation: a) hyperactive or tremor	17	1	7
b) hypoactive	29	22	24

group was characterized by more and sustained crying, they
were more frightened than the other groups and showed more
movement in the testing situation than the non-responder
group. The non-responder group exhibited marked hypo-
activity.

DISCUSSION

We should like to point out that the foregoing is intended as a preliminary analysis, and not as an exhaustive statistical analysis of all the variables. We had anticipated that obstetric data would be available for some 50 - 60% of the children we would examine during the year's testing. However, it became apparent that even when an official record card was traced there was often little information listed which could be of potential use. In general, it appears that there are no consistent differences between the groups as regards their social, pediatric and obstetrical profiles. If any trend is discernible, it is that the low-risk group shows slightly more adverse pediatric indications than the two "risk groups". However, the marked differences between the groups as regards their behaviour during testing corresponds with Mednick and Schulsinger's earlier findings: in a post-test-interview carried out in the 1962 study it was observed that those subjects who exhibited prolonged distress (crying, anxiety, etc.) to the physiological test were represented in the later "first-wave breakdown" group.

As we now have selected our high and low risk groups, we intend to institute a research program in which we will build up a more extensive picture of the child's current and past social and medical family history. Additionally, the retest procedure presently being carried out by the psychophysiology unit will provide us with information on the stability of our measures and in addition ought to give us preliminary indications whether the "preventive" procedures employed in our kindergartens have any significant effect upon the child's physiological responsivity. We expect to obtain funding through various agencies (including WHO) in order to provide resident staff who will carry out behavioural observations with the children in the two schools.*

---

*The observation procedure has now been established in both kindergartens and ratings are being made on a systematic basis together with video-tape recordings which will be evaluated at a later date.

REFERENCES

Ax, A.F. and Bamford, J.L. *Psychophysiology, 7,* 145,(1970).

Bell, B., Gottesman, I.I., Mednick, S.A. and Sergeant, J., Electrodermal parameters in twins. 1974, in preparation.

Gottesman, I.I. and Shields, J.: Schizophrenia and Genetics - a Twin Study Vantage Point. New York, *Academic Press,* (1972).

Gruzelier, J.H. and Venables, P.H. *J. Nerv. Ment. Dis.,155,* 277, (1972).

Kringlen, E., *Heredity and Environment* In-*The Functional Psychoses: an Epidemiological-Clinical Twin Study.* London. Heinemann, (1967).

Mednick, B. *J. Abnormal Psychol. 82,* 469, (1973).

Mednick, S.A. *Psychological Bulletin, 55,* 316, (1958).

Mednick, S.A., and McNeil, T.F. *Psychological Bulletin, 70,* 681, (1968).

Mednick, S.A. and Schulsinger, F. *J. Psychiat. Res. 6,*267, Supplement 1, (1968).

Mednick, S.A., and Schulsinger, F.: Studies of children at high-risk for schizophrenia. In Dean, S.R. (Ed.): *Schizophrenia: The First Ten Dean Award Lectures.* New York: MSS information, 1973, 247-293.

Mednick, S.A., Schulsinger, F., Higgins, J., and Bell, B. (eds.): *Genetics, Environment and Psychopathology.* Elsevier: North-Holland, 1974.

Pollin, W. and Stabenau, J.R. *J. Psychiat. Res. 6,*317, Suppl. 1, (1968).

MENTAL HEALTH IN CHILDREN, Volume I
Edited By D. V. Siva Sankar
Copyright © 1975 by
PJD Publications Ltd., Westbury, N.Y.

THE OFFSPRING OF
MANIC-DEPRESSIVE PARENTS

Julien Mendlewicz and Judith Klotz
New York State Psychiatric Institute
New York, N. Y. 10032

INTRODUCTION

This report is part of an extensive family study of patients with affective disorders. Primary affective disorder is defined as an emotional illness involving recurrent mood swings severe enough to disrupt the patient's life temporarily, but which is episodic rather than chronic in nature and does not entail personality deterioration during remissions. There must be no other preexisting disorder such as anxiety neurosis or other medical illness which may be associated with an affective symptomatology. Two types of affective disease are distinguished: bipolar illness in which both mania and depression are experienced, and unipolar illness in which only depressions are present. The occurrence of manic episodes without depressions is very rare and such individuals are classified in this study as belonging to the bipolar group. Clinical features differentiating the two types (apart from the presence of manic episodes in bipolar patients and its absence in unipolar patients) include an increased prevalence of postpartum disorder in bipolar patients as compared to unipolars and an increase in suicidal behavior in bipolar patients (1-3). Bipolar patients also show more lethargy, less agitation and more hypersomnia during their depression than do unipolar patients (4). The age of onset is also significantly earlier in bipolar psychosis than in unipolar psychosis (3). Most bipolar patients become affectively ill in their thirties while unipolar patients tend to become sick in their mid-forties. Biological differences between the two psychoses were first reported by Perris (4) who noted that bipolar patients in remission had a lower threshold to visual stimuli than unipolar patients. Studies performed at the National Institute of Mental Health reported that bipolar patients had an "augmenting" pattern and unipolar patients a "reducing" pattern of average cortical evoked response (5). The urinary excretion of 17-hydroxycorticosteroids was reduced in depressed bipolar patients as compared to unipolar patients (6). In addition, biochemical studies of enzymes involved in norepinephrine metabolism have provided some support for differentiating depressed patients into bipolar and unipolar types. Erythrocyte catechol-o-methyltransferase activity was found to be lower in women with unipolar illness than women with bipolar illness (7) and monoamine oxidase activity was found to be lower in bipolar patients as compared to unipolar patients (8).

The above clinical and biological differences described between bipolar and unipolar depressive illnesses suggest that these two syndromes constitute different genetic entities. This claim is now supported by family studies showing that bipolar and unipolar depression are genetically different (1-3). It has long been recognized that relatives of people with affective illness have a high likelihood of being affected with the same or similar disorders. Previous family studies (1-4) and especially twin studies (9) have indicated that there is a genetic factor in the etiology of these conditions. For example, the concordance for bipolar illness in monozygotic twins was found to be almost total, whereas dizygotic twins had a much lower concordance rate (about 30%) (9). As suggested by Angst and Perris (2), Winokur (3), and our own studies (10), bipolar and unipolar illness constitute distinct genetic entities. Bipolar illness is very infrequently found in the families of unipolar patients, while the converse is not true. It is therefore conceivable that the widespread unipolar illness in families of bipolars is a variant expression of bipolar illness, and is therefore etiologically distinct from other unipolar illnesses.

Another problem still controversial is the means of genetic transmission which may be operating in bipolar and unipolar families. Polygenic inheritance has been suggested for bipolar illness (11); autosomal (12), and X-linked models have also been proposed (13-14). Kallmann (12) suggested on the basis of twin studies that bipolar illness is determined by a major autosomal gene. Winokur et al. (13) have presented data showing that bipolar illness appears to be transmitted in an X-linked dominant fashion. In our own studies, we have shown strong evidence for linkage between bipolar illness and color blindness (14). Our results also suggest that bipolar illness and the Xg blood group are within a measurable distance from each other (15). Although the above results support the existence of an X-linked dominant factor in the transmission of bipolar illness in certain families, the X-linked model cannot account for instances of father-son transmission of the illness, which have been observed in some studies (2, 4) and in our own material (10). Other modes of transmission may thus determine the bipolar trait, a fact, if confirmed, that would indicate that bipolar illness is a heterogeneous entity.

There are several methodological problems which make some results difficult to compare with one another. Ascertainment biases in family studies are almost impossible to avoid when one studies selected samples of hospitalized patients. There is further variation in the diagnostic and statistical procedures on these samples.

We have recently presented morbidity risks in first degree relatives (i.e. parents, siblings, and children) of bipolar probands in our population (10). The rates we found support previously published data (1-4) and indicate that the risks for all affective illness in the first degree relatives of bipolar patients are not far from the 50% expected in single-gene dominant inheritance.

There have been only scanty data previously reported, either separately or as part of larger studies, relating specifically to the offspring of affectively ill patients. Children of patients with affective disorder not only constitute a high risk population; more than other first degree relatives, they are highly likely to be alive and available for interviews and studies. In this group there are also numerous individuals who have recently experienced, and can accurately recall, their first affective episode; the majority of older relatives would probably have had several episodes since their onset. The presence of childhood behavior problems or other symptoms of emotional illness can be recalled by offspring and their parents in this population more readily than by older patients and their relatives. Offspring thus provide more reliable clinical data on the onset of affective illness and the nature of depressive symptoms in younger children.

One of the difficulties in diagnosing depression in children is the difference in symptomatology between childhood and adulthood for this disorder. For example, the psychological manifestations of adult depression such as guilt and deflated self-esteem are rare in children. Symptoms of affective illness in childhood include irritability, learning problems, and psychosomatic syndromes. The main characteristics of a depressive nature described in children are bodily complaints with various psychosomatic signs, loss of appetite and weight, lack of energy, loss of concentration, irritability, and sleep disturbance. These complaints often lead to school difficulties and interrelational problems with parents.

Since we know that according to any genetic theory there is a vital environmental component in the expression of affective illness, it is also of particular interest to examine offspring of affectively ill parents because environmental variables can be analyzed for their interrelation with the genetic factors. The illness of a parent can in itself be an environmental stress which may entail the partial absence of this parent from the home during the latter's hospitalization or modify familial interactions. Furthermore, the presence of the illness in the family during childhood may have an effect on early symptoms of affective disorder, age of first episode, and other variables.

METHODS

The index cases are patients who were admitted consecutively to the Lithium Clinic at the New York State Psychiatric Institute from 1968 through 1972. 134 bipolar patients and 65 unipolar patients were ascertained. All available first degree relatives (i.e. parents, siblings, children) who were over age fifteen were given a clinical, semistructured interview, Current and Past Psychopathology Scales (CAPPS) (16).

For those relatives who were not examined personally because of distance or infirmity, the probands and all other relatives were questioned as to their mental and physical health and behavior. Clinical data on children below the age of fifteen were collected from their parents and other relatives. On its past section, the CAPPS contains items on childhood psychopathology, adolescent adjustment, and school performance. The diagnostic criteria used for proband relatives were identical and the investigators interviewing the relatives were blind as to the proband's diagnosis. Bipolar probands are patients who experience both mania and depression while unipolar patients experience depression only. The depressive episodes are often characterized by depressed mood along with symptoms of a physiological shift such as decrease in appetite, sleep disturbance, and low energy level, often accompanied by guilt, difficulty in concentration, and suicidal thoughts. Manic episodes include such symptoms as euphoria,hyperactivity,decreased need for sleep, pressure of speech, flight of ideas and irritability. Psychotic symptoms such as hallucinations and delusional ideas are not uncommon during depressive or manic phases. This sometimes leads to confusion between affective disorders and schizophrenia.

To evaluate morbidity risks, the "Weinberg shorter method" was used (17). This was chosen because our population of offspring of current patients contained no individuals over fifty years of age; in fact, most were considerably younger. A method such as Strömgren's (18), which is generally more accurate for estimating morbidity risks, and which we indeed used elsewhere for the entire population of relatives and probands (10) was not applicable because a complete life table could not be constructed as the offspring were confined to younger age groups. The risk period for the Wienberg method was taken to be ages fifteen through sixty-five. Risks in relatives are expressed as morbidity risks, which is an age-corrected estimation. It represents the risk of expressing the disease if the relative survived the risk period. Estimation of morbidity risks is provided by the following formula: $MR = [a]/[b-bo-(\frac{1}{2})bm]$ where "a" is the number of affected relatives, "b" the number of relatives examined, "bo" the number of relatives who have not reached the period at risk, and "bm", the number of relatives currently passing through the risk period. In this formula, the denominator expresses the number of people at risk.

RESULTS AND DISCUSSION

The morbidity risks for affective illness and other psychopathology in the offspring of bipolar and unipolar patients can be seen in Table I. The overall risk for bipolar and unipolar illness combined is 55.5% for children of bipolar probands and 16.4% for children of unipolar probands ($X^2 =$ 13.34, df = 2; p<.002). From the risks of all first degree relatives of the same patients as shown in Table II, it is evident that the risks for offspring are characteristic of first degree relatives of our population in general, as well as consistent with findings of former investigations (1-4).

An excess of females in affective illness has been widely documented. In our population also, both probands and their affected relatives, including offspring, are predominantly female (Table III). It should be noted that this applies to bipolar probands and relatives as well as to unipolar, although the pattern is more accentuated in the latter group. For children of bipolars, the risk for daughters is 97.9% compared to 33.7% for sons to have affective illness ($X^2 = 27.04$, df = 2; p<.0001), while for offsprings of unipolar, we find a risk of 31.2% for daughters but zero for sons (X^2 not significant). This excess of females is consistent with, though does not prove, the X-linked dominant hypothesis of affective disorder. Theoretically, under this mode of inheritance, fathers would pass the gene for the disease to all their daughters but not their sons, and mothers would pass the gene to half of their daughters and half of their sons. This prediction is essentially borne out by our sample as can be seen in Table IV. When probands are separated by sex, an even greater difference in morbidity of sons and daughters can be seen in offspring of male probands.

Additional information on this hypothesis can be gathered by examining offspring according to parental mating patterns. According to the X-linked model, half of the daughters of two ill parents (i.e. dual mating) would have two doses of the gene, while sons have no greater risk in dual matings than if only their mother were affected. Table V shows the data on dual matings: no sons out of twelve, but nine daughters out of twenty-one, were affected with unipolar or bipolar illness. Two sons were drug dependent, one son and one daughter had experienced adjustment reaction of adolescence; one other son had both school phobia and enuresis. None of these offspring were found to be schizophrenic or alcoholic. These numbers are too small to verify these patterns as significant.

There has been a consistent rate of father-son transmission of about ten percent in our own population (10) and in other family studies (2). This indicates that even if the X-linked model is applicable to a portion of families, there must be more than one type of inheritance in affective illness.

In bipolar illness, the age of onset varies between 15 and 65 with a peak at about 35; for unipolar illness, the range is approximately the same while the mean age of onset is later: about 45. Thus, most cases of affective disorder seem to start in adult life as opposed to a generally adolescent onset of schizophrenia. Reports of early onset (i.e. by age 15) in affective illness are rare (19). Studies of children with manic-depressive illness have most often reported sporadic cases (20). On looking at our population of children, however, we found an unexpectedly high incidence of onset before age 20. The proportions of affected offspring who had not yet reached twenty years of age at the time of our last contact is 46% for bipolar probands and 43% for unipolar. Those known to have an early onset (i.e. the number of children who are now less than 20 years old and who are affectively ill plus the number who have passed age twenty but whose onsets occurred prior to age 20) is about half of the total number of affected offspring regardless of the diagnoses of the proband or children (See Table VI).

Table I

Morbidity Risks in Offspring of Affectively Ill Probands

	Bipolar Probands Risk (%) S.E. (%)		Unipolar Probands Risk (%) S.E. (%)	
Bipolar (BP)	23.6	(5.0)	0.0	(0.0)
Unipolar (UP)	31.9	(5.5)	16.4	(6.5)
BP + UP	55.5	(5.8)	16.4	(6.5)
Schizophrenia	2.8	(1.9)	0.0	(0.0)
Alcoholism	5.6	(2.7)	9.8	(5.4)
Drug Dependence	5.6	(2.7)	9.8	(5.4)
Total No. Offspring	184		82	
Total No. Probands	134		65	

Table II

Morbidity Risks in All First Degree Relatives

	Bipolar Probands Risk (%) S.E. (%)		Unipolar Probands Risk (%) S.E. (%)	
Bipolar (BP)	24.8	(2.1)	4.1	(1.4)
Unipolar (UP)	28.3	(2.2)	27.2	(3.2)
BP + UP	53.1	(2.4)	31.4	(3.3)
Total No. Relatives	781		364	
Total No. Probands	134		65	

Table III

Morbidity Risks by Sex of Offspring

| | Bipolar Probands | | | | Unipolar Probands | | | |
| | Sons | | Daughters | | Sons | | Daughters | |
	Risk (%)	S.E. (%)	Risk (%)	S.E. (%)	Risk (%)	S.E. (%)	Risk (%)	S.E. (%)
Bipolar (BP)	18.9	(5.7)	32.6	(9.4)	0.0	(0.0)	0.0	(0.0)
Unipolar (UP)	14.7	(5.1)	65.3	(9.6)	0.0	(0.0)	31.2	(11.6)
BP + UP	33.7	(6.9)	97.9	(2.8)	0.0	(0.0)	31.2	(11.6)

Table IV

Morbidity Risk for All Affective Disorder in
Offspring According to Sex of Proband

	Male Bipolar Probands [N = 56]		Female Bipolar Probands [N = 78]	
	Risk (%)	S.E. (%)	Risk (%)	S.E. (%)
Sons	13.3	(8.8)	37.5	(8.6)
Daughters	100.0	----	97.1	(4.0)
	Male Unipolar Probands [N = 13]		Female Unipolar Probands [N = 52]	
Sons	0.0	(0.0)	0.0	(0.0)
Daughters	40.0	(30.1)	36.0	(14.5)

Table V

Incidence of Affective and Other Illness in Offspring of Dual
Matings (Total No. of Matings = 15)

	Bipolar	Unipolar	Schizo-phrenia	Alco-holism	Drug Depend-ence	Total
Sons	0	0	0	0	2	12
Daught-ers	4	5	0	0	0	21

Table VI

Age of Onset of Affective Illness in Offspring of Bipolar
and Unipolar Probands

	Bipolar Offspring		Unipolar Offspring	
	Before 20	20 or Above	Before 20	20 or Above
Bipolar Probands	9	8	14	9
Unipolar Probands	0	0	2	3

Table VII

Other Childhood Disorders in Offspring Less Than 20 Years of Age

		Neurosis	Speech Disorder	Hyper-Activity	Enuresis	Adjustment Reaction of Adolescence	Autism	School Phobia
Bipolar Probands	Sons	0	1	1	5	2	1	1
	Daughters	1	0	0	0	0	0	0
Unipolar Probands	Sons	0	0	1	0	0	0	0
	Daughters	0	0	0	0	0	0	0

On many offspring we have detailed information regarding childhood adjustment and the presence of symptoms of early emotional illness other than affective disorder. Among those children less than 20 years old, more children of bipolars than unipolars were affected with such childhood disorders (Table VII). (One son of a bipolar proband had both school phobia and enuresis). Although the numbers are small and the differences not significant, it can be seen that enuresis is the most common of these disturbances in children of bipolars, and that there is a preponderance of sons affected among children of both groups.

One of the variables which we examined with great interest was that of childhood bereavement which we defined as the physical absence of either or both parents for six months or more before the age of 15. This could be due to hospitalization of a parent as well as to marital separation or death. Bereavement and loss in early childhood have been considered to be an important predisposing factor to depression in children and adults because of the dependency of children on their parents (21). The number of bereaved children among our ill offspring was surprisingly low (i.e. ten). Our results however, are in agreement with those of Lokare (22) who showed that children with depressive illness show no greater liability than controls to parental deprivation. Another unexpected finding was the presence of only affective illness in the bereaved children of bipolar probands (N = 6), while among the bereaved children of unipolar patients (N = 4) only alcoholism or drug dependence was found.

In summary, the risk for all affective illness in the offspring of bipolar probands is 55.5% as compared to 16.4% in the offspring of unipolar probands. There is a high preponderance of daughters affected from bipolar probands, an observation consistent with our previous studies indicating the presence of an X-linked dominant factor in the transmission of bipolar illness. The offspring of matings where both parents are affectively ill also show an excess of daughters with affective disorder, a result expected with an X-linked dominant condition. Father-son transmission of the illness, although not common, is present in our own population. The findings of X-linkage in some families and the existence of other families in which X-linkage can be ruled out, suggest that bipolar illness is a genetically heterogeneous condition. Affective illness, either bipolar or unipolar is considered to be an adult disease; in our population of offspring of affectively ill patients however, about 50% of them experience their first symptoms before the age of 20. The presence of childhood bereavement considered as an important factor predisposing to affective illness was rare in our sample, and those few offspring who had experienced both childhood bereavement and affective illness were all children of bipolar probands. In those offspring who are now below the age of 20, there is a preponderance of children of bipolar probands having childhood disturbances other than affective illness; among these enuresis is the most common condition and is only found in sons of bipolar probands. Whether enuresis in these children is an early symptom of affective illness or rather a reaction to affective illness in a parent, cannot be determined from these data. Followup studies of these high risk children should provide some information regarding the latter question.

REFERENCES

1. Leonhard, K., Korff, I., and Shulz, H. *Psychiat. Neurol. 143,* 416, (1962).

2. Angst, J. and Perris, C. *Arch. Psychiat. Z. Neurol. 210,* 373, (1968).

3. Winokur, G., and Clayton, P.J. *Rec. Adv. in Biol. Psychiat. IX,* Edited by Wortis, J. New York, Plenum Press, (1967).

4. Perris, C. *Acta Psychiat. Scand., 194,* (1966).

5. Buchsbaum, M., Goodwin, F.K., Murphy, D.L., and Borge, G. *Amer. J. Psychiat., 128,* 19, (1971).

6. Dunner, D.L., Goodwin, F.K., Gershon, E.S., Murphy, D.L., and Bunney W.E., Jr. *Arch. Gen. Psychiat. 26,* 360, (1972).

7. Cohn, C.K., Dunner, D.L., and Axelrod, J. *Science, 170,* 1323, (1970).

8. Murphy, D.L., and Weiss, R. *Amer. J. Psychiat., 128,* 1351, (1972).

9. Zerbin-Rüdin, E. *Zur Genetik der depressiven Erkrankungen, Das depressive Syndrom.* Edited by Hippius, H, and Selbach, H., Munich, Urban & Schwarzenberg, (1969).

10. Mendlewicz, J., and Rainer, J.D. *Amer. J. Hum. Genet., 26,* 692, (1974).

11. Slater, E., Maxwell, J., and Price, J.S. *Brit J. Psychiat., 118,* 215, (1971).

12. Kallmann, F.J. *Genetic principles in manic-depressive psychosis in* Depression. Edited by Hoch, P., and Zubin, J. New York, Grune & Stratton, (1954).

13. Winokur, G., Clayton, P.J. and Reich, T. *Manic Depressive Illness.* St. Louis, CV Mosby Co., (1969).

14. Mendlewicz, J., Fleiss, J.L. and Fieve, R.R. *J. Amer. Med. Assoc.222,* 1624 (1972).

15. Mendlewicz, J., Fleiss, J.L., and Fieve, R.R. Linkage studies in affective disorders: The Xg blood group and manic-depressive illness, in *Genetics and Psychopathology.* Edited by Fieve. R., Rosenthal, D., and Brill, H. Baltimore, Johns Hopkins University press, (1974).

16. Endicott, J., and Spitzer, R.L. *Arch. Gen. Psychiat., 27,* 678, (1972).

17. Weinberg, W. *Z. Ang. Anat. 6,* 380, (1920).

18. Strömgren, E. *Z. Gesamte Neurol. Psychiat. 153,* 784, (1935).

19. Spiel, W. Studien über den Verlauf und die Erscheinungsformen der kindlichen und juvenilen manisch-depressiven Psychosen, in *Depressive States in Childhood and Adolescence.* Edited by Annell, A.L. Stockholm, Halsted Press, 517 (1972).

20. Anthony, J., and Scott, P. *J. Child Psychol. Psychiat., 1,* 53, (1960).

21. d'Elia, G., and Perris, C. Childhood environment and bipolar and unipolar recurrent depressive psychosis, in *Depressive States in Childhood and Adolescence.* Edited by Annell, A.L. Stockholm, Halsted Press, 53, (1972).

22. Lokare, V.G. Neuroticism, extraversion and the incidence of depressive illness in children, in *Depressive States in Childhood and Adolescence.* Edited by Annell A.L. Stockholm, Halsted Press, 142, (1972).

PREADOLESCENCE: A CRITICAL PHASE OF BIOLOGICAL AND PSYCHOLOGICAL DEVELOPMENT

Donald Cohen and Richard Frank
Yale University School of Medicine
New Haven, Connecticut 06510

Although few students of human development would argue that American children today pass directly from childhood to adolescence, we have up to now done suprisingly little to define and explain what happens in the period between the two. We seem to have thus far avoided the crux of the problem by extending "middle childhood" upward and "early adolescence" downward until the two old reliable designations formed a modest curtain in front of our embarrassing lack of knowledge and theory. Yet we know that the "preadolescent" of eleven or twelve years is neither the ideal-typical middle child of nine nor the archetypical adolescent of sixteen. We

---

Acknowledgements

We appreciate the support and suggestions of Dr. Albert Solnit, Professor of Psychiatry and Pediatrics, and Dr. Edward Zigler, Professor of Psychology, and the assistance of Ms. Margrethe Cone. This research was supported in part by Public Health Service Research grant HD-03008, Children's Clinical Research Center Grant RR00125, and the Grant Foundation.

may still prefer to think of him as *in transition* from childhood to adolescence, but we have begun to recognize more clearly that the "pre-adolescent" deserves a period of his own.

In biological terms we can define preadolescence as the period leading up to the earliest bodily changes that we recognize as adolescent--the start of the growth spurt and the emergence of bodily sex characteristics. Recent research has revealed that a period so defined probably coincides with the earliest upswing in levels of important hormones of development in children. This increased endocrine activity of pre-adolescence is generally believed to be the main precursor or trigger of all the unique biological development which takes place in adolescence proper. Changes in hormone levels may have profound effects on the preadolescent's mind and body even before he experiences the commonly observed growth and sexual spurts. Altered endocrine function in preadolescence may itself depend on maturational changes in the central nervous system peculiar to this phase.

Co-existent with this special biological development, observers have also found in preadolescence the emergence of significant new aspects of the instinctual life and of the cognitive life. Preadolescents are beginning to experience a resurgence of sexual and aggressive feelings and a new ability to think in logical and complex ways about themselves and their world, experiences which will reach full flowering later in adolescence. Their social world is also expanding rapidly as they move further from their parents and closer to peers and to adults outside the family. It is no wonder, then, that the conjunction of these new feelings, experiences, abilities and biological changes may impinge upon and upset the relatively stable world of middle childhood, making preadolescence a time of relative emotional disequilibrium.

It is the conjunction of rapid and important changes, biological, social, cognitive and emotional, and the resulting periods of disequilibrium and rapid overall development, which lend a special significance to preadolescence. For here one may expect to find with careful study some greater insight into the mechanisms of biological-psychological interactions in human development. Further, we may learn to use our knowledge more effectively to help troubled preadolescents before all these changes have become integrated in maladaptive personalities later in adolescence and young adulthood.

I. Emotional Tasks

The emotional tasks and problems of preadolescence must be seen in the context of the transition from childhood to adolescence.

Latency or Middle Childhood

In the psychoanalytic scheme of development, the years from six to ten are characterized as the period of latency, or decreased instinctual drive. The period comes into being with the gradual resolution of the oedipal complex, characterized by more firm identification of the child with the same-sexed parent. With this orientation achieved, it used to be said that libido generally declines. Seen this way, the latency period is an exception in psychoanalytic stage theory in that its inception is marked by a decrease in libido rather than a new kind of libidinal attachment.

In fact the child's attitudes and actions are still quite energized, but in new directions. Children now show tremendous drive in taking to learning and to school, in wanting to explore their world intensively. If we wish to conserve the economic model of development, yet emphasize the positive aspects of middle childhood, it may be most appropriate to view these boys and girls as now investing in cognitive functions energy which was previously used in maturation of social relationships within the family. Their libido, previously sexual, becomes primarily aggressive. The modulating influence of the superego developed during the oedipal phase serves to mute and mold this aggressive libido, to allow for sharing and following rules.

In Erikson's terms, the key issue of middle childhood is "industry vs. inferiority" (1). The child's task is to become a good learner, worker and group member. Children reveal their orientation to cognitive tasks and peer activities not only in the intensity of their work, but also quite dramatically in their daily play, as its pattern gradually shifts from the personal fantasy of the oedipal period to the organized games of latency.

Preadolescence

The outstanding emotional quality of preadolescence is shifting cathexis, or unstable feelings and aimlessness. The preadolescent of eleven or twelve invests himself considerably less in cognitive mastery than he had before. There seems to be a breakdown in the normal progressive mechanism of identity development through industry as the initial stirrings of sexual interest and drive appear. Preadolescents often shift between childhood and adolescent behavior. Latency activities are easier to use as defenses against heightened feelings at this stage than they will be later on. They may spend hours, days or weeks working hard on a model or crafts project as in childhood, or brief periods of time in brooding distraction. This kind of shifting continues until the force of biological organizers pushes the preadolescent into puberty. Then it is difficult to maintain childhood postures, although some anxious individuals still try to resist change.

Sexual concerns. Preadolescents show their increased sexual concerns both indirectly, in the symbolism of their work and play, and directly in their expressions of curiosity, exchange of secrets, naive experimentation and embarrassment about their bodies (2). Their sexual feeling and activities are heightened compared to the previous period, but not as reiterative or persistant as in adolescent masturbation and love affairs. For now the activity seems rather aimless and diffuse.

The psychoanalytic view sees in preadolescence a series of conflicts in which boys and girls begin to develop a new set of sexual and aggressive attitudes in relation to family and peers (3). Most preadolescents try to escape from their mother's realm, to show more independence from their primary caretaker. Boys tend to form all male groups which may later develop into gangs. Girls tend more often to regress into infantile behavior, to seek out smaller groups or friendships, and in an awkward way may be curious to see and talk about boys. Preadolescents are beginning to feel their bodies and emotions aroused at a time when they are still quite closely tied to home life. For this reason struggle with family ties may be greater in preadolescence than in adolescence itself.

Upset and change. The stable personality of middle or late childhood seems to loosen up or disorganize in preadolescence (4). Perhaps this instability is a product of the early upsurge of sexual libido whose expression is blocked both by social rules and an immature body. It may also reflect the transitional quality of maturation which leaves the preadolescent suspended between cognitive and sexual concerns, between childish and adolescent behavior. In any case preadolescents often tend to show more restless energy and a shorter attention span, and to neglect and lose interest in work, hobbies, and responsibilities. They may tend to act fidgety, whiny, moody, secretive or depressed, and sometimes return to infantile patterns such as nail-biting or fear of the dark. Physical fighting increases, along with bursts of anger, frequently short-lived and unpredictable. Even preadolescents who previously showed adaptive behavior and adequate defenses most of the time may now show signs of confusion, lability and emotional conflict.

Resurgence of sexual drives and strivings for independence generate two important kinds of conflict--intra-psychic and interpersonal. Preadolescents commonly deal with their conflicts by acting out as well as by compromise and control. It is not unusual for a preadolescent to "show his parents who is boss" by coming home late without informing them, even though he or she may know that an agreeable compromise could have been reached ahead of time. At other times he seems content being treated as a younger, latency age child, accepting his dependence and his desires to be close to his family.

If their powers are yet untested in the world at large, thriving children of ten or eleven are at least knowledgable and capable in the routines of family and home life. Preadolescence is the last period during which their ability to play the role of accomplished "children" will sometimes merit them comfort, security, and feeling of success. But only sometimes. At other times hormonal changes, conflicts and social stresses may trigger a temporary period of psychological depression, intense irritability, or hyperaggressiveness in vulnerable individuals, or less intense but more common emotional reactions in more typical preadolescents. Their ups and downs in moods, attitudes and behavior signify that the stable personalities of childhood have given way to states of flux and reorganization out of which will emerge the more complex personalities of later adolescence and young adulthood.

Early Adolescence-Early Puberty

As the preadolescent enters puberty, the same emotional trends are further sharpened. In particular the early adolescent tries harder and usually succeeds further in separating himself from his family. In doing so, he needs to derive a new sense of strength and perfection relatively independent of his parents. He may be helped along in this endeavor by progress in the fashioning of his *ego ideal* or his imagined ideal self. The ego ideal is a more or less unconscious expression of all the qualities he wishes to have, based on his real successes, his estimation of himself, his hopes, dreams, and fantasies.

Issues of social and sexual identity become clarified as the bodily changes of puberty become obvious to all. When an early adolescent wants to be away from his parents or to explore sexual topics, adults often accepts this as "typical adolescent" behavior. Similar behavior, while less frequently expressed by a preadolescent, is likely to be considered aberrant at that stage. Preadolescents may thus suffer for lack of a label, for not "acting the way they look," although their irregular behavior is often quite normal and adaptive.

Adolescence

The classic psychoanalytic model has been adolescence as an upsurge of libido or sexual and aggressive feeling that reshapes experience and social relationships. In some ways this instinctual resurgence recalls the themes of oedipal development, but it is unique in its explicit sexuality, its direction towards opposite-sexed partners of a similar age group, and its concentration on situations outside of the family.

Family and Peers. Slow detachment from primary objects and the formation of satisfying relationships with peers is in fact a movement characteristic of all phases of development. During adolescence, however, certain important benchmarks in this movement come within reach. For the first time, there is a real possibility of intimate relations with members of the opposite sex, and a real need to break with parents to the extent of separating off activities and decisions from their sphere of influence.

So adolescents characteristically feel like mourning, rebelling and being in love--mourning the loss of comfortable, dependable ties to parents while rebelling against them, and falling in love with new, idealized girl-friends and boy-friends. Sometimes failure to complete emotional tasks smoothly seems to contribute to a clinical disorder (5). For example, the vulnerable adolescent may turn his guilt over the forceful breaking of parental ties into hostility against himself, thereby experiencing a period of anxiety and depression.

Complexity of growth. The contemporary psycho-analytic model still emphasizes the resurgence of instinctual urges, but by no means limits its depiction of adolescence to this phenomenon. It sees adolescent growth as a product of the complex interaction of all the agencies of the mind, each of which has its own developmental history. Drives, autonomous ego functions and superego functions all contribute to the development of defenses and adaptive patterns of coping which arise in adolescence and may be incorporated into an individual's personality. Biological endowment and social environment also play roles in determining these patterns.

The full resurgence of drives in biologically, socially and legally immature adolescents provides plenty of opportunity for intrapsychic and interpersonal conflict to develop even deeper and more complex patterns than in preadolescence. Mental functions, biological functions and the environment are changing rapidly relative to other life periods. New and difficult emotional tasks must be negotiated, including control and expression of increasing sexual impulses and synthesizing of many new perceptions into a meaningful sense of self.

II. Developmental Psychology of Preadolescence

Cognitive Growth

Between the ages of six and ten, middle-class American children think largely in very concrete terms. They spend latency in the Piagetian stage of *concrete operations* (6). The age of ten or eleven, or the beginning of preadolescence, most often marks their earliest entrance into the cognitive stage of *formal operations.* The various achievements of formal operational thought come gradually throughout the next few years, but mental progress is considerably more rapid in preadolescence and early adolescence than later on (7). Gradually adolescents learn to reason more abstractly and logically about real and imaginary situations, to think about thoughts, and to relate relationships as well as objects. They can learn to construct all the possibilities inherent in a situation, including those not directly observable, and to assume a "hypthetico-deductive" attitude--to understand that a belief or statement is a hypothesis, proven true only if the more concrete notions derivable from it are true. A preadolescent of eleven or twelve, asked to explain what determines the period of a pendulum, will often systematically try out one variable at a time (weight, length of string, and so on) in order to arrive at the correct solution. Younger children will usually play with the pendulum unsystematically (6).

Self-examination. In a phase of high instinctual drive and rapid biological growth, young adolescents naturally turn their increasing cognitive powers inwards towards themselves. They think a great deal about their bodies, sexual feelings, successes and failures. They discover subjectivity--the understanding that all experience is really filtered through themselves, whether it originates in the outer world, or in thoughts, dreams and daydreams.

The early adolescent actively searches for the many connections between himself and his environment. He tries out different hypotheses about himself, then sees if his own accomplishments and the reactions of other people agree with his imaginings. In contrast to the younger child, he places great and continuing importance on the complex question, "Who am I?," a preoccupation which led Erikson to emphasize the adolescent's conscious and unconscious efforts to build his *ego-identity* (8). Skeptical of others' words, he wonders what they really think of him. He discovers and examines himself tirelessly.

Examination of the world. Early adolescents are not merely self-conscious egoists. They are budding philosophers as well. For they apply their new cognitive abilities eagerly to the outside world. From preadolescence onward many previously accepted or ignored rules and values are called into question. This new observant and critical attitude derives first of all from emerging powers of logic and abstraction, and from the learning of new facts which seems to contradict preachings and rules. It also stems from the adolescent's increasing attention to and trust in his own impressions, evaluations and responses. Finally, his growing capacity to decenter himself--to see things from another perspective besides his own--allows him more power to compare, generalize and establish abstract concepts and ideals against which self, family and society can be measured.

Cognitive growth is also reflected in the major moral stance which children take at a certain stage. Latency children tend to judge actions good and bad on the basis of their consequences. Older adolescents tend toward developing a series of abstract moral principles. Preadolescent moral views reflect thought processes of intermediate sophistication. They understand, as younger children do not, that an individual's intention to help or to please others can be as important as the consequences of his act. They also tend to see maintenance of family, group and national rules as the ultimate criteria of judgment, a more authoritarian position than that of late adolescence, which allows for conflicts based on higher personal principles (6).

Preadolescent Transition. The rough coincidence in time between the entrance into formal operational thought and the earliest upsurge of instinctual drives is remarkable. The preadolescent seems as much in transition with respect to cognitive powers as with drives and emotions. He is beginning to recognize and analyze his use of language, and to understand ironic and ambiguous expressions. His thought is increasingly oriented towards reality, yet he episodically regresses to daydreams and fantasy, or likes to integrate the two, as shown by reading preferences for science fiction and sentimental family stories (7). He may struggle with abstract and complex principles, and fall back into the familiar usage of concrete notions and simple foolproof rules. Not until age thirteen to sixteen do most adolescents achieve the necessary growth of

attention span, concentration, and verbal exactness and
versitility to allow for consistent use and systematization of
formal operations.   But the decisive changes in cognitive
structure first appear in preadolescence.

The Expanding Social World

Our picture of preadolescent social development comes
largely from studies of middle-class Americans.   The most
noticeable change in the social life of these preadolescents
occurs along the developmental line, with its root in early
childhood--the movement away from family and towards peers.
As the preadolescent grows toward adult size and appearance,
both he and his parents find it more difficult to act as if he were
still a child.   As his confidence and reasoning improves, he
feels less need to rely on his parents' explicit injunctions. He
may seem to deliberately devalue his parents--to disobey,
underestimate and criticize with great gusto. He appears very
sensitive to the exercise of adult power and perogatives,
embarrassed to submit to adult good manners or to accept
adult help openly, revolted by praise or punishment perceived
as infantilizing. In spite of his continuing need and desire for
support and guidance, he may hesitate or altogether cease to
play with or to communicate feelings to adults.

Peer groups. Peer group activities vary from sedate and
benign to active and rebellious. They often reveal the emotional
concerns and cognitive changes of preadolescence. The desire
to revolt against parents and other adults plays a part in some
group members' tendencies to speak and act in vulgar ways, to
flout rules, and to enjoy taking special risks with their pals--all
contributing to an exhilarating sense of peer group bravado.
Increasing cognitive skills, on the other hand, contribute to
cooperation, realistic thought and the rule of law in these
groups.

Boy-girl relationships.   While girls tend toward small
groups linked by secrets, boys more often maintain larger
leader-centered groups over a long period of time. In the past,
boy-girl relationships in preadolescence have usually been
described as mutually hostile, a legacy of latent sexual tensions,
discrepancy in physical maturation and contrasts of interests
and values. Actually, observable antagonism is more often an

expression of mutual striving to strengthen sexual identity. Girls strive to gain the friendship and affection of boys in order to imitate their wild adventuring, and to prove their erotic attraction. Boys may react with hostility if they fear being labeled as sissies, or if they are still limited to expressing erotic excitement as aggression.

In recent years, however, preadolescent boys and girls have seemed to express less mutual hostility and more open affection (9). Perhaps this change is part of the general trend of adolescent social behavior seen at earlier ages. Preadolescent boys who today can strengthen their masculine identity by playing gentlemen and boy-friend do not seem to need much anti-feminine orientation in their peer groups. Preadolescent girls can get proof of their attractiveness directly from the boys' attentions. But the relationships between boys and girls of the same age often weaken in early adolescence when the boys become less attractive to girls developing more rapidly.

Close friendships. For both boys and girls, certain preadolescent peer relationships are likely to become intense personal friendships. These friendships are far more demanding, intense and complex than the casual friendships of childhood. Now each person can adjust his behavior to the other so that the two may achieve mutual satisfaction and security. Close friends make special efforts to get together, to be aware of each other's needs and feelings, and to please each other. In these ways they help satisfy their need for intimacy and support outside of family bounds, and learn to correct unrealistic fantasies and increase self-understanding by seeing themselves through the eyes of others.

Acceptance and achievement. In summary the preadolescent and early adolescent strives for both acceptance and achievement as he enlarges and intensifies his social life (10). One can achieve or be accepted in a peer group, a school group, one's family, or a wider collection of people in a neighborhood or ethnic subculture. Some success in both endeavors is a prerequisite to strong self-esteem. When peer group and adult values conflict minimally, the development of valued skills contributes to both tasks. For example, a skilled ballplayer, good student, or talented musician will more easily find recognition, adult approval and a group of friends who share his interests than would a person who has not developed similar talents, skills or hobbies.

During preadolescence and adolescence individual differences in aptitudes and interests develop greatly. Just as each child develops a pattern of instinctual drives and emotional needs, and a pattern of defenses and adaptations, he also develops a profile of skills, abilities and deficits. He and others recognize that he is good at some things, so-so, or unsuccessful at others. As they move into the wider social world, children discover that they are not praised just for being there, as they are in supportive families. They must accomplish something in order to win acceptance. Thus a sense of confidence and competence in specific skills and abilities becomes increasingly valuable. How a child *perceives* his abilities may be as crucial as the abilities themselves. The preadolescent who *thinks* of himself as more competent is likely to join a group more readily, persist longer in work or play, and eventually achieve more and feel better. Family, teachers and child care workers can do much to bolster or deflate critical skills and perceptions of competence.

III. The Biology of Change in Preadolescence and Adolescence

Puberty may be defined as the phase of bodily development during which the gonads secrete sex hormones in amounts sufficient to cause accelerated growth and the appearance of secondary sex characteristics (11). We have defined preadolescence as the period just before and during the earliest pubertal changes. Preadolescents are thus for the most part prepubertal, but the prepubertal era has its own biological changes. These seem to have more to do with the inner workings of the nervous system and endocrine glands than with body appearance and structure.

Growth and Differentiation (12-16)

For each event of the adolescent growth spurt there is quite a sizable age range in the general population. (13) A good reference point for normal timing is the average age of peak velocity (instantaneous): 12.0 years for girls (9.0 cm./year) and 14.0 years for boys (10.5 cm./year). Over one third of the variability in adult height may be attributed to differences among individuals in the magnitude of the pubertal spurt.

All tissues of the body do not follow the same course of growth. The rate of growth of bone and muscle is always positive, but it decreases steadily between birth and adolescence, when it begins to spurt upward. The absolute amount of subcutaneous fat actually decreases from nine months to six years, increases thereafter in girls through age sixteen, and rises and falls in early pubertal boys before rising again later in puberty. At the age of ten, boys have 80% of their adult height and 55% of the adult weight. Girls have 85% and 59%, respectively. Thus the magnitude of non-skeletal growth in the adolescent spurt is greater than the bony growth.

In general, full body size is achieved before full muscular power. For approximately one year, the boy having completed his physical growth does not have the strength of a young adult of the same body size and shape. Motor coordination skills such as balance usually increase with motor strength. Studies contradict the common notion of a clumsy, overgrown period in adolescence due to readjustments presumed necessary to offset changes in body size and center of gravity. Neither do the physical changes of adolescence cause enfeeblement, even temporarily. If an adolescent becomes chronically weak and easily exhausted, some specific physical or psychological disturbance should be suspected.

Sex dimorphism. During puberty, sex dimorphism becomes more obvious and more differentiated. Relative to the girl, the late adolescent boy has stronger and larger muscles, higher systolic blood pressure, lower resting heart rate, larger heart and lungs relative to size, greater capacity for carrying oxygen in the blood and more power to neutralize the chemical products of exercise, such as lactic acid. Girls lack the rise in red blood cell count and hemoglobin level which boys have, probably a combined effect of increased testosterone in boys and menstrual bleeding in girls.

Sex dimorphism in growth parameters can arise at birth (larger forearm in males), at puberty due to hormonal sex differences (male and female pelvis types), and in later adolescence as a result of the continuation of rapid growth in boys after the spurt in girls has ceased (longer legs in adult males). From birth to maturity, including puberty, girls are generally more advanced in physiological development than boys of the same chronological age. It is suspected that the Y chromosome is responsible for the relative retardation of male development, since XXY children resemble XY boys in this respect, and XO children resemble XX girls.

The most dramatic, outwardly visible and inwardly significant changes at puberty concern the reproductive system. For each sex a succession of five stages of physical maturity based on visible secondary sex characteristics such as pubic hair, breast and testicular development, has come into frequent use. (Table 1) This is feasible because the sequence of events varies far less than the age at which events occur.

Summary of events. The following summary of pubertal changes may be useful: (1) Although girls attain peak height velocity about two years earlier (always preceding menarche) than do boys, they lead boys by only six months in the initiation of the growth spurt in secondary sex characteristics. (2) Girls tend to reach peak height velocity at an early stage of sexual maturity, while boys reach it only after their genitalia are quite developed. (3) Menarche occurs two to two and one-half years after the onset of the first pubertal changes. (4) The development of adult secondary sex characteristics takes approximately four years. (5) There are wide variations in the sequence of changes, and even wider variations in the ages of events. The standard deviation for a given stage or event is about one year. Boys thirteen to fifteen may be found in every stage of sexual development.

Maturation rate. The level of physical or physiological maturity is an important indicator of a child's readiness to tackle various tasks of development. Since children of the same chronological age will be at various stages of physical development, specific physical measures are necessary. Bone development is presently favored because it can be easily rated with an X-ray of the hand. A child whose ossification pattern corresponds to the average for all eleven year olds in the population is said to have a *bone age* of eleven. If his chronological age is nine, one can estimate that his physical development is two years ahead of average.

Other indices of physical maturation include dental eruption and sexual appearance and function. A child advanced in one measure is likely to be advanced in all; similar correlations hold for slow individuals. It is more reliable to predict the timing of one aspect of physical development from the timing of another aspect, than to predict it from chronological age. For example, the earlier a girl shows her first breast and pubic hair development, the earlier she will show her peak height spurt, menarche, attainment of 90% of mature height and complete ossification of hand and wrist. In fact children who are taller and more physically mature as early as age two can be expected to have an earlier menarche and greater bone development at age thirteen. The data suggest that there are children whose general physiological development proceeds more rapidly or slowly than normal, and that we can see this from their earliest years.

When children from roughly equal environments are compared, genetic endowment is undoubtedly the main determinant of the timing and perhaps of the character of the adolescent spurt. One study shows an averge age difference at menarche of 2.2 months for pairs of identical twins as opposed to 8.2 months for pairs of non-identical twins.

The reason for general trend in individuals is that all these growth measures are regulated by the general state of the metabolic, hormonal, and nervous systems over a period of time. The reason for differing maturation rates in the various measures of one individual is that each physiological system responds to the control of *specific* nervous and endocrine mechanisms as well as to general body states.

Endocrine Development

At the physiological level, the special growth and differentiation seen in puberty has its origins in hormonal changes in the *gonadotropic endocrine system*. Adolescent development of reproductive organs and secondary sex characteristics comes about through the action of increased amounts of *sex hormones*: androgens and estrogens. Increased secretion of sex hormones depends, in turn, on a surge in the pituitary gland's production of gonatropic hormones, or *gonadotropins*.

TABLE 1
STAGING SYSTEM FOR PHYSICAL DEVELOPMENT
IN PUBERTY
Estimation of female pubertal development

Stage	Physical changes
P 1	Prepubertal. Elevation of papilla only; no pubic hair.
P 2	Breast budding; some labial hair present.
P 3	Further enlargement of breasts with palpable glandular tissue; no separation of breast contours; labial hair spreads over mons pubis.
P 4	Further enlargement of breasts with projection of areola to form a secondary mound; slight lateral spread of pubic hair.
P 5	Single contour of breast and areola; further lateral spread of pubic hair to form an inverse triangle; onset of menstruation.

Estimation of male pubertal development

Stages	Physical changes
P 1	Prepubertal; infantile genitalia.
P 2	Early testicular enlargement and thinning and reddening of scrotum; minimal straight pubic or scrotal hair.
P 3	Further testicular enlargement; definite phallic enlargement; darker, slightly curled pubic hair and $\pm$ early axillary and facial hair.
P 4	Moderate amount of pubic, axillary, and facial hair and acne; voice change; adult body odor.
P 5	Adult-type body habitus, hair distribution, and genitalia.

Adapted from Kelch, R.P., *et al.* (19).

In males the testes are the main source of androgens. Testosterone is the chief active androgen of male puberty and adulthood, responsible for many masculinizing changes: growth of penis, scrotum and body hair, deepening of the voice, and probably such structural features as the male bony pelvis. In females, ovaries are the main source of estrogens, necessary for development of functional menstrual cycles, fertility and maturation of breast tissue. Adrenal androgens are responsible for the female pattern of hair growth. In general, mature males have ten times higher plasma testosterone levels than females, and only one eighth the estradiol (most common estrogen) of menstruating women at their cyclic estrogen peak (17).

The two known human gonadotropins, *luteinizing hormone* (LH) and *follicle-stimulating hormone* (FSH) have a twofold task in adolescence: (1) to increase the gonadal secretion of sex hormones and to maintain it at adult levels; and (2) to make the gonads functional for sexual reproduction. In women, FSH stimulates the ovarian follicle and LH induces ovulation, the two hormones acting synergistically to stimulate ovarian estrogen production. In men, FSH causes growth of the seminiferous tubules of the testes with consequent sperm production, while LH stimulates the interstital cells of Leydig to produce testosterone.

Time Course of Gonadotropin Changes. (18, 19, 20, 21, 22) The advent of radioimmunoassay techniques in the last decade has enabled investigators to begin to characterize accurately the course of gonadotropin levels during development. A striking discovery has been the small but measurable amounts of LH and FSH in the serum of sexually infantile children.

So far there is some disagreement as to the age at which serum concentrations of FSH and LH begin to significantly exceed the constant low levels of the sexually infantile period. Combining the results of several studies, the mean age of first significant increase in normal children is shown in the Table 2. Data from a few reports indicate that serum FSH in girls and serum LH in both sexes rises rapidly between nine and twelve years. Both hormones tend to rise somewhat earlier in girls, a finding consistent with their slightly earlier observable

Table 2

	FSH	LH
Girls	10	11
Boys	11½	12

onset of puberty. It is notable that the significant increase clearly begins *in the years prior to the appearance of the bodily signs of puberty*--and so coincides with the important personal and social changes of preadolescence.

In the midpubertal adolescents the mean concentration of serum LH during sleep is significantly higher than that during wakefulness, while this difference does not occur in prepubertal children or in adult males (23). Adult levels of FSH are attained before LH reaches a similar plateau. The mean FSH and LH blood levels of adults are approximately two to three times greater than levels in sexually immature boys and girls.

Twenty-four hour urine assays show a pattern of slowly increasing FSH and LH for both boys and girls between 5 and 10 years of age. All urine studies indicate a significant rise in the excretion of gonadotropins during the years prior to the onset of puberty; but the major increase seems to take place during the period of sexual maturation. Adults excrete approximately 12 times as much LH and 6 times as much FSH as pre-pubescent children.

Gonadotropin levels correlate better with stage of pubertal maturation (P1-P5) than with chronological age. The most significant increases occur when the individual is making the transitions between these stages, no matter what his age at the time. Mean values of excreted FSH and LH in group data are almost always significantly higher in stage P3 than in stage P1, and for LH, higher in P5 than in P3. These correlations add strength to the hypothesis that the surge in gonadotropins sets off the mechanisms responsible for bodily sexual development.

In the future, longitudinal studies should give us a much less blurred picture of gonadotropin changes than do the present cross-sectional reports. As such data are collected, we should become increasingly abler to understand the mechanisms which relate hormonal, genital, bodily and psychological changes in each developing individual.

Sex Hormones (Gonadal Steroids) (19, 22, 24). Increases in sex hormone levels tend to follow in time the course of gonadotropin levels and to precede the emergence of sexual characteristics. Blood estradiol in girls rises continuously from very low levels in young children to a level 7 or 8 times as high in menstruating adolescents. Significant increases occur between pubertal stages P1, P2 and P3. Both FSH and LH seem to increase just prior to the trend of higher levels of ovarian estradiol secretion, and the FSH rise seems to anticipate increased ovarian growth. The estrogen increase is in turn well underway before uterine growth accelerates.

In boys, the major rise in serum testosterone concentration occurs between early and mid-puberty. During puberty, testosterone levels increase to more than eight times the level of androstenedione, the weak androgen which is present in relatively greater amounts in infancy. Urinary testosterone increases markedly after 12 years of age (25). The rise in FSH usually precedes the gain in testicular weight, while the rise in LH anticipates the testosterone increase. Just as the estrogen increases in girls predict the rate of uterine growth which will follow, the testosterone increases in boys predict the prostatic growth pattern.

Other Hormones. Serum PBI, BEI, and thyroxine iodine decline from childhood values during adolescence, the lowest BEI values coinciding with the period of the rapid adolescent growth spurt (26). Pituitary growth hormone has been reported by one group to increase more than seven-fold between prepuberty and middle adolescence (27), while others found that 24-hour levels did not correlate with serum testosterone or with stage of sexual maturation (28). Androgens and estrogens increase the growth hormone secretory response to a variety of provocative stimuli, and, conversely, growth hormone facilitates the potency of the gonadal steroids (21).

Physiology of Puberty in Man

Clinical, physiological and anatomical evidence points to an important role for the hypothalamus in the control of the pituitary-gonadal axis. In particular, the hypophysiotropic area, composed of the median eminence, and the arcuate, ventromedial and paraventricular nuclei, has been implicated in the regulation of tonic pituitary gonadotropic secretion. Nerve endings in the hypothalamus secrete small peptide molecules called releasing factors which travel down the portal vessels to stimulate production and release of pituitary hormones. A specific decapeptide, termed gonadotropin-releasing hormone (Gn-RH) has been found to possess both LH and FSH releasing activity (29).

The main clinical evidence for central nervous system control comes from cases of *true sexual precocity*, characterized by normal-appearing but premature onset of puberty before age 8 or 9, with early maturation of the gonads under the influence of the pituitary. Cases in which an associated abnormality can be found often show intracranial lesions, almost always in or adjacent to the hypothalamus (11).

Mechanism of Pubertal Onset. Thus our present model of sexual function and development is a three level hierarchy: the hypothalamus regulates pituitary release of gonadotropins, which in turn regulates gonadal secretion of sex hormones. Sex hormones and direct effects of gonadotropins cause bodily growth and change, and maintenance of sexual characteristics.

Assuming this basic model, how are gonadotropin levels kept low in young children and what makes the levels increase significantly in preadolescence and adolescence? Apparently gonadotropin production in the young is inhibited by the negative feedback to the hypothalamus and pituitary of low levels of circulating sex hormones. This view is supported by both animal experimentation (11) and clinical cases of gonadal dysgenesis or anorchia in which subnormal secretion of gonadal steroids is accompanied by abnormally high levels of LH and FSH in prepubertal children (19, 22, 24, 30).

During preadolescence and adolescence this negative feedback mechanism must be gradually readjusted so that much greater amounts of gonadotropins are secreted than in the immature child. Experimental and clinical evidence seems to locate the site of the critical readjustment in the hypothalamus, rather than in the pituitary, ovaries or testes. Prepubertal gonads can produce adult amounts of sex steroids under the influence of exogenous gonadotropins (19). When the pituitary of a prepubertal animal is grafted into an adult, it secretes adult amounts of gonadotropins. So it seems both the gonads and the pituitary are functionally ready to secrete adult levels of hormones long before puberty begins. However, when the pituitary of an adult animal is grafted into an infantile animal, it will not produce large amounts of gonadotropins (11). Apparently the maturity of the hypothalamus determines gonadotropic output.

The currently accepted hypothesis is that hypothalamic sensitivity to the negative feedback control of gonadal steroids decreases markedly just before and during puberty (21, 30). Low prepubertal levels of androgen and/or estrogen can no longer maintain the low gonadotropin levels of childhood. Consequently, LH and FSH increase, stimulating the gonads to produce more steriods. Readjustment continues until the quantities of sex steroids required for hypothalamic suppression exceed the threshold of sensitivity of the peripheral body tissues; then the steroids bring about the physical signs of puberty. By midpuberty the negative feedback response to gonadal steriods is as low as that of the adult. The cases of true sexual precocity with hypothalamic lesions referred to above, or even those many cases with no observable lesion, may be understood as congenital or acquired abnormalities resulting in overproduction of releasing factor and consequent hyperstimulation of the pituitary at an early age.

At present we have no acceptable explanation for the maturation of the hypothalamic response. One study has shown an invarying mean weight of 48 kg. in groups of girls at menarche, regardless of age. The data suggested that the achievement of a critical rate of amount of body metabolism may signal the hypothalamus (31). Others have speculated on the possible influence of the amygdala or the pineal on the hypothalamus (21).

Cyclic Activity in Girls. In girls there is a second critical hormonal event during puberty: the beginning of cyclic changes and regular monthly ovulation. A different region of the hypothalamus, the anterior preoptic and lateral portions, is responsible for cyclic gonadotropin release. Ovulation requires a midcycle surge of LH, thought to depend on a *positive feedback* response in increased estrogen, a response not usually attained before midpuberty (31). Yet cyclical proliferation of vaginal epithelium has been observed in girls 9 to 12 years old, and cyclic estrogen excretion in a girl 10½ (18). It must be kept in mind that premenarcheal, even pre-pubertal girls may experience periodic hormonal changes which can influence their feelings and behavior.

Clinical data. As alluded to above, clinical disorders or puberty, particularly the hypergonadotropic and hypogonado-tropic states, offer much evidence to support the endocrino-logical model of puberty described. Their response to therapy is generally predictable on the basis of this model. More detailed information and references on both normal and abnormal patterns of development may be found in recent endocrinological reviews (20, 21, 22, 32).

IV. An Interdisciplinary View

In attempting to characterize preadolescent development we have analyzed its features in turn from several separate vantage points: the emotional, cognitive, social, and biological. These are not arbitrary viewpoints. Each has contributed to our understanding because each corresponds to an ongoing *developmental system* in the child. The course of development depends on the continuing complex interactions between these systems as well as the smooth functioning of each one alone. For example, the level of sophistication of thought processes typically used by a child depends as much upon his environment and motivation as on his cognitive maturation.

When the developmental systems are working smoothly together, the child seems "well-balanced"--poised, confident, satisfied, at ease. When the balance is disrupted, he or she seems clumsy, unsure, anxious, upset or depressed. In a phase like preadolescence, when so many new and complex trends are getting underway, and with all the developmental systems affected, many types of disequilibrium are bound to occur. Studies of interactions between developmental systems are necessary not only for our understanding of such periods; they may also yield us further insight into the fundamental processes of normal and abnormal development.

The Social Effects of Biological Growth Rate

Mussen compared the attitudes and self-concepts of boys age 17 at the extremes of retarded or advanced physical development (33). In their TAT responses, physically undeveloped boys expressed more negative self-conceptions and feelings of rejection, more dependent needs, more introspection and more rebellious attitudes towards parents. Jones followed up two similar groups into their early thirties and reported lasting effects: while the differences were not great, the early maturers at 17, more esteemed while in high school, seemed relatively more sociable, enterprising, persistant and dominant 16 years later (34). Such data do not allow us to conclude that differences in physical maturation rate were directly responsible for differences in behavior and personality. Alternative explanations might suffice equally well. The converse might be true--that the psycho-social pattern influenced biological growth. Possibly either the genetic endowment or the environment of the child might have determined both the biological and psychosocial growth pattern. Any or all of these mechanisms might apply in this or other examples of correlations between developmental trends.

Further, there are important exceptions to the useful rule-of-thumb that early-maturers will be held in relatively greater esteem by their peer group. Faust discovered that while sixth grade girls attributed the most prestigious traits to pre-pubertal girls, by eighth and ninth grade late-pubertal girls were leading in prestige (35). During the course of four years, early maturation changed from a social disadvantage to a distinct advantage. It was Sullivan's clinical impression that a boy has serious problems as a result of delayed puberty only if his circle of close friends is broken up (36). The significance of late or early physical maturation can be understood only in social context.

In their examination of children who experience precocious or delayed puberty, Money and Erhardt confront the problem of differential rates of growth in the developmental systems and subsystems of children (17). These children are not all the same developmentally; nor are they equally ahead of or behind other children in all categories. Their "psychosocial age," as judged from thoughts and social behavior, lies somewhere between their chronological age and their physique or bone age. "Erotic age," as measured by mental imagery, may closely parallel physical maturity, while erotic age as measured by dating and sexual experience is more in keeping with similar-aged children.

Toward a Mind-Body Model

In spite of the bewildering complexity of possible patterns of interaction between developmental systems, we expect some regularities because, in the final analysis, genetic influences, prenatal environment and the individual social and learning history all contribute to the build up of a representation in the brain from which all behavior stems. The pubertal endocrine clock is located in the limbic system with the hypothalamus, the cognitive growth clock in the cerebral cortex. This separation may explain the greater sensitivity of cognitive development to the social environment. On the other hand, functional connections between the two brain systems give biological substance to reports of mutual influence between cognitive and biological processes; for example, the observation that girls tend to become more organized, logical and expressive after the menarche (37).

Because they are the least variable, the biologic events of preadolescence and puberty should serve as a guideline against which other kinds of developmental progress can be measured. Yet we must be equally aware that the biologic system is not monolithic. Its several components, including the endocrine glands and hormones, the neurotransmitters and the nervous tissues themselves, are both delicately balanced with each other and continuously interacting with individual experience.

There are many sensitive relationships between endocrine function and catecholamine metabolism. Considerable evidence indicates that monoamines are involved in the control of gonadotropin (38) and growth hormone (39) secretion, and that hormones in turn influence the formation and sensitivity of neural transmitters (40, 41). The highest concentration in the brain of monoamine oxidase (MAO), the main enzyme in the metabolic breakdown of catecholamines, is in the hypothalamus, that part of the brain centrally concerned with emotions and the endocrine system. Plasma levels of enzymes involved in monoamine metabolism (42) and urinary levels of monoamine metabolites (43) may reach their maximum values during preadolescence and puberty, much as in the pattern of gonadotrophins and sex hormones. In the blood, the concentration of MAO is positively correlated with the level of progesterone. Thus, the concentration of MAO increases during the menstrual cycle, reaching its peak during the latter part of the second half of the cycle (44). These cathecholamine-endocrine relationships suggest that upsets in behavior or mood which occur during preadolescence may, at times, be reflections of transient disturbances in the balance between sex hormones and cathecholamine metabolism. Transient metabolic disequilibrium seems particularly likely to occur during pre- and early adolescence when the endocrine system is undergoing rapid and often uneven development.

Abnormalities in either biogenic amine levels or hypo-thalamic-pituitary function have been reported in several types of serious neuropsychiatric disorders in children and adults (45). Combined abnormalities may occur (46). Equally important is the feedback influence of social and psychological experience on biological activity (47), as clearly indicated in the sensitivity of the pituitary-adrenal axis and biogenic amine levels to stress (48, 49). We should not be surprised to discover, then, that experiences such as social rejection, which call forth such affective responses as depression and anxiety, might significantly alter physiological processes, perhaps even delay endocrine maturation. The biologic systems of pre-pubertal and pubertal children, in a state of flux and structural change, should be particularly subject to perturbation by experience. For example, menstruation patterns are seen to be most sensitive to the emotional situation of younger girls (50).

We have much to learn before we can begin to explain how the synchrony of developmental processes is orchestrated.

We do know that normal development depends upon a series of concerted changes--neural, hormonal, cognitive, emotional and social--during critical formative periods. In a complex system in which some important components, such as the genetic, are rigidly defined, limited early dysfunction can easily lead to larger problems, if not compensated by changes in more flexible components. Early experience may pave the way for inappropriate behavior which only becomes obvious years later, under the impact of hormonal and bodily changes. Certain disorders of sexual identity seem to originate in this manner in individuals whose genetic programming appears quite normal (51). In preadolescence as in other periods, the ultimate impact of sex-specific hormones, other endogenous compounds, and drugs as well, depends as much on the past history of the individual as on his more obvious biological and psychological status.

Clinical Phenomena

Disturbances of development in preadolescent children reflect the tasks and resources which are characteristic, if not specific, for children during this period of transition. Running away, excessive moodiness, precipitious adventures, and rapid alternation between overdependence and disgust with parental figures are frequently observed patterns of behavior (3, 5). As seen in clinical practice, the troubles of preadolescence are most often related to the vaguely experienced upsurge of aggression, the social and internal forces towards separation, and the perturbations in body image. The exaggerated troubles of the following two children illustrate the types of disturbance which often confront the clinician.

Samuel. Samuel's father was a bright, eccentric, and self-proclaimed failure who taught school; his mother, an energetic, introspective, and acknowledged depressive. Samuel's only sibling was an older brother of average intelligence who had a neurological syndrome characterized by grand mal epilepsy and rage attacks. A social failure, he was able to hold only marginal, socially isolated jobs. Samuel, in marked contrast, was precocious in every sphere. During his early elementary school years, he attracted wide attention. His father called himself "a son-worshiper," an epithet which was

a remarkably accurate description of his attitude of sub-
servience and respect. Samuel was surrounded by friends. He
was the model child--industrious, respectful of his parents, and
academically, socially, and athletically successful.

At about age 10½, Samuel and his parents slowly began
to part ways. Resisting their demands for Sunday trips and
visits to relatives, Samuel said that he preferred staying home
or going with friends. Unwilling to apply himself to extra
science projects and homework at every moment of leisure,
joint endeavors engaged in previously by Samuel and his
father, Samuel preferred to lounge about or go with pals. To
these early signs of increased assertions of independence and
movement away from industrious occupation, Samuel's parents
responded with concern and increasing alarm. Ferocious
battles became progressively more frequent as Samuel felt
pushed into a corner and forced to strike out and as his parents
felt that only strong demands would save their beloved second
child from following in the path of failure carved out by his
father and older brother.

By age 11½ or 12 years, Samuel often barracaded
himself in his bedroom and engaged in petty destructiveness.
On one occasion, his father felt forced to break down the door
of the bedroom to see what Samuel was doing; Samuel reci-
procally felt forced to break his mother's typewriter. Bathing
created a veritable military campaign. After days or weeks of
parental pestering, Samuel would decide to shower at an
inconvenient moment. Following his shower, the bathroom
would be in shambles and a long stream of water and objects
of clothing would be trailed from bathroom to bedroom. After
such events, which typified Samuel's angry compliance with
the requests of his parents, his mother and father would feel a
sense of victory and of hatred.

Over the course of many months, Samuel's anger with his
family diffused to all activities. His school work fell to barely
passing, and his social relations with peers deteriorated. He
often missed days of school, and he spent his nights wandering
with one or another new acquaintance in the most dangerous
and undesirable areas of the city. From a neatly dressed
youngster, he became totally transformed in his outward
appearance to being shaggy, dirty, and smelly. From a quiet-
spoken and obedient child, he turned into a nasty, terse,

young "delinquent." No longer could he and his parents share trips to the museum, long discussions, or any of the other activities which previously had brought pleasure to them all. His days were preoccupied with thoughts of how to get even with his mother and father; their days were spent with how they could change him back to what he had been and prevent him from becoming a bum or even worse.

Samuel was dragged by his parents to the child guidance center, but the stalemate was obvious. Samuel refused to speak with his parents even in the face of dramatic protestations by therapist and parents. Finally, his father and mother, feeling that they had lost control over their own aggression and on the verge of a murderous attack, reluctantly decided on inpatient hospitalization.

At this time, Samuel was a rather scruffy, rugged, short young adolescent with the first traces of a moustache and a few acne sores. He saw his several years of battling with his parents as the result of their constant, unremitting intrusiveness and his search for some domain in which he, alone, was the guardian of his destiny. That the final domain in which he took refuge was a totally negative one--academic failure, social isolation, personal disorderliness, constant anger, and negativism defined by reaction to parental strictures and ideals-was a price he was only too ready to pay. How Samuel navigated during the next several years to a stance in which he could use his earlier identification with his intellectual father to his own advantage, without feeling that positive social action was a capitulation to the infantile, regressive demands that he felt were personified by his parents, is a story that exceeds the limits of our current discussion.

Sarah. Mr. and Mrs. T. had a long and stormy courtship, marked by mutual passivity and anger that the other partner wasn't decisive enough in separating from parents. Soon after marrying, they recognized the bitterness between them and sought help. On the surface, Mr. and Mrs. T. were models of a struggling, family-minded, middle-class family. Mr. T. devoted himself to his business, Mrs. T., to caring for the house and her part-time work. They looked forward to the birth of their first child and were disappointed with the birth of a daughter, Sarah, rather than a longed-for son. Mr. T., especially, felt added disappointment with the gender of his first-born child when his second and third children were also daughters. During her preschool years, Mr. T. turned toward Sarah with the expectation that, while she could not fully satisfy his wish for a manly and assertive son, that she could at least offer some of the companionship missing from his marriage. Sarah complied. She was surrogate mother to her baby sisters, affectionate daughter for her father. By age 5 or 6, the strains of her many roles were apparent. School phobia, thumb sucking, and social distancing led the family social worker and parents to feel that Sarah required psychological evaluation. With about 1½ years of treatment at about age 8 years, Sarah's school difficulties faded, her enuresis cleared, and she no longer engaged in such activities as hiding under the table at the approach of neighbors or strangers. She became an excellent student; at home she was a delightful companion for her parents. Later, however, Sarah was to recall that she felt that these years of happiness were not genuine, and that she often felt "miserable." During this time Sarah had several close girl friends.

The summer before her first menstrual period (at age 11) was spent in camp. During the summer Sarah, for the first time, felt attracted to a boy her age; at the end of the summer she either kissed or was kissed by him. She felt that this was a deep relationship that would endure past the autumn. When she returned home, she told her parents about this boy and about her feelings. Her father quickly and clearly stated his opinion that the boy would never be in touch with her again and that the relationship was only a passing fancy for him. Sarah protested, but felt he was probably correct.

In the spring before the summer of camp, at times during camp, and during the early autumn after camp, Sarah experienced a return of her feelings of estrangement and tension. Her first menstrual period was accompanied by an exacerbation of these feelings of tension. Her father, on the morning of that special event, came into the bathroom and slapped her in the face, an initiation ritual which was common in the family's subculture. She felt that it was odd that he was so excited by her menstruation; surely, she felt, he would not have acted so enthusiastically the first time his son shaved. She soon became preoccupied by the changing shapes in her body, a tendency which she had noted and had been concerned about for many months before her menarche. Her father, too, became concerned that she might become obese since both parents were, indeed, markedly overweight.

Thus, soon after camp and about the time of her first menstrual period, Sarah decided to go on a diet. This diet first involved the exclusion of certain "fatty" foods, but within several months the diet became a marked reduction of all eating.   Within six months Sarah had lost a considerable amount of weight, was eating only pigeon size quantities at meals, and appeared to be tense and unhappy.   Mealtimes became scenes of violent dispute, as Mr. T. coerced, scolded, and threatened Sarah to get her to eat more, and as Mrs. T. cried and pretended to wish to give Sarah the opportunity to make up her own mind. The family pediatrician, after months of following Sarah's weight during its decline, diagnosed her condition as anorexia nervosa.

By this time, Sarah was a cachectic, but attractive, dark-eyed young adolescent. Her voice was whiny, but she actively sought out friends and activities. All subjects, particularly schoolwork and philosophical issues, were open for discussion; only one subject was closed, food. The mention of eating led to angry denial that this was anything important to her. Eventually, Sarah reconstituted herself into an adolescent and then young adult with a profession of her own; but this story, as Sam's, exceeds the boundaries of our current topic.

In reconstructing Sam's and Sarah's development, it is clear that neither reached the preadolescent phase without difficulty. Sam's over-compliance, excessive goodness, and important role for his father as a surrogate, are warning signals of difficulty. For Sarah, even more clearly, development had moved off track during early and middle childhood. Yet, both Sam and Sarah experienced phase-specific, intense disturbances in development during the months that preceded and the months that followed the onset of puberty. Before either entered into puberty, both showed an increase in their level of drive, need for independence, tendency towards aggressiveness and secretiveness, preoccupation with their bodies, and moodiness. Running away, as Sam did, or obsessive ruminative turning in, as Sarah did, characterize two typical preadolescent stances, neither of which can be characterized as either active or passive. Both youngsters showed rapid swings of mood, and both searched for, but could not accept, support or guidance from anyone, adult or peer. Their affection for adults, and trust in friends, dissolved. Both youngsters felt alone for the first time in their lives, and both wished and feared the forward move into experiences and feelings which were extremely inviting and extremely dangerous.

Sam's and Sarah's parents felt unable to understand their children, whom they saw transformed in front of their eyes over the course of months from intelligible, elementary school children into unintelligible, even bizarre, early adolescents. In their parents, both Sam and Sarah were able to engender destructiveness and rage which had never characterized either set of parents before that time. And both sets of parents felt a sense of terror as they recognized in themselves the urge to destroy the child whom they had, only months before, cherished more than any other.

Programmatic and Research Implications

If our viewpoint on preadolescencse is accurate, there is much to be gained from the recognition of the special developmental needs which characterize this phase of complex biological and psychological reorganization. Child care professionals, particularly those experienced with adolescents, should be encouraged to think about ways in which youth-serving organizations and schoolage day care programs might provide more comprehensive services for preadolescents. Informed, organized, preventive intervention with children and families may reduce the incidence of severe disturbances which mark this transition period, including gang-oriented delinquency, early drug use, school truancy and dropping out, running away, and intra-familial crises.

While major themes and leads so far uncovered are quite stimulating, our information is surprisingly limited in many important areas. There is critical need for further, systematic, basic research in the following areas: (1) development and socialization in the broad range of American subcultures, including urban ghettoes, rural areas, migrant worker societies,

Indian reservations, and one-parent families; (2) longitudinal studies of endocrine changes from childhood into adolescence, correlated with personality and social studies; (3) behavior genetics of normal and deviant development; (4) sexual identity formation in relation to both cultural and biological factors; (5) impact of different cultural experiences, e.g., work opportunities and schooling, both within the U.S. and cross-culturally, and (6) precursors of developmental disability, social and educational problems, and optimal development, based on both new and already available epidemiological and longitudinal data.

We have yet to fully explain the important secular trend in the age of puberty, which has become progressively earlier for the last century and a half in the industrialized nations, and more recently, all over the world (52). Continuously improving nutrition and public health may have originally determined it. Today, increasing stimulation in the child's environment may play a role in continuation of the trend. The earlier onset of puberty presents further problems to youngsters who must now pass through a longer "waiting period" than ever before to prepare themselves educationally for acceptance into adult society. As in other developmental phases, the character of experience in preadolescence, while broadly molded by biology, receives its distinctive shape from the impact of social and cultural forces.

REFERENCES

1. Erikson, E. *Childhood and Society*. W.W. Norton & Co., New York (1963).

2. Erikson, E. *Am. J. Orthopsychiat. 4*, 56, (1951).

3. Blos, P. *On Adolescence*. Free Press, New York (1962).

4. Redl, F. Adolescents, just how do they react, in *Adolescence: Psychosocial Perspectives*. Edited by Caplan G, Lebovici S. Basic Books, New York, (1969).

5. Freud, A. *Psychoanal. Study Child. 13*, 255, (1958).

6. Kohlberg, L., and Gilligan, C. *Daedalus 4*, 1051, (1971).

7. Kohen-raz, R. *The Child from Nine to Thirteen*. Aldine-Atherton, Chicago, (1971).

8. Erikson, E. *J. Am. Psychoanal. Assoc. 4*, 56, (1956).

9. Broderick, C.F., and Fowler, St. E. *Marriage and Family Living 23*, 27, (1961).

10. Gordon, C. *Daedalus 4*, 931, (1971).

11. Donovan, B.T., and Van der Werff Ten Bosch, J.J. *Phsysiology of Puberty*. Williams & Wilkins Co., Baltimore, (1965).

12. Marshall, W.A., and Tanner, J.M. *Arch. Dis. Child. 44*, 291, (1969).

13. Marshall, W.A., and Tanner, J.M. *Arch. Dis. Child. 45*, 13, (1970).

14. Tanner, J.M. *Growth at Adolescence*. Blackwell's Scientific Publications, Oxford, (1962).

15. Tanner, J. M. Growth and endocrinology of the adolescent, in *Endocrine and Genetic Diseases of Childhood.* Edited by Gardner L.W. B Saunders, Philadelphia, pp. 19ff, (1969).

16. Tanner, J.M. *Daedalus* [*Twelve to Sixteen: Early Adolescence*] *4, 907,* (1971).

17. Money, J., and Erhardt, A.A. *Man and Woman, Boy and Girl.* Johns Hopkins University Press, Baltimore, (1972).

18. Saxena, B., Beling, C., and Grandy, H. *Gonadotropins.* John Wiley and Sons, New York, (1972).

19. Kelch, R.P.,Grumbach, M.M., and Kaplan, S.L. Studies on the mechanism of puberty in man, in *Gonadotropins.* Edited by Saxena, B., Beling, C., and Grandy, H. John Wiley & Sons, New York, (1972).

20. Kulin, H.E., Grumbach, M.M., and Kaplan, S.L. *Pediat. Res. 162,* 162, (1972).

21. Root, A.W. *J. Pediat, 83,* 1, (1973).

22. Grumbach, M., Grawe, G., and Mayer, F. *The Control of the Onset of Puberty.* John Wiley and Sons, New York (1974).

23. Boyar, R.M., Finklestein, J., and Roffwang, H., *et al. New Engl. J. Med. 287,* 582, (1972).

24. Jenner, M.R., *et al. J. Clin. Endocrin. 34,* 521, (1972).

25. Gupta, D., and Butler, H. *Steroids 14,* 343, (1969).

26. Hung, W. Physiologic changes in the thyroid during childhood and adolescence, in *Endocrine and Genetic Diseases of Childhood.* Edited by Gardner, L.I. W.B. Saunders, Philadelphia, pp. 206-212, (1969).

27. Finkelstein, J.W., Roffwang, H.P., Boyar, R.M., *et al.* *J. Clin. Endocrinol. Metab. 35,* 665, (1972).

28. Thompson, R.G., Rodriguez, A., *et al. J. Clin. Endocrinol. Metab. 35,* 334, (1972).

29. Flerko, B. Control of follicle-stimulating hormone and luteinizing hormone secretion, in *The Hypothalamus.* Edited by Martini, L., Motta, M., and Frasehini, F., Academic Press, New York, pp. 351-363, (1970).

30. Kulin, H.E., and Reiter, E.O. *Pediatrics 51,* 260, (1973).

31. Frisch, R.E., and Revelle, R. *Arch. Dis. Child. 46,* 695, (1971).

32. Root, A.W., *J. Pediat. 83,* 187, (1973).

33. Mussen, P.H., and Jones, M.C. *Child Develop. 28,* 243, (1957).

34. Jones, M.C. *Child Develop. 28,* 113, (1957).

35. Faust, M.S. *Child Develop. 31,* 173, (1960).

36. Sullivan, H.S. *The Interpersonal Theory of Psychiatry.* W.W. Norton & Co., New York, (1953).

37. Hart, M., and Sarnoff, C.A. *J. Am. Acad. Child Psychiat. 10,* 257, (1971).

38. Coppola, J.A. Brain catecholamines and gonadotropin secretion, in *Frontiers in Neuroendocrinology.* Edited by Ganong and Martini. Ohio University Press, New York, pp. 1384-1393, (1971).

39. Martin, J. *New Engl. J. Med. 288*, 1384, (1973).

40. Frohman, L. *New Engl. J. Med. 286*, 1391, (1972).

41. Landsberg, L., and Axelrod, J. *Circulation Res. 22*, 559, (1968).

42. Weinshilboum, R.M., and Axelrod, J. *New Engl. J. Med. 285*, 938, (1971).

43. McKendrick, T., and Edwards, R. *Arch. Dis. Child. 40*, 418, (1965).

44. Southgate, J. The effect of sex steroids in *Monoamine Oxidases--New Vistas*. Edited by Costa, and Sandler. Raven Press, New York, (1972).

45. Schildkraut, J.J. *Neuropsychopharmacology and the Affective Disorders*. Little, Brown, Boston, (1970).

46. Prange, A.J., and Lipton, M.A. Hormones and behavior: Some principles and findings, in *Psychiatric Complications of Medical Drugs*. Edited by Shader, R.I. Raven Press, New York, pp 213-249, (1972).

47. Miller, N.E. *Selected Papers*. Aldine-Atherton, Chicago, (1971).

48. Cohen, D.J. Competence and biology: Methodology in studies in infants, twins, psychosomatic disease, and psychosis, in *The Child in His Family: Children at Psychiatric Risk*. Edited by Anthony, E.J. John Wiley & Sons, New York, pp. 361-394 (1974).

49. Mason, J.W. *Psychosom Med. 30*, Part 2. (1968).

50. Huffman, J. *The Gynecology of Childhood and Adolescence*. W.B. Saunders, Philadelphia, (1968).

51. Stoller, R.J. *Sex and Gender.* Hogarth Press, London, (1968).

52. Tanner, J.M. *Sci. Amer. 218,* 21, (1968).

MENTAL HEALTH IN CHILDREN, Volume I
Edited By D. V. Siva Sankar
Copyright © 1975 by
PJD Publications Ltd., Westbury, N.Y.

THE DIAGNOSIS, ETIOLOGY AND TREATMENT OF GILLES DE LA TOURETTE'S SYNDROME

Elaine Shapiro, Arthur K. Shapiro, Richard D. Sweet
and Ruth D. Bruun
Payne Whitney Clinic and N. Y. Hospital
Cornell University Medical Center
New York, N. Y. 10021

Gilles de la Tourette's syndrome is characterized by involuntary movements and utterances, and some patients have echo phenomena, such as the repeating of words or gestures of others.

Involuntary Movements

The involuntary movements can be simple or complicated, involving one or more muscle groups. In most cases the first symptom to appear is a facial tic such as an eye blink or twitch of the mouth. However, the onset of symptoms may be multiple consisting of movement, noises, words, or coprolalia.

In a short time the tics usually spread to other parts of the body. Head twitching, shoulder shrugging, arm jerks, and others are reported. In addition, more complicated movements frequently occur, such as jumping, stamping, hitting, and so on.

These movements are involuntary, sudden, rapid, and purposeless. They may be voluntarily inhibited for short periods of time but this results in a build-up of other symptoms. Charact   ically, there is a shifting pattern of symptoms.

New symptoms appear and are added to or replace others. Although remissions are infrequent and last for varying periods of time, the symptoms usually wax and wane.

Involuntary Utterances

The involuntary utterances vary from barks, grunts, coughs, and throat clearing to explicit words and obscenities. Some of the symptoms such as throat clearing, sniffing, and coprolalia are difficult to diagnose because they are blended into the appropriate cultural, environmental and psychological context. Coprolalia, although occasionally a first symptom, usually occurs later, and disappears spontaneously in many patients. Coprolalia does not occur in all patients and is not necessary for diagnosis (1).

Differential Diagnosis

The onset of Tourette's syndrome for 34 patients studied in our laboratory was between the ages of 3 and 13 with a mean of 7 years. The duration of illness between onset and diagnosis averaged 16.3 years (2). This delay apparently grew out of ignorance about criteria for diagnosis. A major diagnostic problem when faced with a child with tics is to differentiate Tourette's syndrome from transient tics of childhood. There are several unique features of Tourette's syndrome which aid in this differential diagnosis.

The first is the spread or progress of the symptoms from a single, simple tic to involuntary movements in other parts of the body.

The second feature is a fluctuating pattern of symptoms characterized by new symptoms replacing or added to old ones or old ones suddenly reappearing.

Third is the inevitable later development of involuntary utterances. In 100 patients seen by the authors, all had noises, words, or coprolalia.

The fourth is the characteristic waxing or waning of the symptoms. For short periods symptoms decrease, exacerbate, or remit, although complete remission is infrequent. In transient tics of childhood remissions are frequent, and symptoms usually disappear after a few months or during puberty.

Fifth is the presence of coprolalia. Although coprolalia need not occur, it was found in about 67.2 percent of our patients. If it does occur, it is pathogonomic for the diagnosis.

Since coprolalia is one of the last symptoms to occur, and in some cases did not occur until 23 years after the onset of symptoms, the diagnosis should not be delayed until it occurs.

The following conditions should also be considered in the differential diagnosis of Tourette's syndrome: The most common are the athetoid-type of cerebral palsy (including status marmoratus), dystonia muscularum deformans, encephalitis lethargica, Hallervorden-Spatz disease, Huntington's chorea (including senile dementia), Pelizaeus-Merzbacher disease, spastic torticollis, status dysmyelinatus, Sydenham's chorea, and Wilson's disease. Other involuntary movement disorders such as manganese poisoning, sequellae following acute Co poisoning, overdosage of amphetamines, phenothiazine extrapyramidal effects, chronic residual effects of neonatal kernicterus, inborn errors of metabolism such as phenylketonuria, infantile gout, acanthocytosis, and hypoparathyroidism, Chagas disease, and Jacob-Creutzfeldt disease can be ruled out on the basis of history and routine laboratory tests. Vascular accidents can result in a variety of bizarre movement disorders. Choreic movements can occur in patients with occlusion of the posterior cerebral artery or its branches, in conjunction with other components of the "thalamic syndrome," and of the superior cerebellar artery caused by damage to the brachium conjunctivum. Coprolalia can occur in patients with aphasias after cerebrovascular accidents, although it does not resemble the coprolalia in Tourette's syndrome. Coprolalia also occurs in klasomania (patients with post-encephalitic parkinsonism in conjunction with an oculogyric crisis) and general paresis.

These diseases can most often be ruled out by clinical history, symptomatology, and occasionally by laboratory tests (3).

Early diagnosis of Tourette's syndrome is important in order to avoid harmful effects of this illness.

Etiological Factors

The syndrome has been considered a psychological illness by many investigators. Psychopathological factors frequently described in medical and psychological literature and commonly believed to characterize patients with Tourette's syndrome include schizophrenia, underlying psychosis, obsessive-compulsiveness, inhibition of hostility, hysteria, somatization, initial high IQ, followed by ultimate deterioration of intellectual and psychological functioning.

On psychological test evaluation consisting of the WAIS, Rorschach, and Bender-Gestalt and psychiatric evaluation of 30 patients, no support was found for these factors which have been extensively reported elsewhere (4).

An alternative hypothesis is that Tourette's syndrome is an organic impairment of the central nervous system. Based on our interpretation of neurological, EEG, psychiatric, and psychological data obtained on 34 patients, Tourette's syndrome is associated often, but not always, with clinical and laboratory evidence of central nervous system abnormality (5).

Neurological evaluation indicated "soft signs" of neurological impairment in 53.8 percent of 34 Tourette patients.

Non-specific abnormalities on EEG records were noted in 50 percent of 32 Tourette patients.

The psychiatrist rated 50 percent of 34 patients as organically impaired based on history of hyperactivity, perceptual difficulties and learning disabilities. This material was obtained from the patients, doctors' records, and when possible, from school records.

The overall percentage of organic impairment on the psychological tests was 76.7 percent. The average IQ of these patients was 103.5. Among patients 16 years of age and over 56 percent had a discrepancy of 19 or more points between their Verbal and Performance IQs with a Verbal higher than the Performance IQ. In addition, moderate to marked abnormalities were found on the Bender. Among patients under 16, only 2 out of 14 had a similar higher Verbal than Performance IQ score, however, 10 out of 14 were judged to have moderate to marked abnormalities on the Bender.

The number of patients with organic indices on three out of four parameters (neurological, EEG, psychiatric, and psychological) was 19 out of 29 patients or 65.6 percent.

In a more recent study, 36 additional patients were evaluated neurologically. The percentage of patients with signs of neurological impairment increased to 55.6 percent. Combining both studies, the percentage of patients with some degree of neurological impairment is 54.2 percent. The psychological test indices and EEG ratings for this recent group of patients has not been analyzed.

We concluded that the etiology of Tourette's syndrome is an undetermined organic impairment of the central nervous system. Definitive evidence about its etiology is likely to arise from neurophysiologic investigation.

Treatment

Many different treatment modalities and drugs have been used in the treatment of Tourette's syndrome. In our experience, based on treatment of more than 85 patients, the most predictable and successful treatment has been with haloperidol. Twenty-one patients in treatment with haloperidol were studied extensively each month for the first nine months and half-yearly thereafter.

Chemotherapy primarily involves careful titration of the dosage of haloperidol until maximum symptom relief and minimum side effects occur. The dosage usually varies between 1.5 and 100 mg per day (occasionally as much as 50 mg per day) during acute treatment which lasts from one to three months before the dosage, effectiveness, and side effects become stabilized. Subsequently, for as long as four years, the dosage is constantly lowered against an endpoint of symptom relief and ability to tolerate side effects, and eventually to a very low dosage. Extrapyramidal effects (primarily dyskinesia, akathesia, akinesia, and parkinsonian symptoms) are frequent and all patients are given concomitant anti-parkinsonian agents.

Most of the 85 patients treated by us had 85 percent improvement after one month of treatment, over 90 percent improvement after one year, and 95 percent improvement after one and one-half years. With time, improvement increases and the dosage of haloperidol and extrapyramidal agents can be decreased. After one and one-half years the dosage is 4 mg per day or less.

Treatment of patients must be individualized because of the marked variation in dosage and clinical response. Recommendations about treatment are described in detail elsewhere (6). The difficulties in successful chemotherapy with haloperidol should not be minimized. A physician experienced in the use of high dosages of psychopharmaceuticals and considerable competence in recognition and management of side effects is essential to successful treatment.

Since haloperidol probably acts by blocking catecholamine synaptic receptors, two other drugs which inhibit catecholamine synthesis or storage were investigated for their effectiveness in treating Tourette's syndrome (7). Six patients were given alpha-methyl-para-tyrosine (up to 3.0 grams per day) and five patients were given tetrabenazine (up to 300 mg per day).

One patient withdrew from the alpha-methyl-para-tyrosine study, three were unimproved, and two patients had greatly diminished movements. However, the therapeutic effect in one patient diminished after seven months.

Tetrabenazine was effective in two patients, for about one month as inpatients but symptoms returned several weeks after discharge in one patient, and in another required concomitant low dosages of haloperidol.

These drugs do not appear to be effective in suppressing the symptoms of Tourette's syndrome. However, research is continuing using a combination of tetrabenazine and haloperidol on an outpatient basis.

SUMMARY

The early diagnosis of Tourette's syndrome is especially important now that effective treatment is available. The delay in diagnosis and treatment has resulted in unnecessary psychological and economic stress to patients as well as their parents.

Characteristically, the symptoms usually begin with a single motor tic but in time become multiple and involve more than one part of the body. The symptoms fluctuate, wax and wane, but total remissions are rare. Involuntary vocal utterances occur in all patients but coprolalia may or may not occur.

Based on our research studies we concluded that the etiology of Tourette's syndrome is an undetermined organic impairment of the central nervous system.

Although research efforts are continuing with other drugs, the treatment of choice, at present, is haloperidol.

REFERENCES

1. Shapiro, A.K., Shapiro, E., and Wayne, H.L., *J. Amer. Acad. Child Psychiat.*, *12*, 702, (1973).

2. Shapiro, A.K., Shapiro, E., and Wayne, H.L. *J. Nerv. Ment. Dis.*, *155*, 335, (1972).

3. Bruun, R.D., and Shapiro, A.K. *J. Nerv Ment. Dis.*, *155*, 328, (1972).

4. Shapiro, A.K., Shapiro, E. Wayne, H.L., and Clarkin, J. *Amer. J. Psychiat.*, *129*, 427, (1972).

5. Shapiro, A.K., Shapiro, E., Wayne, H.L., and Clarkin, J. *Brit. J. Psychiat.*, *122*, 659, (1973).

6. Shapiro, A.K., Shapiro, E., and Wayne, H.L., *Arch. Gen. Psychiat.*, *28*, 92, (1973).

7. Sweet, R.D., Bruun, R., Shapïro, E., Shapiro, A.K., *Arch Gen. Psychiat. 31*, 857, (1974).

MENTAL HEALTH IN CHILDREN, Volume I
Edited By D. V. Siva Sankar
Copyright © 1975 by
PJD Publications Ltd., Westbury, N.Y.

DEVELOPMENTAL EFFECTS OF
EARLY MATERNAL SEPARATION

STUDIES OF THE BIOLOGICAL AND
BEHAVIORAL PROCESSES AT WORK IN A
MODEL SYSTEM

Myron A. Hofer

Albert Einstein College of Medicine
Montefiore Hospital, 111 East 210th St.
Bronx, New York 10467

Clinical studies have related early maternal separation to
a wide variety of psychiatric, psychosomatic and medical
disorders in children. Michael Rutter, in his recent review (1),
lists 6 main syndromes in childhood associated with maternal
deprivation: (a) Acute distress (Robertson's "protest" phase
of separation); (b) Developmental retardation (as described by
Spitz); (c) Intellectual impairment; (d) Dwarfism; (e) Delinquency and antisocial disorder; and finally (f) 'Affectionless
psychopathy' (as in Bowlby's "Forty Thieves"). As Rutter
points out, this list combines responses due to interruption of
an ongoing relationship (a) with those clearly related to
failure to establish any relationship at all (f). The list also
neglects the relationship often described between peptic ulcer

I thank Harry Shair, Hedda Orkin and Lee Kupersmith for
their invaluable assistance in the laboratory.

Supported by Research Scientist Development Award, NIMH
(MH K-1 38, 632) and NIMH project grant MH 16929 (MAH).

or asthma and early separation experiences, the predisposition to depressive reactions and the increased vulnerability to a variety of illnesses (from measles to schizophrenia) supposedly engendered by the early experience of maternal separation.

And, yet, professional opinion is polarized into those who accept all these relationships without critical restraint and those who reject them out of hand as magical thinking. Our understanding of separation is limited to what we have learned from the experiences of bereaved adults and observations of children's behavior when left in nurseries or hospitalized away from their parents. Although many of the syndromes associated with early separation indicate important physiological and biochemical consequences, we have virtually no data on the biological effects of sudden disruption of the mother-infant interaction. Our understanding of the psychological aspects of early separation are based either on concepts of "oral dependence", which have not been studied experimentally, and the concept of "attachment" or "bond formation", which presents difficulties in definition, is thought not to occur before 6-8 months in the human, and therefore cannot deal with separations occurring prior to 6 months' post natal age. Important differences in responses according to age of the infant at the time of separation are relatively unexplored.

Our dilemma is this: we know enough about early maternal separation to strongly suspect that it has profound consequences for development and health, but we have little or no understanding of how that might take place and can, therefore, not adequately prevent or treat children to whom it occurs. And yet, we cannot study it experimentally in humans for the very reasons that would motivate such research--its apparent dangers to the infant. To make matters worse, we have begun to realize that for a mother to be totally confined to child and home is bad for both mother and children in our present day culture. Questions like "won't fathers do just as well for the infant?" remain political rather than researchable issues.

An answer to this dilemma could be provided by an appropriate animal model system. Only by numerous analytic experiments will it be possible to gain some understanding of how the experience of separation from the mother becomes translated into biological and behavioral developmental change in the infant. But as recently as ten or fifteen years ago, one would have little firm evidence to suggest that lower animals show any response to interruption of the mother-infant relationship. The phenomenon appeared to be uniquely human, and in fact we are still heavily prejudiced to regard particularly our social life, as without parallel in the animal world.

The evidence every year forces us to reevaluate our relationship to animal species which we refer to as "lower". Harlow's work (2) convinced a skeptical scientific world that even monkey mothers were good for something besides milk. Kaufman and Rosenblum's studies (3) on early separation in 2 species of Macaques gave us a model syndrome of anaclitic depression which one felt compelled to regard as similar to the human, not the least because of the evocative facial expressions and postures of these infant monkeys.

One can now ask the question: how general a mammalian characteristic is the susceptibility to some kind of early maternal separation reaction? So far, all primate species studied, (2), (3), (4), (5), (6), the dog (7), the cat (8), the chick (9), the rat (10), the mouse (11), and the guinea pig (12) have been reported to show either behavioral or physiological responses, either immediately or long-term, following early maternal separation. Systematic studies are, however, rare and most of the work has simply described phenomena without attempting to go on to discover what processes were responsible for the results.

To my mind, the important question now is: *how* does the experience of maternal absence become translated into altered behavioral and biological function in the infant? This question divides itself into several sub-questions: what are the components that make up the experience of maternal separation? And what are the response characteristics of the infant to each of these components? In attempting to specify these, one is quickly led to confront the mother and infant dyad as an interactional system. The kind and degree of interactions have their own developmental course from conception to the particular age at which separation occurs. Both mother and infant are different biologically (for example different hormonal levels) at different points in the continuum. The infant is very differently organized physiologically from one post natal age to the next, and very different from adults. This means that infants respond unexpectedly to environmental change.

In fact, the mother *is* the environment of the infant, not just in utero, but she provides the most salient aspects of the environment for the infant for a long time after birth. I have found that one of the most useful ways to approach the study of early separation effects is to regard the infant as adapting to an altered environment. This allows us to study the thermal, nutritional, tactile, olfactory and even vestibular input provided by the mother and altered in her absence. To my mind, higher order concepts such as 'attachment' and the production of anxiety in the absence of the attachment object should be utilized only when a response cannot be adequately explained on the basis of similar processes.

Our work has been with the laboratory rat which turns out to be a surprisingly good model for the study of at least some mother-infant separation processes. Work in Czechoslovakia in the past 10 years has shown that adult rats, which were separated prematurely from their mothers, show deficits in learning (13), in development of androgenic and adrenal hormone regulation (14) and in susceptibility to gastric erosions under stress (15). Analytic experiments have identified both nutritional and social factors in the causation of these effects. These long-term effects were sufficiently similar to the kinds of phenomena attributed to early separation in the human to encourage me to proceed with the rat rather than to embroil myself in the immensely expensive and time-consuming process of primate research.

At the time I began 5-6 years ago, there were no observations on the immediate effects of maternal separation on the infant rat. Thanks to Jay Rosenblatt we *did* know a good deal about the normal mother-infant interaction in this species as it developed after birth (16). He showed that there were 3 phases in the early mother-infant relationship extending over the 25 days following birth: an "initiation" phase from days 1-5, "maintenance" days 6-14 and "decline" days 15-25.

The infant rat goes through a period of helpless dependency lasting a long period of time relative to its total life span and quite comparable in duration to the human. Fourteen days marks the maturation of fairly complex sensori-motor capacities. A few days later peer socialization begins, progresses to rough and tumble play, and independence from the mother is completed by 3 to 4 weeks under normal conditions in the laboratory. In the wild, juveniles can still be found with their mother as late as 60-80 days, after sexual maturity has been reached.

If young rats are separated from their mothers at 13 postnatal days or earlier, 90% of them die within the next 6 days. Recent evidence shows that this is not due to simple inanition, since the pups provided with a non-lactating foster mother have only 20% mortality, despite a weight loss pattern comparable to those without any parental surrogate (16). By 14 or 15 days of age, pups generally survive separation, but only after a series of behavioral and physiological changes which we have been studying.

Fig. 1 summarizes the changes occurring in infant rats whose mother was removed from the cage for 24 hours. Many of the changes require as little as 4 hours (heart rate, respiration) or 8 hours (behavior) to develop. What sort of a pattern is it that we have observed, incomplete as our findings are at present? The increase in locomotor, self-stimulating and "emotional" behavior (defecation-urination) when the infant is placed in an unfamiliar test area is reminiscent of the "protest" phase seen in primate (including human) infant separation. The sleep disturbance confirms the heightened arousal and indicates a fragmentation of rhythmic state transitions which could underlie the disruption of much complex, organized behavior. The reduced resting cardiac and respiratory rates do not appear to go along with the behavioral picture, at least as we are used to psychophysiological correlations in the adult mammal. Increased behavioral responsiveness is usually associated with increased cardiac rate. This raises important questions about the processes underlying the translation of the experience into behavioral and physiological change. The exquisite susceptibility of 30 day old early weaned animals to gastric erosion has recently been discovered by Dr. Sigmurd Ackerman in our laboratories, and demonstrates the capacity of this experience to produce pathological stress responses later in life.

FIGURE LEGENDS

FIG. 1
Summary of biological and behavioral changes occurring in
two week old infant rats over the first 24 hours after
maternal separation. The mother is removed from the home
cage without other disturbance of the environment or social
group of 8 - 9 littermates.

FIG. 2.
Cardiac rates during spontaneous activity and inactivity,
basal respiratory rates and activity levels during 3 minute
physiological recordings of 14 day old rat pups separated
from their mothers in the temperature controlled environment,
compared with the control group of littermates left with their
mothers. $N = 6$ in each group. All changes for separated pups
are significant at p less than .01 except activity level. (Reprinted
with permission of *Science*.)

FIG. 3.
Behavior of forty 2 week old infant rats during 10 minutes
observation in unfamiliar plastic test box. Pups separated
from their mothers, but left in their home cages are compared to
their mothered littermates. To allow comparisons of several
behaviors with a single unit of measure, the observed behavior
of both groups in each behavioral category is fractionated
into that percent performed by the separated pups as compared
to the mothered halves of the litters. All differences were
significant at p less than .05. Axillary temperatures were
recorded prior to testing.

Figure 1

12-14 DAY OLD INFANTS - MOTHER ABSENT 24 HOURS

BIOLOGICAL MEASURES

Body Temperature —
Body Weight —

BEHAVIOR

Locomotion **+**   Elimination **+**
Self Grooming **+**

CNS STATE ORGANIZATION

                                State Transition
Awake Time **+**   Frequency **+**
REM Sleep —   Frequent Awakenings
Sleep Onset, Delayed   Fragmentation of Sleep

PHYSIOLOGICAL

Cardiac Rate —
Respiratory Rate —

Figure 2

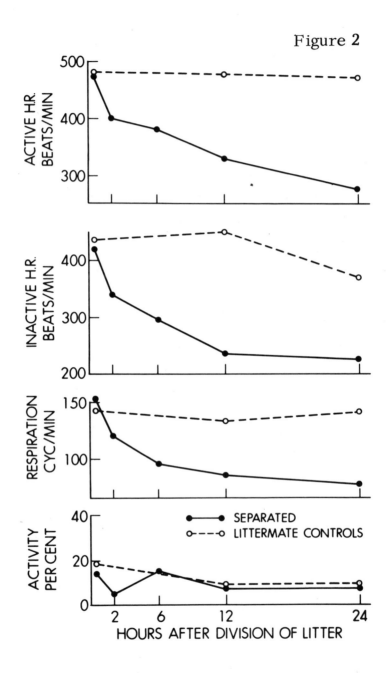

Figure 3

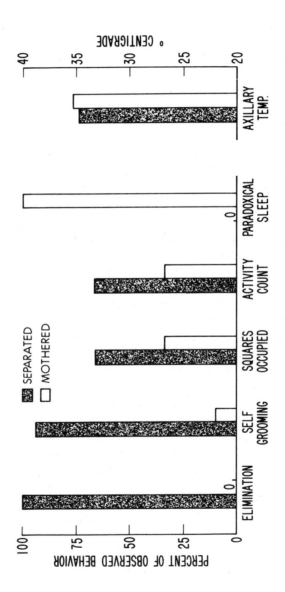

All of the changes occur as listed when the infant's body temperature is maintained by an artificial heat source under the home cage floor. From this we can reason that the absence of the thermal aspects of mothering are not the cause of these changes. How, then, can they originate? I will summarize the results of some of our analytic experiments attempting to answer this question in the case of 2 of the changes listed above, the cardiac and behavioral responses.

Fig. 2 shows the changes in cardiac and respiratory rates observed over 24 hours after removal of the mother from the cage and recorded from freely moving 2 week old infants implanted with chronic subdermal electrodes several days prior to separation. The low heart rates of separated pups are not fixed, but accelerate readily to preseparation levels upon strong sensory stimulation (tail pinching). By using autonomic blocking agents, it was possible to show that the decreased rates were primarily due to a decrease in tonic beta-adrenergic stimulation (18). Surgical removal of the thyroid and adrenal glands and spinal cord section studies demonstrated that the effector route was most likely the sympathetic cardioaccelerator pathway from brain stem to heart via the upper thoracic spinal cord (19). By finding that a non-lactating foster mother failed to prevent the cardiac changes of separation (18) and that providing milk by constant gastric infusion in sufficient amounts *did* entirely prevent these autonomic changes (20), we were able to identify the means by which the mother's absence became translated into physiological change. Milk, but not simple gastric distention, reversed the bradycardia of separation (21). Lactose, or casein, were effective if given intragastrically, but not if given intravenously (19).

These findings have led us to the interpretation that the mother exerts a delicate regulatory control over the autonomic control of cardiac rate by the amount of milk she supplies, and that absence of the mother exerts its effect upon the pups' autonomic regulation through diminution in the pups' nutritional intake. Finally, this nutritional effect does not appear to operate by the usual mechanism of circulatory supply of metabolic substrate. Rather, it involves rapid neural response to the presence of nutrient in the gut, mediated by the central nervous system. This was an unexpected relationship, since nutritional intake was not thought to have an important role in autonomic regulation at any age. No such autonomic cardiac changes occur in starved adults, either rat or man.

Can the behavioral changes, presented graphically in Fig. 3, be linked to the same nutritional-CNS mechanism and the two be viewed as an integrated psychophysiological response? We think not. The same pups which showed maintenance of normal cardiac rates when adequately fed with milk in the absence of the mother for 24 hours had behavioral responses to an unfamiliar test area which were identical with their non-fed littermates and markedly different from normally mothered pups of this age (20). Furthermore, provision of a non-lactating foster mother prevented the occurrence of most of the behavioral changes characteristic of separation (22). These results strongly suggested that the behavioral changes of separation were caused by absence of some aspects of the mother-infant behavioral interaction and were not mediated by an altered nutritional state.

In attempting to understand this behavioral response to the mother's absence we are in the same quandry as the clinicians who first described "separation anxiety" in children. Shall we term this an animal homologue, a prototypical form of separation anxiety, or even an animal "model"? We do not yet know, but when confronted with this phenomenon in young rats, I am reluctant to invoke complex hypothetical constructs before alternate explanation, based on simpler neural processes are explored. For example, could it not be that levels of behavioral arousal, at this developmental age, are regulated simply by the amount of stimulation coming in over certain sensory pathways (e.g. olfactory, auditory, vestibular, tactile, etc.). With removal of the source of specific effective stimulation (the mother) a state of neural habituation dissipates and excitability increases. Such basic processes based on dishabituation are widespread phylogenetically and could have survival value for young mammals through the increased likelihood of a behaviorally hyperactive animal finding essentials such as warmth, food or even its home nest, when in unfamiliar terrain. Combined with vocalization (ultrasonic) it could lead to reunion with the mother. Some recent experiments we have done lend support to such a hypothetical relationship between periodic stimulation and levels of behavioral responsiveness at this developmental age (23).

In conclusion, we have come to view the response of the infant to separation from its mother as quite different from the unitary, integrated responses such as Cannon's fight-flight, or the newer "conservation-withdrawal" of Engel (24) and Kaufman (25). Rather, different systems appear to be under separate control and respond to different aspects of the complex experience which follows separation. For example, while behavioral responses are primarily affected by absence of olfactory and tactile stimulation of the mother (23), cardiac autonomic changes are separately controlled by the milk obtained from the mother. Other central neural functions are apparently unaffected.

These studies are just a beginning, but we hope they will lead to an understanding of some of the basic processes at work in the mammalian mother-infant interaction and responsible for some of the effects of early separation.

REFERENCES

1. Rutter, M. *J. Psychosom. Res. 16,* 241, (1972).

2. Harlow, H. F. and Zimmmerman, R. R. *Science, 130,* 421, 1959.

3. Kaufman, I.C. and Rosenblum, L. *Ann. N. Y. Acad. Sci. 159,* 681, (1969).

4. Kaplan, J. *Dev. Psychobiol. 3,* 43, (1970).

5. Klopfer, P.H. *Z. Tierpsychol. 30,* 277, (1972).

6. Van Lawick-Goodall, J. *Amer. J. Psychiat. 130,* 1, (1973).

7. Scott, J.P., Ross, S. and Fisher, A. *J. Genet. Psychol. 95,* 261, (1959).

8. Sietz, P.D. *Psychosom. Med. 21,* 353, (1959).

9. Kaufman, I.C. and Hinde, R.A., *Anim. Behav. 9,* 197, (1961).

10. Hofer, M.A. Physiological and behavioral processes in early maternal deprivation. In CIBA Symposium No. 8, *Physiology, Emotion and Psychosomatic Illness*, Elsevier, Amsterdam, (1972).

11. La Barba, R.C., Martini, J. and White, J. *Psychosom. Med. 31*, 129, (1969).

12. Astic, L. and Jouvet-Mounier, D. *J. de physiol. 60*,389, (1968).

13. Novakova, V. *Psyiol. Behav. 1*, 219, (1966).

14. Krecek, J. The theory of cortical developmental periods and postnatal development of endocrine functions. p. 233. In *The Biopsychology of Development*. Edited by Tobach, Aronson and Shaw. Academic Press, (1971).

15. Weiner, P. The effect of premature weaning on gastric lesions in the rat. pp. 387-393. In *The Postnatal Development of Phenotype*. Edited by Kazda and Denenberg. Butterworth, London, (1970).

16. Rosenblatt, J., *Amer. J. Othopsychiat. 39*, 36, (1969).

17. Plaut, M. *Psychosom. Med. 36*, 311, (1974).

18. Hofer, M.A., and Weiner, H., *Psychosom. Med. 33*, 353, (1971).

19. Hofer, M. and Weiner, H., *Psychosom. Med. 37*, 8, (1975).

20. Hofer, M.A. *Psychosom. Med. 35*,350, (1973).

21. Hofer, M.A. *Science, 172*, 1039, (1971).

22. Hofer, M.A. *Behav. Biol. 9*, 629, (1973).

23. Hofer, M.A. *Psychosom. Med. 37*, 245, (1975).

24. Engel, G. and Schmale, A. Conservation withdrawal: A primary regulatory process for organismic homeostasis; p. 58-85. In *Physiology, Emotion and Psychosomatic Illnesses,* CIBA Symposium, Elsevier, Amsterdam and New York, (1972).

25. Kaufman, I. C. and Rosenblum, L. A.: *Psychosom. Med. 29*, 648, (1967).

MENTAL HEALTH IN CHILDREN, Volume I
Edited By D. V. Siva Sankar
Copyright © 1975 by
PJD Publications Ltd., Westbury, N.Y.

FAMILY VIOLENCE
AND PREVENTIVE PSYCHIATRY:
AN INNOVATIVE APPROACH

Harvey A. Barocas
Baruch College, CUNY, New York

Intrafamilial violence has become a recurring feature of our society, despite the cultural committment to non-violence. Throughout the nation, violence has become a typical phenomenon in everyday family relationships where family members physically abuse each other far more often than nonrelated individuals. Unquestionably, violence like charity begins at home, with the family circle providing a prime setting for aggressive acting out against individual members. Not only does violence against family mambers and children exist in families, but it is often looked upon as a desirable method of tension reduction and discipline. In fact, there are many familial supports for the existence and perpetuation of brutality toward the young.

Most psychotherapists frequently accept only highly selected patients and view serious emergencies and life-stress situations as contra-indications for traditional treatment. Psychotherapists involved in clinics or office practice frequently observe only the ritualized and socially acceptable expressions of intrafamilial violence and aggression. Acknowledging that the family has become a cradle of violence, our urban police more frequently have the opportunity to observe and intervene in cases of direct family aggression involving children, adults and families. In short, the more serious social and family pathology, ignored by psychotherapists is ministered to by the urban policeman, who is assigned the responsibility for monitoring the dimensions of interpersonal conflict and intervention in a family crisis situation.

In helping to promote the development of preventive psychiatry in the community, the police officer is in a unique position as a case finder in situations of child abuse. He not only performs a service for the child by protecting it from further abuse, but also assists the parents to learn better ways of handling their emotions by making appropriate referrals to agencies who specialize in working with child abusers. What the policeman can provide in a family crisis situation is the crucial service of early recognition and initial intervention which may ultimately determine the difference between sucessful prevention and destructive violence. Intervention in disturbed families is desirable at the earliest point possible in order to prevent a fixed pattern of family interaction which may be impossible to reverse.

Potentially, the policeman has most significant impact in the area of preventive psychiatry. Although prevention in police work has been considered for many years, relatively little has been done to come to grips with the many possibilities that exist. We must recognize that violence at home deserves as much attention as crime in the streets.

Just as relatives are the largest single category of murder victims, so family fights are the largest single category of police calls. More police calls involve family conflict than do calls for all criminal incidents. Police are usually brought into family disputes because people are accustomed to calling them in an emergency, but the reception the policeman gets when he arrives at the door is unpredictable, anything from a cup of coffee to a shotgun blast.

Resort to family violence bespeaks the despair which comes from failure to have on to perceive any alternatives. The fundamental task, therefore, during a police family crisis intervention is to help the individual search effectively for alternatives. By questioning the individual about the immediate threat of violence, about alternatives to it, about the consequences of various possible actions, about his unrealized aims, hopes and needs, the policeman simultaneously fosters the search for violence-avoiding alternatives, and teaches a method of problem solving the individual can learn to use. However, since the police approach is a temporary intervention at a time of crisis, it is imperative that the police engage other resources in whatever supportive or deterrent measures may be required, including social agencies and appropriate psychiatric facilities. The ability of police to work preventively at times of crisis is greatly enhanced by the development of close effective working relationships with the variety of mental health services in the community.

The police are in an unusual position within the community in which they are frequently called upon to perform a variety of mental health and crisis intervention services. In many instances they serve as the front line, 24 hour, urban psychiatric G.P., an ombudsman of the poor, doing our dirty work, without receiving sufficient support, training or recognition. They are indeed an invaluable and ill prepared psychiatric manpower supply providing services to a population untouched by the psychoanalytic profession. Annually, a striking member of family fight calls into police stations and intervention in a family crisis situation has become a routine police function. Paradoxically, although the police are often feared, resented and hated in many of our ghetto communities, they are the first person contacted for help during a family disturbance. The author has been alarmed at the high frequency of social and situational family factors that lead to requests for police assistance during an average city weekend. However, despite the growing importance of rendering family crisis intervention services, relatively little has been done to train and increase the effectiveness of the police in this critical area.

It is generally thought that a person in crisis is motivated to seek help and is uniquely susceptible to therapeutic intervention (1, 2, 3). Timely intervention during a crisis, therefore, can have a significant positive impact on a person's functioning (4, 5). During a crisis period the potential for change is greatly increased and police assistance provided at this point can be very effective and assist in stabilizing family relationships. A family oriented intervention in a behavioral disturbance may produce significant and durable results in a short time. The family's emotional resources could be mobilized into giving each other sufficient support to work through the crisis area. The crisis intervenor wants to halt further family deterioration and help restore the impaired ego coping functions and promote the family's functioning as a stress mediating system again.

However, there is considerable evidence that police handling of family problems via traditional means may be a potential breeding ground for violence (3, 6, 7). Toch (7) in a recent study of violent incidents involving policemen concluded that violence is frequently triggered by person's in authority because they allow themselves to fit into a preconceived stereotype which may engender negative reactions and contribute to acting out behaviors during a crisis. He further reports that there are ways of relating to people which carry a high probability of degenerating into contact of an aggressive nature. Standard police interventions in a crisis situation may meet the "violent man" more than half way in his efforts to create an arena for violence where irrational and destructive forces converge head on. Therefore, there is a reason to suspect a definite relationship between police performance and the potentiation of violence.

Physicians and psychotherapists alike are well aware of their capacity to induce unexpected changes in patients during the course of treatment, especially by their approach, attitude, and general interaction. Harsh or abrupt confrontation by authority figures can readily evoke intense feelings of importance, rage and retaliation. Consequently, in our efforts to promote health, we may inadvertently precipiatate and cultivate more maladaptive mechanisms of defense and further conflict. However, since casualties can be caused by specific intervention styles, they may also be prevented by a modification in intervention style.

Inevitably, in times of high tension, dramatic police intervention may only serve to increase frustration and violence and act as a deterrent to conflict resolution. There is the imminent danger of inducing a further crisis by an abrupt or untimely intervention (8). The crisis context is one of urgency and within that context the policemen must practice a form of dualism: on the one hand, comprehending, participating in and experiencing the urgency; on the other, maintaining the degree of distance that permits his cognitive function to operate effectively. Police must be viewed as reliable, understanding and accepting, and the disputants must have the expectation that the police will be able to help them and their family members. This necessitates that police encourage disputants to tell and retell their traumatic experiences to sympathetic listeners since physical threats and injuries usually result in serious emotional upheavals.

Any policemen knows that one of the most dangerous calls he must answer is the family quarrel, where bitter hot emotion erupts into violence, where injury is as close as a knife blade, and when the despair of misery focuses suddenly on a blue uniform. Family disturbance calls currently represent the single most frequent source of injury and death to police officers by national statistics. Policemen, intervening in family disturbance calls become easy targets of displaced aggression, particularly in cases of wife-beating, infidelity, child abuse and incest. We cannot assume that police are aseptic instruments, since their own life experiences and family values may be imposed on others.

In today's society, in rendering police services during a crisis situation, the very actions undertaken to relieve one disorder may in themselves create further disorder. (i.e., police interventions may precipitate or intensify violent reactions leading to assault, homicide, suicide, etc.) When policemen feel they lack the expertise usually associated with authority, feeling anxious and threatened, they may act hastily, irrationally and in a stereotyped fashion. They may resort to instant arrest, infantilization of disputants, intimidating power plays with themes of white dominance and black subordination, or the use of suppressive force as a deterrent to possible violence. The consequences of such behavior are predictable, hence the danger of iatrogenic violence in the family setting. This explanation may help to clarify the finding that a sizeable proportion of violence during recent years has been carried out by those in positions of authority (6, 7).

As the etiologic vector in cases of iatrogenic violence, the urban policeman must assess his role thoroughly and with considerable self-criticism. Policemen must be helped to differentiate between therapeutic intervention in a crisis situation and non-therapeutic interference, especially if a policeman's own tolerance for anxiety is low and he does not have sufficient awareness and understanding of interpersonal dynamics and neurotic family interaction.   Mental health professionals must recognize that the prevention of family violence is a mental health problem akin to suicide prevention to which similar techniques and principles can be applied.

Policemen must recognize that acute symptoms or problems in a designated individual during a family intervention are usually a reflection of a more generalized disturbance in the basic family system and must avoid perpetuating the family scapegoating. Some people will attempt to use the patrolman's presence to further their own needs, a phenomenon group and family therapists are equisitely sensitized to. If patrolmen are not aware of their own involvement and their own reactions to a family crises, they are highly susceptible to manipulation by family members.   Moreover, if a patrolman takes sides or succombs to the more controlling family member, the intervention is adversely affected.

That murders and serious physical injuries occur more frequently between people who are related, supports the notion "the family that slays together stays together," often in a sado-masochistic bind. Within this family circle, if police are left to draw upon their own biased notions of family psychodynamics, they may actually behave in ways to induce a tragic outcome (e.g., by forming protective-seductive alliances with helpless women against brutal husbands, contributing to the emasculation of male disputants, unconsciously inviting retaliation by intimidating family members, and inadvertently setting themselves up as potential homicide victims).   This situation is further complicated since many father absent families and families with common-law husbands in low-income ghetto areas may rely on policemen as family bouncers or substitute authority figures to compensate for the lack of a male role model.   Moreover, policemen may come to define intervention in a family crisis as an exaggerated personal threat to themselves based on prior interventions as well as their own family life experiences.   Self-fulfilling effects can readily flow from such a definition.

The diversity and complexity of family quarrels where excessive violent potential is present, make police crisis intervention extremely volatile and difficult.   It is impossible to do away with intrafamilial aggression completely, but police can play a crucial role in reducing the potential for violence and helping to regulate it within the family system. However, to serve this cause, we need greater restraints on the use of official violence, impartial law enforcement, meaningful alternatives to arrest, and a more viable mediation system for families in conflict so that we do not continue to innundate our family courts with referrals.

Psychotherapists have much to offer police and society in the control and prevention of human violence. The necessity of having to alert policemen to behaviors contributing to "iatrogenic violence" is rather obvious. Brief emergency crisis intervention police training may work better than the traditional police approaches for defusing potentially explosive family situations. Family crisis intervention provides an opportunity to offer brief emergency psychiatric services, identify unmet needs, and act as a referral to community agencies, however, it also opens the door to reckless approaches and abuses. Frequently, complaints of police brutality arise out of incidents that began as family fights, but escalated into larger conflicts beyond the family system, producing police-community confrontations. Therefore, policemen must be given the psychological skills that are realistically consistent with their daily functioning, or run the risk of exacerbating both family and community conflict. If we accept Toch's (7) position that violent men play violent games because their non-violent repertoire is restricted, and if we acknowledge the phenomenon of iatrogensis, then psychological training in crisis intervention, by increasing the response repertoire of patrolmen, should have a positive influence on general police functioning and assist police in the prevention of violence.

Training police in family crisis intervention is perfectly consistent with the most cherished concepts of psychoanalytic thinking. Since the community is, in a sense, a psychological laboratory, police deal with conflicts that are currently in the forefront of analytic interests. They are constantly exposed to diverse analytic data, including the manifestations of intra-familial aggression, sado-masochistic relationships, disorders of impulse control, incestual relationships and the effect of early experiences on development. However, analytic tech-niques do necessitate modifications when applied to police crisis intervention. Since intrapsychic conflicts are frequently acted out within the family constellation where pathology is more apparent, an action-oriented crisis intervention approach incorporating principles of emergency and family psychotherapy (1, 2, 4, 5) is called for. Such an approach with appropriate community follow-ups can be highly effective in stabilizing deteriorating family relationships at crucial developmental conflict points.

New experimental and educational approaches to the amelioration of family conflict are rapidly emerging in the psychological literature. However, based on considerable clinical experience with several police departments on the East Coast, it became evident that training police in family crisis intervention could not be delivered through the traditional classroom didactic or lecture approach regardless of the scientific rigor of the course content or the expertise of the behavioral scientist.

Unfortunately, many police academy training programs generally address themselves to the technical knowledge necessary for police work and tend to disregard the emotionally-affected uncertainties inherent in family crisis intervention and their ensueing anxieties. Consequently, in additon to traditional mental health lectures, the training programs emphasized a crisis intervention experiential training laboratory which provided a unique opportunity to "learn by doing." This approach utilized professional actors and actresses enacting family fights developed from actual police family disturbance calls. Police teams intervened in pairs during the simulated conflict. The plays were written without conclusions: the outcomes were improvised by the actors in response to the behavior of the policemen. Simulated family fights encompassed such themes as alcoholism, child abuse, wife-beating, infidelity, incest, and unemployment.

All simulated interventions were videotaped and focused videotape feedback was subsequently utilized in small group workshops. Conflict situations were role-played twice to permit different police teams to intervene in the same crisis call and demonstrate differential approaches and intervention styles, as well as the possibility of different outcomes. All the simulated interventions were also subjected to extensive critique and review by police participants in small group discussions. Several issues were explored in group discussions, especially disputants response to the intervention, new problems that emerged as a result of the intervention (iatrogenic reactions) and the officers understanding and reactions to the family conflict.

Focused video-tape feedback, served as an additional vehicle for confronting patrolmen with an immediate, objective audio-visual transcript of their approaches to a family crisis call. Such feedback and group discussions helped alert many patrolmen to blind spots and patterns of maladaptive behavior by giving them information about themselves as they interacted with disputants during an intervention. The feedback process was doubly enhanced by the actors who entered the group discussions and expressed their reactions to the different police interventions.

Policemen found that certain disarming gestures of goodwill were particularly effective in facilitating communication and assisting in conflict resolution without resorting to arrest (e.g., police taking their hats off, introducing themselves, separating disputants, sitting down with disputants, talking about their own families, and offering information about community resources). Other officers found they had more of an impact on disputants when they refused to take sides. They found men were not as hostile toward them when they did not side with women automatically during a domestic quarrel.

Handling family disputes was viewed in three stages: the first stage being the initial intervention, the second consisted of assessment and diagnosis of the family problem, and the third stage involved resolution and/or referral. In assessing the seriousness and chronicity of the family dispute, police would ask non-threatening questions about the frequency of family fights, how long it existed, what precipitated it, and what were the underlying unconscious motives for the family dispute as well as the more obvious ones. They also had to ascertain whether the family disturbance required professional help.

Attempts were actively made to alert policemen to potential counter-transference reactions, sensitize them to principles of psychodynamics, point out particular areas of difficulty, and the role that policemen saw themselves as playing in particular conflict situations. Unless a policeman was continuously alert to his own gut reactions, he was apt to find himself responding negatively and irrationally in many crisis situations, especially against the marital partner who was more obviously abusive and cruel, because of his own identification with the more mistreated spouse and not fully recognizing the latter's less obvious provocative behavior in sado-masochistic interactions. Moreover, violence against children and wife-beating frequently provoked self-righteous outrage and sadistic retaliatory urges in policemen.

During some simulated interventions, two policewomen or a policeman and policewoman would intervene in the family crisis. Although there was considerable resistance to the idea that women could perform patrol duties as effectively as men, particularly in incidents involving family violence, the results were quite surprising. When given the same responsibilities as policemen, women proved to be highly effective in neutralizing family friction and violence and greatly reduced the potential for iatrogenic violence within the family, particularly in instances of child abuse and wife beating. There was less danger of paranoid and homosexual panic reactions in male disputants when confronted by policewomen. Policemen kicking in doors and accepting the challenge of a provocative suspect very often led to physical violence. However, the role of the policewoman in family crisis intervention must be explored further and substantiated by future research.

In time, police began to examine the damaging stereotypes they help toward members of the minority communities and the extent to which these stereotypes affected their behavior during a crisis intervention. In addition, since police were frequently witness to pathological family interactions, they became more alerted to the influence of their own family psychodynamics during an intervention. Many patrolmen saw their own parents as irresponsible and recalled being viciously beaten by alcoholic fathers. This created complications when they were called upon to subdue alcoholic husbands during marital quarrels. Feeling that their competence was being personally threatened, they would sometimes become calloused and belligerent in reading the riot act to disputants and minimizing mediation techniques. Such regressions in the service of intense anxiety were not uncommon.

In order to deal with intense personal reactions, the basic training also included human relations workshops and optional brief counseling sessions which helped sensitize policemen to their own values and attitudes about disrupted family life. To further reinforce the initial training, weekly small group discussions were held over a six month period. Regularly scheduled de-briefings and continuous sensitivity training permitted an on-going review of the methods and biases which affect the crisis interventions.

Although the culture of the police force looks upon psychological training and having compassion for the underdog as offensive to the masculine mystique of law enforces, these innovative training programs have helped patrolmen confront and deal with their reactions toward individuals where behavior is deviant and difficult to understand. An improved self-image, an increased sense of adequacy and self-awareness are fundamental factors in reducing fear and anxiety in police officers and enhancing their skills in serving the community.

Amidst our current social changes and upsurge of family violence and child abuse, innovative approaches to community mental health are rapidly emerging. To help alleviate the current manpower shortage in the mental health area, the Joint Commission on Mental Health and Illness (10) strongly recommended the effective utilization of paraprofessional personnel. Crisis intervention training is currently being utilized by various professional and paraprofessional groups with a wide range of skills (9, 10, 11, 12). Such training will ultimately have widespread use in general police functioning where policemen must act as skilled conflict resolution agents, and where the probability of an iatrogenic reaction is high. Crisis intervention mediation is not a panacea for all conflicts; however, patrolmen feel that it provides them with an alternative to arrest as well as an additional and very necessary psychological skill in the law enforcement process. Moreover, what the policeman can provide in a crisis situation is the crucial service or early recognition and initial intervention which may ultimately determine the difference between successful prevention and iatrogenic violence.

The broader implications of this approach also offer a possible means for relieving the drastic manpower shortage in the field of community mental health and contribute substantially to crime prevention by attacking our high recidivism rates in ghetto communities with a new focus by enabling individuals to remain in their community. Such an educational and action-oriented program can indeed contribute to a reduction in existing police-community tensions in urban areas. In time, crisis intervention in the community will be the hallmark of a new generation of applied social psychiatry.

REFERENCES

1. Caplan, G. In *Principles of Preventive Psychiatry.* Tavistock Publications, London, (1964).

2. Parad, H.J. (ed.) *Crisis Intervention: Selected Readings.* Family Service Association of America, NewYork,(1971). (1965).

3. Bard, M. and Berkowitz, B. *Community Mental Health J.* 315, (1971).

4. Bellak, L. and Small L. *Emergency Psychotherapy and Brief Psychotherapy.* Grune and Stratton, New York, (1965).

5. Hankoff, L. *Emergency Psychiatric Treatment: A Handbook of Secondary Prevention.* Thomas, Springfield, (1969).

6. *Report of the National Advisory Commission on Civil Disorders.* Bantam Books, New York, (1968).

7. Toch, H. *Violent Men.* Aldine Publishing, Chicago, (1968).

8. Chapman, A.H. *Amer. J. Psychother.. 116,* 873, (1960).

9. Joint Commission on mental Health and Illness. *Action for Mental Health.* Basic Books, New York, (1961).

10. Rioch, M. et al. *Amer. J. Orthopsychiat. 33,* 678, (1963).

11. Reiff, R. and Riessman, F. In *The Indigenous Non-Professional: A Strategy of Change in Community Action and Community Mental Health Programs.* U.S. Department of Health, Education and Welfare, Report #3, (1964).

12. Poser, E.G. *J. Consul. Psychol. 30,* 283, (1966).

MENTAL HEALTH IN CHILDREN, Volume I
Edited By D. V. Siva Sankar
Copyright © 1975 by
PJD Publications Ltd., Westbury, N.Y.

THE ROLE OF COMMUNITY AND STAFF EXPECTATIONS IN EFFECTING CHANGE IN A CHILDREN'S PSYCHIATRIC HOSPITAL

Bertram Pepper

Department of Health and Mental Hygiene
State of Maryland
Baltimore, Maryland 21201

and

Erica Loutsch

Manhattan Children's Treatment Center
Ward's Island, New York
New York 10035

OVERVIEW

Over the past 30 years there have been dramatic changes in the role assigned by the community to children's mental institutions. From places once expected to provide housing, sometimes indefinitely, for a small number of severly mentally retarded or psychotic or behaviorally deviant children - with little expectation by either staff or community of any real improvement - the trend has been to expect hospitals to provide adequate active treatment programs for much larger numbers of children who have a wider variety of problems, and return them to the community in improved condition.

However, not many children's programs fully meet these expectations. In turn, many referrals to psychiatric hospitals are still made in despair - because no other solution is available - rather than with the expectation that effective treatment will take place. The purpose of such despairing referrals is to extrude the deviant child from the community. In addition - to further complicate the situation - many acting-out, behaviorally disordered children are still referred to mental hospitals, as opposed to training schools, in hope and in search of more humane custody.

This paper will attempt to trace how, with regard to one children's psychiatric hospital program, changes in expectations and efforts of the community, the children, and the staff resulted in development, over a two-year period, from an institution which had become accustomed to providing long-term custodial care to behaviorally disordered children to one which provides active treatment for many kinds of disturbed children, with prompt return of children to the community.

HISTORICAL REVIEW

The particular Children's Treatment Center we wish to consider began in 1965 as a children's unit in an adult state hospital. It served 40 children from age 6-12 from the East side of upper Manhattan. All the children came from deprived urban areas, and most of them were referred because of bizarre behavior, school failure, or conflict with the law. From 1967 to 1971 the unit only served boys because the staff felt that girls were too difficult to handle, and successfully discouraged their admission.

The authors became familiar with the Unit in 1970, and found that its organization was similar to that of a classical State Hospital; e.g., staff and their services were grouped in five departments: Psychiatry, Psychology, Social Service, Nursing and Education. Every staff member reported to a Department head of the same discipline, who in turn reported to the Unit Chief, a psychiatrist.

There was very little communication across departmental lines. Children went from the ward to the classroom to a session with a psychiatrist or the psychologist, and back to the ward, without anybody communicating with anybody else. It was not uncommon for a teacher who had worked with a child for years to find out that his student had been discharged with no advance notice or planning. The social worker treated the family while the psychiatrist treated the child; lack of a feeling of participation in the child's treatment caused many families to become discouraged and to withdraw entirely. This contributed to prolonged hospitalization for the child, and problems with discharge.

Lack of interdisciplinary communication among professionals, and between professionals and non-professionals, interfered with the children's treatment. Behaviors that were viewed as acceptable in the classroom or the playroom were punished on the ward. The ward staff was viewed as disinterested and excessively punitive by the school staff, and conversely teachers and therapists were seen as too permissive, "letting the kids get away with murder" and then "dumping" hard-to-manage children on the ward staff.

Weekly case conferences, the only vehicle for staff communication, did little to obviate these difficulties. Ward staff was not encouraged to participate and the use of techincal jargon by the professionals discouraged genuine interdisciplinary efforts or understanding. Home visits were sometimes permitted as rewards and withheld as punishment. All children were 7-day a week in-patients.

The effect of these conditions on the children was appalling. In 1971, the average length of stay was over 2 years, and several children had been there since the unit opened in 1965. Of the children who were discharged, 77% went to other residential centers, and those who returned home had great difficulties in adjusting to school and home life in the community. Staff morale was low, as evidenced by the fact that few were interested in any kind of further training or education.

AN ORGANIZATION IN CRISIS

In the fall of 1971, the situation reached critical proportions. Charges were made, and aired by the media, that children were being brutalized by some staff, and that this was a custodial, rather than an active treatment program. The community which had tacitly condoned this state of affairs because it only expected humane detention, now seemed to demand adequate programs and effective treatment. At the same time, dissatisfied staff members were also pressing for change; they wished to play an active role in remediating the child's handicaps and returning him to the community. As a result of these *combined* pressures, radical changes were made.

REORGANIZATION

In June of 1972, the Unit became a programmatically and administratively independent hospital, and moved to a newly built facility. The area served was expanded to include boys and girls from all of Manhattan, and the upper age limit was raised to 16. The majority of the children continued to be from deprived urban areas, presenting with learning disabilities, severe behavior disorders, delinquent behavior and varied psychiatric symptomatology.

Planning for the move into the new building had begun in 1971. At that time the new leadership rejected the concept of developing a psychiatric hospital with secondary specialized services, such as a school program. Instead, program conceptualization and development flowed from an articulated initial planning concpet: these are multiply handicapped children and their psychiatric diagnosis and handicap is not often nor necessarily the child's paramount area of difficulty. Most of the children have major difficulties in several areas, including:

1. General social and family adjustment - which might be addressed by a comprehensive family treatment and a behavioral program.

2. Major educational handicaps - which should be addressed by a special education program.

3. Health problems of various sorts, icluding nutritional, dental, developmental and neurological - which should be addressed by a proper comprehensive medical care program.

4. A variety of psychologic-psychiatric problems- which should be addressed by appropriately individualized treatment, selected from a full range of mental health interventions.

In order to activate the program planning in such a way as to be responsive to the intervention objectives described above, interdisciplinary teams were set up, each to deal with children in a different age band of two years, as defined by birth date in most cases, but also defined by developmental level and physical size in selected cases. Each of the four teams was assigned twelve in-patient beds, and 12 day-care slots, and was asked to evaluate all children referred, with the goal of developing a comprehensive individualized treatment plan for each child. A companion goal of equal priority was to be the selection of the least drastic and confining treatment status compatible with providing the therapeutic programming required.

That is, twenty-four hour seven day a week care was to be used only where programmatically indicated or absolutely necessary. Five days a week in-patient care - with the child returning to his home on weekends - was felt to be somewhat less drastic and disruptive of the child's relationships with home and community. Wherever possible, a child was to be treated on a day basis, and the length of the day might range from a normal school day to extended day care. Currently, the adolescent team is treating several youngsters in a day care status who come to the hospital at 8:00 a.m., and are returned home by hospital staff at 10:00 p.m. Another team (for ages 6-9), has developed a partial day care program in which children spend 2 days in the Manhattan Children's Treatment Center and 3 days in a regular classroom in public school.

One of the basic concepts in developing the program was that the child was but one component of a system which included the family, the school, and the community in general. In order to serve the child, intensive work with the family had to be part of the treatment - Active liaison with the school and referring agency, from the time of admission, was also felt to be essential. This responsibility was distributed among team members, rather than being left to a social worker.

STAFFING

The staff of each team consists of about 23 members: one social worker, one registered or practical nurse, 12 mental health technicians (formerly known as aides), one psychologist, one psychiatrist, a recreation therapist, 3 teachers, and 3 teacher's aides. Each team is responsible for providing *total* care for its 24 children, and team members are not transferred to other teams to fill vacancies due to illness or absenteeism; this has developed team-peer pressure on staff to be responsible for their assignments, since their colleagues have to fill in the deficits. Perhaps as a consequence, absenteeism has been low - in a State civil service system where absenteeism is usually a problem.

Initially, special activities such as music, dance, craft, shop were organized into a separate activities team, but the group was later separated and members individually assigned to the treatment teams in order to further support the integrity of team responsibility for treatment. The present arrangement is generally regarded as more successful even though it narrows the available special activities skills available for each team.

TREATMENT PLAN

The treatment plan has proved to be an excellent device for articulating and orchestrating the needs of the individual child - psychologic, social, physiologic, and educational - seeing that responsibilities are explicitly assigned to staff members for carrying out therapeutic functions, communicating to all team members about the problems and needs of the child so that consistency can be developed, and providing an orderly mechanism for feed-back and up-dating of goals and therapeutic interventions.

Starting with the intake interview, an individual treatment plan is developed for each child by the members of the team. This plan states specific goals in each area - school, behavior at home, behavior with peers, physical health, relationship with the family, etc. Goals are reviewed and adjusted when necessary on a monthly basis, by team members. Each child is assigned and an "advocate" from among the team members, who is responsible for coordinating and implementing his treatment plan. This plan from the beginning, includes a discharge plan and a plan for relating to the family and school. Family treatment and liaison with the community are carried out from the beginning, in an active manner. If a family cannot come to the Center, the staff will go out to the home. As an example of team attitudes on this point, in one case two team members were refused admission to the home for a scheduled family visit. They demonstrated their commitment to family and community participation by holding their conference on the stoop. Family counseling was continued within the apartment on the occasion of the next session. Similarly, team members go to the school to talk to the principal and teachers, and to the local voluntary agency to ensure aftercare. This has resulted in a high degree of family and community cooperation.

RESULTS

The results of these changes have been extremely encouraging. The median length of stay was reduced from over 700 days before reorganization, to 390 days during the first year, to 339 during the second, and it continues to go down. The more recent lengths of stay include *any* status, including day-care. Sixty % of the children are on some form of day-care, and of the other 40% more than one-half go home on weekends. New programs have begun, including variants of day-care and night-care. Only 38% of the children are now on medication, compared to virtually 100% in 1971.

Effects on children: Even though the Treatment Center is a completely open institution, there have been few escapes, despite the prior training and experience of many of the children in running away from locked institutions. On the contrary, several children, seeking refuge, have requested to be admitted to 24 hr. care because of difficulties at home. Some have referred their friends and siblings for treatment at the center.

Effects on staff: Staff attitude and morale have improved. Sixty-nine per cent of ward staff have complete in-service training, and many have asked for further, more advanced courses. Fifteen per cent are working on high school diplomas and 13% are enrolled in college level programs.

Effects on community: The attitude of the community has changed, and is reflected in the nature of referrals and in the reaction to discharges. Children are now referred much earlier, and the program is seen as a placement of choice, not as the last resort after everything else has failed. Schools and community agencies are more open to accepting the children on discharge, since they have participated in the treatment plan. Families usually remain involved and cooperative. Only 40% of our children are discharged to residential treatment centers now, as compared to 77% in 1971.

CONCLUSIONS

The goals and objectives - and hence the policies and specific programs of a child mental health service - represent a series of compromises: these compromises are negotiated between and among the following factors, in an extremely complex equation:

1. The scientific orientation of some staff.

2. The guild orientation of other staff.

3. The personal needs and demands of parents.

4. The requirements of the community-the societal uses of the mental health system. These may include: selecting out children whose behavior is deviant, labelling them, segregating them, and modifying their behavior.

5. The children themselves, with their needs, requests, demands, and responses.

6. The expectations and requirements of community agencies - such as schools and clinics - which also serve children.

From the above, we conclude that to call for a purely scientifically determined program in a children's psychiatric center is naive and counter-productive. Even the value of treating a child with respect and dignity - which we support fully and unequivocally - is more social and political than it is psychiatric and scientific.

This acknowledgement of an old reality permits a degree of honesty in our shaping of child mental health programs which, if combined with modest determination and tactful firmness, can permit programs of scientific merit to deveop with the understanding and support of their non-scientifically oriented constituencies and communities.

MENTAL HEALTH IN CHILDREN, Volume I
Edited By D. V. Siva Sankar
Copyright © 1975 by
PJD Publications Ltd., Westbury, N.Y.

THE OFFENDER CHILD
OR THE OFFENDING SOCIETY?
A UNIFIED SERVICES APPROACH

Dorothy F. Berezin
NYC Department of Mental Health
New York, N. Y.

New York City children and adolescents involved with the law
have been casualties of a nonsystem of unilateral and uncoordinated planning, hampered by bureaucratic obstacles and
jurisdictional barriers, with the result that individual children
and families have been deprived of needed services. The
development of psycho-social-educational-rehabilitative
programs through the combined efforts of an Inter-Agency
Action Task Force On Children And The Law and The New
York City Department of Mental Health and Mental Retardation Services' local office in each borough, represents a firm
commitment to collaborative planning, inter-agency funding
and joint supervision.

The Child and The City
At the moment a child is born in New York City, part of what
he might ever become has been decided by the nature of his
biological inheritance and the rest will be decided by the
nurture or lack of nurture offered by the existing key integrated
social systems (family, health, school, peer group) in which he

will grow and develop. His heredity was handed to him. He could not ask for it nor could he ask to be conceived or request that he might not be born. His society was also handed to him.

Retrospective study of the "offender child"* would probably indicate that life was thrust upon him in a municipal hospital and that his mother, probably black or Hispanic did not receive prenatal care. He may be premature or a "high risk" infant. His mother will take him home to a small, crowded, dirty,deteriorating apartment in a poor, deprived neighborhood in the city. For his first years he will probably receive inadequate care and supervision. His parent or parents will be forced by circumstances to be overwhelmingly concerned with survival, striving unsuccessfully for better housing, food, better health and longer life with some dignity. In the inner city these concerns take precedence over the recognition of the developmental needs of infant or young child. His parents may not be able to cope with his behavior or their own personal problems, unable to provide sufficient care, supervision, love or understanding. If he is involved in any day care system, it will probably have insufficient resources to help his parents in their struggle to survive.

Studies of the "offender child" indicate that he has problems from a very early age, in the cognitive, social and emotional spheres. Because he has lacked adequate stimulation as an infant or his environment has been inconsistently over-stimulating or reenforcing of inhibitory rather than exploratory behavior, he will probably evince little curiosity or eagerness to learn. As his learning difficulties magnify and his behavior becomes more disruptive he is fated to be examined and diagnosed by school based or community services often utilizing a battery of tests standardized on white, middle class children which discriminate against black and Hispanic children. Often there is no recognition of the need for bi-lingual communication with the child and parent or of special ethnic or cultural patterns. Our "offender child", therefore, follows a well-known path starting as described above, going

*A boy or girl before his 16th birthday found to be a habitual truant, incorrigible or out of lawful control or a delinquent child, that is one who has committed an act that is criminal when done by an adult.

on to increased non-attendance at school and behavior problems at school and at home and in the community, of truancy, suspension from school and involvement with the legal system.

This is a child whose rights have been violated. His rights as enunciated by the Joint Commission Report (1) are: the right to be wanted; the right to be born healthy; the right to live in a healthy environment; the right to satisfaction of basic needs; the right to continuous loving care; the right to acquire the intellectual and emotional skills necessary to achive individual aspirations and to cope effectively in our society; the right to receive care and treatment through facilities appropriate to his needs and which keep him as closely as possible within his normal social setting.

This same child has usually experienced abusive treatment or violence by his parents, who themselves were probably abused as children, who want and need help which is not presently available to them. He may have been a baby who was burned with a hot iron or beaten with a strap. Prior to the enactment of the Child Protective Services Act of 1973, a child received little protection. Even now people often express more outrage at the plight of an abused animal than an abused child. A recent publication, Violence Against Children (2) is a mandatory consciousness-raising document for all mental health professionals. It explores child abuse and corporal punishment at home and in school, the institutional and familial supports for the existence and perpetuation of violence against children, as well as discussing problems of prevention and treatment.

Although the New York urban society is rich in resources, expertise and commitment, it is also competitive, racist and with violence deeply rooted and rationalized. A poor, minority child, whose developmental needs were not met in infancy, early childhood, middle years or early adolescence, is a stigmatized child. In addition he also tends to be a casualty of the City's non system of unilateral, uncoordinated planning, hampered by bureaucratic obstacles and jurisdictional barriers.

The Action Task Force

To respond to the special needs of these children and the many demands for action on their behalf, the New York City

Department of Mental Health and Mental Retardation Services took the initiative in establishing an Inter-Agency Action Task Force on Children and The Law. This was done with the awareness that the Family Court system in the City of New York deals with approximately 60,000 families per year. The overwhelming majority of the Court's cases involve children and adolescents, many of whom are seriously disturbed and whose behavior has brought them to the attention of the Family Court through a variety of channels. The Advisory and Working Committess of the Task Force are composed of specialists and child advocates from public and private, medical and non-medical settings and from different geographical areas of the City. Represented are the Department of Health, The Board of Education, The Judicial Conference of the State of New York, The State Department of Mental Hygiene, the Council of Voluntary Child Care Agencies, Special Services for Children, The Office of Probation, in addition to central staff and staff from the local offices of DMH & MRS. Thus, gathered together are almost all of the City and State agencies responsible for providing services to children involved with the law.

There was agreement by all concerned that the Task Force should concentrate on action, utilizing recently completed investigation, studies and research, rather than initiating new surveys; that planning for children should be based on their needs, rather than on static, diagnostic categories or legal definitions; and that unilateral planning, jurisdiction and funding of agencies concerned with these children should be replaced by coordinated and collaborative efforts. The objectives of the Task Force, therefore, were: to identify different groups of critical problems and needs of children involved; to establish priorities of needs; to pinpoint and eliminate unnecessary procedures and steps in the establishment of publicly funded facilities.

Our Department, through the Office of Child and Adolescent Services created the Task Force and Committees. There was not, nor was there intended to be, a single authoritarian leader who could completely dominate, control or manipulate the many large planning and caring systems represented in this group, and in the additional groups involved in program development, namely municipal hospitals and voluntary agencies. Many months of discussion and communication development were required before even preliminary decisons could be reached. Only after a series of intense meeting of the several groups, did there begin to emerge a dynamic, inter-active process that moved responsible, committed people closer toward common goals. Each individual would surely have stated in response to a direct query, "My single concern is the welfare of the child."

It was quite apparent that the agencies had sharply defined territorial rights and authority and strong possessive-ness of the child or children. There were strenuous objections to any intrusions on turf, overt as well as covert resistance to actions that might limit independence, maneuverings for visibility or credit, competition between methods of per-suasion and clout. The hashing and rehashing of these issues and feelings has started a process of new insights and the working through of ambivalences. (3)

In the group there were ardent advocates for many different procedures and techniques. As there was an increase in individual willingness to re-examine knowledge, attitudes, beliefs and prejudices it appeared that there had been a shift from "The child belongs to us" to "We belong to the Child."

Methodology

The Task Force tried to pursue an integrated, develop-mental, Unified Services approach to the needs of children, with input from consumers, as well as providers through the Department's local offices in each borough. Such an approach was expected to individualize and stabilize psychiatric care for children and adolescents in the community; to eliminate the "revolving door" situation and the exclusionary admission policies based on residence and to provide judges with more than the two alternatives of sending the child to a state training school or back to his community with no help at all. To restate a point of view expressed above, the Department considers the disturbed, learning disabled, "offender child" as a victim in the breakdown of a system composed of child, family, neighbor-hood, school and community. It proposes to deal with children at the lowest intensity of care consistent with their problems, always considering the child as a complete indivisible entity; to seek to develop comprehensive programs to meet the total needs of the whole child, to move beyond the present intolerable situation where individual facilities or agencies are equipped to deal only with particular aspects of the child or one or two specialized needs.

New Models of Service

The development of the programs reflected the goals, objectives, composition and struggles of the Task Force. They represented the first steps in a series of interrelated actions to provide services for children and families within their own communities enabling as many children as possible to remain at home when appropriate and providing brief respite services when indicated. In regard to non-secure, semi-secure and secure facilities, it is essential that there be a graduated series of settings so that each child may be provided with services according to his needs. The definition of security must encompass not just physically restricting construction, hardware and procedures, but specially trained staff able to provide a wide range of services that help the child develop his inner resources and his "sense of security." Programs at five Municipal Hospitals and in at least three community residences utilize the services of psychiatrists, psychologists, social workers, mental health workers, activities therapists, special education teachers, nurses and lawyers. Several different therapeutic models are offered including day therapeutic communities providing therapy, education, social, recreational and vocational services to court-involved adolescents and their families, as well as mental health teams providing a variety of treatment oriented services to children and their families, as well as to children residing in shelters or residences during the Family Court process. One component of a particular hospital program will serve the children of mentally ill hospitalized mothers with a view toward preventing the placement of such children.

The Task Force concurred that children within existing shelters are in need of high priority attention. Because of inadequate mental health staffs in the shelters, these children many of whom are seriously disturbed have not in the past received mental health services. The Bureau of Institutions and Facilities of Special Services for Children (Human Resources Administration) has been in the process of converting the large City shelters to small, community-based, diagnostic and reception centers and group residences. The children residing in these facilities are largely referred to the Family Court as Persons-In-Need-Of-Supervision (PINS) and are identified as being uncontrollable with severe behavioral problems.

The recent report, "Juvenile Injustice", (4) noted that a major reason for the failure to deal with these children is "the fragmented and compartmentalized delivery of service systems" that allow each department and agency to say "let someone else provide for that child." The report concludes, as its principal recommendations:

> "An absolute top priority must be given to the development of services for children before the Family Court of the State of New York.
>
> The services that are required for court children range from a much stronger probation staff, supportive services in the community, special programs in the schools, half-way houses, to a wide variety of residential facilities."

The decision of the Bureau of Institutions and Facilities provides a unique opportunity for a coordinated and collaborative planning effort by this Department with other agencies to meet the needs of court-related children, in line with the recommendations of the Judicial Conference. Additional funds have been requested to permit five contracts to be entered into with mental health providers based on this model of service under which the providers will assume responsibility for providing to the Diagnostic and Reception Center and Group Residence the following services: quality diagnostic psychiatric and psychological services, on-going in-service training, individual and group treatment, family work, chemotherapy and remedial education.

Obstacles and Constraints

It appears then that the "offender child" is a child in crisis who is constantly "on trial" even prior to his first encounter with the legal system and during his court relationship especially in the referral process to a child caring or treatment facility. Each agency takes considerable time in deciding whether the child will fit into its program before accepting or rejecting the child. There are many reasons for rejection, all of which were described in preliminary remarks.

The "offender child" is subjected to an extraordinary length of time to bring his case to final disposition. Juxtaposed to this situation is the inordinate amount of time to make a program operational; or to comply with the numerous, complicated regulations and procedures of the City and State agencies that are involved. It thus becomes necessary for program directors to maintain, not patient flow but paper flow, to wrestle, not with diagnostic criteria but with space within a facility withheld because of professional rivalries or within a community because of lack of knowledge about emotional disturbance.

CONCLUSIONS

A Unified Services approach to the multiplex, multi-level, multi-problematic planning process for mental health services for children and adolescents in New York City has been analyzed.

This analysis strongly supports the thesis that the term "offender child" is misleading. There are only children with special needs. It is an offending society* that violates the rights of children from birth to adolescence; that stigmatizes them because of poverty, race and religion; that interferes with their cognitive, emotional and social development; that keeps them in crisis and "on trial" until adolescence. Then they are designated as casualties of the system requiring intensive psycho-social-educational and rehabilitative services to enable them to cope even partially with society's pressures and demands.

It is essential that clinicians, systems analysts, administrators, lawyers, child advocates, concerned citizens and consumers who form a knowledgeable segment and an influential coalition in New York City endeavor to work harmoniously, cooperatively and collaboratively through a Unified

---

*Therefore the total group and institutional framework and the process of living together and being knit together within it as a "socii" or members of the same commonality. (5)

Services approach for the promotion and protection of the mental health of children and adolescents.

REFERENCES

1. The Joint Commission on Mental Health of children: Crisis in Child Mental Health: Challenge for the 1970's. New York, Harper and Row, (1970).

2. Violence Against Children. *J. Clin. Child Psych. 11,* (1973).

3. Jones, M., Bonn, E. *Hosp. Com. Psychiat. 24,* 675, (1973).

4. Faber, S., and Schack, E. *Juvenile Injustice,* report of Judicial Con. of St. of N.Y. 74-77, (1973).

5. Lerner, M. America as a Civilization. New York, Simon & Shuster, p. 60, (1957).

MENTAL HEALTH IN CHILDREN, Volume I
Edited By D. V. Siva Sankar
Copyright © 1975 by
PJD Publications Ltd., Westbury, N.Y.

THE SIGNIFICANCE OF SYMBIOSIS AND SEPARATION-INDIVIDUATION FOR PSYCHIATRIC THEORY AND PRACTICE

Bernard L. Pacella and Marvin S. Hurvich

Roosevelt Hospital, New York

In recent years, child analysts and research workers in child development have been observing, almost microscopically, the behavior of infants and children during the first 2-3 years of life. Foremost among these observers have been Piaget, (1) Spitz, (2) and Mahler (3).

In the course of her studies over a period embracing more than 20 years, Mahler developed her concepts concerning symbiosis and the separation-individuation (S-I) phase of life which involves the first three years of existence. This (S-I) phase begins as an outgrowth of the symbiotic period (3-6 months of age), takes on momentum after the 8th month of life and proceeds through several sub-phases which she carefully describes. Her observations of these sub-phases represent a first attempt to follow carefully and systematically the emotional development and maturation of an infant in relationship to the love object (the mother), and provides a major advance in the understanding of the endless subtle interactions between mother and child. Of greater importance is the potential impact of symbiosis and the separation-individuation concepts upon psychological theory and practice. The significance of these concepts is beginning to be reflected in the general body of theory and practice of psychoanalysis, psychiatry and psychology, but like all new understandings, there is always a time lag before syntheses into and integration with the main body of psychiatric thinking occurs.

Prior to the onset of the separation-individuation phase the infant is described as being in the objectless or preobject phase of development, which has been referred to as the autistic period of development during the first 2-3 months of life, and the succeeding symbiotic period of existence with the mother, during which time ego boundaries are indistinct; the infant apparently lacks the capacity to differentiate between mother and self. There is an important shift in perceptual organization in the transition from the autistic phase to the symbiotic phase, in which the primitive coanesthetic organization gradually evolves toward the more mature diacritic perceptual system. This reflects a shift from largely internal and contact sensations to visual and auditory distance perception. This shift from contack (primal) perception to visual perception in the course of the first few months of life is of paramount significance for the infant's development as is mediated through the instrumentality of object relations (Spitz), which Dr. Mahler has studied in detail. During the nursing period, while the child experiences the sensations of the nipple in his mouth in addition to all of the other associated sensations, he also sees the mother's face, which has become the crucial early sensory percept, and as a consequence, contact perception blends with distance perception and they become partially fused as one total experience. Visual perception attains the position of greater constancy and reliability and subsequently becomes the leading perceptive modality in man, of vital importance in psychic development and in the adaptive process. The later visual perceptual experiences (at first non-specific relating to any adult and at the 5th or 6th month becoming very specific to the mother) supersede in importance the original perceptual experiences.

It is during this period of early developing diacritic sensory organization, and the early formation of visually dominated engrams plus visual distancing in relationship to the mother, (from the 3rd to the 6th month) that Mahler speaks of the phase of symbiotic unity or the mother-child dual unity.

During this time, the face gestalt of the nonspecific adult and the infant's early smiling response is of major importance in the development of the child's mental apparatus, according to Spitz and others. Thus, we can conceive of the mother and the self as the fused primal love object of this symbiotic phase of infant development when all sensory phenomena, early motor activity and affects are fused with maternal representations, comprising the total life of the infant with relatively complete gratification of its needs, and an unconflictual existence.

The separation-individuation phase, divided by Mahler into three sub-phases, gradually evolves out of the mother-child diadic unity, or symbiotic phase, during which time the infant recognizes the mother as a need-satisfying object rather than as a libidinal or love object (not in the phallic sense of the oedipal period); and finally as the "ambivalently-cathected" love object from which it wants to separate itself while at the same time holding on the object.

The first sub-phase of separation-individuation is the differentiation sub-phase, from 5 to 10 months of age; the second or practicing sub-phase spans an approximate period from 10 to 15 months; and the third, the rapprochment sub-phase extends from 15 to 25 months; naturally, there is considerable overlapping of these periods. Following these sub-phases, the child is described as being on its way to object constancy, in which the image of the good mother is maintained regardless of day to day variations in gratifications and frustrations.

During the differentiation or hatching sub-phase, the infant begins to move out of the "symbiotic orbit", as Mahler describes it, develops distance perception, recognizes the mother as a specific object, and frequently exhibits stranger anxiety-a phenomenon which points to the specificity of mother and the infant's clearer recognition of other specific objects. Sitting up, creeping and standing develops during this phase, and specific objects take on new dimensions as the infant moves cautiously away from the mother, then rapidly back to her before crawling away from her again.

In the second, or practicing phase, there is an increasing tendency to explore objects and areas distant from mother, as only to return again for emotional refueling (Furer), always keeping her in sight, and may react to strangers with anxiety while attempting to familiarize their features by comparing them visually and tactilely with mother's. Dr. Greenacre (4) describes the 12-15 month old infant as carrying on a love affair with the whole new world as if the world were his oyster. During this phase, the infant seems to be relatively impervious to the various injuries and hurts he sustains in bumping into objects, falling down, etc.

During the rapproachment, or third sub-phase, from 15 to 25 months, the infant has greater mobility and greater neuromuscular development and the push for independence from the mother, so characteristic of the practicing phase, continues. But in addition, he now seems more desirous of being close to mother, not only physically but through the use of language and other activities for communication and game playing. He is even more resistive now to being separated from her, yet wants to be assertive and function in many ways as a separate individual. Interestingly, the toddler now seems more sensitive to hurts and falls, and reacts more vigorously to these injuries than in the practicing phase.

Thus, from the point of view of object relationship, we see two major developments almost antithetical in nature occurring during the separation-individuation process:

a) The investment of the mother as a specific love object; and the tendency to be close to her and intimately involved with her. Mahler has described this as active approach behavior.

b) The increasing tendency to separate self from the mother, and to exercise, practice and develop one's own resources and potentials.

Optimal development of the child is enhanced when the mother is able to accept both the child's increased separation and independence on the one hand, and his wishes for intense interaction on the other. Mahler sees the rapproachement sub-phase as epitomizing the universal life-long struggle against fusion on the one side, and isolation on the other, perhaps an early important root for the development of ambivalence.

Some of the important contributions of separation-individuation will be mentioned.

1. It has clarified important diagnostic issues in the area of childhood psychosis and provided the basis for technical advances in the treatment of autistic and symbiotic child psychoses, which Mahler has described.

2. It has underscored the importance of a satisfactory and satisfying symbiosis between mother and infant for adequate growth and development during the separation-individuation phase, and its disturbance leads to the child's later inadequate internalization. This results in a failure of optimal separation and of the mother representation, and increases proneness to both adolescent and adult psychopathology.

3. It has provided a framework within which to observe and to understand central aspects of ego development, and the development of object relations. This increases our ability to understand the behavior and clinical phenomenology of young children during the first three years of life.

4. It has led to an understanding of some effects of separation-individuation upon later childhood, adolescence and adult life; how the developmental movement into the oedipal phase of life and beyond may be shaded and permenently affected by the psychic developments during the separation-individuation process. Thus, a defective symbiotic and S-I phase development may make it difficult for a child to deal adequately with the stresses imposed by oedipal conflicts. It is as though the first 3 years of life provide a maternal anchor from which the child may progress into the later stages of life.

Mahler systematized and clarified the area of childhood psychosis by focusing on pathological disturbances in the early mother-infant relationship (5). She distinguished autistic infantile psychosis (first described by Kanner in 1942) (6) from symbiotic infantile psychosis (first described by herself in 1952). For the autistic children she underscored the failure to progress beyond a mother-infant symbiotic relationship to a separation of the infant's self-image from that of the mother, i.e., to self differentiation. Mahler described behavioral characteristics of these two syndromes, the mechanism and function of the autistic and symbiotic disturbances, and differential diagnostic considerations.

Her later work confirmed for Mahler the validity of the two categories of infantile psychotic syndromes, with the qualification that there is a broad spectrum of combinations of the two kinds of characteristics, with either autistic or symbiotic defenses predominating in a particular child.

Mahler's approach to the treatment of young psychotic children is based on her formulations of the normal autistic, symbiotic and separation phases, and on her understanding of the characteristics of the infantile psychoses described above. Such concepts as the corrective symbiotic experience, and the use of a mother-child-therapist framework within which to aid the child in reliving missed infantile experiences at a pace congenial to him suggest some of the technical advances developed in the framework of separation-individuation theory.

Where the symbiotic experience is not satisfactory and the infant is unable to utilize the mother to maintain homoeostasis, where mutual cuing between infant and mother is deficient or defective, there results a failure of separation of the mental representation of the infant from that of the mother, and an interference with the individuation process, which renders the infant vulnerable to serious psychopathology. This may cast its shadow upon the later sub-phases of separation-individuation which will interfere with a proper resolution of the oedipal conflict.

The problems of separation anxiety would seem to have its roots in the separation-individuation phase and is clearly discernible during the practicing and rapproachement periods of life. Anaclitic depression, described by Spitz as occurring in the last third of the first year of life, precipitated by the long absence of the mother, becomes more understandable in the light of the S.I. phase studies.

The origins of ambivalence, which have been discussed in the literature largely in relation to anal drives may be seen in nuclear form during the rapproachement phase and in what Mahler calls the rapproachement crisis, which is at the crossroads of the conflict between separation and fusion with the mother. This adds the dimension of certain ego factors as well as anal conflicts in the consideration of ambivalence.

The entire question of object constancy development has been more clearly defined by separation-individuation studies, although we cannot elaborate upon this complicated question in this paper.

In conclusion, the increased understanding of psychological development in relation to the quality of mothering and the specifics of the mother-child relationship during the first three years of life has been greatly extended and amplified by Mahler's work on symbiosis and the sub-phases of separation individuation. Many of her observations emphasize the need and gives promise for the increased utilization of early preventive and therapeutic measures.

ACKNOWLEDGMENT

We would like to thank Dr. Margaret Mahler for her constructive comments and criticisms.

REFERENCES

1. Piaget, J., and Inhelder, B. *The Psychology of the Child;* Basic Books, New York, (1969).

2. Spitz, R., *The First Year of Life,* International Universities Press, New York, (1965).

3. Mahler, M. *On Human Symbiosis and the Vicissitudes of Individuation,* International Universities Press, New York, (1968).

4. Greenacre, P., *Psychoanal. Study of the Child, 12,* 47, (1957).

5. Mahler, M. *Psychoanal. Study of the Child, 7,* 286,(1952).

6. Kanner, L. *Child 2,* 217, (1942).

MENTAL HEALTH IN CHILDREN, Volume I
Edited By D. V. Siva Sankar
Copyright © 1975 by
PJD Publications Ltd., Westbury, N.Y.

AN ECO-STRUCTURAL APPROACH TO SYSTEMS CHANGE: A BRIEF DISCUSSION

Harry J. Aponte
Philadelphia Child Guidance Clinic
Philadelphia, Pennsylvania

This paper is an effort to confront the therapeutic dilemma faced by clinicians who in their work wish to address themselves to the individual, the family, the schools, places of employment and other societal entities that in their experience are directly related to the clinical problems they deal with every day. The author's clinical foundation in family therapy is the source of the theory which here suggests a framework for a therapeutic approach that takes into account the various levels of social organization.

Psychotherapeutic work with families was first called family therapy about 20 years ago by clinicians who redefined emotional problems of individuals as family problems. They moved away from the concept of mental illness as a phenomenon contained strictly within the individual personality and asserted a view that the individual's psychological problems are manifestations of interpersonal conflict within his family. Family therapy brought in a new dimension to the conceptualization and treatment of emotional problems. It was a step away from a concept of mental illness, limiting it to a dysfunction contained in the individual personality, and a step towards a more comprehensive conceptualization of human functioning, based on social systems.

The influence of social systems theory has manifested itself in an approach to therapy which is labeled here eco-structural.* The term contains the word ecology to describe human behavior as a product of the dynamic relationships among social systems** in the human context, individuals, family, and the complex of functional groupings that make up the community. The word structure as a part of the term eco-structure focuses on the manner in which people who constitute systems structurally organize their relationships with one another to fulfill the functions of these systems.

The theory underlying the eco-structural approach to therapy proposes that in the ecology of society conflict arises when the enhancement of one system or subsystem endangers another system. For example, in a classroom the promotion of a gifted teacher to an administrative position may benefit her with an increase in salary and prestige, but will deprive the children in the class of this teacher's talents and may upset an immature youngster who has been personally attached to her. In a family the birth of a child may have been eagerly anticipated, but may imperil the emotional equilibrium of a jealous sibling or the harmony of a fragilely organized marriage.

A THERAPEUTIC APPROACH

In the context of therapy, when a problem is presented to a therapist with an eco-structural orientation he or she approaches it by:

1) Identifying what social systems or subsystems are dynamically most closely implicated in this systemic conflict and how.

2) Determining in what ways the relationships of the people in these systems can be altered to remove the symptoms and resolve the underlying structural problems.

*A term suggested by Lynn Hoffman.
**A social system is determined by the persons who compose it and the function for which they come together.

3) Contracting with the persons in these systems to reorganize structural relationships in ways specifically geared to achieve agreed upon goals.

The systems the therapist will examine are the individual, his or her family with the various subsystems in the family, and the other societal systems that most immediately impinge on the problems presented. The clinician includes in the therapeutic effort the persons from those systems whose participation will most efficiently facilitate the problem-solving work of therapy. He intervenes in the patterns of relationships formed by the members of the system as they carry out the functions of the system through its operations.*

In the case of a depressed woman, the therapist will examine in what operations of what context (or systems) of her life this woman behaves in a despondent manner. Is she depressed because of her relationship with her husband? If so, under what circumstances (or operations) of that relationship does she act depressed? When she is out socializing with him? When he is away on business trips? Or in everything having to do with him? The therapist also considers the woman in other relationships, with relatives and friends and in other life contexts, such as work and community. The behavior of the woman in all these systems and in the context of the therapy forms the basis of the therapist's hypotheses about the functions of the depressive stance.

With a child who is having trouble in school the therapist may choose to hold an interview with family and relevant school personnel at the school. In a session that includes family and school the therapist selectively elicits interaction between the child and school personnel, the child and family members, and the school staff and family. Choice of area for interaction depends on the operations where the problems are manifested, such as homework or truancy. When the members of the family system and school system deal with one another within their respective systems and across the boundaries of their systems, they assume varying positions in relation to one another according to the issue under consideration. Consequently, the clinician has the opportunity to observe how these

---

*Operations are discrete modules of activity. A system is actualized through its operations, which taken together make up the fabric of the system in action.

systems organize when engaged in the conflict-producing operations.

The structural aspects of relationships in the pertinent systems that the therapist will look at are: the boundaries of the system which define who are in and out of the activities of the system, the force or power of the system which energizes its operations through a patterned distribution of force among the component social units* of the system, and the system's alignments which tell you who among the component units is working together, is opposing whom and is indifferent to whom in any particular operation. The therapist will also examine the communication process among the components of the systems in question since the structure of a system develops through the interchange of information among the units as they interact in their operations.

Is a woman reacting psychosomatically because she must live in her in-law's home where she has no area of responsibility that is her own, (a problem of shrinking boundaries)? Is the youngster asserting himself through delinquent behavior in a power struggle with a dominating parent because he has no means of affirming his autonomy? Or does a child react with anxiety and insomnia because she feels herself isolated in a family situation in which her father, her only ally at home, is comprising his support of her because of his effort to placate the insecure and demanding mother, (an issue of alliances)? In any of these instances, the family could have been communicating conflicting expectations to the identified patient, a double bind in the family's communications about the organizational relationships. In each of these examples, a different aspect of structural relationships is emphasized but one can readily see how a change in any one aspect of a relationship affects the other structural aspects in some way.

To change the functioning of a system the clinician acts as part of the structural dynamics of the system as its members tackle the problematic operation. The therapist becomes a

---

*A component unit is the basic element in the structural composition of a system. A hockey player is that unit in a team. A team is the component element in a league of hockey teams.

powerful component in the patterning of interactional behavior in this operation, employing her or his central position to shift alignments, tilt the balance of forces, alter boundaries within the structure, and influence the system's modes of communication. The therapist employs any one in a spectrum of techniques depending on the purpose of the intervention and on the system in which he/she intervenes. Techniques differ according to the social unit, whether it is an individual, a family or larger network.

When engaged therapeutically with these systems, the therapist obtains data through techniques that are calculated to inform him/her most fully about the structural dynamics of the system in action. For example, the therapist employs techniques in the interview itself that have the individuals from a family system engage in the actual problematic operations or analogous operations both to assess how the family organizes when activated and to begin in the interview itself to alter these structural relationships. Where anorexia in an adolescent girl is the presenting symptom, an interview with the entire family organized around a meal represents the problematic operation in this instance (1). If the girl's struggle for personal power and boundaries within her family is thought to be the germaine structural issue underlying the anorectic symptom, the family may be asked to negotiate this issue in the context of the meal they are eating or in another family operation, such as, TV program selection for that evening.

The therapist involves himself or herself with the system through techniques that essentially are geared towards reorganizing interactions among the component members. For example, to augment a timid husband's position *vis-a-vis* his wife, the therapist may insist during a period in an interview that a wife not interfere with her husband's talking to the therapist. Assuming that the structural basis of the problem they came in for was a power struggle, the short term goal of this tactic may be to buttress the husband. However, the long range purpose is to redistribute the balance of force in the structural pattern of this husband-wife relationship so that the habitual effectiveness of their interactions in the marital operations will be enhanced. While the therapist may align himself with the husband to exclude the wife in certain operations of the clinical interview, he may work at other times to move the strengthened husband to give on his own initiative to his wife the affection she has tried to extract through intimidation. In the example just cited, the timing and manner of the therapist's intervention take into consideration the effect on the wife of being temporarily excluded from the husband-therapist communications.

The assignment of tasks is another technique that flows from this theory that stresses active intervention in current dynamics. A task is a therapist-prescribed operation constructed to alter some structural pattern within a system. With a task, the therapist faces a challenge of how to weave a set of prescribed actions within a social group so as to influence, as planned, an essential aspect of the system's structural pattern. Out of a diagnosis of the source of the problem the therapist decides on an activity that embodies the desired structural changes. The members of the system who the therapist selects for the task will not only alter the relationship but will impact on others in their environment. The therapist plans the task anticipating its effect on the surrounding ecological context. A task, because it is a time limited agreement to focus on altering a sequence of actions, can have a dramatic impact on the lives of people and consequently on the lives of those around them. The clinician, therefore, carefully plans a task on his/her assessment of the structural basis of a problem and carries out its assignment attentive to its possible repercussions on the social field as a whole and on each unit within it.

The interdependence of systems in an ecological chain suggests that the work for change in one system will probably necessitate a series of treatment contracts for change with interlocking systems in the focal system's supporting ecological structure. (2) For example, the success of a therapist in helping an adolescent towards maturity who is overly involved with his lonely, divorced mother may be linked to expanding the social life of that youngster's mother. The therapist will contract with the boy to view and handle himself more maturely, and with the youngster and his mother to draw more distinct boundaries between themselves in their relationship, and with the mother to establish closer social connections with her peers. The therapist makes contracts with each of three interrelated systems: the boy, mother and son, and mother as an adult within her peer context. The therapist will coordinate his/her efforts with all these systems and subsystems. The clinician attempts to respond to a system or subsystem in terms that will meet the needs of that system without sacrificing, but supporting the other systems in its social environment.

CONCLUSION

Eco-structural theory stresses conceptualizing the structural relationships among components within systems and among the systems themselves in their social context. It is a viewpoint that includes context at various levels of complexity in a continuum of interconnected systems. Human problems approached through this perspective can be understood in terms of the dynamics in the ecological field that are currently creating and sustaining them. Consequently, the therapist's interventions can be executed within the scope of the immediate and continuing implications for the structural relationships of the components of the systems being affected. This requires detailed analysis of the most discrete interactional sequences in an operation of a system as well as a perspective of the intersystematic connections within the larger ecological context.

The paper offered an outline of eco-structural theory and attempted to demonstrate how this view of therapy carries with it techniques specific to it as well as commonly used therapeutic interventions which, however, would be employed within the purview of the theory.

FOOTNOTE

1. Aponte, H. J. and Hoffman, L., "The Open Door: A Structural Approach to a Family with an Anorectic Child", *Family Process*, Vol. 12, No. 1, pp. 1-44, 1973

2. Aponte, H. J., "Organizing Treatment Around the Family's Problems and Their Structural Bases", *The Psychiatric Quarterly*, Vol. 12, No. 2, pp. 209-222, 1974

REFERENCES

1. Buckley, Walter. *Modern Systems Research for the Behavioral Scientist.* Aldene Publishing Company, Chicago, (1968).

2. Buckley, Walter. *Sociology and Modern Systems Theory.* Prentice Hall, Inc., Englewood Cliffs, New Jersey, (1967).

3. Caplow, Theodore. *Two Against One.* Prentice Hall, Inc., Englewood Cliffs, New Jersey, (1968).

4. Haley, Jay. *Uncommon Therapy.* W.W. Norton and Company, Inc., New York, (1973).

5. Lane, Michael. *Introduction to Structuralism.* Basic Books, Inc., New York, (1970).

6. Minuchin, Salvador. *Families and Family Therapy.* Harvard University Press, Cambridge, Massachusetts, (1974).

7. Piaget, Jean. *Structuralism.* Basic Books, Inc., New York, (1970).

8. Rubington, Earl and Weinberg, Martin S. *Deviance, The Interactionist Perspective.* The Macmillan Limited, London, (1968).

9. Taylor, Howard F., *Balance in Small Groups.* Van Nostrand Reinhold Company, New York, (1970).

MENTAL HEALTH IN CHILDREN, Volume I
Edited By D. V. Siva Sankar
Copyright © 1975 by
PJD Publications Ltd., Westbury, N.Y.

THE SELF-CONCEPT OF THE CHILD IN RELATION TO LEARNING

Hilmar Wagner
University of Texas, El Paso, Texas

"The self-concept is a better predictor of a child's future success in school than is intelligence" (6). This statement by Coopersmith and Silverman is the premise of this paper and is a recurring theme throughout much of the literature in child development. Not only will the self-concept be treated in relation to learning, but the mutuality of other factors such as peer identification, the physical self, and the psychological climate of the classroom will be considered.

For the purposes of this paper the self-concept will be defined in terms of the child's realistic and positive acceptance of himself and his role in relation to his perception of how significant others view him. This definition will in turn cause a distinction to be drawn between the real and ideal self.

Background

There is enough evidence to support the theory that if the child has self-esteem he likely has it made not only academically but also socially and emotionally. An above average intellect does not assure one of the success and happiness. Very few people develop the maximum of their potential ability.

Among failures, suicides, and non-performers there are many with high I.Q.'s. A positive self-image produces desirable traits, and makes for a happier, better-adjusted person, which in turn opens the way for learning. The plastic surgeon, Maxwell Maltz, has indicated that how a person sees himself influences and determines everything he thinks, feels or does. This self-image is the result of the experiences an individual has had and how he has viewed or interpreted these experiences.

Murphy (10) writes of the amount of attention paid to the self-concept, indicating that as a person feels about himself, so will he act, linking this to the self-fulfilling prophecy. She suggests charting two profiles, showing the outsider's viewpoint of the child and the child's viewpoint of himself, with the second of these being more important since decisions are based on it. Highly self-critical children are more anxious, insecure. cynical and depressed than are self-accepting children. The self-concept thus serves as a boundary, acting as a limit to the actions of the child. According to Survan (12) a child with a good self-image is unafraid in new situations, makes friends easily, experiments with new materials, shows trust to the teacher, and is cooperative, responsible, creative and independent. Children make significant improvement in what they try to do when they are free of self-doubt.

The importance of self-esteem is expressed by Briggs in the following statements:

> How your child feels about himself affects how he lives his life. High self-esteem is based on your child's belief that he is lovable and worthwhile. Your child must know that he matters just because he exists. He needs to feel competent to handle himself and his environment. He needs to feel he has something to offer others. High self-esteem is not conceit; it is your child's quiet comfort about being who he is (3, p. 1-9).

Perhaps some of the most significant research regarding the relationship between the self-concept and school achievement was conducted by Brookover (5) and his associates. In a six-year longitudinal study of a population of seventh through twelfth graders, attempts were made to enhance the "self-concept of ability" among low-achieving students. Their evidence supports the theory that positive changes in significant others' evaluation will raise the child's "self-concept of ability" and positively influence his academic achievement. Earlier research by Brookover and others (4) indicated that the "self-concept of ability" functions quite independently of measured intelligence in influencing academic adjustment, and provides a better indication of academic potential than measures of intelligence.

The need to meet challenges to the best of one's ability is very strong in our culture. Glasser's position on "reality therapy" notes that man has two basic needs: the need for love and the need for self worth, both forming pathways to successful identity (7, p. 12).

The Classroom and Success

Children who are successful in school tend to set realistic and reasonable personal goals. Success in school often leads to a good self-concept and helps individuals deal more effectively with any setting in which they find themselves. Children who have been unsuccessful and feel that they cannot win, regardless of their efforts, often feel that it is not worth the risk of failing to even try, and thus behave accordingly. Personal sureness provides the child with the courage to try new tasks.

The psychological climate of any given classroom is dependent on interpersonal relations among the student and other students and the student and the teacher. The self-definition pupils and teachers have of themselves has a tremendous impact on classroom climate. If children feel that they are valued, they often develop a healthy self-respect, which they likely transfer to others. As the writer indicated in an earlier paper,

> In the classroom there is the opportunity to achieve, whether scholastically or socially. The teacher supplies the approval of which the child has been deprived. In satisfying this need, the teacher may approach the situation by helping the child achieve a sense of mastery in subject matter content or by encouraging him to seek peer acceptance which will serve his internal needs (14, p. 14).

The curricula of the schools should contain experiences designed to improve the intellect. Praise, even for small successes, is uplifting. Children need some form of recognition for their efforts with success being built only on success.

To engender a healthy self-concept the teacher provides for genuine encounters in a psychologically safe climate involving trust and free from judgement. Here the child can have his own feelings without the teacher withdrawing approval. The teacher must have a healthy self-concept of his own in order to help his students improve their self-concepts.

Teachers want life's positives for their students: inner confidence, a sense of purpose and involvement, meaningful and constructive relationships with others, success in school and work, all adding to the child's happiness. Happy children are usually more involved with others, whereas the child who fails often receives more scolding and rejection, adding to his lack of self-confidence.

When a child enters school he comes with an idea of self resulting from his pre-school experiences. If his self-concept is good, he will face new learning tasks with expectations of success rather than being anxious. This success will likely lead to a healthy teacher-pupil relationship producing a cycle of successes. Children who feel worthy perform better in school. A learning atmosphere free from anxiety allows the child to realize both his abilities and his limitations and to accept both without guilt feelings or blaming others.

Shaw and others (11) report that male achievers feel more positive about themselves than male underachievers. Female underachievers, however, are ambivalent with regard to their feelings toward themselves according to the Shaw study. When the child fails in relation to those around him and he stays back while his peers progress, he is likely to have an unbalanced ego. This is especially humiliating and frustrating for the student for whom learning is difficult. Learning is avoided when it is perceived as threatening. Experience with success is what counts, speaking much louder than words of praise from parents and teachers.

The Influence of Peers

The feelings which children express toward each other serve to reinforce and strengthen or limit the child's feeling of self-worth. Only with peers can the child relate as an equal. Through peer interaction the child is helped in clarifying his feelings and is more open in expressing his attitudes toward self and school.

As the author wrote in another source (13), the peer group allows the child the opportunity to build a healthy self-concept through development of his talents and strong suites. How the peer group treats him and whether they regard him favorably or unfavorably will largely determine how he will appraise his own self-worth and the picture he will get of himself. Briggs reinforces this position in the following words:

> Every child has the potential of liking himself. Your child needs to see himself as the important people around him do. He builds his self-picture from the words, body language, attitudes and judgements of others. He judges himself according to his observations of himself in comparison with others and others' responses to him. High self-esteem comes from positive experience with life and love (3, p. 9-20).

If the peer culture values social and extracurricular activities more than academics, the self-concept of the child will adjust itself to these demands, often to the neglect of academic subjects. "The student who cannot afford to participate (financially) in the school activities which are provided and who sees his peers taking part in them might develop a poor self-image and consequently lower his level of aspiration, in a sense giving up his dreams of the future" (8, p. 5-6).

The research of Zimbardo and Formica suggests that youngsters with low self-esteem are less popular and are less effective within their groups, but are hungriest for group acceptance. Beatty writes, "Studies show that children who are highly involved in the classroom peer group are better liked, make greater use of academic abilities, and express more positive attitudes toward self and school than those who are less involved in peer activities" (1, p. 365).

The Child as an Individual

Every child needs individual recognition and attention, where interest is focused at some time solely on him and where there is unqualified acceptance of him as an individual. Objectives aimed toward social and emotional adjustment appear to this writer much more important than our traditional educational goals. A child with a healthy self-concept can reach most of our educational goals. If the teacher expects children to succeed, they likely will. Becker, Englemann and Thomas (2) write that many psychologists conclude that educators should quit worrying about teaching kids and focus all efforts in making kids happy, confident, loved and respected.

Regardless of class size, the child must be dealt with as an individual. Any significant changes in behavior must come through a change in self, a change which Carl Rogers refers to as "unconditional positive regard." Children who are labelled as uneducable usually become just that. No question from the child is too trivial for an adult to answer sincerely. Friedenburg's research (9) points out that schools, either directly or indirectly, pressure students to relinquish their autonomy, including the sacrificing of their own personal desires in behalf of trivial institutional considerations.

The Physical Self

The physical self of the child, including his physique, size, sex-role identification, personal appeal, determines the reactions of others toward him. Every society has a criteria by which individuals are judged, such as the right height or weight or having the prescribed body-build. Constant integration of the self to rapid body changes is necessary for a healthy self-concept in the child. Age of maturation has an impact on the self-concept and the independence granted the child. The child's physical structure may have an influence on his interest in people and the activities which he chooses.

The child's self-concept is influenced significantly by the physical self since the actual presence of the body is more real than any other aspect of personality. The significance of the body, not only physically, but socially and emotionally as well, integrates the self-concept with reality. Early training by parents and other adults concerning modesty and morality complicate the task of self-identity in relation to the body.

Recommendations

The following recommendations have been successful for some teachers attempting to improve learning conditions by enhancing the self-concept.

(a) Help the child pull together his two self-concepts, the real and the ideal. Opportunities for role-playing, especially playing parts where the child is successful, can change the child's self-image. Accept the way he is and the things he does. Be honest in this respect, but always use positive reinforcement.

(b) Help the child live with his established self-concept. Solicit his suggestions and use them. Make him feel his ideas are worthy. Story-telling, based on suggestions, situations, or pictures may make him begin to think of his own feelings.

(c) Group activities and group guidance techniques can help peers aid children with low self-concepts. Here students are allowed to be judiciously and appropriately open with their concerns, prejudices, and ambivalences. The teacher changes his role from that of a judge to a reactor. Efforts are made to make each child feel an important member of the group, though initially children may fear close physical contact in a group.

(d) Help the child compliment those strengths which he has going for him. Much verbal reinforcement and encouragement can help in this respect. Be careful here in showing favoritism and be sure that each child feels that his strengths are recognized.

(e) Allow the child opportunities for success in activities and responsibilities in which he can achieve. Interesting and challenging tasks within the child's ability range should be carefully selected by the teacher, accompanied by much teacher verbal encouragement.

(f) Help the child become realistic in his levels of aspiration. Children with poor self-concepts often are reluctant to enter into new situations. In making assignments and allowing the child choices, carefully weigh the child's opportunities for completing the task to a degree in which he is satisfied and in which he feels pride through accomplishment.

(g) Allow the child to maintain his individuality. Working within time restrictions, listen to each child attentively. Encourage children to respond individually and to feel free to actively participate in learning activities.

REFERENCES

1. Beatty, W., "The Feelings of Learning," *Childhood Education*, (1979).

2. Becker, W., Englemann, S., and Thomas, P., *Teaching: A Course in Applied Psychology*, Chicago, Science Research Associates, (1971).

3. Briggs, D., *Your Child's Self-Esteem: The Key to his life*, Garden City, New York, Doubleday and Company, Inc., (1970).

4. Brookover, W., Patterson, A., and Thomas, S., "Self Concept of Ability and School Achievement, *"Final Report of Cooperative Research Project #845, U.S. Office of Education*, East Lansing, Michigan State University Press, (1962).

5. Brookover, W., LePerre, J., Hamacheck, E., Thomas, S., and Erickson, E. "Improving Academic Achievement Through Student's Self Concept Enhancement, *"Final Report of Cooperative Research Project #1636, U.S. Office of Education*, East Lansing, Michigan State University Press, (1965).

6. Coopersmith, S., and Silverman, J., "How to Enhance Pupil Self-Esteem," *Today's Education*, *58*, 28, April, (1969).

7. Dinkmeyer, D., and Carlson, J., *Consulting*, Columbus Ohio, Charles E. Dinkmeyer Publishing Company, p.8-12, (1973). (Quoting Glasser's Reality Therapy).

8. Evans, B., and Wagner, H., *The Cost of a High School Education*, El Paso, The University of Texas at El Paso Print Shop, (1970).

9. Friedenberg,E., *Coming of Age in America*, Random House, New York, (1963).

10. Murphy, M., "Values and Health Problems," *The Journal of School Health, 43,* 23, (1973).

11. Shaw, M. and others, "Self Concepts of Bright Under-achieving High School Students as Revealed by an Adjective Check List," *Personnel and Guidance Journal, 39,* 193, (1960).

12. Survant, "Building Positive Self-Concepts, *The In-Structor,* Feb., (1972).

13. Wagner, H., "The Increasing Importance of the Peer Group During Adolescence, " *Adolescence, 6,* 53, Spring, (1971).

14. Wagner, H., "To What Extent Do Teachers and Their Pupils Enjoy School and One Another?" *Texas A.S.C.D. Journal, 1,* 13, Nov., (1970).

15. Zimbardo, P. and Formica, R., "Emotional Comparison and Self-Esteem as Determinants of Affiliation," *Journal of Personality, 31,* 141, (1963).

MENTAL HEALTH IN CHILDREN, Volume I
Edited By D. V. Siva Sankar
Copyright © 1975 by
PJD Publications Ltd., Westbury, N.Y.

CHILDHOOD SOCIAL COMPETENCE AND BEHAVIOR STYLE IN RELATION TO PSYCHIATRIC DISORDER IN EARLY ADULTHOOD

John H. Fryer

Veterans Administration Hospital
Bedford, Massachusetts

and

Norman F. Watt

University of Massachusetts

ABSTRACT

In the study of the development of psychopathology, various life history research strategies have begun to supplant the traditional clinical retrospective approach. Although less vulnerable to certain data distortions, the life history approach has often been hampered by serious sampling restrictions which limit the extent to which the findings can be generalized. The present study utilizes teachers' comments in school records to study the childhood behavior of a relatively unbiased sample of persons hospitalized for functional psychiatric disorders in early adulthood. Analysis of these concurrently-recorded premorbid data generally provides confirmation of Phillips' maturational theory of psychopathology. The patients are distinguished from their matched controls by their lower social competence and greater aggressiveness in childhood. Premorbid interpersonal competence and internalization of aggression are positively related to adult outcome, while withdrawal is negatively related to outcome. Congruently, interpersonal competence in childhood is associated with internalization of aggression, rather than withdrawal, in adulthood symptomatology. Furthermore, there is evidence of significant continuity in life style from school behavior to adulthood psychiatric symptomatology, in terms of role orientation. These findings suggest the theoretical and practical utility of approaching the study of psychological disorder from a developmental perspective in terms of maturational and stylistic dimensions.

The purpose of the research to be reported here is two-fold: First, to augment descriptive knowledge of the childhood behavior patterns of adult psychiatric patients; and, second, to provide an empirical test of certain aspects of the Phillips (1) maturational model of psychopathology. Until relatively recently, most of what was known of the childhood characteristics of adult psychiatric patients was based upon retrospective reconstructions of developmental histories from the recollections of the adult patient and his relatives. A number of authors, especially Mednick and McNeil (2), have pointed to the inherent methodological weakness of this traditional clinical retrospective approach. Data derived from this kind of historical reconstruction are subject to intractable distortions attributable to faulty recall, repression, and knowledge of the patient's adulthood psychiatric status. This last source of possible bias affects the clinician's interpretation, as well as the informants' report. In view of these methodological difficulties, Roff and Ricks (3), among others, have argued for the efficacy of the "life history" approach to the study of psychopathological development. Life history research relies upon data generated by the direct observation of childhood behavior, before adulthood outcome is known.

Two major subtypes within the life history strategy may be specified: The prospective method, and the childhood records method. Because of the low base-rate of severe psychopathology in the general population, prospective studies have focused on samples of children thought to be vulnerable to psychological disorder. The longitudinal study of children of schizophrenic mothers conducted by Mednick and Schulsinger (4) is the most ambitious example of this type of research. In contrast to the planned longitudinal observation of vulnerable or "high-risk" children, childhood records studies rely upon examination of the child guidance center records or school records of children ultimately identified as suffering from mental disorder in adulthood. The Judge Baker Guidance Center Schizophrenia Project (5) and the follow-up study by Robins (6) exemplify the child guidance center records strategy. The school records method has been utilized by Lane and Albee (7, 8) and by Pollack et al. (9) to study preschizophrenic intellectual development, and by Barthell and Holmes (10) to study the social participation of preschizophrenics.

Each of these life history strategies shares the methodological advantage of being founded upon data generated by direct observation of childhood behavior, and each is thereby free from the distortions which plague clinical retrospective research. However, certain additional methodological difficulties are encountered by these life history research designs. The genetic high-risk selection criterion excludes the approximately 85% of the preschizophrenics who do not have a schizophrenic parent. The child guidance center records method includes in its samples only those adult psychiatric patients who have a history of psychiatric referral in childhood. This method is further limited by the use of abnormal control groups consisting of children who manifested various forms of psychopathology, notably aggressive behavior. The school records method carries the potential for selection of more representative samples of future psychiatric patients. However, school records studies have frequently been hampered by failure to control for social class. The present study employs sample and control group selection procedures designed to overcome these methodological problems in an effort to investigate the premorbid behavior patterns of a representative group of psychiatric inpatients.

The prolific research by Leslie Phillips (1) and his colleagues suggests that adaptive potential and behavior style may be of crucial importance in the development of psychopathology. In this theoretical formulation, adaptive potential is defined as the individual's relative potential for coping with the tasks set by society, as compared to others of the same age-sex class. Behavior style refers to attitudinal sets and habitual patterns of response in the areas of interpersonal relations and mode of expression. In operational terms, adaptive potential may be equated with the concept of "social competence", defined as the individual's past (optimal) level of performance in society. Interpersonal behavior style, or "role orientation," may be measured on the basis of the relative predominance within the individual of the orientations of "self-deprivation and turning against self," "self-indulgence and turning against others," or "avoidance of others." Expressive style may be viewed in terms of the relative predominance within the individual of expression in the spheres of "thought," "affect," or "action." A maturational correspondence is presumed to exist between level of social competence and characteristic behavior style. That is, internalization of anger rather than externalization of anger or interpersonal withdrawal is presumed to represent a relatively high level of psychosocial maturation and social competence. Similarly, predominance of ideational expression rather than affective or motoric expression is presumed to correspond to a higher level of maturation and competence. If level of social competence and characteristic behavior style are relatively stable within the individual over time, knowledge of these premorbid behavior patterns could lead to the prediction of risk, form, and outcome of subsequent psychiatric disorder.

Extensive evidence for the validity and utility of this theoretical model has been produced by the Phillips research group for the paramorbid and outcome phases of psychological disorder. Adulthood premorbid social competence has been shown to be related to psychiatric diagnosis (11), sphere dominance in psychiatric symptomatology (12), and outcome (13). Furthermore, it has been demonstrated that paramorbid behavior style is related to outcome of psychological disorder (14). One of the most impressive findings to emerge from this group of studies is that the behavior style variables of role orientation and sphere dominance collectively account for essentially all of the variance in major diagnosis, up to the limit of diagnostic reliability (15).

Nevertheless, the essentially cross-sectional design of the Phillips studies has lacked the capability of providing an empirical test of the central, developmental, aspect of this theoretical formulation. Particularly in need of empirical confirmation are the hypotheses that behavior style is longitudinally continuous and that childhood social competence and behavior style are related in the predicted manner to risk, form, and outcome of subsequent psychological disorder. The research to be reported here is designed to provide a test of these major hypotheses on the basis of a subject sample which is quite representative of all psychiatric inpatients who are first admitted for functional mental disorder in early adulthood.

METHOD

Subjects and Controls. The Massachusetts Department of Mental Health maintains records of the names, dates of admission, and diagnoses of all patients admitted to any private, state, or Veterans Administration psychiatric facility in Massachusetts. The present study utilizes this central data bank in an attempt to follow the psychiatric careers of all functional psychiatric inpatients first admitted in early adulthood from a large representative sample of the general population. The matching of public school enrollment lists with the psychiatric admissions lists maintained by the state constitutes an effective tracing procedure for the achievement of this kind of sample selection. The Boston suburb of "Maybury" was chosen for this purpose on the basis of its large size, demographic representativeness, and superior school records.

A computer list was obtained from the Massachusetts Department of Mental Health containing the names of every patient 15 to 34 years of age who was first admitted to any inpatient psychiatric facility in Massachusetts during the fiscal years 1958 through 1965. Of the 19,179 patients listed 15,811 were diagnosed as manifesting some form of functional psychiatric disorder. This list of 15,811 psychiatric patients was checked against the enrollment lists from the files of the Maybury school system. Cumulative school records were located for 160 of these patients. Examination of the school records showed that 145 of the 160 students had attended Maybury schools long enough to have received at least one year of annual teachers' comments in the record. These 145 individuals whose school records contained at least one year of teachers' comments, and who were subsequently hospitalized in Massachusetts for functional mental disorder, constitute the sample on which the present research is based.

The size of the school population from which the sample was drawn can be estimated to be approximately 6800 (16). On the basis of Public Health Service survey data for mental hospital admissions in the United States (17), a representative population sample of this size would be expected to include approximately 150 persons who will be initially hospitalized for functional mental disorder prior to age 35. Since the research sample is of the same order of magnitude as this (hypothetical) target sample, it would appear that the loss of subjects due to defective follow-up procedures or permanent out-of-state migration has been minimal.

The research sample, then, may be presumed to be rather representative of all psychiatric inpatients first admitted for functional disorder prior to age 35. However, as this age-range restriction would imply, the sample is considerably more representative of those psychiatric disorders which tend to have early, rather than late, onset. The research sample of 74 male and 71 female psychiatric inpatients is comprised of the following major diagnostic groups: 59 schizophrenics, 41 personality disorders, 31 neurotics, and 14 depressive psychotics.   This would include approximately 85% of all the schizophrenics, two-thirds of the (nonalcoholic) personality disorders, half of the neurotics, and one-third of the depressive psychotics that the population of 6800 would ultimately be expected to yield.

One matched control record was selected randomly from the school files of the same graduating class as the index case. These controls were matched with the index case for age, sex, race, father's occupational level, and father's education. The initial criterion for regarding these controls as "normal" was that, as of 1965, none had been admitted to any psychiatric facility in Massachusetts. Subsequently, a direct follow-up located two-thirds of these control subjects and confirmed that almost all had achieved an adequate social adjustment in adulthood. (Only one control had been hospitalized for psychiatric treatment and one had been sentenced to a long prison term). As a result of these control selection procedures, the premorbid behavior of the patients can be evaluated in terms of deviation from the behavior of normal children of similar circumstance. Two of the 145 control records proved ultimately to contain insufficient information for use in the research. Hence, the reported subject-control comparisons are based upon the sample of 143 patients for which there were usable matched control records.

Measures. The Maybury school records format reserves a good deal of space for teachers' annual comments regarding the social development, work skills, and scholastic achievement of the student. Following the work of D'Andrade (18) and Conger and Miller (19), Watt *et al.* (16) developed a coding system for categorization of the teachers' comments in terms of 37 bipolar dimensions. Subsequently, this coding system was revised by the elimination of infrequently scored and redundant categories (21). Reliability tests on this revised system of 24 bipolar categories demonstrated that the interrater reliability was superior to that of the original coding system. Research assistants, unaware of the research rationale, scored the school records by simply counting the number of teachers' statements which were judged to fit each of the 48 coding categories.

Childhood social competence and behavior style were measured on the basis of these coded teachers' comments. Two aspects of childhood social competence were distinguished: work skills competence and interpersonal competence. The raw score for work skills competence was obtained by subtracting the sum of coded comments indicating low work skills competence from the sum of coded comments indicating high work skills competence. The actual score on work skills competence was computed by dividing this raw score by the total number of years for which annual teachers' comments appeared in the student's record. Interpersonal competence was measured in a similar manner. The score for total social competence was obtained by summing the scores for work skills and interpersonal competence.

The measurement of behavior style in childhood was somewhat more complex. As before, raw scores were obtained for each of the behavior style variables by subtracting the sum of "negative" comments in each behavior style category from the sum of "positive"comments in that category. Division of these raw scores by the total number of years of teachers' comments yielded "ratio scores" for each of the three roles and spheres. Standard scores were then computed on the basis of the group distributions of these six ratio scores. Ipsative scores were calculated by subtracting the individual's mean standard score on all three role orientation variables from his standard score on each of the three roles. This produced sigma deviation scores indicating the relative predominance of each of the three role orientations within the individual. A parallel procedure was followed in the computation of sigma deviation scores for sphere dominance within the individual. These computational procedures yielded measures of childhood behavior style which are not subject to the effects of differences in absolute scoring frequencies between categories or differences in amount of case material across subjects.

Paramorbid behavior style was measured on the basis of psychiatric case records on symptomatology at first admission. Access to the psychiatric case records of the 145 patients in the sample was sought, and detailed information on behavior during hospitalization was obtained for 132 of them. A reliable system for coding psychiatric case records in terms of 34 unipolar and 36 bipolar symptom categories was developed and applied to these 132 cases by research assistants who were unaware of the research rationale. Classification of psychiatric symptoms in terms of the role orientation and sphere dominance categories adhere as closely as possible to the method developed by Phillips, Broverman, and Zigler (15). Raw scores for the three roles and spheres were derived by subtracting the sum of the symptoms coded as "absent" in each category from the sum of the symptoms coded as "present" in that category. "Ratio scores" for the three roles were calculated by dividing each of the three raw scores by the total number of symptoms coded as present or absent in any of the role orientation categories. A similar procedure was followed to compute ratio scores for the three spheres. On the basis of the group distributions for the ratio scores, standard scores were computed for each of the roles and spheres. Ipsative sigma deviation scores were then calculated for role orientation and sphere dominance by a procedure identical to that employed in the calculation of the sigma deviation scores for childhood behavior style. As a result of these score derivations, both the childhood and paramorbid behavior style measures reflect the relative predominance of the three roles and the three spheres of expression within the individual.

Psychiatric outcome data in the form of diagnosis and dates of hospital admission and discharge were available for the entire sample of 145 patients. Outcome of disorder was measured on the basis of a six-year (2190-day) follow-up period commencing on the day of each patient's first inpatient psychiatric admission. Two types of outcome indicators were employed: global ratings of outcome, and length of hospitalization. The global ratings are assigned on a three-point scale (1=poor, 2=fair, 3=good). From the dates of admission and discharge, the number of inpatient days for first admission and for all admissions combined were computed. Because of the skewness of the distributions, the actual scores for length of hospitalization were derived from the number of inpatient days by logarithmic transformation.

RESULTS

Table 1 presents the paired t-test analysis of patient-control group differences for the childhood social competence and behavior style variables. This analysis shows that, in childhood, the patients were lower in total social competence (p less than .05) and were oriented more "against others" in their social behavior (p less than .01) than their matched controls. Nonsignificant trends (p less than .10) suggest that the patients were lower than their controls on both work skills and interpersonal competence in childhood, and that the patients may have been *less* avoidant than their controls (contrary to prediction). The patients are not distinguishable from their controls in terms of sphere dominance in childhood. Thus, it may be concluded that, in comparison to developmental norms, the childhood behavior of persons vulnerable to mental disorder in adulthood is marked by low social competence and externalization of aggression.

The results of the correlational analysis of the relationship between childhood role orientation and the role orientation manifested in adulthood psychiatric symptomatology are shown in Table 2. This analysis reveals that paramorbid role orientation is significantly and congruently related to childhood role orientation in terms of the relative predominance of the "against self" (p less than .01), "against others" (p less than

TABLE I

Childhood Behavior and Vulnerability to Psychiatric
Disorder in Early Adulthood

CHILDHOOD BEHAVIOR MEASURES	MEAN PAIR DIFFERENCE SCORE: PATIENT MINUS CONTROL (N = 143 Matched Pairs)
Social Competence:	
Work Skills Competence	-.23*
Interpersonal Competence	-.20*
Total Social Competence	-.43**
Role Orientation:	
Against Self	-.04
Against Others	.19***
Avoidance of Others	-.15* [a]
Sphere Dominance:	
Thought	-.04
Affect	.03
Action	.01

[a] Two-tailed test of significance. All other tests are one-tailed.

* p < .10   ** p < .05   *** p < .01

TABLE II

Childhood Role Orientation and Role Orientation in
Subsequent Psychiatric Symptomatology

CHILDHOOD ROLE ORIENTA- TION MEAS- URES	PRODUCT-MOMENT CORRELA- TIONS (N = 132 for each correlation) PARAMORBID ROLE ORIENTA- TION MEASURES		
	Against Self	Against Others	Avoidance of Others
Against Self	.21***	-.07	-.17**
Against Others	-.14*	.24***	-.09
Avoidance of Others	-.11*	-.16**	.29****

* p < .10 ** p < .05 *** p < .01 **** p < .001
All significance tests are one-tailed.

TABLE III

Childhood Sphere Dominance and Sphere Dominance in
Subsequent Psychiatric Symptomatology

CHILDHOOD SPHERE DOMIN- ANCE MEAS- URES	PRODUCT-MOMENT CORRELA- TIONS (N = 132 for each correlation) PARAMORBID SPHERE DOMIN- ANCE MEASURES		
	Thought	Affect	Action
Thought	.22***	-.03	-.17**
Affect	-.04	-.02	.05
Action	-.19**	.04	.13*

* p < .10 **p < .05 ***p < .01
All significance tests are one-tailed.

TABLE IV

Childhood Social Competence and Behavior Style in
Subsequent Psychiatric Symptomatology

PARAMORBID BEHAVIOR STYLE MEAS- URES	PRODUCT-MOMENT CORRELA- TIONS (N = 132 for each correlation) CHILDHOOD SOCIAL COMPE- TENCE MEASURES		
	Work Skills Competence	Interperson- al Compe- tence	Total Social Competence
Role Orientation:			
Against Self	.21***	.32****	.32****
Against Others	-.15**	-.01	-.11*
Avoidance of Others	-.08	-.36****	-.26***
Sphere Dominance:			
Thought	-.08	-.24***a	-.19**a
Affect	.24***a	.20**a	.27***a
Action	-.18**	.01	-.11*

a Two-tailed tests of significance. All other tests are
one-tailed.

* p < .10
** p < .05
*** p < .01
**** p < .001

TABLE V

Childhood Behavior and Outcome of Psychiatric Disorder
in Adulthood

CHILDHOOD BEHAVIOR MEASURES	PRODUCT-MOMENT CORRELATIONS OUTCOME MEASURES		
	Global Rating	Length of Hospitalization [b]	
		First Adm.	All Admissions
	(N=145)	(N=145)	(N=143)
Social Competence:			
Work Skills Competence	.18**	.06	.02
Interpersonal Competence	.17**	.14**	.19**
Total Social Competence	.22***	.12*	.13*
Role Orientation:			
Against Self	.19**	.12*	.10
Against Others	-.06	.03	.07
Avoidance of Others	-.15**	-.17**	-.18**
Sphere Dominance:			
Thought	.05	-.05	-.10
Affect	-.12*	-.15**	-.09
Action	.05	.18** [a]	.18** [a]

[a] Two-tailed tests of significance. All other tests are one-tailed.

[b] Signs of correlations on length of hospitalization have been changed so that a positive value indicates a positive relationship with favorable outcome.

* p < .10   ** p < .05   *** p < .01

.01), and "avoidance of others" (p less than .001) orientations. Furthermore, the against self orientation in childhood is negatively related to the avoidance orientation in subsequent psychiatric symptomatology (p less than .05), and the premorbid avoidance orientation is negatively related to predominance of the against others orientation in the paramorbid phase of disorder (p less than .05).

With regard to the interrelationship of childhood and adulthood sphere dominance, the results of the analysis are less consistent. These results are summarized in Table 3. Thought dominance in childhood is positively related to paramorbid thought dominance (p less than .01), and negatively related to paramorbid action dominance (p less than .05). Similarly, action dominance in childhood is negatively related to predominance of ideational symptoms (p less than .05), and a nonsignificant trend (p less than .10) suggests that childhood action dominance and paramorbid action dominance are positively related. In contrast to this developmental continuity for the thought-action dimension, predominance of affective expression in childhood is not associated with paramorbid affect dominance. With this notable exception, the analysis supports the hypothesis that form of symptom expression reflects premorbid behavior style.

Table 4 summarizes the correlational analysis of the relation of childhood social competence to behavior style in subsequent psychiatric symptomatology. Total social competence in childhood is positively associated with predominance of the against self orientation (p less than .001) and negatively associated with predominance of the avoidance orientation (p less than .01) in symptom manifestation. A nonsignificant trend (p less than .10) also suggests that total social competence in childhood is negatively related to a paramorbid orientation against others. The two components of childhood social competence show a somewhat different pattern of relationships to paramorbid role orientation. While both work skills and interpersonal competence are positively related to the paramorbid against self orientation (p less than .01 and p less than .001, respectively), work skills competence is negatively associated with the against others orientation in symptomatology (p less than .05) and interpersonal competence is negatively associated with the paramorbid avoidance orientation (p less than .001).

In contrast to the interrelationship of childhood social competence and paramorbid role orientation, paramorbid sphere dominance is generally not related to premorbid social competence in the manner predicted. Contrary to theoretical prediction, total social competence in childhood is negatively associated with paramorbid thought dominance (p less than .05) and positively associated with paramorbid affect dominance (p less than .01). A nonsignificant trend (p less than .10) suggests that total social competence may be negatively related to paramorbid action dominance, as predicted. Once again, the components of childhood social competence show a different pattern of relationships to paramorbid behavior style in terms of sphere dominance. Both work skills and interpersonal competence are positively associated with predominance of affective expression in psychiatric symptomatology (p less than .01 and p less than .05, respectively). However, work skills competence is negatively related to paramorbid action dominance (p less than .05), while interpersonal competence is negatively related to paramorbid thought dominance (p less than .01).

Table 5 presents the correlational analysis of childhood social competence and behavior style in relation to outcome of psychiatric disorder in adulthood. Total social competence in childhood is positively related to favorable outcome rating (p less than .01), and there is some evidence that total social competence is also related to favorable outcome in terms of length of first admission (p less than .10) and total length of all admissions (p less than .10). While work skills competence is positively related to favorable outcome only in terms of global rating (p less than .05), the interpersonal component of premorbid social competence is significantly related to favorable outcome as measured by all three outcome indicators (p less than .05).

As predicted, the premorbid against self orientation is positively related to favorable outcome rating (p less than .05), and the premorbid avoidance orientation is negatively related to favorable outcome rating (p less than .05). However, the against others orientation in childhood is not significantly associated with outcome of disorder. Only the orientation of avoidance in childhood is significantly related to (unfavorable) outcome as measured by length of first admission (p less than .05) and total length of all admissions (p less than .05).

Childhood sphere dominance is not significantly related to outcome rating, although there is a trend suggesting that premorbid affect dominance is negatively related to rated outcome (p less than .10). As predicted, premorbid affect dominance is associated with long hospital stay at first admission (p less than .05). However, this relationship does not hold for total length of all admissions. Contrary to prediction, action dominance in childhood is positively related to favorable outcome as measured by length of first admission (p less than .05) and total length of all admissions combined (p less than .05).

CONCLUSION

A brief descriptive survey will serve to clarify the main findings of the foregoing analysis. In comparison to their childhood peers, the patients were more likely to have had low social competence in terms of work skills and interpersonal skills. In childhood, the patients were more likely than their controls to have been oriented against others, and less likely to have been oriented to avoid others. Role orientations against self, against others, and avoidant of others remain constant from childhood through adult psychiatric hospitalization. Thought dominance in expressive style is also constant longitudinally, whereas action dominance shows only trends in this direction, and affect dominance shows no such continuity. A child who is competent in work skills and interpersonal relations is more inclined to turn against self and to express disturbance in the affective sphere if hospitalized as an adult. On the other hand, a child with poor work skills is likely to turn against others and to express disturbance in the form of action if hospitalized as an adult, and a child with low interpersonal competence is likely to avoid others and to express disturbance in the thought sphere as an adult psychiatric patient. The socially competent child, particularly the interpersonally competent child, will get better after psychiatric hospitalization, whereas the child who avoids others has the poorest prognosis. Generally speaking, the child who turns against self and the child who is inclined to action have good psychiatric outcome, while the affect-dominated child has poor outcome.

Viewed theoretically, this analysis based upon teachers' comments recorded in the school histories of the subjects and the psychiatric evaluations recorded in their psychiatric case histories generally provides confirmation of the hypotheses generated by the Phillips maturational model of psychopathology. High social competence in childhood is a favorable prognostic indicator in terms of vulnerability to, and outcome of, psychiatric disorder in adulthood. In accord with the theoretical formulation, the interrelationship of premorbid social competence and paramorbid role orientation indicates that the orientations of "avoidance of others," "against others," and "against self," fall along a maturational continuum. The finding that the formal, stylistic, qualities in psychiatric symptomatology reflect longitudinal continuity from the premorbid phase has application to the traditional psychoanalytic problem of symptom "choice," as well as to the Phillips formulation. This result provides empirical support for the notion, perhaps best articulated by Shapiro (20), that the stylistic aspects of character, as well as the nature of instinctual conflicts, may play an important part in determining the form of manifest psychopathology.

In one major respect, the results of the present analysis fail to support the Phillips model. With the exception of the finding of longitudinal stability for the thought-action dimension, the analyses on sphere dominance generally produced findings which are contrary to theoretical prediction. Action dominance in childhood is apparently a favorable, rather than unfavorable, prognostic indicator, and affect dominance in childhood shows no relationship to paramorbid behavior style. One might speculate that the prognostic significance of sphere dominance is largely dependent upon the situational context in which it is measured. Thus, affect dominance in school behavior may signify serious emotional disturbance, while affect dominance in the psychiatric hospital setting may be indicative of a capacity for experiencing emotion and a potentiality for coping with emotional problems. Furthermore, as Phillips and Zigler (14) suggest, the experience of adaptive failure is more likely to precipitate an affective reaction of guilt and anxiety in those patients who have achieved a high degree of internalization of societal values. These patients would tend to have a higher level of achieved premorbid social competence, a greater potential for coping with psychosocial stresses, and hence would have a better prognosis for speedy and permanent recovery than patients who evidence little affective reactivity during the morbid phase of disorder. Similarly, action dominance in the school situation may be associated with an adaptive active approach to the accomplishment of age-appropriate social tasks, while action dominance in the psychiatric setting may simply reflect a deficiency in judgment and impulse control (as Phillips' theory presumes).

One set of apparently divergent findings from the present research should serve to call renewed attention to the methodological commonplace that interpretation of results must take due account of the nature of the sample and comparison groups. The results of the present analysis indicate that abnormally high aggressivity, rather than withdrawal, in childhood is the more crucial variable in predicting subsequent psychiatric hospitalization. However, within the group of children destined for future psychiatric hospitalization, withdrawal rather than externalization of aggression is the more ominous prognostic indicator. Thus, the parameters of any future mathematical model for prognosis may prove to be quite different, depending upon whether the aim is early identification of persons vulnerable to mental disorder, or differential prognosis within this vulnerability group.

Previous analyses of the childhood behavior of the schizophrenics in the present sample reveal that male preschizophrenics show a different pattern of behavioral deviation from their matched controls than do the female preschizophrenics (16, 21, 22). Generally, the male preschizophrenics are characterized by aggressiveness and disagreeableness, while the female preschizophrenics manifest a childhood pattern of interpersonal withdrawal and passivity. These findings suggest the need for separate analyses of premorbid behavior patterns for males and females. Furthermore, the unitary aspect of the Phillips model of psychopathology cannot be tested empirically in the absence of separate analyses for the major diagnostic groups. This series of subsample analyses is currently underway and, hopefully, will help to determine the extent to which the obtained relationships between these maturational and stylistic variables transcend traditional diagnostic classes.

FOOTNOTE

This paper is based upon a doctoral dissertation submitted to the Department of Psychology and Social Relations, Harvard University. The research reported here was supported by the Schizophrenic Research Program of the Supreme Council 33° A. A. Scottish-Rite, Northern Masonic Jurisdiction, by Public Health Service Research Grant MH-13280 from the National Institute of Mental Health, and by Office of Education Research Grant OEG-1-71-0021 (059). Additional support for this research was provided by NIMH predoctoral research fellowships MH-38253 and MH-51127, as well as National Science Foundation dissertation support grant GS-37679.

The authors gratefully acknowledge the research assistance of Roberta McGovern, Joy Corsi, Barbara Fryer, and Sally Ives. Special thanks are due Dr. George Grosser, Dr. Thomas Pugh, and former Commissioner Dr. Milton Greenblatt of the Massachusetts Department of Mental Health, and the public school authorities of "Maybury," for their invaluable cooperation in this research project. Dr. Robert Stolorow, Dr. Amy Lubensky, and Professor David McClelland were primarily responsible for developing the basic system for coding of the teacher's comments in the school records.

* Presented at the Eastern Psychiatric Research Association conference on *Psychiatric Problems of Childhood*, held January 31 to February 2, 1974, New York. Conference Program Chairman: Dr. D. V. Siva Sankar, Queens Children's Hospital, Bellerose, New York.

REFERENCES

1. Phillips, L., *Human Adaptation and Its Failures.* Academic Press, New York, (1968).

2. Mednick, S., and McNeil, T. *Psychol. Bull.* 70,681, (1968).

3. Roff, M., Ricks, D.F. *Life History Research in Psychopathology.* Edited by Roff, M. and Ricks, D.F. The University of Minnesota Press, Minneapolis, (1970).

4. Mednick, S.A., and Schulsinger, F. A longitudinal study of children with a high risk for schizophrenia: A preliminary report. In *Methods and Goals in Human Behavior Genetics.* Edited by Vandenberg, S. Academic Press, N.Y., (1965).

5. Nameche, G., Waring, M. and Ricks, D.F. *J. Nerv. Ment. Dis. 139,* 232, (1964).

6. Robins, L.N. *Deviant Children Grown Up.* Williams and Wilkins Company, Baltimore, (1966).

7. Lane, E.A., and Albee, G.W. *J. Abnorm. Soc. Psychol. 68,* 193, (1964).

8. Lane, E.A. and Albee, G.W. *Amer. J. Orthopsychiat. 35,* 747, (1965).

9. Pollack, M., Woerner, M. G., and Klein, D. F. A comparison of childhood characteristics of schizophrenics, personality disorders, and their siblings. In *Life History Research in Psychopathology.* Edited by Roff, M. and Ricks, D. F., The University of Minnesota Press, Minneapolis, (1970).

10. Barthell, C.N. and Holmes, D.A. *J. Abnorm. Psychol. 73,* 313, (1968).

11. Phillips, L., Broverman, I.K. and Zigler, E. *J. Abnorm. Psychol. 71,* 209, (1966).

12. Phillips, L. and Zigler, E. *J. Abnorm. Soc. Psychol. 63,* 137, (1961).

13. Zigler, E. and Phillips, L. *J. Abnorm. Soc. Psychol. 63,* 264, (1961).

14. Phillips, L. and Zigler, E. *J. Abnorm. Soc. Psychol. 68,* 381, (1964).

15. Phillips, L., Broverman, I.K. and Zigler, E. *J. Abnorm. Psychol. 73,* 306, (1968).

16. Watt, N.F., Stolorow, R.D., Lubensky, A.W. and McClelland, D.C., *Amer. J. Orthopsychiat. 40,*637,(1970).

17. Taube, C.A. *Characteristics of Patients in Mental Hospitals: United States-April-June 1963.* Public Health Service Publication No. 1000, Series 12-No. 3, Washington, D.C., (1965).

18. D'Andrade, R. *Amer. Anthropologist 67,* 215, (1965).

19. Conger, J.J. and Miller, W.C. *Personality, Social Class, And Delinquency.* John Wiley and Sons, New York, (1966).

20. Shapiro, D. *Neurotic Styles.* Basic Books, New York, (1965).

21. Watt, N.F. *J. Nerv. Ment. Dis. 155,* 42, (1972).

22. Watt, N.F. Childhood roots of schizophrenia. *J. Cons. Clin. Psychol.,* (in press).

MENTAL HEALTH IN CHILDREN, Volume I
Edited By D. V. Siva Sankar
Copyright © 1975 by
PJD Publications Ltd., Westbury, N.Y.

TOILET TRAINING, A MAJOR MILESTONE?
An inquiry into delayed language development
and its significance in the social history

Robert J. F. Stepney
Essex Child Development Center-Garden School
Belleville, New Jersey 07109

Early childhood development is dependent upon the successful completion of various milestones, such as, weaning, crawling and walking, toilet training, and the onset of speech. Delay or failure of one or more of these milestones can result in maturational problems for the child which become exacerbated by the time he enters nursery school or grade school.

For the seriously emotionally disturbed children, who are frequently excluded from public classes because of the severity of their emotional problems, the lack of language development would appear to be most crucial. The child who is expected to learn in school is expected to be able to communicate with his peers and mentors. Without speech, he is immediately thrust into a disadvantaged situation which requires an exhaustive and intensive effort on the part of many professionals within the educational system to, at first, understand the etiological factors at work and, second, to undertake a program to remediate the problem.

It is also generally accepted by most educators that a child with a pronounced disability or handicap will often manifest anxieties and fears that further add to his inability to respond to normal or appropriate learning situations in the classroom. This gives rise to a failure to learn, a syndrome that is characterized by a wide variety of symptoms along a broad spectrum of psychological aberrations. This study examined one specific area of difficulty which focused upon the relationship, if any, between the completion of toilet training, bowel control, and the growth of speech or language.

Psychoanalysts, in their study of young children, have pointed to the significance of early experiences if such experiences are surrounded by stress, catastrophic anxiety, and fear of loss, abandonment or death. Struggles between parents and children around the area of achieving 'acceptable' toilet habits may very well be devastatingly disruptive to normal developmental processes; the "damned pattern of toilet training", as it was described by the mother of a hospitalized youngster, who, herself, had suffered a psychotic breakdown.

It may, therefore, be speculated that, if the child fails to meet the needs of the parents in this important societal expectation, the child may, in turn, be denied the opportunity to express himself in his moments of fear and, ultimately, withdraw within his own frail psyche, electing to become mute. Such a condition brings us very close to the description of the autistic child-the child whose total sensory mechanism remains primitive, at an infantile level, usually socially unresponsive to the human beings in his grossly circumscribed world.

REVIEW OF THE LITERATURE

While the literature on early childhood development is extensive, that which deals with specific events or stages, such as toilet training, would appear to be sparse suggesting that more often than not a global or holistic view is taken of child growth. Spock (1), who is both a pediatrician and psychiatrist, has probably influenced vast numbers of parents in the western world in a most comprehensive work on child care. In a volume of almost six hundred pages, a few are devoted to toilet training. For the normal youngster, the third year is considered to be the year of success, the year of accomplishment. Interestingly, the author devotes a paragraph to the parents' feelings about toilet training:

"The subject of toilet training has been made more complex for parents by the studies of psychiatrists, psychologists, and pediatricians."

Laing (2) had written extensively about the quality of experience in interpersonal relationships. While so often educators and other professionals discuss, deliberate upon, and study behavior, frequently they do this in such a manner as to neglect the quality of the experience as an essential factor of the behavior.

"Some theories are more concerned with the interactions or transactions between people, without too much reference to the experience of the agents. Just as any theory that focuses on *experience* and neglects behavior can become very misleading, so theories that focus on behavior to the neglect of experience become unbalanced."

It would seem as if the literature-with a few major exceptions-has ignored the quality of experience in the very crucial area of toilet training.

Bettelheim (3) reminds us again that it was psychoanalysis that made us aware of...(how) "personality can depend on...the individual experiences around toilet training." He is at pains to point out the crucial nature of the experience of giving up one's own stool, perceived by the child as giving up a part of the self. The anxiety inherent in this situation is very much a personal matter. For some, where the self is well established, it is not threatening, while for others, particularly disturbed youngsters, giving up of the feces is a fearful experience. The author philosophizes about this as follows:

"The issue is important because of the underlying anxiety: if part of what was self (stools) can become non-self, then all of self may become non-self and disappear."

Here, Bettelheim is talking about the significance of the individuation experience, that is, differentiating between self and non-self or the first rudimentary steps to establish the individual psyche.

Child psychiatrists have been puzzled and confused by children thought not to be mentally retarded but showing a profound lag in the area of speech and social relatedness. Kanner (4), who described such youngsters, observed at the John Hopkins Hospital in Baltimore, felt quite strongly that, if language did not flourish by six or seven years of age, then the prognosis was exceedingly poor. Many of these children he diagnosed as autistic and Kanner's syndrome of autism has been the basis for much subsequent work in this perplexing area. He was also able to discern a pattern of parental characteristics which he thought might be significant in the child's development, although today this is considered to be less conclusive than it was first thought to be.

Lenneberg (5) argues in an excellent paper on language that its development is best understood in the context of developmental biology. There is a universality of language behavior found around the world and it is possible to show a correlation between motor development and language development. A child of two years is found by Lenneberg and others to have a repertoire of some fifty words.

> "Children have the capacity for language but do not use it, either because of peripheral handicaps, such as congenital deafness, or because of psychiatric disturbances, such as childhood schizophrenia..."

In summary, it will be helpful to look at the work of Sears, Maccoby and Levin (6) and the studies they made of toilet training as part of a wider view of child rearing in American culture. While the authors were not looking for a relationship between speech and bowel control, they were able to show that many children were "emotionally upset" by the demands of toilet training. Children who were started early (around five months) were found to have a greater difficulty, but the authors emphasize that other "cross-cultural" factors have to be considered, one important one being the mother's attitude towards sex.

> "Although early starts on training tended to require a longer period for completion than the late starts, the

mothers who started early and had a high sex anxiety pushed the task through to completion more rapidly than those with low sex anxiety who started later."

Where mothers had been found to be 'severe' in their approach to training, that is, a great deal of pressure was applied accompanied by scolding and punishment, than as many as 55% of the children displayed emotional upset. Freud's (7) speculations on the development of the anal personality have meaningful application here.

It is clear from studies of this nature that bowel control is a perfectly natural activity, common to many species, and that sphincter release is probably a regulatory activity which becomes inhibited when interfered with by the demands, or over-demands, of toilet training performance. In other words, in the learning process which, in some ways, is a maturational process, the concepts of a critical period, that is, the period when the development of the child is most fortuitously poised for successful completion of a given task (bowel control in this case) is a most important concept.

It would not be surprising then to find that the beginnings of speech, or rather, the moment of optimum speech development, has also its own critical period. Further, we might expect to find that both critical periods overlap and, therefore, the quality of early pattern of child training may have profound significance for all children but, especially, for those children found to be high risks, as it were, to severe emotional trauma.

REPORT ON INVESTIGATION OF TOILET TRAINING FOR THIRTY SERIOUSLY DISTURBED CHILDREN

The study, an investigation into the development of bowel control and the onset of speech in severely emotionally disturbed children, postulated that meaningful speech is delayed until bowel control is successfully achieved.

Bowel control is defined as the satisfactory acquisition of toilet habits resulting in the elimination of feces (bowel movements) at regular intervals in an acceptable manner and place as designated by the parents.

The onset of speech, or development of meaningful language, here means the use of sentences of five words or more in a typically normal manner found in the everyday practive of language useage as a means of verbal communication. This rules out the echolalic responses of some children first using vocal sounds, such as 'go to toilet'. However, 'Billy go to the toilet', or 'I want to go to the toilet' would be acceptable.

Seriously emotionally disturbed children in this study are those youngsters who have been prevented from attendance in a regular public school because of the nature of their disturbance. This is an educational classification ruling out the use of psychiatric nosology in a primary way but, nevertheless, including children diagnosed as psychotic, schizophrenic, autistic, neurologically impaired, etc., and any combination of these psychiatric categories. Intellectual functioning is not a consideration, as the intelligence range will be found to follow the normal distribution, but may be depressed by the severity of the mental or emotional handicap.

DISCUSSION OF FINDINGS

The major hypothesis is supported by the findings of the statistical data. That is, the group of thirty seriously emotionally disturbed children experienced a delay in the development, or onset, of meaningful speech. In addition, we found that seven children in this particular group failed to develop any speech as a tool of communication so essential to satisfactory educational growth (see Table 3). While for the control group, speech onset was developed earlier than for the seriously emotionally disturbed group, for both groups there appeared to be no significant difference in regard to age of bowel control completion.

It is not possible to isolate the factors determining the cause of speech failure for the seven seriously disturbed children. Indeed, the study was not attempting to do this, but only to investigate the relationship, if any, between the two all-important milestones of toilet training and speech development.

As a delay in speech development for the seriously disturbed group was found, with seven failing to master speech at all, then a discussion of the meaning of these findings enters the realm of speculation to a large extent.

While the control group seemed to fair considerably better, in that all subjects developed speech without the same delay as the seriously disturbed group and perhaps independently of toilet training progress, one crucial consideration looms large. Palpably, both groups of children had the same parents, and presumably, the same social development. Variables such as divorce, death, or social mobility to name a few, are clearly beyond control but, conceivably, may have a profound effect upon a particular child of either group.

The nature of the social contract between mother and infant is clearly a matter of importance, especially as mothers in our society respond to societal pressures; in other words, social mores are conditioned by prevailing attitudes and customs. The mothering pattern is very often an inherited pattern, from one generation to another, but since the advent of mass media and new forms of mass communication, old ways are probably breaking down and new attitudes and practices are being adopted.

What is certain is the fact that the social environment for the child is of primary importance. As Winnicott (8) has pointed out:

> "In the case of any individual, at the start of the process of emotional development, there are three things: at one extreme, there is heredity; at the other extreme, there is the environment; and in the middle, is the individual living and defending and growing."

The author goes on to describe a psychotic breakdown as 'the reversal of the maturational processes of earliest infancy'. It becomes clear then that an infant, unknowingly to the parents, is having difficulty from any of the three areas; heredity, environment, or within the self (or the internal environment) and may be unable to respond healthily to demands such as toilet training. This results in a distorting relationship in the social contract. Where the parents' original inclination was innocently poised and harmlessly projected towards the infant, a new and frustrating element enters, gratification in the

Table I

Sub. No.	Age	T.T. Cpd.	Speech Dvpd.
1	6.2	2.	4.
2	10.2	4.	6.
3	5.6	7.	-
4	8.6	4.	5.
5	8.11	7.	-
6	6.8	5.	5.
7	5.6	5.	4.
8	8.7	6.	-
9	20.0	2.	2.
10	5.11	5.	-
11	11.10	4.	4.
12	10.3	3.	5.
13	11.7	7.	2.
14	10.6	5.	-
15	9.6	9.	2
16	10.10	4.	4.
17	13.8	2.	2.
18	6.6	3.	-
19	6.3	3.	3.
20	13.5	1.	2.
21	8.8	5.	4.
22	7.1	3.	4.
23	8.3	5.	5.
24	15.8	5.	5.
25	6.2	3.	3.
26	18.3	3.	13
27	5.3	5.	3.
28	8.6	4.	5.
29	9.2	3.	3.
30	8.0	5.	-

N = 30

Above table shows age of toilet training completed and speech developed for thirty seriously emotionally disturbed children.

Mean age for toilet training was 4.3 years.

Mean age for the 23 subjects who did develop speech was 4.1 years.

Table II

Sub. No.	Age	T.T. Cmpd.	Speech Dvpd.
1	3.0	2.	5.
2	8.5	3.	4.
3	8.9	2.	3.
4	10.4	2.	2.
5	7.0	2.	2.
6	10.1	2.	2.
7	7.10	3.	2.
8	6.6	3.	2.
9	24.0	2.	2.
10	7.0	3.	2.
11	10.4	2.	1.
12	19.6	3.	2.
13	9.8	3.	2.
14	8.0	4.	3.
15	14.3	2.	2.
16	8.8	2.	1.
17	8.0	3.	2.
18	4.1	2.	2.
19	10.5	3.	2.
20	10.8	2.	2.
21	6.9	3.	2.
22	6.0	3.	3.
23	4.9	2.	2.
24	13.3	3.	3.
25	10.5	3.	2.
26	23.4	3.	2.
27	22.7	2.	2.
28	4.2	2.	1.
29	5.3	2.	2.
30	13.11	2.	2.

N = 30

Above table shows age of toilet training and speech developed for thirty children, siblings of group in Table I and considered to be normal.

Mean age for toilet training was 3.5 years. Mean age for speech development was 3.3 years.

All developed speech consequent with or a little earlier than toilet training was completed.

Table III

Subject Number	Age	Toilet Training Completed	Speech Developed
*			
3	5.6	7	0.
5	8.11	7	0.
8	8.7	6	0.
10	5.11	5	0.
14	10.6	5	0.
18	6.6	3	0.
30	8.0	5	0.
	Mean	5.4	0.

*female

Above table shows those emotionally disturbed children who failed to develop any speech.

Six males - representing 20% of group. One female - representing 3.3% of group.

Mean age of completing toilet training was 5.4 years, whereas the mean for control group was 3.5 years or, as Spock suggests, the third year is the year of success.

Table IV

	First Born	Last Born	Middle Child
Group A (subject)	14 (47%)	11 (37%)	5 (16%)
Group B (control)	6 (20%)	9 (30%)	15 (50%)

N = 30 in each group.

The above table shows the ordinal position of the child for both the severely emotionally disturbed group and the control group of siblings.

mothering role diminishes and perhaps ceases for both child and mother. The environment no longer facilitates, the maturational process halts or slows down, and the infant fails to thrive or live up to expectations. With this developmental, biological constriction, the way is paved for both emotional and organic upheaval, the one being involved in the other, as the concept of psychosomatic symptoms are often manifested.

While the findings suggest that, for some severely emotionally disturbed children, the onset of speech may be related to successful achievement of earlier milestones-particularly bowel control-it does not follow that we have discovered a causal relationship. Palpably, the infant organism is subjected to a multiplicity of significant experiences and the task of extrapolating the crucial ones, that is, isolating the chain of cause and effect, is beyond our present state of knowledge. We do know, however, that good preventive social medicine for the pre-school child is only available for the few who can afford it. Even in such cases as these, pediatric knowledge leaves much to be desired. One has only to be involved in the social history-taking function, as a psychiatric social worker, to learn from parents of the bewildering and, often contradictory, advice offered to them when they have realistically concerned themselves with attempting to discover what ails their emotionally disturbed child. While it is true that parents pursue their search for information to extreme lengths, often because of their overwhelming anxiety, the state of their perplexity is enhanced by professional misinformation. Very few professionals appear able to acknowledge their own ignorance concerning severe states of mental illness in children.

Unfortunately, public schools become involved in the situation much too late and even those infants who are fortunate enough to be enrolled in nursery schools or similar preschool programs may go undetected or denied service because of being unable to meet certain prescribed criteria for admission, such as bowel control and other self-care functions.

SOME BROADER SOCIAL IMPLICATIONS

While there have been some isolated attempts to set up services for severely disturbed pre-school age children, there

has been no wide provision or general application of appropriate
mental health care for infants.   Most child guidance clinics
serve school age children, while schools have resisted accepting
children before their fifth birthday. This has resulted in poor
detection of children at risk, and usually delayed detection until
after unsuccessful attempts to adjust to the demands of school
life and work.

It is common knowledge that mental health services have
been woefully inadequate, and demonstrably ill-financed, while
frequent criticism of such services invariably fails to take into
account the economic climate which allows poorly staffed
services to grapple with a plethora of patients.

In New Jersey, especially, such services have been
dismally supported and, following a recent American Psychiatric Association statewide hearing which reported-as a
major reccommendation-the need for a commissioner of mental
health, the public reception of this, as represented by the press,
seems to be negative or, at least, ambivalent.   Economic
stringency is always the response to those urging implemen-
tation of new services.   Economic stringency is, itself, an
administrative disease process resulting from the folly of not
reordering priorities which will enhance human survival rather
than destroy it. The economic problem, the ecological problem
and the provision of social services are all related and must
command an integrated approach to a solution.

At the community level, all children should have access
to proficient health services with kindergarten enrollment
available, alongside counselling and therapeutic services geared
to the needs of inexperienced mothers and fathers. Preventive
services-rarely tried-can be made to succeed and, thereby,
avoid the costly provision of rescue or rehabilitative services
which, currently, are creaking under the pressure of human
demand.

An extensive study by Hollingshead and Redlich (9)
dwelt at great length on the provision of mental health services
over a decade ago, much of their findings remain relevant
today:

"Our scientific knowledge is rapidly increasing
and shifting emphasis on our ideas about mental illness.

Theories which were considered true and accepted yesterday are disproved today and forgotten tomorrow. Solution of the mental health problem is one of the great challenges of our time. Is our society ready to meet this challenge?"

It would seem as if the schools have enrolled a new generation of children, but the challenge has not yet been met.

REFERENCES

1. Spock, Benjamin, *Baby and Child Care.* Pocket Books, N.Y. p. 248, (1960).

2. Laing, R.D. *The Politics of Experience and The Bird of Paradise.* Penquin Books, London, p.42, (1967).

3. Bettelheim, B. *The Empty Fortress, Infantile Autism and The Birth of The Self.* The Free Press, New York,p.34 (1967).

4. Kanner, L. *Child Psychiatry.* Chas. C. Thomas. Illinois, (1957).

5. Lenneberg, E.H. *Annual Progress in Child Psychiatry and Development.* Brunner-Mazel, New York, (1970)

6. Sears, R.R., Maccoby, E.E. and Levin, H. *Patterns of Child Rearing.* Harper & Row, New York, p. 112, (1957).

7. Freud, S. *Character and Anal Erotism.* Collected Papers. Vol. II, Hogarth Press, London, 1924.

8. Winnicott, D.W. *The Maturational Processes and the Facilitating Environment.* International Universities Press, New York, p. 137, (1965).

9. Hollingshead, A.B. and Redlich, F.C. *Social Class and Mental Illness, A Community Study.* John Wiley & Sons, Inc., New York, p. 380, (1958).

MENTAL HEALTH IN CHILDREN, Volume I
Edited By D. V. Siva Sankar
Copyright © 1975 by
PJD Publications Ltd., Westbury, N.Y.

THE RECOGNITION OF UNDETECTED MENTAL ILLNESS IN SOCIAL AGENCIES

Adelaide S. Hulse and Francis P. Kehoe

Diocese of Long Island, Jamaica, N.Y. 11435

Schizophrenia has been described as psychiatry's number one riddle. It is the most prevalent and incapacitating of the major mental illnesses and recently it was suggested that the incidence of schizophrenia may figure prominently among the causes of social turbulence and disorder (1).

The greatest problem involved in the treatment of schizophrenia is the lack of skill in diagnosing this illness. While it is generally accepted that the earlier in the course of the illness the patient receives treatment, the more favorable the prognosis. Often schizophrenia goes unrecognized until florid symptomatology is displayed. Often the manifestation of problems in social and interpersonal areas cause schizophrenics first to seek help in a social agency.

Family agencies serve as a place where all kinds of problems are presented and sorted out, referrals to other more appropriate services are made and services on a wide range of problems by staff members are provided. Essentially family agencies differ from mental health clinics in that the former employ primarily social workers and offer as a basic service *counsel on interpersonal relationships* in family, child and marital problems. It is known that in the process of resolving environmental problems, emotional disturbances are often found to be contributing factors. Many people may be more willing to accept assistance when they see the problem arising from environment or from family relationships than they would be to seek service from a designated "psychiatric" agency.

Theoretically, when persons with mental illness such as schizophrenia *are recognized* family agencies serve as a bridge to their reaching the appropriate medical and psychiatric facility. The crucial issue being the *early* recognition of such persons, particularly adolescents, so they may as quickly as possible enter the most appropriate treatment facility. However, a recent study reveals there is little contact, much less collaboration between family agencies and mental health clinics (2), mutual isolation being the rule.

The remainder of this paper will describe the innovative efforts developed by one particular family agency and the startlingly high incidence of previously undetected schizophrenia found throughout the caseload especially adolescents.

Based on this agency's experience great savings in anguish, time and financial cost for both the counselled and the counsellor are suggested.

The Youth Consultation Service, Diocese of Long Island is an Episcopal Church related, voluntary social agency founded in 1919, serving children, youth and their family. As in many such agencies insufficient funding to meet community needs have been a chronic problem.

Historically it was agency policy under advisement of the psychiatric consultant to refer any patient diagnosed as schizophrenic to a psychiatric setting. The staff at that time, however, felt the caseload contained few schizophrenics. Those recognized were usually seriously impaired and had often had toured the various mental health facilities. They were sources of much staff frustration as were the number of persons seen over a length of time with no improvement, while perplexing the staff regarding their appropriate diagnostic and treatment considerations. In past staff could not determine with any client the problem to be dealt with.

In exploration of various ways to improve staff acuity in diagnosis we learned about the Hoffer-Osmond Diagnostic Test used to uncover schizophrenia through a series of cards relevant to the patient's perception of how he views the world by answering true or false. The authors felt strongly by asking the appropriate questions (the cards), determination could be made of the presence of the schizophrenic illness. Osmond said "we invite the patient to give us a window on his or her experience to increase our joint understanding of his or her affairs."

The test consists of 145 cards covering perceptions of all the senses: visual-auditory; tactile; time taste; olfactory; thought and feelings.

As the staff began its use, we became both intrigued and skeptical. We were not easily persuaded that we could have such a high incidence of the illness on our caseload. We found by its use we became more comfortable in relating with the patient to his perceptual world.

It was not our intention to try to prove or disprove the reliability of the testing instrument. We knew of the extensive research on its usefulness and reliability. Our project was designed to supplement the workers clinical assessment to serve as a guideline for deciding which clients should be referred to appropriate psychiatric resources for medical confirmation of the illness.

PROJECT:

For eight months (1968-1969) we made extensive use of the H.O.D. as part of our initial evaluation of new applicants for service. The focus was on our adolescent population.

The patient was given the test in a private office, instructed to read each card and answer it by placing it in either the true or false box. When the test was completed, the patient was asked to bring both boxes to the worker's office. Prior to scoring each true answer was checked with the patient to be sure no external or situational events might realistically account for the response. The technique led to enhancing the worker-patient relationship as they both gained a common understanding of how the patient viewed his problem. Staff scored the test in order to familiarize themselves with the patient's choice of response as well as a check on reading ability not always known at the point of referral.

Interestingly those teenagers who obviously were not schizophrenic seemed delighted in taking the test. This was significant in view of the staffs' fear such a test might turn off the teenager from accepting service. Only one refused to take the test.

At the conclusion of the study approximately 30% of referrals based on the H.O.D. scores had a high probability of schizophrenia, this as compared to our former contention that we served few schizophrenics.

Those with these scores were urged to accept immediate referral to a variety of psychiatric resources in the community. Rarely did subsequent medical confirmation disagree with the conclusion reached from the H.O.D. screening.

CONCLUSION:

Our experience in the main substantiated the valuable use of the H.O.D. as an economic tool both in cutting administrative costs and saving staff time enabling the worker to screen those persons more properly referred to a medical clinic. More families could be served, a high risk population (adolescents) could promptly reach medical service and be aware of the basis of their distress and dysfunctioning.

FURTHER USES:

Based on our experience we have firm conviction that the H.O.D. can be useful for early detection of schizophrenia in similar client populations and that the incidence of schizophrenia would be equal to or higher than our findings.

Borderline cases would be uncovered.

Davidman (3) in a brief, informal paper described the high incidence of undiagnosed and unreported schizophrenia found in a study of prisoners incarcerated in New York City. This incidence was far greater than generally perceived. The H.O.D. would afford an excellent screening tool for this population.

Use of the H.O.D. by high school and college personnel especially for those evidencing learning problems, decreased school performance, disruptive behavior and/or depression would serve as a valuable detection tool.

We submit routine screening of social populations as foster case, public welfare, reception centers, drug programs, Family Court, job-training, maternity shelters would prove eye-opening and have great social planning and treatment implications.

We reiterate the H.O.D. is particularly invaluable to social workers, as well as fellow partners in the mental health field such as physicians, nurses, clergy and para-professionals in allied fields by which much can be learned of the nature of schizophrenia.

REFERENCES:

1. Turner, F.J. In *Differential Diagnosis and Treatment in Social Work*. The Free Press, New York, (1969).
2. Hill, W., Lehmann, J., and Slotkin, E. In *Family Service Agencies and Mental Health Clinics*. Family Service Association of America, New York, (1971).
3. Davidman, H. The Problem of Undiagnosed Schizophrenias in Prisoners. In *Schizophrenia: Current Concepts and Research*. Edited by D.V.S. Sankar, P.J.D. Publ., Westbury, New York, (1969).

MENTAL HEALTH IN CHILDREN, Volume I
Edited By D. V. Siva Sankar
Copyright © 1975 by
PJD Publications Ltd., Westbury, N.Y.

CHILDREN'S BEHAVIOR DISORDERS AS PRODUCTS OF FAMILY MILIEU

Richard L. Jenkins

State Psychopathic Hospital, Iowa City, Iowa

Although it is axiomatic that human character is deeply influenced by parents and by the family milieu, and although people are very widely ready--indeed often too ready--to blame parents for the misbehavior or maladjustment of their children, yet there seems in general surprisingly little professional understanding of the relationships between particular kinds of family milieu and particular kinds of behavior problems in children. In judging parental shortcomings, people in general have been more willing to condemn, than to study, to understand, or to help. There has been little or no recognition of *specificity* of relationships between particular types of family milieu and particular types of behavior disorders.

The behavior problems children show are understandable efforts, albeit faulty efforts, to cope with their environment. Particular behavior disorders relate themselves statistically to particualr kinds of environment, especially to the family milieu of developing children.

Parenthood is an extremely complex matter. It is possible, however, to describe in a broad way certain functions which are a necessary part of any successful parenthood for the human child.

The first and most essential of these functions is providing security for the continuance of the child's life. This involves providing food and drink, warmth and protection from the weather and other stresses and dangers. The assurance of such continuing protection is communicated to the child by rocking, cooing, cuddling, and other methods of the nursery which from time immemorial have been used to reassure infants and convey parental interest.

Without some parental source of security the human infant cannot survive. Sometimes parental care is adequate for the survival but inadequate for any reasonable degree of emotional security. It is from this group that our most fearful children, our chronic runaways, typically come. Lacking the courage to stand and meet life, they become the undependable fringers of the juvenile gang, the punks of more aggressive delinquents, often trading sexual submissiveness for some measure or hope of protection, or some small element of material gain.

What would predispose an adolescent toward fear? What more than an early lack of confidence or basis for confidence in the continued care of his parents? For without the care of parents persons, the young child will die. People instinctively understand the response of running away. One runs away from danger, from threat, from that which is unbearably unpleasant. Yet, people often do not understand how particular types of family background contribute to the *runaway reaction*. The backgrounds which do so are those which enhance insecurity and minimize self-confidence. As one might expect the backgrounds of the children who chronically run away are conspicuously filled with elements which predispose toward insecurity and fear. Compared with other delinquent children, runaway children show a significantly higher incidence of illegitimacy, of being unwanted children, of gross parental rejection, and institutional and foster home placement.

These children do not have confidence in their parents nor good relations with their parents, and show this, not only by running away, but by stealing in the home. Group delinquents seldom steal in the home. Stealing in the home is characteristic of the runaway children, and is often a preparation for running away. While the stealing of group delinquents is often aggressive, the stealing of runaway children is nearly always furtive. Emotional immaturity, apathy and seclusiveness are all disproportionately common in these children. The environment has afforded little opportunity for healthy personality growth.

Girls are more prone to the runaway reaction than to other forms of delinquent behavior. This behavior of course may represent an effort to realize, in actual life, daydreams of escape from the confining bonds of childhood into the freedom of adult status by running away to be rescued by an adult male sexual partner.

Childhood experience contributing to insecurity and fear predisposes toward the runaway reaction.

Beyond providing some basic security, the process of mothering normally develops in the child a capacity for empathy, for *feeling with* others.

The empathic person gets a lift from the joy or pleasure or happiness of another, and feels a sympathy for unhappiness or misfortune of another. Empathy, and sympathy, which is a special form of empathy, are sharing experiences. One cannot learn to extend them *to* others without first having experienced them as extended *by* others. It is necessary to learn first a measure of emotional resonance with a person in a more or less parental role. Then the relation can be extended to others in different roles. However, the capacity for feeling with others is normally learned in early childhood and depends upon the development of that kind and degree of emotional rapport which begins in a parent-child relationship extending gradually into the child-parent relationship.

The care of the infant and young child usually falls to the mother and is commonly called mothering, regardless of who carries out the function. If the mother person, whether by reason of unwilling motherhood or otherwise, lacks capacity or disposition for rapport with the child, this matter of empathy is not learned, or is learned very inadequately in early life. The result is an egocentric individual unconcerned with the rights or feelings of others.

Without a good experience in sharing joys with a mother figure and having sorrows and hurts soothed away, a child never develops the capacity to share feelings with others, and the result is a hostile personality, usually aggressive when he dares to be. The typical background of such children is one of some parental rejection, although not as severe and undiluted rejection as is typical of the chronic runaway. Further more, this rejection is often partially compensated by some parental overprotection.

Morality begins with loyalty, usually initially loyalty to a parent person. These children fail to develop loyalty, or at least fail to develop it to a normal degree. Some totally fail to develop it and consequently are without morality and without conscience.

The result is a person who feels hostile and has the courage to show it. He may take it out on younger children, or on animals. He is inclined to be cruel. This kind of family milieu is particularly likely to give rise to the *unsocialized aggressive reaction*. Of course inconsistency in the parents, and in particular the failure of parents to set limits for the hostile child contributes enormously to the problem. These children are particularly disposed toward quarrelsomeness, violence, vengefulness, and destructiveness.

Another type of reaction, different in its cause but shading into the foregoing, is that of the spoiled or overindulged child. Here the mother has met the child's physical and emotional needs but has not had the firmness or the courage to set reasonable limits. These children are often charming and outgoing, until crossed. I believe that the type of parental management which contributes to this type of problem was exemplified by a Kentucky mountain mother who was taken to task by a public health nurse for breast nursing her son so long. The mother explained, "Well, I did try to wean him two or three times, but when I do he swears at me so much I give in to him."

Childhood experience which fails to develop empathy and loyalty yet does develop or encourage a measure of self-confidence predisposes toward the development of the unsocialized aggressive reaction.

In some contrast with the foregoing are the children who show the *overanxious reaction*. These are the sensitive, worrysome children, chronically anxious, crying easily, predisposed to frequent nightmares and other sleep disturbances. These are most typically children in upwardly mobile, middle class, educationally amibitious families. These children have typically not been given a warm acceptance for simply being a member of the family. They are expected, by their behavior and achievement, to reflect credit on the standing of the family and so to earn their status in the family. They come to feel that their acceptance and standing in the family is conditional upon good behavior and a good report card. This creates conflict and anxiety--conflict between the perfectly natural desire to follow their own wishes, and the sense of obligation to do well scholastically, with anxiety about examinations and grades. Other common and obvious contributing factors are illness in the child and anxieties in the mother. The infantilizing, overprotective mother is particularly frequent.

These children have developed the pattern of seeking to insure parental favor and parental protection by being very good children, by observing parental prohibitions and parental demands.

Childhood experience in which parental acceptance is or seems to the child to be dependent upon adherence to exacting parental standards predisposes toward the overanxious reaction.

Although most of the overanxious children are boys, the preponderance of boys (about 2 out of 3) is very significantly less than in any of the other behavioral groups or in the clinic population at large.

There is still another behavior disorder with a characteristic background on another dimension--the *group delinquent reaction.* The great majority of those who show this reaction are boys. These adolescents typically may be considered more psychiatrically normal than any of the foregoing groups, for the problem is less of a psychiatric problem and more of a social problem than any of the foregoing.

The group delinquent reaction is a reaction of group rebellion against the established order of society, expressed in group delinquent activity, stealing, and truancy from school.

The group delinquent reaction is of course the product of the delinquency are, typically the impoverished area, on the wrong side of the railroad tracks. The residents of these areas, by reason of poverty, get the fewest of the material benefits of our culture, and are most likely to regard or experience the police as a foreign, aggressive force. Persons living in such areas are naturally likely to feel that they have the least to gain by conformity with the law, and the most to gain by violating it.

The adolescent who shows the group delinquent reaction typically had adequate mothering and acceptance as a young child, which typically rendered him capable of empathy, loyalty, and social exchange. He grew up in a large family in a crowded household, most typically without any adequate paternal direction. His father is most likely to be dead, to have deserted his family, or to be an alcoholic.

Under these circumstances, the boy leaves his crowded home to play on the street. He picks some older street habitue as his masculine model. He becomes a member of a street gang which becomes a delinquent gang by a natural process of growth. His meaningful loyalties are to other members of the juvenile gang.

Childhood experience in which a boy has adequate mothering and lacks a satisfactory masculine pattern in the home predisposes toward the selection of a delinquent masculine pattern and toward the group delinquent reaction.

It is my impression that the *withdrawing reaction* is prone to occur when communication with others, and particularly a parent, is grossly unsatisfying to a child. The verification of this hypothesis will depend on more adequate data than we have acquired.

The foregoing patterns of family milieu were found by looking at the families of particular types of behavior disorders. If we look at the typical social class differences of American families, we find that differences of social class have more effect upon adult behavior and specifically upon parental behavior than they do upon child behavior.

In a study of 1500 case records of children examined at the Illinois Institute for Juvenile Research in Chicago, we compared three hundred and two children who clearly came from "middle class" backgrounds with the remainder, who were for the most part, at lower economic and educational levels.

These comparisons clearly brought our contrasts in the families and the clinic population as a whole.

In the middle class group, referral to the clinic was by parents or a physician, not by a social agency or a school. Race tended to be white, the families were disproportionately of Protestant or Jewish religion. The principal wage earner was a professional, or a proprietor, manager, foreman, or craftsman. The pregnancy was planned. Marital maladjustment was relatively infrequent. The social worker and psychiatrist were both likely to see the mother as overly ambitious, as controlling, rigid, and as pushing the child toward too early responsibility. The father was seen as tending in these same directions. Overt rejection of the child by either parents was exceptional. In intelligence tests the child tended to test above average rather than below average and his interest in the tests tended to be focused, sustained, and goal-directed. After the examination the mother was likely to be referred for treatment at the I.J.R.

There was no type of problem characteristic of the child from the middle class home, but certain types of problems were conspicuously infrequent. Stealing, lying, truancy from school, and bullying were relatively very infrequent, as was hostile disobedience. However, these children were described as submissive to their parents less often than the remaining children were.

We made a parallel study of another group of 265 children who clearly came from impoverished family backgrounds and contrasted these with the cases not classified as coming from impoverished backgrounds.

These children were more likely than the remaining children to be black and Protestant. Referral was typically by the social agency. The prinicpal wage-earner was likely to be an operative or kindred worker. Probably because economic deprivation rather than home conflict was a factor in the selection of these cases, marital maladjustment was less frequent in this group than in the remaining clinic population. The social worker typically saw the mother as having reasonably wholesome attitudes toward the child, as not being controlling, rigid, nor critical, depreciative and as not pushing toward too early responsibility. The father also was considered to have reasonably wholesome attitudes and conflict between the parents about child rearing was not usual. Mental health problems were significantly less frequent with these parents than with the clinic average. In the psychiatrists' judgement there was some tendency for these mothers to be overprotective and infantilizing. They were not punitive nor critical, depreciative, but there was some lack of consistency. These children tended on intelligence tests to do less well than the average.

Speech defects or lack of speech were significantly more common in this group of children than in the clinic average. The children tended to be judged immature and to have difficulty in separating from the mother. Sex problems and hostile disobedience were a little less common than with the remaining children.

All in all, our efforts to compare the types of behavior problems developed by children of different social classes did not yield much. Apparently, there are no conspicuous differences, in the effect upon the child, of the way families of middle class and working class background meet children's needs, nor are there conspicuous differences with impoverished families.

SUMMARY
In summary our studies indicate that:

1. Childhood experience contributing to insecurity and fear predisposes toward the runaway reaction.
2. Childhood experience which fails to develop empathy and loyalty yet does develop or encourage a measure of self-confidence predisposes toward the development of the unsocialized aggressive reaction.
3. Childhood experience in which parental acceptance is or seems to be dependent upon adherence to exacting parental standards predisposes toward the overanxious reaction.
4. Childhood experience in which a boy has adequate mothering and lacks a satisfactory masculine pattern in the home predisposes toward the selection of a delinquent masculine pattern and toward the group delinquent reaction.

In our studies, middle class status is associated with a relatively high incidence of maternal behavior rated by clinic personnel as overly ambitious, controlling, rigid, and pushing the child toward too early responsibility. It is also associated with a relatively low incidence of delinquent behavior in children.

Impoverished family status, on the other hand, is associated with a low incidence of the foregoing maternal attitudes, but a relatively high incidence of overprotective and infantilizing maternal behavior. The children tended to be immature and to have difficulty in separating from the mother.

The influence of social class on parental behavior is much more evident than its influence on child behavior.

REFERENCES

Hewitt, L., and Jenkins, R.L., *Fundamental Patterns of Maladjustment: The Dynamics of Their Origin* (Monograph). State of Illinois, Springfield (Ill.), (1946).

Jenkins, R.L. *Behavior Disorders of Childhood and Adolescence.* Charles C. Thomas, Springfield, Illinois. (1973).

Motivation and Frustration in Delinquency
------:*Am. J. Orthopsychiat. 27,* 528, (1957).

Problems of Treating Delinquents
-----:*Federal Probation, 22,* 27, (1958).

------: *Breaking Patterns of Defeat.* J. B. Lippincott, Philadelphia, (1954).

------: Delinquency as Failure and Delinquency as Attainment. Reprinted from *Illinois Twenty-sixth Annual Governor's Conference on Youth and Community Service,* (1957).

The Psychopathic or Antisocial Personality
------: *J. Nerv. Ment. Dis. 131,* 318, (1960).

------: Diagnoses, Dynamics and Treatment in Child Psychiatry. *Psychiat. Res. Rep.* No. 18, Am. Psychiat. Assoc. pp. 91-120, (1964).

------: Psychiatric Syndromes in Children and Their Relation to Family Background. *Am. J. Orthopsychiat. 36,* 450 (1966). Reprinted (Second ed.) in *Readings in the Psychology of Adjustment* (ed. by Leon Gorlow and Walter Katkovsky), McGraw-Hill, New York, (1968).

------: The Varieties of Adolescent Behavioral Problems and Family Dynamics, Adolescent Psychiatry (Proceedings of a conference held at Douglas Hospital, Montreal, Quebec, June 20, 1967(. Ed. by S. J. Shamsie, Schering Corp., (1968).

------: Classification of Behavior Problems of Children. *Am. J. Psychiat.*, *125*, 1032, (1969). Reprinted (Second ed.) in *Readings in Human Development* (ed. by Harold W. Bernard and Wesley C. Huckins). Allyn and Bacon, Boston.

------: The Varieties of Children's Behavior Problems and Family Dynamics. *Am J. Psychiat.* *124*, 1440, (1968). Reprinted (Second ed.) in *The child: A Book of readings* (ed. by Jerome Seidman). Holt, Rinehart and Winston, New York, pp. 149-155, (1969).

------: *Am. J. Psychiat.* *128*, 168, (1971).

Jenkins, R. L. and Boyer, A., Types of Delinquent Behavior and Background Factors. *Int. J. Soc. Psychiat.*, *14*, 65, (1968).

Jenkins, R.L., Gants, R., Shofi, T., and Fine, E., Interrupting the Family Cycle of Violence. *J. Iowa. med. Soc.*, *60*, 85, (1968).

Jenkins, R. L., and Glickman, S., Common Syndromes in Child Psychiatry. *Am. J. Orthopsychiat.* *16*, 244, (1946).

Jenkins, R. L., and Glickman, S. Patterns of Personality Organization Among Delinquents. *Nervous Child*, *6*, 329, (1947). Reprinted in *Readings in the Psychology of Adjustment* (ed. by Leon Gorlow and Walter Katkovsky). McGraw-Hill, New York, (1968).

Jenkins, R. L., and Hewitt, L., Types of Personality Structure Encountered in Child Guidance Clinics. *Am. J. Orthopsychiat.* *14*, 84, (1944).

Jenkins, R. L., NurEddin, E., and Shapiro, I., Childrens'Behavior Syndromes and Parental Responses. *Genet. Psychol. Monogr.*, *74*, 261, (1966).

Jenkins, R. L. and Stahle, G., The Runaway Reaction. A case Study, *J. Am. Acad. Child. Psychiat.* *11*, 294, (1972).

MENTAL HEALTH IN CHILDREN, Volume I
Edited By D. V. Siva Sankar
Copyright © 1975 by
PJD Publications Ltd., Westbury, N.Y.

RETHINKING CHILD AND
FAMILY TREATMENT

Leonard Hollander

C.M.D.N.J.-Rutgers Medical School

Piscataway, New Jersey 08854

In the struggle between child and family ideologies, stances tend to become fixed and polarized. Troublesome issues may remain unresolved, and communication between practitioners in these two fields cut off by mutual suspicions and formulary maneuvers. Adversaries tend to exaggerate incompatabilities, minimize similarities, and stereotype opponents and their work. The interests both groups hold in common are obscured in the heat of controversy (1,2).

This presentation aims to clarify concurrences and differences by a comparative approach from the viewpoint of a child psychiatrist.

To work with a family systems orientation, a change from the more traditional emphasis on the youngster, the child psychiatrist must be willing to modify his professional identity through training in new skills and the redeployment of old skills. He already uses his knowledge of developmental factors in children's lives, is skilled in utilizing play and fantasy techniques, and has advised and guided parents. These skills and experiences will continue to be useful in family therapy. In fact, the psychiatrist who is limited in knowledge and understanding of developmental problems, and uncomfortable in clinical approaches to children should work closely with child consultants to treat families with children, particularly when the youngster is designated as the patient.

The age-appropriateness of behavior, coping mechanisms, and defenses can be judged within the family context. Interpersonal factors contributing to retardation and distortions in development may be discovered through observations of the family roles children play and the transactions between family members (3,4,5,6).

Examination of the youngster's place in the family does not imply exclusion from consideration of individual features, such as variations in temperament, maturational lags, and other biologically related differences. The correlation of child characteristics and parental concerns is a familiar task to the child psychiatrist.

So is the giving of advice to be used outside the consultation meeting. Not as familiar is the shift in emphasis to change in parent-child relationships here and now in the family treatment session. The immediate availability of actual parent-child transactions, graphic and vivid samples, rather than parent-selected and described examples, leads to more effective on the spot moves and rapid information feedback to family members and therapist. Advice-giving is just one of a variety of strategies which can be designed to influence the family system.

Play and fantasy techniques foster communication between parents, children, and therapist, particularly at points of impasse in treatment. Parents can observe child play, use the child-therapist relationship as a new model, participate in sculpting, role playing, painting, and child play, discuss with the child wishes for changes in the family and ways to reach these goals, etc. The sharing of fantasies and the attention to imagination and play for adult as well as youth help release creative energies for change from habitual, fixed, dysfunctional patterns of relating. The promotion of play and fantasy facilitates spontaneity, helps the family rediscover potential for pleasure, and work out alternate solutions to problems.

Seeing the child individually can be a point of entry to family change. However, this is only one means of access the child psychiatrist can choose (7). One of his goals is to make the family more aware of the dysfunctional family system, rather than confirming their view of the youngster as the problem. Thus he may decide to meet with the whole family, or some of the subsystems, such as parents, or children.

Planning treatment strategies requires a comprehensive view of the family system. Redefinition in these terms may confront the child psychiatrist with troublesome issues he prefers not to consider. Some will feel the acute strain of efforts to integrate concepts which appear to be incompatible, or at least to use different vocabularies. Others will be able to encompass several languages of discourse and conceptual models for treatment.

Meetings with the family require observations of processes as well as individuals. The multiple exchanges cannot be fully noted by one observer. His observations can be supplemented by adding another professional and/or recording the session. Attempting a session alone with a large, or disorganized family, or one with many children can be an overwhelming experience.

Some child psychiatrists prefer to continue satisfactory one to one sessions with children, and do not want to treat families.

The special art of psychotherapy with the individual child is an important part of the child psychiatry training program, and will continue to be used in treatment sessions, even by those who treat families.

Another aspect the child psychiatrist may find troublesome has to do with whom he treats. The criteria for family as contrasted to individual treatment are neither adequate nor clear cut. The pressure to pick one modality of therapy prematurely *must* be resisted. Rather than pursuing one course of action, different decisions as to whom to see have to be made at different times. Making these decisions requires a tolerance for uncertainty and ambiguity. An analogous phenomenon in the physical sciences is represented by Heisenberg's indeterminacy or uncertainty principle (8).

Introductory statements relating to the policy of seeing the family conjointly, and the youngster and other members of the family separately when necessary, are often more acceptable to the family than recommendations for family treatment. The timing and manner of presentation of recommendations have to be worked out with an appreciation of the set of the family towards *child* treatment. Their child orientation is determined by unconscious needs and defenses, as well as customary ways of regarding the disturbed youngster as the focus of attention. This is re-enforced by the attitudes of referring sources, medical and non-medical.

The following vignettes illustrate these points:

(1) An 8½ year old girl was referred because she was "too bossy". She was described as a tomboy. She play acted she was a boy and pretended she had a penis. A 5½ year old sister, who had fears of dying, also wanted to be a boy. Father, 35, and mother, 33, ran a bridal shop. After initial evaluation, recommendations for further study of the family were rejected. Mother stated she wanted girls, was glad *she* was a *girl*. Father said, "We can't blame ourselves."

(2) A 6 year old boy was seen because of soiling, stubbornness, and stealing. He was the youngest of four children, with an 8 year old brother, a 12 year old sister, and a 16 year old effeminate brother. Both father 47, and mother 45, were depressed, showed little warmth, and kept a distance from each other. The 16 year old boy and the 6 year old boy were close to mother. The 8 year old boy and his 12 year old sister were close to father. Sleeping arrangements kept the parents in separate rooms, with the children. They differed on ways to bring them up. Father came alone to the final session although his wife had also been invited. Reasons for not continuing were given as 1. the problem is almost over, 2. his belief the soiling has to do with mental retardation, 3. seeing the family together might add to the 6 year old's inferiority problem, 4. his worry that the 16 year old might learn of his father's concern over his possible homosexuality, 5. psychiatrists betray confidences, 6. seeing the family makes it appear like the whole family has a problem when "it has nothing to do with us."

(3) A 7 year old boy's behavioral and school problems initiated his mother's request for a psychiatric interview. He was an overactive child, a bedwetter disturbed from sleep by nightmares. He fought with his 10 year old sister. She also had school problems, had difficulty expressing herself, and

was unhappy. A 13 year old sister was characterized as "bad tempered" (formerly a behavior problem), had reading difficulties. Mother, 35 was dyslexic as a child. She over-identified with all 3 of her children in terms of school problems. Mother requested a family interview. In the initial meeting father, 35, voiced his doubts about a family approach, which his wife had told him about on the way to the session. He wanted an individual evaluation of the boy. He called several days later for a second appointment for the family which they did not keep. What happened was that one of the children was not at home when they were ready to leave, and he and his wife had an argument. The family was then sent to the psychiatrist to whom they were originally referred. He saw the boy indi-vidually, the parents together, the 3 siblings together, and then the whole family. Next a five session contract was set, the goal being the functional restoration of a poorly operating family system. The following hours were marked by father's insistence on having his son seen (nightmares, bedwetting continued). He missed some appointments, and eventually voiced his concern that his wife would not be able to change her ways of relating to the family.

Two common elements in these situations are the stated purpose of having the youngster interviewed by the psychia-trist, and reluctance to pursue the family ramifications. In all three families, the parents wanted to prevent further exploration of marital relationships. Particular attention must be paid to such reluctance, since it may be a crucial factor in termination. The therapist who is skilled with children has the option of continuing to focus on the child or children in the family, a less anxiety provoking approach to the parents. As adviser to the parents, he may find that a trusting relationship built up in the interim allows parental exploration of their marital difficulties.

The next two cases are examples of a focus mainly on the child:

(1) Treatment was requested for a 9 year old girl described as hostile, disobedient to her stepmother, lying, and unhappy. Her mother died when she was 2½ years old, and her father remarried one year later. Father, 35, and stepmother, 30, had a 2½ year old and 6 month old daughter of their own. Step-

mother had less patience than her husband with the 9 year old. The 9 year old was seen on a weekly basis for a period of 3 months. Her erotic anticipations at the outset were handled by definition of the therapist's role and the function of therapy. Some time after therapy sessions were spent conferring with stepmother who brought her. Occasionally, stepmother and father were seen together. No major differences emerged between the parents. The stepmother's complaints about her stepdaughter diminished in the course of treatment, and in the end she said she probably was the problem and needed the help rather than her stepdaughter.

(2) An 11 year old boy in the 5th grade came because of unhappiness, anger, reluctance to do school work, and lack of friends. The third of four children (sisters 20, 14 and brother 7) he had three seizures between the ages of 1½ and 4. Father, 47, was a busy administrator. Mother, 43, a housewife and artist, was over anxious and over involved with this son. Parents differed in their views, mother stressing his disabilities, and father emphasizing his abilities. Mother's mother, a strong willed woman she resented, lived in the home.

School report was that he was of normal intelligence, and functioned well when motivated, but was unproductive otherwise. He had some gross motor difficulties, as well as fine motor incoordination. He gave various excuses at home and at school for not doing his work.

He was seen weekly for five months, with occasional parental conferences, particularly with mother who brought him. Individual sessions with the boy were characterized by formal conversation and avoidance by him of discussion of his problems. Recommendations at a parent conference following a home visit were that the boy stop coming, and that the parents return for guidance. The father was asked to become more involved (and his wife less involved) with the youngster. The next two visits occurred one year later, precipitated by his outburst of anger in school and at home (particularly at his mother) and his lack of productivity in school. Recommendations were that alternate residence plans be considered for mother's mother, a disturbing influence in the home, and that mother and father regard each other more as a husband and wife who need time for each other as well as themselves. Her obsessive preoccupation with her son continued and she began to criticize his teachers as unfair and demanding. Again, further meetings with the parents to work our their differences were recommended.

The case material has been presented to afford an opportunity to discuss a broad approach to the study of the youngster in his family. In an exchange of the experiences of both family and individual therapists, the emergence of new ideas not limited to the either/or dichotomy is anticipated. A re-examination of the assumptions we accept as "fact" is called for. We can rethink our practices both for the sake of scientific inquiry and in the interest of more efficient and more successful outcomes.

Treatment plans which are effective require flexibility, and openness to the use of techniques clinically determined by the needs of the situation, rather than rigidly labeled and fixed as *individial* or *family*. This approach allows the clinician to divide his time for individual members or parts of the family, as well as the whole family.

In charting the course of future inquiry, such questions as the following still remain:

(1)   When is conjoint family therapy necessary and appropriate?

(2)   On what grounds does the therapist select the members of the family he decides to see in a session?

(3)   Which goals of family therapy are relevant?

(4)   What alternate methods work as well or better?

(5)   If the family is not ready for conjoint approaches, should the parents be allowed to "write the prescription" in terms of separate individual help for the youngster and guidance for themselves?

(6)   Does the use of this prescription confirm the family's concept of the named patient as the one needing help and therefore, does this make more difficult the task of conjoint family therapy?

(7)   If such difficulty does arise, how could it have been avoided?

Summary:

Clinical considerations related to the transition from a child-focused area of work to a family systems viewpoint have been discussed. The changeover expands the child psychiatrist's professional skills and options in treatment. Further research on treatment outcome would help in choosing among these options. The benefits of closer collaboration between family and child clinicians and researchers outweigh the potential risks of ideological clashes.

REFERENCES

1. Hollander, L. *Child psychiatry versus family diagnosis and treatment.* Paper read at the annual meeting of the American Academy of Child Psychiatry, Ann Arbor, Michigan, (1967).

2. McDermott, J., Char, W. *The undeclared war between child and family therapy.* Paper read at the annual meeting of the American Academy of Child Psychiatry, Washington, D.C. (1973).

3. Rollins, N., Lord, J., Walsh, E., *et al.* Some roles children play in their families. *J. Amer. Acad. Child Psychiat. 12,* 511, (1973).

4. Framo, J. Symptoms from a family transactional viewpoint. Family therapy in transition. *Int. Psychiat. Clin. 7,* 125, (1970).

5. Hollander, L., Karp, E. Youth psychopathology and family process research. *Amer. J. Psychiat. 130,* 814, (1973).

6. Bermann, E. *Scapegoat.* U. Of Michigan Press, Ann Arbor, (1973).

7. Haley, J. Strategic Therapy when a child is presented as the problem. *J. Amer. Acad. Child Psychiat. 12,* 641, (1973).

8. Heisenberg, W. *Across the Frontiers.* Harper and Row,

9. Montalvo, B., Haley, J. In defense of child therapy. *Family Process 12,* 227, (1973).

MENTAL HEALTH IN CHILDREN, Volume I
Edited By D. V. Siva Sankar
Copyright © 1975 by
PJD Publications Ltd., Westbury, N.Y.

ECOLOGY IN CHILD DIAGNOSIS AND INTERVENTION: A THIRD DIMENSION

Don Shapiro
Queens College Educational Clinic, New York

The classroom is the setting of choice for studying a school-age child. While we have been groping our way back towards working with children in their natural group, the family, we may have been neglecting this natural setting, the classroom. The classroom which offers a child an environment for growth offers a third dimension to the child psychodiagnostician.

As a consultant to a teacher-training program at Queens College, I was guided by Caplan's model of levels of mental health consultation (1) as applied to psychological services in the schools by Meyers (3). I will present observations of individual children in open classrooms which illustrate an emphasis on each of four levels of intervention. I could not have known where to place this emphasis had I dealt only with the interaction of child and clinician in office. It was the third dimension, the ecological aspect of the classroom, which was crucial. I will also discuss two children seen in a clinic setting in order to specify some parameters of classroom observation.

Direct Service to the Child

Ernest had the benefit of fine teaching in a fine school--
but he wore a weird smile and behaved in a strange, sneaky
manner. He floated, never settling down to anything. Shortly
after I entered the room, the open-classroom coordinator
arrived and began working individually with Ernest. With her
intense energy and warmth, she could charm almost any child
(or adult) into following her. But there was no charming
Ernest; the weird smile was fixed on his face. I watched this
scene for a moment, then stationed myself at the opposite end
of the room. It took a long while, but finally Ernest approached
me.

"I locked my little brother in the bathroom once", he
began. "Oh you've probably done worse things than that",
I commented to him. And in the next ten minutes he cata-
logued a list of "worse things" that was truly quite horrible,
some of which he had undoubtedly done, others were perhaps
"imagined". In school, everyone had been too busy being kind
and helpful to believe his guilt. The burden was too much
for one little boy to carry alone. After his long list, he turned
from me abruptly and began to work purposefully in school
for the first time in years. He could begin to make some sense
out of reality once he had received feedback which supported
his own knowledge of himself.

The best, most concerned teachers often have the
greatest difficulty accepting the evil lurking in children's
hearts, but some adult had to accept this child's hostile feelings
and memories before he could seek more adaptive behaviors. It
is more likely that someone experienced with pathology will
grasp the possibility of such intensely violent feelings underlying a "strange" character structure.

Indirect Services, Focus on the Teacher's Interventions

I was invited to observe George, a six year old in an open-
corridor arrangement of several classrooms whose teachers and
student teaching internes worked together. Though it is better
to stay in the background to allow sufficient time for observation, in this instance immediate intervention was called for.
No sooner had I been introduced to the teachers, when I saw
little George race by, smash a huge block building a group of

children had been constructing, and race into another room. I mimicked George, racing right after him. When he turned towards me with a gesture of surprise, I made a similar gesture. This was followed by a number of other gestures, mostly hostile, all of which I mimicked. This finally turned into an orderly game, which first one and then another boy wanted to join.

The teachers had reported that George was unreachable, unpredictable, had no friends, could suddenly be destructive. They needed a demonstration of an immediate intervention when George was destructive. The crucial element of this intervention was the demonstration to George that I had the potential to be just like him, that he was not such a "different" kind of person, and that therefore he could be understood. He was then able to ritualize our intense gestures into an inviting game. I stayed with him, as his special person, for a few minutes. When he was about to squirt water from his mouth at some passing children, it was possible to tell him that he was supposed to keep the water in the sink--confident that he would do what was suggested. He now welcomed help in guiding his behavior.

Then it was lunch hour, time to meet with the staff. They shared their observations of the intervention, as well as what they knew about George's past behavior. They began to discuss how a teacher might do what they had just seen a clinician do, and turned to the practical issue of making one teacher available to George as soon as he began to get into trouble. The teachers recognized the economy of devoting fifteen minutes to George while it was still possible to avert a crisis.

This kind of intervention must usually be modelled for teachers, but once they have seen how to become part of the special world of special children they can do so as long as the need remains. It is just as often a withdrawn child who requires this kind of help. Tom, for example, was a physically handicapped child who had just come to a regular school from a school for the handicapped. He lived and worked in a world all his own, it seemed, talking to no one but himself. He began to be the butt of cruel humor from the other children, but he was indifferent even to this. I went over to the table where Tom was diligently tracing books through transparent paper for no obvious reason. I picked up a copy of the same book and did precisely what he was doing. Once again this was a demonstration that he and I were the same kind of creature. He soon began to apply standards of relevance to the work he did, and finally to approach the teacher for help.

It is reasonable for teachers to demand that children be reasonable. With children who cannot meet that demand, teachers often need help in communicating their willingness to be helpful. Since reason is not effective, a clinician's understanding of the child's special difficulties and ways to resolve them may be necessary.

Focus on Teachers' Behavior

John was direct in his demand on his teachers. He reached for and talked about sex incessantly. The teacher favored strict prohibition, the student teacher interne favored permissiveness, and John remained an incorrigible little boy, tuned out--on work, on friends, on life. I had sat near John for just a few minutes, watching him "make out" with the interne, when he approached me to find out if I might be her lover. One could of course explain this situation with a description of his wild home life; I had heard all about that, but what was the teacher supposed to do? I listened intently while John began to express his terrifying fantasies: school burning down, walls crumbling, everyone killed, etc.

When it was time for the group to go to the lunchroom, John as usual demanded of the interne that she hold his hand and walk right out with him. I asked if he could wait a few minutes, instead of being first to go. He thought he could wait. Then the teacher insisted that he go without the interne. I asked the teacher and John if he might go with the last children in the group and wait in the lunchroom a few minutes for the interne to join him. Everyone agreed, and for the first time John left the room without holding the interne's hand.

John needed strict discipline, but it was the teacher's need to impose it all at once that was problematic. The teacher had to receive a small dose of discipline herself; that was the function of pressing her to permit the interne and John to be together in the lunchroom. This discipline was presented to the teacher in a flexible way that she could accept.

John also needed to feel human warmth, as the interne knew, for he was terrified of being overwhelmed by his cruel fantasy world--still, he would remain as terrified of human closeness as he was of distance until he could feel confident of his ability to protect himself to some extent. The interne, out of her own experience, could share the fear of loss of closeness. In fact this shared experience was strong enough to prevent her from helping John to move away to a safer distance. By increasing the distance for a brief period and then being close again, the interne could learn to build her tolerance for appropriate frustration through planning and anticipation.

The ability to measure the dosage of discipline as well as to plan in order to increase tolerance for frustration are essential for teachers. They are better able to relate to children when they themselves have experienced such measured discipline and purposeful frustration. This can be stated as a Golden Rule: Do unto teachers as you would have them do unto children.

Children have a remarkable propensity for finding adults' weak points. Among the large group of children to whom a teacher relates, it is almost inevitable that one child will bear down on at least one weakness to the extent that an outside clinician's consultation can be useful.

Focus on Changing School Structure

While it might seem that giving each child precisely what he needs requires enormous energy, the process is actually somewhat like learning to swim: once you are in tune with the water, swimming is easier than walking. But there are children like Annabelle for whom this analogy does not hold: something too basic has been left out. Where John had to be "weaned", so to speak, Annabelle had yet to be "nursed". She was no trouble in school, yet her teachers were disturbed that she should be so totally engaged in another realm. She gazed into the eyes of whoever was talking, the consuming gaze of the nursing infant. Nothing else mattered, nothing else existed.

The teacher was asked if there were other children like this in other classrooms; she invited her colleagues to join in discussion. They seemed to recognize this phenomenon as a regular, if rare, by-product of slum life. It was suggested that internes spend half an hour of quiet time alone each day with each of these children, who may never have had the luxury of undivided maternal attention in their home environment.

I had observed Annabelle from a distance, I had felt her gaze and smiled in return, without making any further approach. It is clear that what she needed was response but not initiative--she was still to fragile for that. One could hardly demand of "school" that it provide such a one-to-one relationship, but it is lucky for such children when their needs can be considered in school and when an attempt is made to meet them.

Every school has groups of children with needs that are not met by the ordinarily adequate classroom. When the school moves beyond identifying the "problem child" towards assuming the initiative for meeting the challenge, the system itself inevitably experiences growth.

Parameters

That third dimension of the classroom is not always helpful. Mary, for example, was quite happy in a class for the retarded--but at the age of six, she never said one word. While children may be "tested" too often apart from the classroom setting in which their problems are most apparent, Mary's difficulty was actually masked in school. In the natural classroom setting, I could not discover what the total absence of language was about.

In the more controlled privacy of the office, one could use graphic material to explore concept development. One could ascertain that she drew spontaneously, as children do in all cultures by the age of 2, but that she could imitate only her own patterns. She did develop "circular reactions" to her own work to the level of a three year old, with consistent, continuous patterns, not merely random motoric exercise (DiLeo).

One could also pay sufficient attention to the sounds she produced to note that they were beyond the level of her speech development. This suggests that Mary's was not a motoric problem, but rather that the vocal act had not been integrated with cortical organization to produce speech. And while there were no word combinations, no syntax or semantic, Mary's approach to intelligence test tasks suggested intellectual functioning at the 3.6 year level. It could then be said that neither intellectual deficit nor motoric deficit were the critical problems; it could also be said that hearing loss alone could not explain her inability to imitate others, nor could central damage alone explain the total absence of speech.

Now a program for training imitation of gesture, presented simultaneously with speech, could be devised for Mary. Her mixed central and peripheral aphasia with well-developed emotional and inter-personal growth required careful "two-dimensional" study. No classroom observations could have provided the confidence to prescribe interventions.

Similarly, Charlotte's wide range of emotional functioning required careful clinical assessment apart from the third dimension of the classroom. Charlotte could swing from total inattention to gay playfullness, from suspiciousness to stubborness, from depression to sadism. It would have been difficult to observe a sufficient sample of her diversity in one particular setting; she was too complex for that. Could one have discovered that the poised little girl who enters asking "What do I do here" can be very frightened by a slight unexpected noise--or that the impulsive girl who says abruptly "I'm going now" can become deeply depressed when she gets her own way?

It requires the isolation of a two-person clinical setting to distinguish Charlotte's "false-self" competency from underlying emptiness. In such a setting the clinician is free to respond with the feelings and behaviors that match immediate, rapidly shifting needs. It was small wonder that Charlotte's teachers, sensitive and inventive though they had been, had always been frustrated just when they thought they were making progress with her.

Summary

The classroom is a natural setting for psychodiagnostic observation and interaction with children. Only after such "ecological" observation and interaction can there be a three-dimensional approach to intervention, an approach which can achieve maximum effect with minimum effort. For then the optimum level of intervention becomes apparent. Examples have been presented of interventions at each of these four levels: direct service to the child; indirect service, focus on the teachers' interventions; focus on teachers' behavior; focus on changing school structure. Examples have also been presented of parameters in which the added clarity of a two-dimensional clinical approach justifies the sacrifice of the natural setting.

The ecological approach extends the growing interest in working with children in the natural group, the family, to working with children in the natural setting of the classroom. For professionals who work with children, it shifts the emphasis from regular clinic settings with occasional school involvement to regular classroom settings with occasional clinic involvement.

REFERENCES

Caplan, G. *The theory and practice of mental health consultation.* Basic Books, New York, (1970).

Di Leo, J.H. *Young children and their drawings.* Brunner/ Mazel, New York, (1970).

Meyers, J. *School Psychol. 11,* 5, (1973).

MENTAL HEALTH IN CHILDREN, Volume 1
Edited By D. V. Siva Sankar
Copyright © 1975 by
PJD Publications Ltd., Westbury, N.Y.

THE "MYTHMAKING" PROCESS
IN THE PRESCHOOL CHILD

Paul N. Graffagnino
Institute of Living
Hartford, Connecticut 06114

The purpose of this paper is to propose the consideration of the "mythmaking" process as a significant, active,
coping mechanism for the young child between the ages of
three and seven. Sandler and Nagera in their study on fantasizing in 1963 observed that in this age group there are
"many thoughts which occupy an intermediate position"
between fantasy (which has a defensive connotation) and
reality oriented thoughts (1).

The child at this age is a primitive ontologist, faced
with any number of exhilirating, as well as terrifying experiences. The mythmaking process is a common one in human
history. Indeed the young child is in an analogous position to
primitive man who tries to conceptualize difficult to under-

Dr. Graffagnino is Director of the Child Psychiatric
Services of the Institute of Living, 17 Essex Street, Hartford, Connecticut 06114, and Associate Clinical Professor of
Psychiatry, Division of Child Psychiatry, University
of Connecticut School of Medicine.

stand and frightening experiences by means of his limited range of prior knowlege and his prior cognitive abilities.

As a process, mythmaking has been studied extensively in the anthropological and social sciences, but relatively neglected in developmental psychology. Early psychoanalysts, for example, Freud, Abraham (2)*, Ferenczi (3), Reik (4), Jung (5), and Rank (6) were interested in myths and in their relationships to magic thinking in children, animism, and dreams. In *Totem and Taboo,* Freud noted: "An intellectual function in us demands the unification, coherence and comprehensibility of everything perceived and thought of and does not hesitate to construct a false connection, if, as a result of special circumstances, it cannot grasp the right one" (7).

Within the present century, studies by anthropologists and social scientists such as Levi-Strauss, Campbell (8), Kirk (9), Kluckholn (10), and others, have created a considerable body of knowledge on myth and the process of mythmaking. Henry Murray, the clinical psychologist, in 1960 attempted to correlate the anthropological and psychological thought on the subject of mythmaking (11). He pointed out the usefulness of the myth to primitive as well as to modern man. It is true that when a myth is surpassed by a more definitive truth or scientific fact, the myth no longer serves a purpose and can actually become a destructive force, as did the Nazi and Aryan myths in the 1930's.

Levi-Strauss embarked nearly twenty years ago upon the monumental task of trying to elucidate a science of mythololgy. In *The Raw and the Cooked,* he analyzed the content of almost two hundred myths of the Indians of Central Brazil. One of his conclusions is: "Myths signify the mind that evolves them, by making use of the world of which it is itself a part. Thus, there is simultaneous production of myths themselves by the mind that generates them and by the myths, an image of the world which is al-

*From Abraham, reference 2, p. 208: "The myth is a surviving fragment of the psychic life of the infancy of the race, whilst the dream is the myth of the individual."

ready inherent in the structure of the mind" (12). His studies also reveal the complicated interplay of creative and destructive forces in human societies as reflected in their myths.

The present paper then, will examine how the concept of mythmaking may be applied to the mental activities of the young child.

Definition: As Murray points out, one of the most useful definitions of mythmaking is that of Schorer: "Myths are instruments by which we continually struggle to make our experiences intelligible...A myth is a large, controlling image that gives philosophical meaning to the facts of ordinary life, that is, which has organizing value for experience. A mythology is a pantheon of such images, Without such images, experiences are chaotic, fragmentary and merely phenomenal" (13).

Types of mythmaking in young children: The preschool child probably creates an endless variety of myths. The following categories represent a preliminary attempt to examine the types of mythmaking in both normal and abnormal development.

1. The normal evolution of the myth. Though often myths are evanescent, many probably have a life history which one could postulate as follows: The myth originates either in the child's mind spontaneously or in response to an outside communication. The creative process occurs when he makes the myth his own and elaborates on it. There then follows possibly a more protracted period during which the myth is made a part of the lifestyle of the child, during which time it is usually continually modified. This is a very exciting but sometimes frightening process for the child. As Anthony points out, the child at this age has "an astonishing capacity for answering any question, and disposing of any difficulty with the most far-fetched and unexpected reason or hypothesis" (14).

Finally secondary process thinking becomes dominant as the child moves into the latency years (or in Piaget's terminology, as he moves from the intuitional phase to the stage of concrete operations). The child can now begin to resolve the myth into its realistic and non-realistic components, if it is still accessible to consciousness. As time goes by, he also comes to understand better the affective truths which had been embodied in the myth.

    a. The evolution of the Santa Claus myth. In the American culture a two or three year old child begins to react to the story of Santa Claus. The child soon makes the myth his own. Each child elaborates on the story in his own private way. A seven or eight year old is usually not quite ready to give up his belief. By the time the child reaches fourth grade, at age ten, a statement such as the following can be heard: "In fourth grade nobody believes in Santa Claus, but we *want* the little kids to believe in him." Normally the myth gets gently put to rest by the child by means of sublimating thoughts such as Santa being a symbol of "the spirit of Christmas" (which was nearer to the truth all along).

    b. The onset of the mythmaking process in a young child's life: In the following example, the psychotherapist of a four year old child had the occasion to help the child initiate the process. A.B., a four year old girl, who had had a severe developmental arrest due to maternal neglect during the first two years of life, had made significant strides in object relations under the care of a loving foster mother. At four, her speech development and her cognitive functioning were still retarded. She had never shown any active creative use of verbal fantasy in her play.One day her therapist decided to introduce make-believe symbols as she rolled a metal ball through a plastic labyrinth game. The game was somewhat difficult for a child this age. As she manipulated the game, the therapist suggested that it looked as if the ball were going from "one room to another, down hallways, maybe". This opening remark of his, together with her own anxiety over manipulating the game, triggered a quite spontaneous and joyous fantasy on the girl's part. She discovered that she could elaborate on these ideas as she rolled the ball. She "invented" verbally different rooms such as the "bedroom", "the t.v. room", "the bathroom", and so on for different parts of the labyrinth. She described the ball's affect as if it were a person who wanted to get to a certain room and who was happy or angry, depending on whether or not the ball reached the proper "room".

This is an example of how an adult can help the young child introduce fantasy play into his life at its very earliest and how the child converts it even then into a coping process.

c. *The termination of mythmaking as a dominant process.* As the child grows past age seven, the ideas involved in mythmaking evolve toward reality. The "family romance" fantasy, typical of the latency child occurs when the child has begun to be disillusioned with his own parents. This new daydream replaces the earlier mythic belief in the omnipotence and goodness of his own parents, which belief is now left behind. Many other examples could be given of this phase of transition toward secondary process thinking.

2. *Mythmaking as used constructively in development:* There are many ways in which the oedipal child must come to understand his perception of his inner drives, his interpersonal relationships and the environment outside the family.

A vivid description of a child's speculations on sexual topics for example, was given by Freud in 1908 in his paper "On the Sexual Theories of Children". He noted how a child can create several confused theories about where a baby comes from, how it gets into and later, out of the mother's body and what is the father's role in this. Freud added: "These speculations and doubts...become the prototype of all later thought-work on problems..." (15).

The parents' role during these years is important in guiding the mythmaking process. At first parents indulge it and cultivate it but their goals must be gradually to lead the child to a more comprehensive set of skills for understanding himself and his world.

3. *Mythmaking as a negative factor in child development.*

a. *Prohibition of the mythmaking process.* Prohibition or inhibition of the mythmaking process between the ages of three and seven may cause trouble later. For example, a twenty-five year old man, remembered that his parents had instilled "strict realism" in their children from the very earliest years, as soon as they could begin to speak. They had immediately prohibited fanciful stories or make believe. The patient had become an overly realistic adult who was hypercritical of his loved ones at home and of his colleagues at work. While his candor was at times refreshing and led to success in his rigorous professional life, his failures in close personal relationships caused him much anguish. It seemed clear that his having been deprived of mythmaking adversely affected his later development.

   b. Overstimulation of the process. On the other hand, overstimulation in mythmaking can lead to difficulties, for example in the child whose parents overutilize frightening stories to help to discipline him, or in another child whose parents, perhaps out of their own needs, overindulge him in fairy tales and make believe. The extreme example would be found in cases of folie a deux in which the preschooler accepts, and makes his own, the distorted thinking of his parent as the price he pays for continued love and protection (16).

   4. Mythmaking as it occurs in child psychotherapy: Examples of myth-making and myth formations in children can frequently be found during child psychotherapy (17). The therapist is in a good position to observe the life history of a myth and to help in its resolution.

   K.L., a six year old girl, was referred for persistent stuttering. Her mother had ejected her father from the house and divorced him when the girl was three years old. She had contributed misinformation, which led to the girl's creating a myth about her father. She told her that the father was away in the armed forces, which was not true. She fostered a false hero's image of the father which the girl elaborated on. However, at the age of 5½ years, the mother told her in anger the story was not true, that the father had left the family, was living in a distant state and would not return. The girl was extremely upset. At the time of the referral six months later she still did not accept her mother's latest statements and held onto the earlier "myths" that her father was away in the army and would return some day.

   M.N., a nine year old boy who had been immature and dependent, demanding undivided attention of peers, parents and teachers, had been in psychotherapy for two years before he painfully revealed a repressed belief centering around his mother and his beloved older sister who had died of a malignancy when she was eight years old. The patient had been four years old at the time. The sister had been a mother-figure for him. The repressed belief or "myth" came out over a four week period during which he was quite upset. He became angry at his therapist whom he accused of saying that his mother had given "cancer" to his sister. This turned out to be a projection onto the therapist of his own accusatory belief that his mother had "given cancer" to his sister by sleeping with her in the last months of the girl's life. A second part of the "myth" was that he believed his sister would reappear any day in reincarnated form. It turned out that the mother admitted that she indeed believed in something like this herself and had shared this thought with the boy. In subsequent months the therapist helped the boy to put these beliefs to rest and to substitute a more realistic understanding of the situation, including his own angry feelings. He made significant steps toward maturity thereafter.

Discussion: Mythmaking in this developmental context may be defined as an intellectual, coping device available to the three to seven year old child in which he uses his primitive cognitive abilities to deal with his ever-expanding inner and outer experiences. It is a technique for mastery as contrasted to defensive mechanisms such as counterphobias and "denial in fantasy" (18). As Anna Freud points out "the children whose outlook for mental health is better are those who cope with...danger situations actively by way of ego resources such as intellectual understanding, logical reasoning, changing of external circumstances, aggressive counterattack, *i.e.*, by mastery instead of retreat" (19). Lois Barclay Murphy has referred to activities like these as coping devices (20). Spitz has described "psychic organizers" in the first eighteen months of life (21). Mythmaking seems to be one of the organizing processes which helps the preschooler toward the higher integration of his personality which occurs by age six or seven. Thus during the preschool years fantasizing, mythmaking and realistic thinking can be seen as interrelated processes for dealing with new experiences, with the three processes being understood as on a continuum from the more defensive to the more adaptive.

The similarity of the thinking processes of the pre-schooler and primitive man is nowhere better seen than in comparing one of the constructive daydreams that Little Hans reported at age five at the end of his analysis, with the myth of the Bororo Indians which Levi-Strauss used as the key myth with which he began his study. In the former Hans told his father that he thought a plumber had come and taken away his buttocks and his penis with a pair of pincers, but only so as to give him larger and finer ones (22). In the myth of the Bororos, the youth, who had raped his mother in the jungle and who then had barely excaped being murdered by his vengeful father, began to emerge as the hero of the story when (after he had been injured by his father) vultures chewed away his own hind-quarters (the penis was not mentioned). After the vultures had been satiated, they proceeded, (like Little Hans' plumber) to help the youth, by carrying him to safety. The youth rebuilt his buttocks magically out of materials nearby and went to seek his own vengeance by bringing the destructive forces of wind, cold and rain to his tribe from then on (or, in another version of the ending, by killing his father and all of his father's wives, including his own mother) (23).

Mythmaking is also similar to the intuitive and pre-logical phases through which the mind of the scientist proceeds before he formulates a new and creative hypothesis (24, 25). He differs from the young child in that his intuition has a much more solid base of prior information and experience on which to work.*

---

*From Anthony, reference 16, p. 573-595. Anthony points out that before the child can move on to a more scientific way of thinking he has to leave behind the hallmarks of this stage of thought and has to give up and move away from, among other things, the use of primitive argument, the use of compulsive questioning, the use of reasoning by juxtaposition, the"syncretic"mode of thinking, and above all, the ways of primitive ontology, that is, animistic thinking and magic. He has to turn away from anthropomorphism and his egocentric perspective.

Because of the nearly universal prevalence of infantile amnesia, it is most difficult for adults to recapture the intensity of the cognitive world of the child between the ages of three and seven. Among the possible approaches to further study of the mythmaking process the techniques of longitudinal studies, and child psychoanalysis (or preferably a combination of both) can be employed (26,27). Other techniques for analyzing the thought content and progression of thought content in young children may be used, such as those used in the sequential analysis of the content of children's stories by Taylor and Glazer (28) or in the studies on causal thinking by Larendeau and Pinard (29). Techniques for analyzing myhtmaking being developed in anthropology may also be applied to the study of the children's myths.

Conclusion: This paper has suggested that the process of mythmaking in the child between the ages of three and seven may be identified as an active coping mechanism by which the child tries to understand himself and his surroundings. It would seem that recent researches in the anthropological field on the subject might stimulate research in child development. A preliminary description of the types of mythmaking and of the evolution of the process in the young child have been presented. Some of the pertinent literature has been reviewed. It is hoped that focusing on this concept will help to further the understanding of the development of the young child. Mythmaking appears at about the same time in development as the process of fantasizing but serves more of a "coping" function than the latter.

REFERENCES

1. Sandler, J., and Nagera, H. *Psychoanalytic Study of the Child, 18,* 159, (1963).

2. Abraham, K. *Clinical Papers and Essays on Psycho-analysis, Volume II,* edited by Abraham, H., Basic Books, Inc., N.Y., p.204, (1955).

3. Ferenczi, S. *Problems and Methods of Psycho-Analysis,* ed., by Bolient, M., Basic Books, Inc. Publishers, N.Y., pp.328, (1955).

4. Reik, T., *Myth and Guilt,* George Braziller, Inc., N.Y., (1957).

5. Jung. C.G., *Psychological Types,* Kegan Paul, Trench, Trubner, and Co., Ltd., London, p. 241, (1944).

6. Rank, O. *The Myth and the Birth of the Hero,* Robert Brunner, N.Y., (1952).

7. Freud, S. *Totem and Taboo,* Kegan Paul, Trench, Trubner and Co., Ltd., London, p. 158, (1912).

8. Campbell, J. The historical development of mythology, *Myth and Mythmaking,* Edited by Murray, H.A., N.Y., George Braziller, Inc., pp. 19, (1960).

9. Kirk, G.S. *Myth: Its Meaning and Functions in Ancient and Other Cultures,* University of California Press, Berkeley, (1971).

10. Kluckholn, E. Recurrent themes in myths and mythmaking in *Myth and Mythmaking,* Edited by Murray, H.A., George Braziller, Inc., N.Y., pp.46, (1960).

11. Murray, H.A., The possible nature of a "mythology" to come, in *Myth and Mythmaking,* Edted by Murray,H.A., George Braziller, Inc., N.Y., pp.318, (1960).

12. Levi-Strauss, C. *The Raw and the Cooked, Introduction to a Science of Mythology*, Volume I, Harper and Row, New York, p. 341, (1969).

13. Schorer, M. The necessity of myth, in *Myth and Mythmaking*, Edited by Murray, H.A., George Braziller, Inc., N.Y., p. 355, (1960).

14. Anthony, E.J., The reactions of parents to the oedipal child, in *Parenthood: Its Psychology and Psychopathology*, Edited by Anthony, E.J., and Benedek, T., Little, Brown and Company, Boston, pp.276, (1970).

15. Freud, S. (1908), On the sexual theories of children, in *The Collected Papers of Sigmund Freud*, Vol. II, The Hogarth Press, London, (1948).

16. Anthony, E.J. The influence of maternal psychosis on children - folie a deux, in *Parenthood: Its Psychology and Psychopathology*, Little, Edited by Anthony E.J. and Benedek, T., Brown and Company, Boston, pp.573 (1970).

17. Anthony, E.J., *J. Amer. Acad. Child Psychia. 3*, 106, (1964).

18. Freud, A. *The Ego and Mechanisms of Defense*, International Univerisities Press, New York, p. 78, (1946).

19. Freud, A. *Normality and Pathology in Childhood: Assessments of Development*, International Universities Press, Inc., New York, p. 136, (1965).

20. Murphy, L.B. and collaborators, *The Widening World of Childhood: Paths toward Mastery*, Basic Books, Inc., N.Y., (1962).

21. Sptiz, R.A., *The First Year of Life*, International Universities Press, Inc., N.Y., (1965).

22. Freud, S., A phobia in a five year old boy, in *Collected Papers of Sigmund Freud*, Vol. III, The Hogarth Press, London, p. 240, (1948).

23. Levi-Strauss, C., *The Raw and the Cooked, Introduction to a Science of Mythology*, Volume I, Harper and Row, N.Y., pp. 35, (1969).

24. MacCorquodale, K., and Meehl, P.E., Hypothetical constructs and intervening variables, in *Readings in the Philosophy of Science*, Feigel, H., and Broderick,M., eds., Appleton-Century-Crofts, Inc., pp.596, (1958).

25. Quine, W.V., On what there is, in *Semantics and the Philosophy of Language*, Edited by Linsky, L., The University of Illinois Press at Urbana, pp. 189, (1952).

26. Freud, A., *Normality and Pathology in Childhood: Assessments of Development*, International Universities Press Inc., N.Y., p. 24, (1965).

27. Robertson, J. *Psychoanal. Study Child. 11*, 410, (1956).

28. Taylor, W.R., and Glazer, W.M., *J. Amer. Acad. Child. Psychiat., 12*, 554, (1973).

29. Laurendeau, M., and Pinard, A., *Causal Thinking in the Child*, International Universities Press, Inc.,N.Y., (1962).

MENTAL HEALTH IN CHILDREN, Volume I
Edited By D. V. Siva Sankar
Copyright © 1975 by
PJD Publications Ltd., Westbury, N.Y.

PSYCHIATRIC CHARACTERISTICS OF THE RELATIVES OF SCHOOL PHOBIC CHILDREN*

Rachel Gittelman-Klein **
Long Island Jewish Hillside Medical Center
Glen oaks, New York 11004

Recently, a placebo controlled study was conducted at Hillside Hospital investigating the clinical efficacy of imipramine among children with school phobia (3, 4). As is generally recognized, the central difficulty in school phobia is severe separation anxiety. The children are not afraid of school *per se*, rather they are unwilling to venture into any situation which requires separation from the parent.

The rationale for using imipramine in the treatment of separation anxiety in children is presented briefly since it is

*This study was supported, in part, by the United States Public Health Service Grants MH 14514 and 18759.

**Assistant Professor, Queens College, City University of New York, Flushing, N.Y. 11367
Director, Child Development Clinic, Long Island Jewish Hillside Medical Center, Hillside Division, Glen Oaks, New York 11004

related to the hypotheses concerning the psychiatric characteristics of the parents. Serendipitously, Klein observed a marked
therapeutic imipramine effect among adult agoraphobes. The
value of this pharmacological therapy was subsequently
established in placebo controlled, double blind studies (5).
Clinical investigation of adult agoraphobes revealed that about
half of them had been fearful, dependent children with marked
separation anxiety frequently associated with difficulty
adjusting to school. The high prevalence of early separation
anxiety among adult agoraphobes led to the postulation that
the two states reflected a common psychopathological process
and therefore might respond to the same pharmacological
intervention. The latter conjecture was borne out in our study
of imipramine effects in school phobic children. Bowlby, in his
recent book on attachment behavior, concurs with Klein's view
that early severe separation anxiety and adult agoraphobia
may be manifestations of the same psychological disorder (2).
Further, several clinical considerations have led to the postulation that agoraphobia, which is currently diagnosed in the
DSM II as a Phobic Neurosis, along with fears of specific
objects such as animals, heights, etc., might be better categor-
ized as a separate diagnostic entity (6, 7), the hypothesis
being that pathological separation anxiety may be related to
the affective disorders. I wish to stress that the phobic patients are not typically depressed and that phenomenologi-
cally do not present with a mood disorder. Nevertheless,
agoraphobia shares several characteristics with affective
illnesses: 1. women are over-represented within the disorder,
2. it has a fluctuating cyclic course with periods of complete
remission, 3. when a psychological precipitant is identifiable, it
is regularly one which involves an object loss, as is the case in
depression, 4. it is alleviated by antidepressants. Any one of
these considerations in itself would be insufficient to lead to
the conjecture of a relationship between agoraphobia and
affective disorders, but the cluster of the four characteristics
is suggestive.

As a result it is hypothesized that the parents of school
phobic chidlren have histories characterized by a higher preponderance of depression than do the parents of children treated
for other psychiatric disorders. Further, since it is conjectured

that pathological separation anxiety is related to affective dysregulation, a greater prevalence of separation anxiety symptomatology is predicted for the relatives of school phobic children. No specific prediction is made with regard to concordance of phobic symptoms, since these are not felt to be clearly related to affective disorders.

Procedures

Subjects

The parents of the 42 school phobic children who completed the drug study were all interviewed. For comparison purposes, data were obtained from parents whose children were being treated in a research program for behavior disorders, specifically Hyperkinetic Reaction of Childhood.

The children were matched for race and social class. It was not possible to match children for sex since hyperactive boys greatly outnumber hyperactive girls, and no such sex distribution exists among school phobic children. As a matter of fact, it would be unwise to match for the sex of the phobic children since one would then select a highly unrepresentative sample of hyperactive children. Similarily it was not possible to match all children for age. The two disorders have different age onset patterns, hyperactive children tend to be referred for treatment during the first three years of elementary school, and the diagnosis is not used in adolescence. On the other hand, we found that referral for school phobia was most frequent for 11 to 12 year olds, coinciding with the onset of Junior High School. Therefore, the age distributions of the two samples differ. The phobic children had an age range from 6 to 15, the hyperactive children from 6 to 12. All younger children were matched for age, SES and race. The mean age of the phobic children was 10.2 years, of the hyperactive children 8.2 years. The age discrepancy is reflected in the parents' ages, so that the parents of the phobic sample were older (mothers and fathers of phobic Ss respectively were 41 and 46 years old; those of the hyperactive Ss were 35 and 39). The school phobic sample consisted of 20 boys and 22 girls. Thirty-nine were white, three black. Social class tended to be low, one family in Class II, 17 in Class III, 17 in Class IV, and seven in Class V.

Among the hyperactive Ss there were 39 boys and three girls, their race and SES distributions are identical to those of the phobic group.

Measures

The parents were interviewed individually, data were recorded on forms. Specific inquiry was made regarding depressive episodes, phobic symptoms, severe separation anxiety in the patient's parents, and a history of school phobia in the siblings. Whenever possible both parents were interviewed; if not, the mother alone was the source of information.

Relatively narrow criteria for depression were used. Reports of feeling unhappy or depressed were not sufficient. The functional capacity of the individual had to be impaired significantly so that usual role-appropriate duties (i.e., jobs, housework, etc.) had to be affected over a month or more. If such a reaction was reported as the result of the death of a close relative it was discounted since it was felt that a distinction between grief and depression could probably not be made accurately. Reports of depression in the parents prior to the age of 18 were not tabulated.

In almost all cases rated positive for depression there was convincing diagnostic evidence such as suicidal attempts, shock treatment, improvement with anti-depressant medication, no improvement with minor tranquilizers, reports of agitation.

Typical phobic symptoms were fear of heights, bridges, trains, planes and crowds.

Separation anxiety had to be documented in terms of being unable to move freely from one's parents or children, such as inability to take trips away from the family, chronic morbid concerns about members of the family when away from them.

School phobia was rated positive if the siblings had refused to go to school, or specific severe somatic symptoms such as vomiting had been present prior to going to school over an extended period of time. School refusal or severe somatic distress at the beginning of the very first school year, either kindergarten or first grade, were discounted.

Results

Since the sample consists of 42 children, there are a total of 84 natural parents in each group. Siblings below the age of six were eliminated since it was felt they were too young to have had the opportunity to develop the target symptomatology. The phobic children had 67 siblings age six or over, the hyperactive children had 66 siblings above six.

Parent's History

Three aspects of the parents psychological characteristics were recorded: depression, specific phobic symptoms, and severe separation anxiety.

Depression. Of the 84 parents of the phobic children seven were rated as having experienced incapacitating depressive episodes, six mothers and one father. Among the parents of the hyperactive children, eight were similarly rated, two were questionable with regard to a depressive history, all mothers. Obviously, prevalences of 8.3 vs. 9.5% do not discriminate between the two clinical groups.

TABLE I

History of Depression Among Parents
of School Phobic and Hyperkinetic Children

| Parents of | History of Depression | | N |
	Present	Absent	
Phobic Ss	7	77	84
Hyperkinetic Ss	8	76	84

The hypothesis that the parental histories of phobic children would have a significantly greater amount of depression was not supported. As a matter of fact one could argue for greater potential depression in the hyperkinetic sample since the parents were younger.

Phobic Symptoms. Data regarding this group of symptoms as well as separation anxiety were not available for one mother in the phobic group; she had committed suicide during a depressive episode.

Eighteen of 83 parents of phobic children had clear cut specific fears, 11 mothers and seven fathers. Among the 84 parents of hyperactive children, twelve had phobic symptoms, ten mothers and two fathers. The types of phobic objects did not differ between the two groups.

TABLE II

History of Specific Fears Among Parents of School Phobic and Hyperkinetic Children

Parents of	Specific Fears Present	Absent	N
Phobic *Ss*	18	65	83
Hyperkinetic *Ss*	12	72	84

$X^2 = 1.55$, n.s.

The prevalences of phobic symptoms of 21% and 14% for the parents of phobic and hyperactive children respectively are not different ($X^2 = 1.55$, n.s.).

Separation Anxiety. Of the 83 parents of phobic children 16 were rated as having severe separation anxiety, 12 mothers and four fathers. Two parents of the hyperactive children were rated positive on this measure. The difference between the two groups is highly significant ($X^2 = 12.4$, p less than .005).

Siblings' History

School Phobia. Among the 67 siblings of the 42 school phobic children, 11, almost 20%, had a clear-cut history of

TABLE III

History of Separation Anxiety Among Parents of School Phobic
and Hyperkinetic Children

| Parents of | Separation Anxiety | | N |
	Present	Absent	
Phobic Ss	16	67	83
Hyperkinetic Ss	2	82	84

$X^2 = 12.4$, $p < .005$, one-tail

school phobia. None of the 66 siblings of the hyperactive
sample were reported to have had a history of school phobia.
The difference between the two groups is highly significant
($X^2 = 11.81$, p less than .005).

TABLE IV

History of School Phobia in The Siblings of School Phobic &
Hyperkinetic Children

| Siblings of | History of School Phobia | | N |
	Present	Absent	
School Phobic Ss	11	56	67
Hyperkinetic Ss	0	66	66

$X^2 = 11.81$, $p < .005$, one-tail

Since the phobic children were older, their siblings also
tended to be older and therefore had more opportunity to
develop difficulties in school attendance. Though this factor

might mitigate to a small extent the difference between the two groups, it could not be such as to render the concordance for school phobia among the siblings insignificant. On the other hand, had phobic reaction to school during the first year been included, the contrast between the two groups would have been even more marked since two siblings in the phobic groups had such a history, none did in the hyperactive sample.

Relationship Between Parental Depression and School Phobia in Offsprings

Though no significant difference was found in rates of depression between the index and control group, the question may be raised whether the families who had a parent with a history of depression were more likely to be the ones to have more than one affected child. This did not turn out to be the case. A history of depression in the parents did not correlate with concordance for school phobia in the offsprings.

A similar question can be raised with regard to separation anxiety. In this case as well, a report of separation anxiety in the parents was not correlated with the presence of school phobia in the siblings.

Discussion

The findings of this study are considered heuristic and not conclusive since the parents' verbal reports were the only source of information and no objective validating data were available. The shortcomings of these procedures are too well known to elaborate on them. However, whatever biases and omissions result from this procedure, there is no reason to belive that they played a differential role within the two groups with regard to reports of depression. It is of interest that in both groups prevalence of affective disorder is higher than expected in the general population. Though a normal control group is mandatory to establish the above observation.

The fact that a parental history of depression was not associated with severe separation anxiety in the offsprings raises a question regarding the association between the two disorders.

There appears to be significant concordance for pathological separation anxiety between index cases and their relatives, parents and siblings. Obviously, the mechanisms of transmission of separation anxiety cannot be elucidated by this study. Only results from crossfostering are conclusive. If indeed separation anxiety has a genetic component, it will be very difficult to establish. As a group, individuals with great propensity for separation anxiety and therefore for attachment behavior, would be least likely to give up their children for adoption. Therefore, using the genetic model, one would predict a lower rate of pathological separation anxiety among adoptees than among nonadoptees. Ideally, one should study children of non-separation anxious parents adopted by individuals who are positive for the disorder. However, the likelihood of identifying such a group seems remote.

The postulation of genetic transmission of pathological separation anxiety makes use of the concept of attachment behavior as described by Bowlby (1). Namely, separation anxiety is a universal biological process whose adaptive goal is to elicit the mother's care and obtain retrieval for the child.

Any normal psychobiological adaptive mechanism can become dysregulated. It is felt that a large proportion of children with severe separation anxiety may be experiencing a dysfunctioning of a psychobiological interpersonal regulatory function.

REFERENCES

1. Bowlby, J. *Child Psychol. Psychiat. 1*, 251, (1960).

2. Bowlby, J. *Attachment and Loss. Vol II. Separation.* Basic Books, N.Y., (1973).

3. Gittelman-Klein, R., and Klein, D. F. *Arch. Gen. Psychiat. 25*, 204, (1971).

4. Gittelman-Klein, R., and Klein, D. F. *J. Nerv. Ment. Dis. 156*, 199, (1973).

5. Klein, D.F. *Psychopharmacologia,* 5, 397, (1964).

6. Klein, D.F. Drug therapy as a means of syndromal indenti-fication and nosological revision. Paper presented at the Annual Meeting of the American Psychopathological Association, New York, (1973).

7. Klein, D. F. and Davis, J. H. *Diagnosis and drug treatment of psychiatric disorders.* Williams & Wilkins, Baltimore, (1969).

BIRTH FACTORS IN SCHIZOPHRENIA

Elaine Mura

The significance of various birth factors in the occurrence and development of many forms of human deviance has long been of interest. Recently, researchers have been able to demonstrate that one or another of these factors seems to correlate with specific physical and/or mental pathology.

This paper shall discuss the relationship between many birth factors and the incidence and course of psychosis--especially schizophrenia. Only studies which are probably or definitely unrelated to purely genetic elements or in which these play a minor role will be evaluated.

To establish some order in this broad field, birth factors have been subdivided into two areas--central and peripheral. The former will cover research into some predominantly organic questions: pregnancy difficulties, unfavorable fetal environment associated with maternal factors, paranatal complications, prematurity, and weight at birth. The latter will deal with circumstantial occurrences surrounding the event of birth:

This article was reproduced from, *"Schizophrenia - Current Concepts and Research"* published in 1969. The Editor hopes that there have been no errors in the reproduction.

1. Order of birth and other familial predictors
2. Sex
3. Season of birth
4. Social factors
   a. Race
   b. Migration
   c. Intelligence
   d. Culture
   e. Social class

CENTRAL FACTORS

The fact that individuals can be affected by occurrences and circumstances in their fetal life has been well demonstrated. Jackson (1) describes a number of such cases:

Nutrition: Fetal rickets among the offspring of starving Chinese mothers showing up at one month in X-Rays despite breast feeding (2).

Altered oxygen supply: Mongolism being associated with hemorrhage and resultant threatened abortion (3).

Increased fetal movement of arms and legs in severe hemorrhage and premature separation of placenta with its hemorrhage (4).

Endocrine system: Insulin content in pancreases of fetuses of diabetic mothers being twenty-four times that of normals (5).

Fetal goiter possibly resulting from maternal inadequately functioning thyroid (6).

Pseudo-hermaphroditic female infants being born to women who were administered progestins in their pregnancies (7).

Placental barrier: Increased incidence of congenital deafness in children whose mothers were heavy users of quinine during malarial season (8).

Increase in fetal heart rate comparable to that of many adult cigarette smokers when the mother smoked during the last three months of pregnancy. Byproducts of tobacco were found in the fetal bloodstream (9).

To measure fetal activity, Sontag and Richards (10) placed a block of wood on the mother's abdomen and struck it with a doorbell vibrator; they got what was probably a startle reflex in the fetus. Jackson (1) noted what looked like fetal learning when he stimulated the fetus at one minute intervals and measured changes in the heart rate; he found both negative adaptation and recovery.

In contrast to the foregoing physiological effects, Plum (11) felt that subnormal intelligence in spastic cerebral palsy was less related to pregnancy or birth factors than to family history (like palsies, subnormal intelligence, psychosis, or epilepsy among close relatives). Previously, in surveying 543 cases of cerebral palsy, Plum (12) found that, except for toxemia and metrorrhagia, pregnancy factors seemed to be of little etiological significance. However, he did find that birth complications occurred more frequently than normal with certain types of problems related to different varieties of the disease. Observing only birth trauma in 35 children, Schachter (13) uncovered some personality correlates related to whether or not the individual experiences birth abnormalities, with deviance appearing in adulthood in one-third to one-half of the afflicted group (particularly alcoholism and subsequent neuropsychiatric disorders). He found that asphyxia did cause some retardation compared to a control group of one hundred normal children. When Ucko (14) investigated two groups of 29 boys each longitudinally for five years, he found no differences in either intellectual or emotional development between the asphyxiated and normal group. However, he did discover some significant differences in temperamental characteristics, with the asphyxiated being unusually sensitive, overreactive, having a tendency to "disequilibrium" when their normal routine was broken.

When Pasamanick and Knobloch (cited in 15) found pregnancy difficulties to be associated with cerebral palsy, epilepsy, mental deficiency, behavior disorders, reading disabilities, and tics, they distinguished between prolonged or difficult labor and employment of operative procedures (like Caesarian, forceps, breech) and stated that, the association occurred rather with prolonged anoxia, producing complications of pregnancy like toxemia and maternal bleeding. Weidon (16) also found toxemia to be significantly higher (46.4% in schizophrenic patients and 22.2% in controls). Pre-eclamptic toxemia is known to produce a thrombosis of part of the vascular system of the placenta that becomes fibrosed, thus cutting off the oxygen supply to the fetus. It is not unusual for one-third or more of the placental tissue to be destroyed by long-standing toxemic pregnancy.

These studies, as Jackson (1) suggests, "offer further evidence of the importance of fetal environment as a determinant of behavior postnatally, perhaps, as well as prenatally."

Certain women are reported to be vulnerable to pregnancy complications and produce abnormal offspring with behavior disorders. In studying families with two or more hospitalized for psychiatric illnesses, Lucas, Rodin, Simson (17) found a very high incidence of paranatal complications. This concurs with world-wide epidemiological studies which have shown that whenever disturbed children are studied, there is a much higher percentage of them who have had atypical birth experiences (18).

The majority of studies relating birth and pregnancy complications to psychosis and schizophrenia have been carried out with children. Analysis of five studies discussing childhood schizophrenics by Pollack and Woerner (19) revealed a significant association between complications of pregnancy and psychosis in children; they ascribed the ambiguity of findings regarding birth complications to differing categories used by the authors. A summary of this study illustrates the type of study, methodology, and findings typical of this area.

Comparing 43 psychotic children and their 66 siblings, Whittam, Simon, and Mittler (20) found that the psychotic group contained a significantly higher proportion of children (67%) with one or more abnormalities in the pre-, peri-, or early post-natal period than the sibling group (33%). Interestingly, the patients had a lower incidence of toxemic history suggested by some authors to be the crucial factor than either their siblings or the general population. They also found that children with retarded motor milestones tended to be those with a history of abnormal delivery (highly significant). None of the psychotic children showed normal speech development--true for 12% of the sibling group, which is also an unusually high proportion. Besides complications of pregnancy and birth, health of the psychotic children in the first year of life was also poorer, suggesting higher risk disposing to a handicapping condition. Gittelman and Birch (21) also found excessive perinatal complications in 97 schizophrenic children attending a day school for disturbed chidlren, particularly characterizing those children with subnormal mentality. Twenty-five per cent of that group, as a matter of fact, was subsequently rediagnosed as mentally subnormal and/or chronically brain damaged. In the entire group, central nervous system pathology was evident in 80 per cent, revealing that neurologically damaged may also be encountered outside an institution. By contrast, Osterkamp and Sands (22) found that birth difficulties alone did not differentiate schizophrenic and neurotic children--but that when a patient had experienced both birth difficulties and feeding difficulties (especially a difficult and short period of breast feeding), he was more likely to fall into the schizophrenic group. This is consonant with Osterkamp's finding (22) that mothers of schizophrenics more often try breast feeding unsuccessfully (both frequency and lack of success characterizing the group). Investigating 286 psychotic group (including hospital admissions, outpatients in both a child guidance clinic and consultation with a private psychiatrist), Bender and Faretra (23) found that a significantly high number had pregnancy and birth complications. They especially found maternal illness, bleeding, toxemia in the period of pregnancy and delivery and respiratory disturbances related to anoxia in the period of birth to be most frequent among schizophrenics. In disagreement, Patterson, Block, Block and Jackson (24) found no significant differences between schizophrenic, non-schizophrenic but disturbed, and normal children on this axis. The findings specifically related to autistic children have been inconclusive, with Kanner (25) showing significantly increased rates of pregnancy complications, Lotter (26) showing significantly fewer than non-autistic but handicapped controls, and Rimland (27) showing no significant difference between autistics and normals. He did, however, find that many mothers had experienced bleeding and had a history of previous miscarriage and stillbirth, reminiscent of Terris Monk and Lapouse's finding of a definite association between childhood schizophrenia and previous fetal loss (28).

In deviant adolescents, Pollack (29) found a significant incidence of pre- or peri-natal abnormalities, especially in the group with a history of learning defects and behavior disorders in childhood. Pollack, Levenstein, and Klein (30) also found that early minimal brain damage of a pre- or para-natal origin may be the significant factor in the development of adult psychopathology in some patients. Those in this category had a poorer prognosis: as the severity of their damage increased, almost one hundred per cent of their hospitalized schizophrenic patients fell into the "very poor" group of chronics. In a third study, Pollack and Greenberg (31) also found a significant relationship between paranatal complications and psychosis, with the highest incidence of such complications being significantly correlated with personality disorders and almost none appearing in the history of affective disorders. In their 71 consecutively admitted patients, they also found that onset was significantly associated with birth abnormalities, with those having severe complications also having a lower age of onset. In fact, twice as many in the severe group (as compared to none or moderate) were treated in adolescence. Specifically in schizophrenia, a younger onset was noted for those with both moderate and severe paranatal abnormalities; 78 per cent in the moderate and 89 per cent in the severe group were treated under the age of 18 compared to 14 per cent who had no birth complications.

When comparing monozygotic twins discordant for schizophrenia, Stabenau and Pollin (32) found that birth complications differentiated the index from the health--specifically neonatal asphyxia. They suggested that this might be due to the index twin's often being second born, thus being more likely to experience periods of anoxic cyanosis during delivery or respiratory distress thereafter. Rosenthal (38) also reported severe pregnancy and birth complications in quadruplets concordant for schizophrenia; however, this might have been an artefact of multiple birth of this size in an older woman.

Studies discussing the association between pregnancy and birth factors and psychosis using adult subjects have been few--suggesting either that their being farther away from the event of birth causes researchers to think less in terms of these factors and more in terms of psychological stresses in developing theories of etiology or simply that fewer significant correlations have been drawn in this population. The foregoing empirical evidence suggests the former possibility.

Prematurity

If a correlation could be drawn between prematurity and psychosis, this would also tend to support an organic etiology in schizophrenia, the rationale being that either more fetal complications have resulted in birth before full term or more fetal complications have caused a prematue birth. Pasamanick and Knobloch (cited in 15) found that prematurity was probably involved in brain injury, especially when precipitated by toxemia or bleeding. If this is considered as lowering the threshold to stress in an individual already predisposed to schizophrenia, then the incidence of mental illness should be higher.

Studies have found prematurity to be related to several other subsequent events. Graham, Ernhart, Thurston, and Craft (33) found that 16.7 per cent of a group of premature children performed abnormally on one or more tests of cognitive functioning compared to 6.9 per cent of the normal full-term group. Cutler (34) also found depressed intellectual functioning in premature Negro babies which she attributed to the high incidence of neurologic damage, especially among males. However, even without neurological abnormalities, she found depressed IQ and gross motor scores in comparison with full-term matched controls. In mental deficiency, Lilienfeld, Pasamanick, and Rogers (35) noted significantly more retarded Negro children to be premature even with no significant difference in pregnancy complications. They also concluded that complications of pregnancy and prematurity were significantly associated with epilepsy, behavior disorders, reading disabilities, and cerebral palsy. Studying cerebral palsy, Plum (11) also found a large number of prematures, especially girls who were also smaller. Pasamanick and Knobloch (cited in 15) attempted to separate the effects of prematurity and birth weight--often confused in these studies since, of course, premature infants are usually lighter in weight--and found that 44 per cent with a birth weight under 1500 grams had abnormal conditions of serious magnitude, compared to 8.6 per cent in the rest of the premature group and 2.6 per cent in full-term controls. They also designated more prematures as having "minimal damage."

The majority of studies investigating the variable of prematurity found significantly higher rates of prematurity in schizophrenics. Lane and Albee (36) noted that in 52 schizophrenic adults, five were premature at birth compared to five in a control group of 115 siblings; this represents a significant difference which they felt might even be larger in future since some of the siblings might also become schizophrenic. Three studies investigating children also were relevant. For the autistic child, Kanner (25) found very significantly higher rates of prematurity when organic entities were removed from the sample; these were, however, similar to children who were organically impaired but without autism. Keeler (37) pointed out the same for autistic children as well as a lack of movement before birth in most of them. Bender and Faretra (23) also concluded that prematurity was a significant factor in schizophrenic children. Terris Monk and Lapouse (28), on the other hand, found no significant differences between 463 children diagnosed as schizophrenic and matched controls (9.2 per cent rate for cases and 8.4 per cent for controls).

In twins, Rosenthal (38) found no increase in rate of schizophrenia despite their high incidence of prematurity (even making them, he adds, a deviant sample in this respect). In a sample of 10,000 cases of premature monozygotic twins, in fact, he found only seven who were said to be schizophrenic. On the other hand, Pasamanick and Knobloch (cited in 15) found twinning to be more common among cases of neuropsychiatric disorders--possibly relating, they feel, to the significantly higher incidence of prematurity. Havelkova (39) commented on the unusually high number of twins in 29 families with schizophrenic children.

The empirical data reveals a possible but still ambiguous relationship between prematurity and schizophrenia. Of interest is the number of studies utilizing children which reached significance, possibly suggesting that prematurity effects are more readily discernible in children, with adult compensating-- or simply that researchers interested in childhood psychosis tend to analyze birth data like this more closely.

Birth Weight

For those interested in establishing a relationship between organic damage or physiological weakness (leading to high risk) and incidence of psychosis, the question of birth is especially important. If birth weight could be shown to be lower for the mentally ill than for normal siblings or the general population, some link inferring organic causation would appear plausible. Studies which have been carried out have illustrated that birth weight is in fact lower for those afflicted with cerebral palsy (12). Knobloch, Rider, Harper, and Pasamanick (40) have also found that the rate of neuropsychiatric abnormalities increased as birth weight decreased.

Several explanations have been offered to explain the existence of a correlation between birth weight and psychosis. One is, of course, the organic theory which suggests either a higher risk for a lighter baby or simply that a less adaptive baby is born smaller. Another theoretical possibility is that birth weight is really reflecting the lower class membership of the mother. When comparing 377 high income mothers with 1019 low income mothers, Baird (41) found that smaller women in the lower wage group had a higher proportion of light babies than women of the corresponding size in a well-to-do group. He explained this as being reflective of the poorer diets of the low income group who were undernourished in their youth and grew about three inches shorter on the average --and shorter women tend to have lighter babies. The fact that maternal diet may affect birth weight has been suggested by the finding that children born in the summer are significantly lighter (cited in 15), when maternal dietary intake (especially protein) decreases. The relationship of diet to birth weight has also been studied by Ebbs, Tisdall, Scott, Moyle, and Bell (42) who followed babies from pregnancy through six months of age for three groups of mothers: a poverty group with poor diets, a poverty group whose diets had been liberally supplemented, and a middle class well-nourished group. Surprisingly, they found that the heaviest babies (averaging seven pounds ten ounces) were born to the unsupplemented poorly fed women, while the other two groups were almost the same (seven pounds seven ounces). However, two weeks later the babies in the unsupplemented poverty group were judged to be generally poorer in condition compared to the other two--with the supplemented diet babies being in the best condition! Six months later the influence of a well-nourished mother apparently finally became noticeable when this group of babies was found to have significantly fewer illnesses--of course, this may reflect differential class hygienic standards or postnatal care. Paffenbarger et al.'s study (43) noted that alive infants born to women suffering

TABLE I

Year	Author	Subjects	Controls	Methodology	Results		
1960	Vorster	15 schiz. children (10 M, 5 F) 4-14 seen at guidance clinic--no organic problems	33 normal sibs (19 M, 14 F) 2-25	Retrospective questionnaire, maternal interview, hospital records in 2/3 cases	Preg. comp.		.05
					Birth & neonat comp. including prematurity		
					Prematurity		.01
					Infantile ill.		NS
					Abortion just pre or post		.01
							NS
1962	Knobloch and Pasamanick	50 early infant autism in Ohio (34 M, 16 F) 11 weeks 9 years some organic problems	1. 50 abnorm without autism but some organic disorders (23 M, 27 F) 2. 50 norm lower socio-ec status (27 M, 23 F)	Retrospective maternal interview		Abn	Norm
					Preg. comp.		
					Abnorm del.	NS	.01
					Premat (BW)	NS	NS
					Neonatal abnorm.	NS	NS

Year	Author	Sample	Control	Method	Variables	Significance
1963	Hinton	62 psychotic outpatients in Ontario 46--evidence of organic brain disorder 10 mean age (39 M, 23 F)	62 consecutive admissions to children's hosp. for tonsilectomy 6.1 mean age (29 M, 33 F)	Retrospective parental interview, hospital records	Preg. comp. Birth and neonat compl. including prematurity Prematurity Severe Infantile illness or feeding difficulties	.01 NS NS .01
1964	Taft and Goldfarb	29 schiz. inpat. NYC 6-11 (21 M, 8 F)	1. 39 sibs (20 M, 19 F) 2. 34 pub sch ch socio-ec, age matched (17 M, 17 F)	Retrospective maternal interview physician and hospital records	Preg. comp. Birth and neonat comp. inclu. Prem.	Boys .05 Girls .05 Boys .001 Girls .10
1964	Terris and Lapouse Monk	463 schiz. ch. Bellevue 2-12 (372 M, 91 F)	463 matched ch. NYC	Retrospective maternal interview Hospital records	Abnorm del. Premat (BW) History of previous stillbirths or abortions	NS NS .02

from post partum psychosis weighed less than average; perhaps the mother's attitude of her physiological condition might affect the weight of the child. Paffenbarger found more hypertension and headaches during pregnancy--but suggested that this might reflect organic dysfunctions which he hypothesizes as etiological in post-partum psychosis.

Drawing an empirical correlation between birth weight and schizophrenia has yielded ambiguous results. Some studies uncover no significant differences between cases and controls (19, 28, 44, 45, 47). Some studies have shown birth weights for schizophrenics to be significantly lower. Lane and Albee (36, 48) found a significant difference: 52 schizophrenic adults with 115 siblings were found to have an average mean difference of six ounces less with schizophrenics averaging seven pounds and siblings averaging seven and one-half pounds. Seventy per cent weighed less than the average for siblings, while 61 per cent weighed the least in the family at birth no matter what the number of siblings. Whittem, Simon, and Mittler (20) similarly noted that a higher proportion of psychotic children weighed five and one-half pounds or less (but this just failed to reach significance at .06).

In multiple births, the twin lighter at birth has been found to be the schizophrenic one in later life (32, 49). A single case of quadruplets (38) concordant for schizophrenia revealed that the two lighter at birth became in later life the chronic, sicker patient, while the heavier two achieved a more satisfactory (although minimal) life adjustment. The Stabenau-Pollin twin study also found the schizophrenic one to be shorter and weaker, comparable to Simon and Gillies study (50) which noted that when the physical characteristics of 34 psychotic children were compared to the normal standard, the psychotics were significantly below their peers in weight (above and below the fifth percentile), bone age (over half below the 25 percentile and one-third below the tenth), and height (the majority below the tenth percentile). Although controversial, the empirical findings lean slightly in the direction of no significance. In contrast, the results in prematurity studies show a more frequent association, interesting in light of the fact that some analyses seem to have defined prematurity in terms of lighter-than-average birth weight.

Maternal Factors

Many relationships have been documented between the physiological and mental state of the pregnant woman and the fetus. Masland (cited in 15) mentions empirical links drawn between a number of maternal factors and the outcome of pregnancy:

1. Nutrition
2. Physical activity (like heavy manual labor)
3. Maternal immune reactions
4. Physique
5. Heart volume
6. Illness or infections
7. Massive X-Ray
8. Toxin intake (like abortive agents, tobacco)
9. Hormones (like cortisone and insulin)
10. Electrophoretic pattern of blood proteins
11. Emotional status

The relationship between emotional states and fetal reactions is probably largely an endocrinological event--for example, blood sugar and ultimately epinephrine being liberated by emotional excitement, passing through the placental barrier, and affecting the endocrine balance in the fetus. In the study at Fells Research Institute, Jackson (1) observed both pre- and post-natal effects of maternal emotional stress. In a group of 300 children, the pregnancies of five women were traumatic (that is to say, husbands died or abandoned their wives, etc). In each, fetal heart rate increased by 20-25 beats a minute--this phenomena lasting over weeks. After birth, all five babies were also found to be hyperactive, irritable and restless; they cried more, had more interruptions in sleep, had more hyperactive gastrointestinal tracts so that they experienced more bowel movements, a greater intolerance for food, and more spitting up. Stott (23) found a significant association between frequency of emotional shock and other psychosomatic stress in pregnancy and defective children--suggesting other abnormalities resulting from maternal emotional state.

It, therefore, seems reasonable to assume that maternal factors might enter into the production of psychotic offspring.

In fact, some studies have shown a relationship between emotional stress and schizophrenia. Ricks and Nameche (36) found that traumatic pregnancies (defined as "crises levels of mental disorder in the mother during pregnancy or immediately thereafter, extreme disruption of family life at the time of pregnancy, serious physical illness in the mother, and illegitimacy") differentiated mothers whose infants later became schizophrenic adults from a group of controls. They suggest that since the birth was associated with a period of tension that exceeded other pregnancies of the same mother, she was less well organized and able to cope with the child--clearly a different interpretation of the data strongly leaning to a psychological etiology. Similarly, a psychological attitude has been shown to have little effect on offspring. Patterson, Block, Block, and Jackson (24) found that mothers with unplanned pregnancies had more physical symptoms than those who had planned pregnancies, but that these probably psychosomatic complaints were not correlated to later schizophrenia, psychosis, or normality in the infant.

The mental status of the mother could also affect the offspring. Paffenbarger, Steinmetz, Pooler, and Hyde (43) found that mothers who later suffered from post-partum psychosis tended to complain of headaches and manifested hypertension during the pregnancy. They also had more respiratory illnesses and dystocia. This might be linked to the lower birth weight of their infants and their tendency to be premature. As a matter of fact, although this seems at first glance to be an association based on emotional factors, Paffenbarger hypothesizes that this is in fact a physiological disorder associated with hormonal imbalance due to pregnancy. Actual physical increase in ovarian insufficiency has also been found in hebrephrenic and catatonic patients (51). Perhaps a factor of this nature might ultimately explain the higher incidence of schizophrenia in offspring of schizophrenic mothers or at least their deviance. Fish (52) described such a difference in the children of hospitalized schizophrenic mothers, with children showing some evidence of disturbance in the functioning of the nervous system; they were described as either excessively quiet or excessively irritable. Fish hypothesizes a similarity between this behavior and the motility, excitability, and perceptual disturbances she has observed in older schizophrenic children.

Even the moment of conception has been linked to psychosis in the offspring. Heuyer, Lebovici, and Roumajon (53) suggested that an association might exist between the fact that a woman was intoxicated at the moment of conception and her son's psychosis. However, Caplan dispels this connection "adduced to hide our ignorance."

Table 2

CENTRAL FACTORS: Survey of Studies Cited in this Section

Factor	Significant	Not Significant
Pregnancy Complications	M and F--7	M and F--1 1 fewer
Birth Complications	M and F--12 M only--1	M and F--3 F only--1
Prematurity	M and F--4 M only--1	M and F--5 F only--1
Birth Weight	M and F--3 M only--1	M and F--5 F only--1
Infantile Illness	M and F--2	
Abortion or Stillbirth	M and F--1	M and F--1
Neonatal Abnormality		M and F--1

Theories

Several organic theories have evolved from the work on birth and pregnancy factors and psychosis which is similar but have a different emphasis. The first will be referred to as the genetic-precipitation theory. The major proponent of this view has been Lauretta Bender. In essence, schizophrenia is described as being initially an inherited predisposition decompensated by an intrauterine or paranatal noxious or traumatic event. This brain damaged or otherwise defective or traumatized infant who might have had only a marginal handicap will suffer more from deprivation, hospitalization, and separation from the mother, even for shorter periods, than the potentially normal child. Recently Bender (1955) has defined schizophrenia as "a maturational lag at the embryonic level in all areas which integrate biological and psychological behavior; and embryonic primitivity or plasticity charaterizes the pattern of the behavior disturbances in all areas of personality functioning. It is determined before birth and hereditary factors appear to be important. *It may be precipitated by a physiological crisis which may be birth itself, especially a traumatic birth.*" Stabenau (1968) states a similar view: "There is evidence to postulate a genetic component to the etiology of schizophrenia; however, detailed family study of monozygotic twins discordant for schizophrenia suggests there are pre- and/or post-natal experiential environmental components necessary for schizophrenia to emerge in a given individual."

Pollack also postulates an organic theory which will be referred to as the cognitive disorganization theory. In contradistinction to the former theory, which based much importance on the genetic component in schizophrenia, he describes a model based on the interaction of cerebral dysfunction, childhood social deviancy, and increasing stress of changes created by advancing age. A crucial factor in his hypothesis is the presence of early minimal brain damage of a pre- or para-natal origin. While this is not especially radical, he goes on to suggest that "neurological as well as psychiatric dysfunctions in the child originate from organic disorders in central nervous system integration" (54). *"The critical factor seems to be cognitive disorganization, not paranatal complications per se, and the temperamental patterns resulting from interference with normal brain development"* (31).

In discussing infantile autism, Rimland (27) postulates a similar problem in conceptual impairment; however, he more specifically suggests a malfunction of the reticular formation as the direct cause since this portion of the brain "provides the driving force in facilitating cortical activity and is felt to be the site at which sensory input is integrated and converted to a code which makes it compatible with the retrieval system used in making available a wide range of content of memory." Hyperoxia, he specifies, is a possible factor in the malfunction of the reticular formation. He also cites the biological law which states that organisms destined to reach higher states of development are most vulnerable to damage by adverse environmental conditions. "Autistic children were genetically vulnerable as a consequence of inborn capacity for high intelligence."

Pasamanick and Knobloch (cited in 15) have hypothesized the existence of a continuum of reproductive assault, with abortions, stillbirths, and neonatal deaths on one end and varying degrees of neuropsychiatric disability (like cerebral palsy, epilepsy, and child behavior disorders) at the other. *They base their model on the theory that maternal and fetal factors causing anoxia, toxemia, hemorrhage, and prematurity result in either lethal damage to the fetus or sublethal damage to the brain.* They mention that the continuum is at least partially socio-economically determined and suggest preventive programs in the prenatal and even pre-conception period.

Another theoretical conception might be termed polycausal. Jackson (1) suggests that although nutritional, endocrinological, toxic, and emotional factors in the fetal environment bear no known relationship to the etiology of schizophrenia, they do indeed bear a relationship to constitution. "...Such modification of a constitutional character in the biochemical and physiological nature of the brain cells may be influenced adversely by fetal environment, and that at a later date they may be responsible for grave behavioral deviation." "It seems to me, therefore, that it is only rational to think of schizophrenia as a somatopsychic disease, one in which the cerebral physiology, determined and modified as it may be by genic inheritance and by prenatal and postnatal environment, that is adverse at least to that individual, to create psychologically inappropriate and inadequate for the organism's protection."

In contrast to most of the foregoing theories, Brackbill and Fine (55) clearly differentiate two different etiologies, depending on whether the patient is diagnosed process or reactive schizophrenic. They suggest that the former is reflective of central nervous system involvement (the result of infection or trauma) while the latter might be primarily psychological. This might explain the different course and functioning observed in the two groups.

In summary, most authors investigating pregnancy and birth factors in the etiology of schizophrenia suggest that in an individual predisposed to the illness such assaults seem to raise the risk for the emergence of schizophrenia. In combination with unfavorable social factors, the disease entity we know as schizophrenia emerges.

Critique

The birth and pregnancy factor studies may be criticized severely on several counts. The first problem is in the selection of the subjects. If hospitalized patients were used, the assumption is that their psychopathology is serious enough to warrant institutionalization. Since more than half of schizophrenics are out patients (56), this may not make generalization over the entire population feasible. Diagnosis is another difficulty, since diagnoses are usually subjective and often change in the course of treatment or with the change of expectations accompanying the increase of age. Definition of the defect can also be difficult because some conditions (like mental deficiency or behavior disorders) are not entities but symptom complexes related to a variety of etiologies. Lumping them together may invalidate results. Specifically in twin studies (considered especially enlightening when discordance is present since genetic similarities are erased as a variable), some glaring problems are present. According to Rosenthal (38), same sexed twins may live in the same geographic area (contributing to a sample error). Males may migrate more (bringing the later to be described variable of migrant disposition into play), while females may stay and be maintained at home. Furthermore, the healthy-unhealthy ratio may be disturbed by later onset of psychosis in the "normal" twin. Two physiological factors may enter into the interpretation of findings: monozygotic twins, who share maternal circulation, may be differently affected, with one being disadvantaged. Twins are anyway a deviant sample, being more prone to both prematurity and fetal death than singletons. Especially in this field of central factors, the inclusion of so many children and so few adults in studies might lead one to question the generality of the findings.

Another problem is in the collection of relevant data. Hospital records are notoriously unreliable (cited in 15). In Oppenheimer *et al.*'s 1957 report, hospital records were often found to be incomplete; the following percentages of completeness suggest the unreliability of such data:

Table 3

Data	Hospitals			
	1	2	3	4
Rh Factor	32	13	84	93
Serology	78	13	83	99
Anaesthesia	64	5	100	100
Weight of infant	89	90	100	100
Infant Physical Exam	93	51	100	55

As is readily obvious from even cursory examination, the quality of hospital reports varied considerably. The retrospective interview (usually maternal) also has serious drawbacks. Wenar (57) summarized his investigations into this area of recall as follows:
1. Information on pregnancy and delivery
   Good for overall gestation and delivery
   Poor for health during pregnancy, duration of delivery, maternal injuries during delivery, use of instruments, immediate difficulties with neonate

2. Factual development data
   Good for motor development
   Poor for weight after first year
3. Illnesses
   One third of major and one half of minor forgotten
   (including pneumonia and tuberculosis!)
4. Child rearing practices
   Good for breast feeding
   Poor for thumb-sucking, toilet training, personal and
   social independence encouragement
5. Interpersonal relationships
   Poor in all areas

Wenar also found that the passage of time did not matter: what a mother remembered was well-remembered; the forgotten was forgotten forever. Boys' mothers recalled better than girls'. Social class did not affect the frequency of errors, but rather the type. Robbins (58) studied this problem with similar results. In 47 upper middle and upper class Jewish families with mothers and fathers both being well educated (most college plus) and many holding advanced degrees in medicine, law, or even psychology, the inaccuracy of recall was striking. Even with frequency of interviews (they were in a longitudinal study), they did not improve. Their inaccuracies were greatest in items dealing with age of weaning and toilet training, occurrence of thumbsucking, and demand feeding; they tended to be in the direction of the recommendations of experts. In contrast to the evident unreliability of retrospective reports, Pollack and Greenberg (31) suggested that parental reports may be less distorted than one is led to believe, since in their study one group (personality trait disturbances) reported such difficulties and one (affective disorders) did not. Clearly they saw no reason to assume a differential bias in one mother over another.

Another important problem is the formulation and interpretation of results. Dependent variables are built right into the studies: for example, authors have shown prematurity to be correlated significantly with lower social class and height of the mother. The danger of focussing on a specific factor (like toxemia) might well result in ignoring the other important variables which might be interrelated or independent.

With the many difficulties existing in carrying on these studies and interpreting the results, it is surprising that the data seems to hold in so many of the pregnancy and birth studies.

Problems specifically related to birth weight and prematurity findings are similar--however, a few added difficulties present themselves. Birth weight and prematurity are often pooled or confused in these studies. Some use the two interchangeably, with prematurity being defined as lower birth weight. When authors have attempted to divide the two, they have often found no significance where it existed before. Another ambiguity in interpretation is present. Perhaps, these are not the important variables at all, but merely causative of later poorer adjustment due to differential maternal treatment--with the mother tending to overprotect the smaller and weaker. In the case of the Genain quadruplets, the opposite was found to be true; the fact that the two smallest and lightest became the sickest might have reflected their mother's rejection, this pair constantly being shoved aside in favor of the other. Social class variables are apparently important as well. For example, Pasamanick, Knobloch, and Lilienfeld (59) discovered that prematurity and social class seemed significantly correlated. In their sample, five per cent were upper class whites, 14.6 per cent were lower class white, and a whopping 50.6 per cent were lower class Negroes--suggesting as well a confounding racial variable. Baird (41) found the same overrepresentation of prematurity in lower class English mothers, with 8.38 per cent in this group as compared to five per cent in an upper class group. The latter were also almost always for the usual medical reasons (85 per cent) while the former were often unexplained (52 per cent). If such strong class effects show up, it should not be surprising that significant differences are often found in child psychotics who have been found to reflect this variable more than adults (60).

PERIPHERAL FACTORS

Birth Order

A relationship between ordinal position in the family constellation and incidence of psychosis has been the topic of serious investigation since the 1950's. When in 1959 Schachter

(61) formulated some hypotheses regarding the psychological effects of being born first or last in the family, he renewed interest in this subject. Briefly, Schachter's position was that first-born children were more affiliative--that is to say, they prefer social outlets for their anxieties and prefer to be with others when in stressful situations. His rationale was that first-born children spend more of their earlier life with adults and are more dependent on them (their parents have sufficient time to lavish attention on them and the inexperience to pay doting and overprotective heed to every untoward movement they make). On the other hand, laterborn children get little parental attention and tend to spend more time alone, thus becoming more self sufficient and tending to handle their problems in an asocial manner. If in fact such differences in personality (the gregarious vs. the withdrawn approach to anxiety) do exist, then birth order should have an effect on the occurrence, course, and treatment of psychosis. The organic approach to psychosis would postulate a similar tendency for the later-born to show more deviance; however, the reason would stem instead from the less favorable intrauterine environment to which the later-born is subjected. In support of this prediction, Pasamanick and Knobloch (cited in 15) found that increasing birth order increased the risk for mental deficiency. The implication of heightened fetal and neonatal risk of damage could have ramifications in the occurrence of psychosis, but thus far most of the studies have theorized regarding the psychological rather than the physiological possibilities. A third interpretation might be cultural: since expectations and stresses differ (especially in non-Western cultures) different families position could affect adjustment. Generally, the prediction has been in the direction of more breakdown among the more stressed group, the first-born children.

Some early studies into this question investigated the relationship of ordinal position and deviant behavior. For example, Bakan (62) found that later-born siblings were significantly overrepresented in the alcoholic population--the likelihood of becoming alcoholic increasing as the number of older siblings increased, so that younger children in larger families had the highest probability of becoming alcoholic. The psychological causality of this fact was evolved by Schachter (61), who suggested that having fewer social outlets, the younger in the family would turn to an isolated means of facing problems-- alcohol--rather than to talking them out or seeking therapy (61). However, a physiological explanation might be inferred from Schachter's study (13), which found that one-third of a group of individuals who had suffered a serious birth trauma became alcoholics in adulthood (among other defects including 47 per cent retardation and 42 per cent neurologic manifestations). As the alcoholic group was correlated with subsequent appearance of neuropsychiatric disorder, one might question whether the appearance of alcoholism and psychiatric disturbance both might not be a function of undetected or minimal paranatal damage occasioned by later birth. Both Bakan's and Schachter's studies could be criticized for possibly presenting data confounded by social class variables; however, Schachter (61) found that the birth order effect held in duration of therapy even when the increased size of the family suggested increased lower class participation. The evidence linking ordinal position and other behavior deviances is contradictory. While Sletto (63) noted more early-born siblings and Burt (64) more only boys to number in the ranks of the delinquent, Baker, Decker, and Hill (65) and Slawson (66) found no relationship whatever. The same seem true for childhood behavior disorders, where Rosenow and Whyte (1934) and Bender and Faretra (1952) found first or second-born children to preponderate, while Levy (1932) also uncovered no relationship. Earlier Rosenow and Whyte (67) found that the middle child in the three-sibling family was more often treated in guidance clinics. Measuring for psychological problems by the Taylor Manifest Anxiety Scale was attempted by Schachter (61), who administered this test to 298 undergraduates; he found no significant relationship or systematic trends between birth order and disturbances. However, this author's reanalysis suggests sexually differentiated trends in the direction of more middle-born males manifesting anxiety, compared to females, who seem more anxious if the oldest in a large family or the later-born in a small family. Neurosis has also been empirically found to occur significantly more often in all position in the family constellation (68) or to be insignificant (69).

Table 4

Author	Year	Subjects	Family Size	Results
Wahl	1956	568 schiz. in Navy compared to 100,000 Naval recruits and 392 schiz. from his 1954 study	Significantly larger than average (4+)	Later-born slightly predominated
Schooler	1961	25% of all hospitalized female schiz. in 1959 from 17-65 at Springfield State Hospital, L Bldg. more than 18 mths.	2-4	Significantly more patients in last half; in several studies she analyzed, later-born sig. but difference due entirely to 4+ families. In this sample, similar but N. S.
Caudill	1963	All admissions in 1958 to 3 private and 1 public hosp. in Tokyo (psychot, neurotic, and sch)	All sizes only children excluded	In schiz. and psychot. eldest son and youngest daughter overrep'd, esp. unmarried males in traditional families. N. S. for neurotics
Schooler	1964	Female schiz. admitted in Maryland 1942-49; All male	2-3 show effects; not 4+	First-born in lower class males; last born in middle class males; Sig. more

Author	Year	Sample	Size	Results
		schiz from 18-40 in 2 state hosp. in 1958		last-born females but class N. S.
Granville-Grossman	1966	1244 schiz. (562 males, 682 females) in U. K.	All sizes	Later-born and last-born overrep'd in males N. S. for females. N. S. when both sexes pooled
Barry and Barry	1967	1009 schiz. (320 males, 689 females) in Pa.	2-3 group 1 4+ group 2	In group 1 sig. more first-born males. In Group 2 2 sig. more born in second half
Solomon & Nuttall	1967	291 males schiz. in 5 mental hosp. in Mass.	2, 3, 5 sig. for chronicity	First-born for high socio-ec. class. Earlier-born recover more quickly and are more likely to have an acute onset; later-born more likely to become chronic and manifest undesirable ward behavior after an insidious onset.
Nowicki	1967	1400 psychot. patients in U. S. V. A. hosp. over 7-yr. period.	small (4+ excluded)	Middle-born group also deviant; all groups differed sig.

With inconclusive findings such as the above in the birth order literature, it is not surprising that research linking order of birth and psychosis has been controversial.

The typical study has utilized male and/or female hospitalized patients--primarily adults and often chronic. It has generally been carried out in countries with Western European culture (although recently a few studies have appeared from Asiatic countries). Numbers have varied from sparse (32) to huge (2227), with occasional use of control groups. Many times, however, birth order effects have been tangential findings either thrown in to fill space or pulled in to explain confusing results. Most U. S. studies after 1959 have relied on Schachter's rationale if at all possible, while cross-cultural results have been explained in terms of traditionalism. Some researchers have examined the first or last ordinal positions. Others have suggested that first half and last half siblings are statistically stronger due to the increased number. The research abounds in both types of analysis; some authors, in fact, use both to achieve significance.

The following studies illustrate the type of research and findings in the field.

A summary of the results of studies carried out in the last twelve years reveals the following patterns: some studies have shown schizophrenic males to be first born (69-72); others have shown them to be later or last (73-75), born. One study (76) stresses the deviance of the middle born, and several studies qualify their findings: first-born males in small (2-3) families or upper-class families (77, 78). First-born males have also been found to be more socially isolated (chronic hospitalized patients) by Schooler (70).

For schizophrenic females, results are somewhat more confirmatory. Most studies found that they are more often last or later born (69, 79-81). Two studies found no significance but were in the direction of last (82) and first (72), while one uncovered no significant trend at all (75). Schooler and Scarr (83) and Schooler (70) found first-born females hospitalized for schizophrenia to be more sociable and later born to be less sociable (with only children, in contrast to Schachter, being the least sociable of all).

Two investigations uncovered birth order effects which held for both male and female schizophrenics--the prevalence of first born (Bender and Faretra, (1952)) and first half (71). Interestingly, the former study investigated childen and the latter Indians. In a large family (4+) Barry and Barry (77) found that schizophrenics tend to be in the second half, while Lotter (26) found no significant trends at all in autistic children but Phillips (84) did with the autistic child tending to be a first-born male.

Table 5

	Male	Female	Both
First Born	4 (plus 1 aut., 1 small family, 1 upper class, 1 socially isolated)	1 N. S.	2
Middle Born 1			
Last Born	3	4 1 N. S. 2 less sociable	1 large family
N. S. (and no trend)		1	1 aut.

In analyzing previous data, Barry and Barry (77) found early-born children to be generally overrepresented in large families in non-Western cultures (India), but later-born children to be overrepresented in large families with Western culture (England and U. S.), especially for women. Only in small families in the U. S., they found first-borns to be more common. Apparently, they did not look comprehensively enough into available data, since this author's investigations yielded questionable results. The birth order effect appears to hold most

(according to the empirical data cited in this paper) for schizophrenic females, who seem to be more often later or last born.
In schizophrenic males, all ordinal positions seem to be overrepresented, depending on the study. Numerically, the data favor
first-born as being overrepresented; however, the bulk of these
are qualified by family size, social class, culture, etc. At least
the smaller number of studies relating later birth to psychosis
in males is more clean-cut. For schizophrenics in general, the
evidence is completely useless in formulating a hypothesis,
except to say that the birth order effect seems to be very closely
related to sex and that pooling data flattens or totally negates
most significance.

Family Size

One cannot speak of ordinal position in the family without
investigating the effect of family size on incidence of psychosis.
Schooler and Scarr (83) suggest that small families may be
less cohesive than large, with the parents of the large having at
least stayed together long enough to produce more children.
They feel that this may be a crucial factor in the development of
schizophrenia, whereas in normals it may be trivial. Wahl (73,
74) found that the families of his schizophrenics were larger
than average (4+ compared to the national norm of 2.2) with
the youngest overrepresented. Farina, Barry, and Garmezy
(79) and Barry and Barry (77) noted that when families were
larger than average (4+), a significant number of patients came
from the second half. Generally, when the use of large families
is specified, later-born siblings tend to preponderate; on the
other hand, the use of small families results in ambiguous find-
ings--either not significant or equal occurrence of all ordinal
positions. Perhaps small family constellations tend to flatten
effects which appear as number of siblings increases. Furthermore, incidence of schizophrenia might not be the relevant
factor in family size. Farina, Barry, and Garmezy (79) suggested instead that recoverability is related to large family size: the
larger the number of older siblings, the more likely the patient
was to be hospitalized for schizophrenia and the less likely he
was to recover; the same was true for only children. In their
sample of 167 schizophrenic patients admitted to two state
hospitals (82 male and 85 female), they also found that females

had more older siblings--perhaps offering an explanation for the greater number of female chronic patients present in mental hospitals, perhaps also throwing a statistical monkey wrench into their data. As mentioned earlier, an obvious criticism regarding large family findings is that this may be a social class related factor (especially in state hospital and chronic populations) with lower classes tending to have larger families. It may also be a valid correlation and supportive of both Schachter's psychological view and an organic view of schizophrenia.

Maternal Age

Another variable which is difficult to separate from birth order effects is the age of the mother. If mothers of schizophrenics could be shown empirically to be older than the average, the implications for physiological causation would be enormous, indicating less favorable fetal environment, greater biological stress, etc. Interestingly, maternal birth rank has a greater effect of producing fraternal twins than her increasing age or the presence of older siblings in the family she has mothered (81), suggesting that her own birth order may actually affect her physiological process of conception. This does not rule out the relevance of maternal age to psychological factors as well (for instance, how might this affect the child rearing practices she employs). The results nicely uphold the suggestion that maternal age is greater for mothers of schizophrenics--that is to say, they confirm this finding until one peruses the studies which have included maternal age data and finds that practically every study mentioning older mothers also found an overrepresentation of mental illness in later or last born siblings. A study which only used three-sibling families (85) found no significance in psychosis or neurosis. However, in some specifically organically related difficulties, mothers were found to be older. Ucko (14) found that when comparing 29 boys asphyxiated at birth with 29 boys not asphyxiated, the mothers of the asphyxiated boys were significantly older. This was an especially powerful finding since first born children in both groups were compared (erasing the effects of family size), although when all ranks were pooled, significance disappeared. Of course, it might also represent a statistical artefact created by the small number. Paffenbarger, Steinmetz, Pooler, and

Hyde (43) noted that rates increased with age in para-partum psychosis. Since they suggested that at least post-partum psychosis may have an organic etiology, this seems to suggest that increased age renders women more vulnerable to physiological difficulties relating to birth. As age has also been found to be significantly related to mental deficiency and mongolism (86), there seems to be some justification for expecting older women to experience more pregnancy and birth difficulties, which in turn may lead to more neuropsychiatric disorders. By contrast, Pasamanick and Knobloch (87) found that very young or older women had a significantly higher risk of producing mental defectives, but this is not necessarily inconsistent with organic causation theories if one sees both extremes as a typical or higher risk ages. In studying parental (rather than maternal) age, Dennehy (88) found a slightly higher than average age for parents of all groups he investigated (depressives, schizophrenics, alcoholics, combined) except drug addicts. Granville-Grossman (89), on the other hand, found a similar but not significant trend for parents of schizophrenics but concluded that parental age--especially paternal age--was not a factor.

Familial Factors

Perhaps searching for birth order effects in order to predict incidence or course of schizophrenia is an attempt to oversimplify a complex family constellation with innumerable individual variations. Both genetic-organic factors and social factors seem to enter into the picture. The former cites the higher incidence of schizophrenic offspring when the mother is schizophrenic herself (16 per cent probability as compared to one per cent without a psychotic parent) (90). When a group of children with such a family were compared with children with a normal background, Heston (91) found that the children who did not become schizophrenic showed a higher incidence of emotionally labile neurotics and psychopaths--but also individuals living a more interesting, varied, and creative life than the controls. Perhaps Huntington's findings (92) that more great men are born in the same season as more schizophrenics reflects the line between constructive and destructive creativity. These might be particularly relevant findings today when schizophrenics have been found to be experiencing relatively greater increases in marriage and total reproduction than the general population--particularly in the case of schizophrenic women (93). Social factors are many and complex, but suggest that the mother-father-child triad might be the relevant one with siblings playing a very minor role in the process, certainly quite contradictory to ordinal position theories, especially in the case of the later-born siblings (1). Clausen and Kohn noted in the Hagerstown study (1) that schizophrenic families differed from controls in that there was more often a strong maternal and weak paternal figure (particularly among paranoids); they also found that males said that they felt closer to their mothers and females to their fathers. When comparing schizophrenic and neurotic children, Block, Patterson, Block and Jackson (1) found that the mothers of schizophrenics tended to be hostile, distrustful and manipulative, while fathers were more direct in expression of hostility than mothers and were assertive to the point of being counterphobic. By contrast, Creak and Ini (94) noted that the parents of 102 psychotic children were heterogeneous, representing the full range of emotional warmth, which they consider evidence of a constitutional or pathogenic etiology. Similarly, Bender and Grugett (95) found that the emotional climate of the family of the schizophrenic child was not unfavorable but considerably more favorable than that of the non-schizophrenic behavior disorders in terms of cohesion, stability, interest in children, etc. The latter may represent the clear-cut diagnosis of middle class children as schizophrenic when compared to lower class children, who are usually difficult to differentially diagnose (60). The findings of Lowe (96), Levine and Olson (97), Lotter (26), and Rimland (27) that autistic children have parents who are better educated and intelligent, in a higher socio-economic class, and more stable might also reflect the class difference or possibly that (as Rimland and Sankar suggest) autistic children are in fact different from schizophrenic children. Interestingly, Lotter (26) did find that while there was no greater incidence of psychotic illness in relatives, there was a greater incidence of other serious mental illness in the families of autistics when compared to her normal controls.

Occurrence of other mental illness in the family, not being married, and having an absent father appear at first glance to

Table 6

Author	Year	Subjects	Country	Years under Study	Results
Tramer	1929	2100 schiz, psychot, alcoholics, paretics from private clinic	Switzerland	1871-80 1901-10	Significant difference Winter--Dec. to May smaller number in May
Lang	1931	3976 schiz; 1879 manic-depress. 17379 control psychiatric hospit. pats. Total monthly rate and total birth rate in Bavaria, 1905-14 All S's in public hospitals	Bavaria	1905-14	Somewhat higher for schiz. from Jan to Feb and lower in Aug and Nov, but N. S. N. S. for sibs, manic-depressives, or psychopaths compared to general population
Petersen	1934	3467 schiz; 691 manic-depress. in public hospitals; Control Monthly birth rate in U. S., 1917-29	U. S. U. S. Ind., Md., NY, Mass., Mich., Ohio, Pa.	1917-1929	Winter--Dec and Jan higher for schiz. Summer--June to Sept. lower for schiz. Manic-depress. above controls in March-May.
Huntington	1938	10420 schiz; 3683 manic-depress. Control total monthly birth rate for Mass, 1885-1914		1885-1914	Both schiz and manic-depressives higher in Winter (Feb-April) and lower in Summer (June-Sept)

Nolting	1934 1951 1954	2589 schiz; 1556 manic depress. 2090 schiz; 1228 manic-depress. 3253 schiz. Controls for all birth rates for Neth. in years studied	Netherlands	1920-53	Winter (Dec-March) higher for schiz; Summer (June-Sept) lower; N. S. difference between manic-depressives and controls
Barry and Barry	1961	1453 schiz (pub. hos.) from N.J. & Mass.; Controls 1-1/2 million from general population in Mass.	U. S.	1883-90 1903-10 1923-30	Jan-April highest for schiz; May-Aug Lowest; Sept-Dec intermediate; N. S. for manic-depressives but similar to schiz.
Norris and Chowning	1962	3617 schiz. in pub. hosp.; Controls total Canadian birth rate for 1923, 34, 37, 40 (randomly selected)	Canada	1959 (S's born 1919-44)	Jan-May higher for schiz; June- Sept lower but N. S. for other randomly selected years in span of 1919-44
Barry and Barry	1963	6751 schiz from 2 private hosp. (2416 males, 3261 females--1907; 455 males, 619 females--1931) Controls monthly birth rate for total years	U. S.	1907-62	N. S. but suggested sex difference with males highest in Jan-April and females highest in May-Aug; also suggested that the higher the social class, the closer to the norm.

predict significantly better hospital adjustment for schizophrenics (98). However, these authors feel that such negative
qualities do in fact merely characterize chronic patients or
militate against their being discharged from the hospital. They
suggest that other mental illness in the family merely prepares
the patient early for life among deviants and dulls the distinction between being inside and outside the hospital. Some
studies have attempted to correlate religion and psychosis, but
these investigations have yielded little, with religion simply
reflecting the composition of the particular population (73, 74,
95). Schooler (70) found significantly more schizophrenics to be
Catholic and Jewish compared to Protestant even though
guessing ethnic background by name showed all to be equally
represented.

Criticisms of birth order findings are usually made because of the lack of control for many of the familiar factors
described above. Of course, some of these variables are difficult to control for, since maternal age and larger family size
must almost certainly be correlated, as must ordinal position
and birth rank (the first born must also be the oldest). Some
statistical artefacts also enter the picture--for example, does
larger family size really increase the likelihood of schizophrenia
or does it increase the likelihood that a statistical significance
will be obtained? And what about studies which have not found
first born but have found first half significant? Is this a legitimate statistical manipulation as Schooler (81) suggests or does
it cast doubt on the validity of the findings? A further question
has been asked which casts doubts on interpreting the results
at all. Couldn't it be, as Sundararaj and Rao (72) suggest, that
the patients admitted to hospitals are not representative of
schizophrenia in general who do not seek admission? For
instance, in the rural population, deviants are more readily
assimilated in India. They go on to ask whether in fact early
born individuals (more frequently psychotic in their population)
might not only have a better chance of hospital admission while
other disturbed siblings are kept at home. Perhaps a family is
ashamed or discouraged after one hospitalization and maintains other family ill at home. Since a U. S. sample (99) found,
however, that younger siblings seem to have an earlier onset of

disease (as measured by hospital admission), this might not be a tenable hypothesis in this country. This is also suggested by the finding that the closer blood relationship in the family, the smaller the age difference between onsets. Schooler (70) also suggests that birth rank might not reflect incidence, but rather symptomatology--with the last born female being less competent socially and prone to bizarre or self-destructive behavior.

The implications of birth order data to the two major theoretical entities are interesting but inconclusive. When postulating an organic etiology in schizophrenia, the sex differences which seem to enter into most of the results could reflect the variable occurrence of fetal and paranatal injury with later born females less able to withstand the increased risk but all males (in any ordinal position) more susceptible to damage. If as the slight trend suggests, schizophrenic males tend to be first born, could this be consistent rather with a psychogenic explanation (with first born siblings being more subject to reactive stress or react violently to the inability of the environment to stand their overassertiveness) while the evidence showing high incidence of later born schizophrenics especially among chronics could be consistent with Brackbill and Fine's theory that process schizophrenia is organic or biochemical in etiology with later borns being exposed to more biological stress (78). However, if order of birth (at least in females), is relevant, why has it been found that all siblings of schizophrenics including those who develop normally have been found to have more pregnancy and birth complications (23)? Moreover, if cultural differences seem to affect data (69, 71) how can physiology be causally involved?

Birth order effects may be related to several psychological variables postulated by Schachter. In terms of sex role in greater dependency and need to verbalize and interact socially may be more acceptable in the first-born female (these elements being consonant with the female role in the American culture) while the tendency to withdraw or be more self-sufficient and inner directed (characteristic of later born) may be less acceptable in the later born female, heralding at least the beginnings of poorer societal adjustment. On the other hand, the latter constellation would be more acceptable for the male in our culture while the former would not--suggesting greater adjustment problems for the first-born male. However, the inability to verbalize could also get him into more "hot water" in this society, as could the exaggerated need for self-sufficiency. Thus the male might be prone to more difficulties no matter what his mode of adjustment or ordinal position. If childhood treatment does in fact influence ability to withstand later assaults, then females--especially first born--who experience greater approval and attention in the family should be healthier. On the other hand, greater interest in the first-born male may be coupled with our demands and responsibilities--again tempering a positive with a negative aspect. This has been postulated in both the Japanese (69) and the Indian (71, 72) cultures in traditional families. The additional finding by Caudill that the youngest female is more poorly adjusted due to enforced dependency and responsibilities to the father suggests the power of parental expectations and attitudes in developing stress situations. If birth order then does have an effect in the social sphere, why do schizophrenics tend to have more poorly adjusted siblings (including marital discord, mental defectives, delayed speech, schizophrenia), the conclusion of Havelkova (39). And why have normal siblings been found at least to suffer from marked constriction of personality (1). Schooler (81) suggests that environmental factors related to birth order have a transitive effect--that is to say, either the number of schizophrenics is highest for the first born and decreases steadily thereafter or is highest for the last born and steadily increases, nicely taking all results into account, explaining family size variables, and getting rid of genetic explanations since this would assume a random distribution.

The variety of findings regarding birth order factors in the occurrence of schizophrenia suggest that something is going on--but no consistent pattern has emerged and at present the results must be considered inconclusive.

Sexual Factors

Whether an individual is born a male or a female appears to have a definite correlation with the probability of his becoming psychotic and even the course of his psychosis. Even before birth, in fact, this factor has an influence. The varieties of such effects run the gamut from predispositions to actual incidences of all manner of deviances.

Very few serious organic diseases have been found to be more common in females. Most diseases of the gastro-intestinal tract, respiratory tract, blood vessels, heart, bones, joints, and urinary tract have much higher frequency in males, while some are limited to males alone (thromboangiitis obliterans). On the other hand, females are more subject to functional diseases like hypertension, migraine, hysteria, and chronic nervous exhaustion (possibly sub-substantiating the finding that females are more prone to experience anxiety and react to stress made by Sontag in 1947). This apparent inherent sex-linked weakness in the male even holds true for the animal kingdom, where the male is shorter lived (100).

In terms of pregnancy, birth, and maladjustment, males have been found to be more prone to:

1. Pregnancy difficulties in utero (cited in 15) (Gittelman and Birch, 1967)
2. Paranatal complications (56) (Gittelman and Birch, 1964)
3. Fetal death (Bellack, 1962)
4. Higher infant mortality (101) (Birch, 1964)
5. Higher mortality from childhood diseases (102)
6. Higher mortality rates at any age (100) (Bellack, 1962) (cited in 101)
7. Cerebral palsy (103, 104)
8. Epilepsy (105)
9. Mental deficiency (cited in 47, 106)
10. Reading disabilities (107)
11. Behavior disorders (18)
12. Neuropsychiatric disorders (35) (Gittelman and Birch, 1967)
13. Higher suicide rates both in adulthood (3:1) and old age (10:1) (108)

In incidence of pscyhosis, males also seem to have the edge--at least until the adult years. Males are more likely to be psychotic in infancy (20, 109), autistic (26) and hospitalized for psychosis (and schizophrenia) in childhood (20, 47). In fact, up to the age of 12, males outnumber females in ratios variously quoted as 5:1, 4:1, 3:1, or 2:1 with the former larger ratios predominating (95). Pollack, Levenstein, and Klein (30) found that male adolescents also outnumber females in schizophrenia. However, during the child-bearing years, Jaco (110) and Pugh and MacMahon (111) both found that mental illness is higher for females than males. Pollack (29) suggested a ratio around 3:2 (F:M). Of course, this increase in females may be reflecting three diagnostic categories other than schizophrenia-- parapartum psychoses and involutional melancholia (to which only females are obviously subject) and manic-depressive psychosis, which Malzberg (1935) and Spiegel and Bell (68) found to be more prevalent among females. In schizophrenia Erlenmeyer-Kimling, Rainer, and Kallmann (112) found that in New York State from 1934-6 and 1954-6 at approximately age 35 the prevalence of males was reversed and females thereafter consistently outnumbered males. Malzberg (68) cautioned that in New York State this might be due to the use of state hospital populations in the figures; more males were probably being admitted to Veteran's Administration Hospitals and not state hospitals after World War II. With advancing age, more females are found in the ranks of the chronic patients (113); their rate of hospitalization also increases until they definitely lost any advantage and catch up with males (68). One could argue, naturally, that with increasing age, life expectancy, which is higher for females, begins to enter the picture. The higher ratio of F:M senile psychotics tends to corroborate this impression (68, 114).

Rosenbaum (90) noted other sex-linked probabilities in schizophrenia by investigating twins and relatives of schizophrenics. In the primary family group, an individual of the same sex as the patient is more likely to become schizophrenic. This is especially true if the patient is a female. Rosenthal (113) found that brother pairs of twins exceeded by more than one-half number of all brother-sister pairs when they were concordant for schizophrenia. Concordance rates were higher, however, for female pairs compared to male pairs. In dizygotic twins, he discovered that the female-male ratio was 4:1--but cautioned that this might be a sampling error due to the greater number of female chronics in hospitals which are used for such research.

In an attempt to understand the reason for the sex differences in distribution and course of psychosis, researchers have formed a number of hypotheses related to either biological or psychological factors. The first of these attempts to causally link the well-known fact that males are biologically less able to withstand physiological assaults, both before and after birth. Thus they would be more apt to sustain organic damage. In point of fact, a number of researchers (34, 47, 54, 101) (Gittelman and Birch, 1967) have found that more males than females are organically brain damaged.

For example, Taft and Goldfarb (47) investigated the difference between boy and girl schizophrenics (21 boys to 8 girls reflecting the usual male:female ratio in childhood schizophrenia). They found that boys outnumbered girls significantly in organic involvement (8:3), whereas girls outnumbered boys significantly in nonorganic, functional etiology (7:1). Rosenthal (1962) found a similar cluster when he compared male and female twins who were schizophrenic. Four times more often than females, males had a history of trauma or infection; females, on the other hand, had a psychic etiology more often than males (the first finding was highly significant while the second just fell short of significance but was in the right direction). The results might demonstrate, as Stabenau (1968) suggests, that "there is evidence to postulate a genetic component to the etiology of schizophrenia; however, detailed family study of monozygotic twins discordant for schizophrenia suggests there are pre- and/or post-natal experiental environmental components necessary for schizophrenic symptomatology to emerge in a given individual."

Birch (101) asks whether there could not be a connection between boys' significantly larger head sizes at birth and their higher incidence of the organoid syndrome. He also postulates a correlation between paranatal mortality and organicity: "If you want to find a high incidence of organic and organoid syndromes, look for a population with high paranatal mortality rates." He does, however, offer an alternate explanation to the usual which suggests biological weakness in the male, suggesting instead male strength. Males, Birch hypothesizes, might

tolerate brain damage in fetal life better than females, who die
in early pregnancy. Therefore, the preponderance of males with
brain damage may be reflecting the fact that they tolerate
damaging experiences fatal to females. The higher male birth
rate also might be called into evidence for such a position.
Actually, Record and Smith's Birmingham data (115) on mongolism show that paranatal mortality rates are higher in female
mongols than in male, whereas a few years later, male mongol
death rates are higher than female.

Shearer and Davidson and Finch (116) even postulated
differential chemical reactions in the ova of schizophrenic
women which prevented the development of males. They found
that in women who had an onset of schizophrenic symptoms
within one month before or after the theoretical date of conception, no males and 14 females were born. They postulated that
perhaps some chemical substance interfered with the viability
of the ovum to the Y chromosome carrying sperm or its development in the fertilized ovum which was not lethal at a later stage
of development.

Sex Role

A second set of theories revolves out sex role factors.
Several researchers (69, 72, 77, 98, 117-121) have stated that
sex role identification or expectations might account for differential sexual incidence and course of psychosis. For instance,
Gardner (117) suggests that sex role indentification might
account for the fact that girls who later became schizophrenic
after being seen in a child guidance clinic for a period of time in
their childhood had severely disturbed mothers significantly
more often than those in the same group who became well-
adjusted adults. On the other hand, this was not important
for boys who became schizophrenic. Such a finding would also
be consistent with Rosenbaum's conclusion (90) that same sex
(and especially female) primary family members had a higher
probability of also becoming schizophrenic. By contrast,
Costello, Gunn, and Dominian (122) found that three background events seemed common in schizophrenic males; absence
of a father, early childhood single illness (perhaps consonant
with Bowlby's theory (123) of maternal deprivation), and less
adolescent illness. It would appear, therefore, that having an

unhealthy same sex person with whom to identify--or none at all--predisposes towards poor mental health later in life. Another possibility is cross-sexual identification, suggested by Clausen and Kohn (cited in Bellak, 1962) who noted in their Hagerstown study that schizophrenic males often said they felt closer to their mothers, while schizophrenic women often stated a preference for their fathers.

Schooler and Long (118) divided a group of 144 regressed chronic schizophrenics (half male and half female) into three experimental conditions: benevolent, hostile, and control. In the first, the patient was told that a paired patient would receive a dime every time he correctly completed a task; in the second, a paired patient would lose a dime for every error; in the third, no money was involved. Analysis revealed no initial significant sex or condition differences between patients and controls but unexpected and interesting differences in subgroups. Male catatonics were found to begin the task with hostility; then over time they became more benevolent. The same was true for female paranoids. Male paranoids, on the other hand, began more benevolently and over time became more hostile. This pattern was also found in female catatonics. The initial sex difference was explained by sexually determined defense mechanisms and sex roles (for instance, females being culturally conditioned to be less aggressive). However, the authors had to resort to "complexity" explanations when the behavioral changes described appeared over time. Schooler (119) also found differences between schizophrenic males, schizophrenic females, and normal controls when investigating affiliation preferences. The higher the level of intellectual functioning, the more likely the schizophrenic male was to want to work with someone who would want to make friends and express both positive and negative opinions. Female schizophrenics, by contrast, preferred the co-worker to keep negative feelings hidden. Schooler explained this desire in females for harmony by denial to be a function of culture--the tendency for females to feel helpless in the face of aggression and to want to avoid it. On the other hand, McClelland and Watt (120) found that female schizophrenics tended to react assertively like normal males, while male schizophrenics reacted sensitively like normal females. Since the same might be said for career women as schizophrenic women, they suggested that sex role alienation might not be the relevant explanation, but rather the self-image disturbance in schizophrenia. Schooler and Parkel (98) also noted that male and female chronics differed qualitatively, with females being more ideationally disturbed, holding more implausible ideas, and showing greater conceptual disorganization--in other words, being better able to see both the real and unreal connections between phenomena. Possibly this is also a function of the greater sensitivity that this culture expects of a woman.

One obvious criticism of the studies disclosing differences between the sexes related to incidence of psychosis is that they have rarely been investigating that factor when they almost accidentally found it. Therefore, they often have been working with unequal numbers of each sex (weakening their statistical conclusions) or have not been following up their studies with interpretive discussion. Again has a looseness of diagnostic categories been applied, making understanding and generalization difficult. The use of hospitalized patients-- usually chronic--leads one to wonder if this might not be the reason for some "sex" differences. For example, might not the higher number of male hospitalized childhood disorders really be reflecting the fact that boys are harder to handle at home, or that families somehow feel more responsible for little girls? Of course, in all relationships between psychosis and sex, there must be weighed the inescapable fact that generally males experience most forms of neuropsychiatric disorder more frequently than females. Therefore, might not the higher incidences of psychoses (especially in childhood and adolescence) merely be reflecting this general tendency? In old age, might not the longer life span of females be the relevant variable?

At present the two explanations of sexual differences-- level of biological risk and sex role factors--both seem to interact in the differential incidence (especially the former) and of course (especially the latter) of psychosis.

Season of Birth

Since the late nineteenth century, researchers have exhibited an interest in a topic which has intrigued man since the dawn of recorded history: How does the month of birth effect the life of the individual? At first glance for today's scientists, this question smacks of pseudopsychological or even magical flavor; after all, astrology has long passed from the realm of serious scientific pursuit into the nether world populated by charlatans and quacks. Yet is a relationship between time of birth and subsequent events entirely implausible? After all, the fetal and neonatal periods are highly sensitive ones in which vicissitudes of environment could conceivably have an effect--and a lasting one--especially if an unfavorable season coincides with a critical stage of development, such as the first three months of fetal life or immediately before or after birth. Already many authors have uncovered what appear to be definite links between physiological ailments or deviations and season or even months of birth. For example, Rutstein, Nickerson and Heald (124), showed that the highest incidence of newborns with arteriosis was in the late autumn, logically following the spring prevalence of maternal rubella, often considered an antecedent factor if occurring in the early months of pregnancy. Barry and Barry (125) also cite a seasonal correlation for anencephaly and congenital cranial osteoporosis, as does Plum (11, 12) for cerebral palsy. Pregnancy complications (87), perinatal mortality (125), and prematurity (15) seem to occur most frequently in the winter, as do births later found to be mentally deficient (126, 127) or less intelligent (128). Possible connections between winter birth and social or personality deviance like criminal insanity or "the problem child" have even been suggested (125). It is therefore not surprising that some psychologists have attempted to investigate the possible relationship between psychosis and season of birth.

The typical study in this field--consisting of only about two dozen in over fifty years--had certain features in common. It was usually conducted in a country manifesting Western European culture and concerned statistics gathered for hospitalized psychotic patients (the majority diagnosed as schizophrenic or manic-depressive). The size of the sample was typically in the thousands (the range covering anywhere from 1453 to 23,000) but more often around two or three thousand. While both sexes were included, this was usually in random proportion in the year or years of the sample. Most studies have been conducted with adults and have included all patients newly admitted into a mental institution for a span covering from one to 25 years (the median being around seven years). Controls were average monthly birth rates taken from census statistics for the general population for one or more years (usually in the range of birth years for the subjects) for either a delimited area (like a particular state or city) or a nation (like Canada). This year was divided into 12 months, 4 seasons, or trimesters (1: January-April; 2: May-August; 3: September-December), with the latter predominating.

The following eight summarized studies are representative of some of the more important work done in the area. The results of these and other investigations are surprisingly confirmatory, each supporting the other with amazing accuracy. The majority found that schizophrenics are more often born in the winter (if the year was divided into four seasons) or in the first trimester (92, 125, 126, 129, 130) (Tramer, 1929; Nolting, 1934, 1951, 1954; Pile, 1949). Others who found no statistically significant difference nevertheless discovered that the results were in the direction of the preceding studies (128, 131). A few found no significant differences at all in the incidence of schizophrenia and season of birth (130) (Pile, 1949). On the other hand, Goodenough (1941) actually found that more schizophrenics were born in the spring and fewer in the winter.

When these results are compared with those for other behavioral deviances--for example, problem children--they yield similar findings: more individuals with severe personality problems are also born in the winter (cited in 125). As a matter of fact, so are more great men--a positive personality deviation? --(92), less intelligent men (128) and retardates (126, 127). More pregnancy difficulties are also noted by the latter authors to occur in the winter. In fact, the only deviations which appeared to more often correlate with the third trimester were those which might be termed neurological (11, 12, 124, 125).

The following gives an overview of the season of birth-psychosis findings.

A variety of hypotheses for the observed season of birth-psychosis connection have been proposed by authors interested in the question.

Table 7

Finding	Number of Studies
Winter or first trimester	10
N. S. but in the direction of above	3
N. S.	2
Spring	1

Parental Considerations

Many of these theories have tried to relate cultural, sub-cultural, and socio-economic class behavior of the parents to season of birth. One such theory suggests that parental mating habits may account for the greater number of deviant individuals born in the first trimester. As Hollingshead and Redlich (132) have clearly demonstrated, different cultural groups do in fact have different seasonal mating habits. Therefore, Barry and Barry (125) ask if parents of psychotics might not comprise a subgroup with atypical mating habits. Thus far no studies have investigated this possibility. Huntington (92) suggests that the favorable and pleasant climate of spring would appeal to procreation among basically unfit and impulsive people and cited material showing the large number of illegitimate births in the winter; he generalized unfit and impulsive to include criminals and psychotics who would in turn have less than fit offspring. Barry and Barry (92) point out, however, that unstable parents also offer the poorest home environment and often come from the lowest socio-economic classes. In fact, they found that psychotic patients do come predominantly from the lowest socio-economic strata and suggested that the lower class may have a different seasonal distribution of birth which is being reflected in the supposed season-psychosis correlation. When studies have attempted to control for this variable, some of the striking correlations found between winter and mental illness have disappeared (131), although a few authors have found that class differences do not affect the results which are the same for all groups (126) (Goodenough, 1941). Other authors have simply concluded that lower classes show greater deviation from the norm (131, 133). Still, Pasamanick and Knobloch (134) have found that neuropsychiatric disorders are more common among lower classes. Perhaps, as Barry and Barry (131) suggest, the middle and upper classes are better able to modify the deleterious effect of climate and feed and care for their pregnant women. In fact, Pasamanick, Dinitz, and Knobloch (133) virtually ruled out the postulated increased rate of lower class births in winter when they found that both Negroes and whites included in all social classes had fewer deliveries in winter in a five-year period in Baltimore.

Fetal Environment

Other hypotheses have attempted to show the connection between fetal environment and season of birth. A relationship between weather and time of conception has been shown in a study by Pasamanick, Dinitz, and Knobloch (135). They found that when all 1955 births in the U. S. were compared by month and geographic distribution, certain patterns became clear: in the South, there was a marked decline during the spring; in the Midwest and Northeast, there was only a slight trough in the spring; in the Northwest (Washington and Oregon), there was no spring trough; in fact, births were slightly higher in the spring than expected. Thus summer conception would appear to be less likely in the hotter South than in either the Midwest and Northeast, whereas it would seem that in the cooler summers of the Northwest conception was actually more likely. Although the obvious criticism could be leveled that this was found to be true only in 1955 and that the results could be an artefact of that particular year, the study is still suggestive of the types of investigations which are possible and the type of inferences which have been drawn.

One of the leading theories has related this idea of summer heat to deviant development. A lowered threshold to stress through the hypothalamico-pituitary-adrenal-cortical axis serving as an additional organic percursor in an individual already genetically predisposed has been postulated by Pasamanick and Knobloch (cited in 15). In fact, Knobloch and Pasamanick (126) did find a significant increase in the rate of both schizophrenia and mental deficiency in individuals born in years following hot summers as compared to cool.

A second effect of summer heat might be nutritional reflecting maternal diet. Knobloch and Pasamanick suggest a possible protein deficiency caused by decreased dietary intake (inferred from their discovery that in one year all children born in the summer were significantly lighter in birth weight and such weight is largely accumulated by the fetus during the last three months of pregnancy (15)). Nolting (1934) suggested a Vitamin C deficiency was the crucial factor. He stated that winter birth is related to schizophrenia since in this critical period when normal mental development is taking place (a few weeks before or after birth) Vitamin C is lacking. In a later study among mental defectives, Nolting (1951) found that the highest birth rate was during June and July, when he rapidly changed the critical period of Vitamin C deficiency to the last three months of prenatal development. Pasamanick, Dinitz, and Knobloch (cited in 15) state that summer conception would seem to have some effect on twinning--possibly due to the teratogenic effect of heat stress on the embryo--since the peak season of twin births (which show significantly higher infant mortality, prematurity, and neuropsychiatric disorders) was in the spring. Males (usually considered more susceptible biologically) have lower birth rates just prior to and during the descending curve of the spring depression as well as increased pregnancy complications. Again these events coincide with summer conception as does the neonatal death peak in spring (135).

Pasamanick, Rogers, and Lilienfeld (18) also found that more births in the first trimester were preceded by complications of pregnancy (specifically eclampsia or preeclampsia, uterine bleeding, and heart disease). Pre-maturity has also been found to occur most frequently in the winter (cited in 15). Many of these birth and pregnancy complications have been linked to schizophrenia. Petersen (129) also stresses the importance of season of conception--the critical period, however, being spring, when the fetus is overstimulated and fatigued by meteorological instability.

One investigator (128) even suggested that the increased incidence of winter births found among schizophrenics really reflected differential intelligence. More intelligent patients were born in the second and third trimesters and less intelligent in the first: since more patients were found to be born in the first, this must reflect the inferior level of performance of most schizophrenics.

In summary, the hypotheses regarding reasons for a correlation between season of birth and psychosis have grown out of many studies linking season and birth and other atypical or generally deviant subsequent events like brain damage or mental deficiency. These theories have considered the parents (especially the mother) in terms of mating habits and social class. Fetal environment--including climate, nutrition, pregnancy difficulties, and complicating factors of birth--have also been cited in explanation. At present not enough uncontested data is available to select a probable hypothesis; however, theories revolving about fetal environment seem to offer the most promise if in fact a relationship between season of birth and psychosis exists.

The whole area of study is open to severe criticism, especially on methodological grounds. This was perceived and actually investigated statistically by Norris and Chowning (130), whose original study is presented in the Table preceding. After finding significant results in the usual direction (more schizophrenics born in the first trimester), they compared prior research and their own study and found that almost none of them had controlled for variables which could turn out to be relevant: geographic area, socio-economic class, yearly differences in control census figures. The use of representative years taken from the range of birth dates of the subjects was questioned. Their initial study, which found significant differences between schizophrenics and normals when the years of 1923, 1934, 1937, and 1940 (randomly selected) were averaged to give a monthly birth rate, yielded different results when different randomly selected years were compared. For instance, the results were not significant for the years 1925, 1935, 1937, and 1945--but they were significant for 1922, 1934, 1944, 1939; 1922, 1929, 1931, and 1944 also was not significant. Neither was a monthly birth rate based on all the years of the study, 1921-1946. Norris and Chowning then compared several pairs of years randomly and found that 1922-1940 and 1935-1946 differed significantly, while 1935-1944 and 1935-1941 did not. In fact, fifty per cent of monthly birth rates in Canada differed significantly from each other in any year and/or from themselves in different years. As the most common control in nearly all the studies in the field has been figures from randomly selected years, this criticism many negate many of the conclusions found. They also found that the birth rate for one province could differ significantly from another province and/or itself from year to year; as the control for patients in one hospital or clinic has often been the national norms, a geographic artefact might interfere with interpretation of results. They also found that most studies did not control for social class, a possible significant variable, although the few that have executed this control have not found it important, except for Barry and Barry, whose 1963 study was published after Norris and Chowning's and found that the higher the social class the less deviation from the norm.

In this study Barry and Barry criticized Norris and Chowning on several counts: as they used months rather than trimesters, they felt that the number per month might have been too small to be valid. They also questioned whether the difference in Canada's climate (where summers are relatively cool) might not have explained their absence of significant differences, especially when compared to American studies. Finally, they suggested that Norris and Chowning's cases probably had fewer lower socio-economic representatives since they included both public and private hospitals. If social class does play a significant role in the statistics of prior studies, this could explain the different results. This study also found a non-significant but clear tendency for psychotic males to be born in the first trimester and psychotic females in the second. This could be due to the fact that in the general population fewer male births occur in the spring (135) and more neonatal death (to which males are more subject than females). Still, sex is a possible relevant variable which has rarely been controlled for.

Another possibly relevant variable is intelligence. The only study which controlled for this (128) revealed a connection between spring and summer birth and more intelligent patients and winter birth and less intelligent patients. This data is somewhat substantiated by studies showing that mental defectives are also more often born in the winter (126).

In fact, might not the whole area really be reflecting deviance in general rather than psychosis, one subheading in this broad topic. The many previously mentioned investiga-relating all types of deviations from the norm to season of birth certainly enhance this possibility.

The two criticisms which could be leveled at nearly all birth factor studies might be confounding the findings further: Does the inclusion of hospitalized patients only effect the results? Do the diagnostic categories (and the considerable looseness with which they are applied to seasonal studies) influence the results? In other words, can results found for "psychotics" be generalized to schizophrenia? Can results found for schizophrenics be accurately ascribed to all schizophrenics or only those in a particular geographic area, year, hospital?

Social Factors

A number of social factors have been found to be relevant when investigating the problem of birth in psychosis. These include such elements as race, migratory tendencies, functioning level in society, culture, and social class.

Race

Most postulated racial differences appearing in birth factor-psychosis studies have discussed the Negroid and Caucasoid, particularly in terms of their relative positions in U. S. society. Other "racial" differences have been interpreted as due to different norms rather than skin color. These will be discussed in the section related to culture.

Generally, Pasamanick (136) found that Negro babies matched the Gesell norms set up for white children in almost all areas except two: language and gross motor behavior. Com-

parison of Negro premature babies and Negro full-term babies
at 30 months (34) revealed similar findings. However, Pasamanick and Knobloch (15) found that when comparing white
and Negro babies at 40 weeks and again at three years a significant difference appeared. At 40 weeks both groups showed
no disparity in a general development quotient; at three years,
on the other hand, they found that the white mean was 110.9,
while the Negro mean was 97.4.

Negroes have been found to differ from Caucasians in the
occurrence of some deviant physical events. For example, they
have been noted to have a higher incidence of:

Pregnancy abnormalities (137)
Prematurity (59)
Cerebral palsy (103)
Mental deficiency (106)
Behavior disorders (18)
Neuropsychiatric disturbances (134)
Epilepsy (not significant but in the right direction) (105)
Postnatal injuries like head injury, lead intoxication, and
    infection (cited in 15)

In hospitalization for psychosis, diagnosis and course of
illness, Negroes have also been found to differ. Malzberg (138)
discovered that Negro rates of hospitalization in New York
state hospitals from 1939 to 1941 were twice as high as rates of
admission for white patients in the same period. Upon investigating further, he found that the two most common diagnostic
categories for Negroes were paresis and alcoholic psychosis.
When comparing Negro and white male and female schizophrenics, Lane (139) found that significantly more Negro males
were diagnosed process schizophrenics, while significantly more
white females were diagnosed reactive schizophrenics, with
Negro females and white males falling into intermediate positions. She hypothesized that if process was defined as withdrawal and turning against others, this might often in fact fit
the Negro male patient; if reactive was defined as reacting by
turning against oneself, this might often in fact describe the
white female patient. When comparing the two extremes, she
also suggested that the white female might encounter enough
childhood acceptance to alter the inexorable course of schizophrenia, while the Negro male might be the most rejected of the

four groups. Furthermore, culturally, the white female would be encouraged to repress aggressive behavior and introject, in the process becoming more self-critical. On the other hand, the Negro male tends to be both more aggressive due to positive culture sanctions and more isolated. The white middle or upper class mental health worker would certainly be more comfortable with the former mode of behavior than the latter and so would be more disposed to diagnosing the white female in the less severe and more hopeful diagnostic category.

Basically, two different approaches have evolved in the attempt to explain the differences connected with race in birth factor-psychosis studies. The first cites organic etiology; the second, social.

Organic theories stress the preponderance of pregnancy abnormalities and prematurity complications in the Negro group. Lilienfeld, Pasamanick, and Rogers (35) have hypothesized a relationship between such physiological factors of birth and any number of neuropsychiatric disorders, including cerebral palsy and childhood behavior disorders. Such disorders have, in fact, been found to be more prevalent in the Negro group. These theories also point out that Negroes do in fact have a more chaotic physical history after birth, with infections and injuries more common and thus more likely to traumatize the individual.

The major criticisms of this line of reasoning come under the heading of the second type of theory: social factors. Such theories stress the different family life and social environment to which Negroes have been exposed. For instance, Kardiner and Ovesey (140) found the Negro home to be mother dominated, with a lack of respect for the father, who was usually either absent or if present passive and remote (except for occasional violence). If process schizophrenics come from mother-dominated homes, as Chapman and Baxter (141) suggest, could this not explain Lane's results (139) cited above? However, Kohn and Clausen (142) have noted that mother-dominated homes also correlated with other deviances, including ulcers, anorexia nervosa, juvenile delinquency, and drug addiction. They suggest that the inclusion of this factor in schizophrenic etiology may be premature. Perhaps the absence or passivity of the father is the important variable, as Costello, Gunn, and

Dominian (122) suggest. Since these subjects were white male schizophrenics, however, this flattens rather than heightens the racial difference. Bender and Grugett (95) feel that parents of Negro children seem less sensitive to childhood problems, another environmental variable which could be relevant in explanation. Malzberg (143) suggests that the migratory habits of many New York State Negroes (who float back and forth between North and South, often with little economic stability) might explain the high incidence of mental illness. Socio-cultural deprivation might also account for the inflated inclusion of Negroes in the ranks of the deviant. Intellectual functioning, for example, is often found poorer among Negroes. However, when Lilienfeld and Pasamanick (137) investigated mental deficiency among Negro and white patients, they uncovered some interesting differences. Below the I. Q. of 50, Negroes and whites alike were found to have experienced one or more pregnancy or paranatal abnormalities. Above 50, however, this ceased to be true for Negroes but remained significant for whites, who had such abnormalities equally at all I. Q. levels. The results strongly suggest that atypical birth factors are operating in the occurrence of mental deficiency for all whites but only those Negroes termed most retarded. The authors state that the "less retarded" Negroes may in fact be suffering from socio-cultural deprivation. Finally, Malzberg (138) suggests that both paresis and alcoholic psychosis, the two categories with the majority of Negroes, are really socially-determined illnesses stemming from an unstable and unhealthy environment.

When evaluating the studies which have found significant differences between the races, several critical problems arise. The first of these is the bias imposed by testing instruments and individual items. For instance, Lane (1968) questions the use of items relating to aggression, which she feels impose negative bias on the Negro, whose subculture sanctions a-mounts of violence intolerable to the middle-class white, as well as on the male, who can be acceptably more aggressive, especially among Negroes of the lower class. Carlson (1966) also found a cultural bias on the Bender-Gestalt test. When she administered it in Alabama to two groups of 31 each (one Negro schizophrenic and one white schizophrenic), she found that although the Negro were better educated than the white, they did more poorly--both on Designs 4, 6, 7, 8 and in total time.

A second problem is an examiner bias. Lane (139) suggests that in her study the interviewers offering the diagnoses might have felt more antipathy towards the Negro males than any other group, consonant with findings by Hollingshead and Redlich (132). Paffenbarger (80) found that female Negroes were more apt to be diagnosed psychotic than female whites when both were suffering from parapartum psychoses. Consistent underrecording of Negro symptomatology was discovered by de Hoyos and de Hoyos (144), which they attributed to status differences between Negro patients and white therapists in the direction of overcompensation. Pasamanick (136) questioned his own finding that Negro children are less verbally responsive because of their possible inhibition in speaking to a white examiner.

A third problem seems to be the almost constant confounding of two separate but interrelated variables, race and social class. So many of the findings related to Negroes seem to be related as well to inclusion in the lower class that it is difficult to separate the two or to decide which is in fact the relevant factor. For example, prematurity is more common among Negroes (59). However, as there is a significant correlation between size of mother and prematurity and as undernourished women from the poverty classes tend to be smaller in adulthood, might not prematurity really be related to lower class membership? This was, in fact, what Baird (41) found. A variation of the same argument can be applied, as a matter of fact, to all of the organic deviances described above.

In summary, studies relating race to psychosis leave much to be desired, primarily because of the many relevant variables which are not controlled for and because of the ambiguity of interpretation possible.

Migration

Although only a handful of researchers have delved into the relationship between migratory groups and psychosis, some relevant findings have emerged. Several authors (145-151) have found that mobile populations had a disproportionately high incidence of psychosis. Specifically in schizophrenia, Faris and Dunham (149) found this rate to be highest in the areas of highest mobility and social disorganization. When they divided the city of Chicago into a number of differing neighborhoods, they found that the rate of schizophrenia varied from a low of 111 per 100,000 in outlying wealthier suburban districts to a high of 1195 per 100,000 in central city areas devoted to housing transients (rooming houses, for instance). The drift hypothesis has been formulated to explain this fact--that is to say, people in poorer mental health tend to drift into the slum and transient neighborhoods of the city. Of course, others have aksed if in fact the stressful situation of living in these areas did not result in poorer mental health or an actual psychotic break. Dunham and Faris (cited in 1) suggest that social isolation--prevalent in the slums--is a necessary precursor to schizophrenia, especially in the child. The phenomena of higher rate of psychosis and living in the central city seems limited to the megalopolis. By contrast, Clausen and Kohn (cited in 1) found this to be untrue in the Hagerstown, Maryland, study. They concluded that the small size of the city explained the difference and suggested that poor adjusted individuals tended to leave (to the very large cities nearby?).

Malzberg (152) uncovered similarly high rates among migrants hospitalized in New York State. Upon investigating further, he found that the psychosis was not always manifested immediately after the move, but might be delayed for extended periods of time. He also felt that the high rate of native born Negro admissions might be partially explained as a drift function of their migratory habits.

Comparisons of native born and foreign born hospitalized psychotic patients have usually shown that a relatively larger number were foreign born. For example, Malzberg in 1936 found that a higher percentage of immigrants numbered in the ranks of hospitalized schizophrenic patients than the comparable rate for natives (2:1). In a later study, Malzberg (152) found that when comparing foreign born Norwegians and the later generations with the same Norwegian origin, the natives had a lower rate than their migratory forbears. Wedge (148) also found that migrant Okinawans in Hawaii had a far higher rate than would be expected from their small numbers and their rate of schizophrenia reflected in hospitalization on Okinawa (their native environment).

Some significant differences were also found in diagnostic categories when looking at foreign born admissions to U. S. hospitals. For instance, Malzberg (152) found that the Norwegian patients (foreign born and later generations both) had a lower rate of inclusion in all categories except paresis and alcoholic psychosis. He found the same to be true for Negroes (1956) in even higher percentages--so much so, in fact, that this group outnumbered all others. Opler and Singer (153) also uncovered some significant qualitative differences in hospitalized schizophrenics in New York City with Irish and Italian backgrounds (37 of the former and 40 of the latter). Alcoholism was found more important to the Irish, while the Italians tended to sublimate their problems in hypochandriasis and somatization in general. Irish tended to exhibit latent homosexuality, were more quietly anxious and paranoid, and were more prone to defenses like fantasy and withdrawal. On the other hand, Italians tended to exhibit overt homosexual behavior more frequently, were more excited and confused (generally in the schizo-affective category), and were more prone to poor control.

Various rationales have been cited by these authors in the attempt to explain their results. Odegaard (147) hypothesizes that the individual psychology of the patients is the important factor, with schizoid personalities tending to emigrate. A more anthropological explanation was attempted by Wedge (148), who investigated mothering practices and found no differences between the two groups. Therefore, he postulated vulnerability to schizophrenia despite positive mothering practices (like breast feeding) and described the two types of Okinawan patients he had encountered in Hawaii, one matching the schizoid designation of Odegaard (shy, suspicious, and withdrawn) and one being evaluated as aggressive and overcompensating. Both, he states, are probably reactions to the status of Okinawans in Hawaii--that of a despised minority. The latter position of the migrant is consonant with the third theory regarding the causality of such a high incidence of psychosis: the lower social status of the migrant.

Malzberg reanalyzed his 1936 data on 15704 native-born white patients and 10987 foreign-born white patients admitted to New York State mental hospitals from 1928 to 1931 in an attempt to ascertain whether such factors could account for the fact that foreign-born patients outnumbered native-born two to one. When he corrected for the different age composition of the two groups (with foreign-born immigrants tending to be older), he found that the ratio of 1.2 to 1 (F.B.:N.B.) was reduced by twenty percent. When he corrected for the different level of urbanization (with immigrants tending to be more highly urbanized), and socio-economic environment (with immigrants tending to belong to a more indigent economic and occupational class), he found that ratios became insignificant. The total reanalysis revealed no important difference between native and foreign groups, who only exceeded the natives by eight percent when the above variables were taken into account. He also found no significant differences between them in representation in different diagnostic categories.

Braatoy (154) noted that migrants also had a higher total mortality and a higher suicide rate than native-borns and concluded that unfavorable living conditions imposed upon the immigrants were in fact responsible for their higher rates of schizophrenia.

It seems plausible to suggest that some relationship exists between place of birth, tendency to move, and psychosis when one looks at the available figures regarding incidence of psychosis and migratory behavior. However, the present quantity of investigation seems to leave enough doubt regarding what is happening to make the formulation of hypotheses premature. The major criticism of the literature is the lack of control of what might eventually turn out to be crucial variables.

Intelligence

The relationship of birth factors and psychosis cannot be complete without at least a brief look at the research regarding intelligence and level of functioning. Much of the relevant research in the area of pregnancy and birth complications are their subsequent effects has been related to the later functioning of those so damaged in the fetal or neonatal periods. For instance, studies have revealed a correlation between both mental deficiency (106) and reading disabilities (107) and such abnormalities--the former a generalized deficit in functioning and the latter a more specific decrement. As such complications are also associated with neuropsychiatric disorders (35), one would be tempted to look for lower intellectual abilities in those so afflicted. In fact, using the 1916 form of Stanford-Binet, Roe and Shakow (155) found a significantly lower mental age for schizophrenics (141 months compared to 164 for a control group). Similar findings were made by Kendig and Richmond (157) and Shakow (158). The major criticism of these studies has been that no premorbid I. Q.'s were available--leaving unanswered the obvious question: Are schizophrenics in fact less intellectually able or is their functioning being impaired by the onset of the disease? Winder (cited in 1) suggests that "...for organic theories, the implication is that dementia or deterioration begins well before the time of overt psychotic symptoms and introduces the possibility that often there is no significant decrease in intellectual performance during a large part of even all of the psychotic period."

In studying childhood school records of adult schizophrenic patients, Lane and Albee (48) found that future schizophrenics scored significantly lower than their own siblings, while a control group of neighborhood children and their siblings did not differ significantly. In a suburb study of 114 middle and upper class schizophrenics, they discovered that when the patients were compared with their own siblings, the crucial variable in terms of premorbid intellectual functioning seemed to be the later type of schizophrenia which developed. In process schizophrenics, she found a lower I. Q. even in childhood, but in reactive schizophrenics, she found no such decrement and the patients scored as well as their healthy siblings. Other researchers have noted that diagnostic category is important in assessing intellectual functioning. Kendig and Richmond (156) found that paranoids scored the highest of the schizophrenic group, as did Harper (158). In fact, Mason (159) found that when comparing army induction I. Q.'s for normals and individuals who later became schizophrenic, paranoids did not at that time differ from normals. Neither, he also found, did catatonics. Manic-depressives, as a matter of fact, were to be above the control group in I. Q. Taken together, the deviant group (schizophrenics, alcoholics, neurotics, manic-depressives and character disorders) did not differ from the normals. Roe and Shakow (155) found catatonics to function slightly above the normal group; by contrast, Kendig and Richmond found them to be similar to paranoids but slightly lower. All researchers found hebrephrenic and simple schizophrenics to have the lowest level of intellectual functioning even before onset of illness. Pollack and Greenberg (31) found that a group of schizophrenics with paranatal abnormalities scored lower than those without. On the V. I. Q. those with complications scored significantly lower (including those with moderate or severe dysfunction). Generally, schizophrenics with "minimal brain damage" have been found to score less on tests of cognitive functioning. The implication is, of course, that some schizophrenics (perhaps those with particular diagnoses) might be functioning less efficiently due to physiological damage occasioned by irregularities of pregnancy or birth.

A number of criticisms have been leveled at theories which relate less adequate intellectual functioning with psychosis. The majority of the studies utilized hospitalized patients--usually chronic. Miner and Anderson (160) found that chronics do in fact score lower than less chronic patients. This could be considered supportive of Lane's findings as well, since chronics would be largely classified as process schizophrenics. Another criticism must be acknowledged when perusing the literature--the lack (especially in some of the early studies) of adequate controls of such variables as social class, sex, age, and education. As a matter of fact, some studies have equated educational level and intelligence, although the correlation between the two have yielded a weak correlation. Shakow (157) noted that among 723 schizophrenics admitted to a Massachusetts State hospital, the educational levels were almost exactly comparable with the general population at that time (66 per cent grammar school, 29 per cent high school). However, in college attendance he found that schizophrenics only had a six per cent rate, while normals had a ten per cent rate. Of course, many reasons might exist to explain the difference, including less ability among schizophrenics, interruptions in education among schizophrenics occasioned by the onset of the disease, or even the tendency for state hospital patients to be from lower socioeconomic classes (and thus less likely to seek a college education). Another difficulty in measuring intellectual functioning is the tests themselves. These may impose a number of biases: 1) a negative bias for socio-economic deprivation, 2) a design which specifically attempts to minimize sex differences, 3) a bias favoring cooperative subjects (or those without organic difficulties, since organics will doggedly try and try but never succeed).

The literature regarding relationships between intellectual factors and psychosis reveals some enlightening intraschizophrenic differences; however, these may in fact be a function rather of differential reality contract. Unless studies are undertaken which attempt to compare non-hospitalized schizophrenics with normals, many of the effects noted must be taken very cautiously. In terms of birth factors affecting intellectual functioning, investigations revealing deficits should be reanalyzed to determine how much of the lowered functioning might be due to specific organic defects like impaired verbal or perceptual abilities and how much might be due to actual generalized poorer functioning. Furthermore, instruments differentiating between sexes and races should be developed so that the "I. Q." difference might be understood apart from other variables.

Culture

There is evidence that schizophrenia or schizophrenic-like reactions occur in all the known cultures of the world (161). The apparent paucity of mental illness in primitive societies could be explained in terms of their not being hospitalized as often as Europeans or Americans (cited in 161) and by the ability of these societies, often organized around much magic and mysticism, to assimilate those we would term psychotic into acceptable and even highly desirable roles like shaman (162). Of course, the lack of complexity in these societies when they are compared to the Western culture could be cited to show that in fact less mental illness does exist in the primitive world; however, researchers have found that the rate of hospitalization increases with the decrease of tribalization and increase of acculturation (161). In fact, the major difference seems to be qualitative rather than quantitative, with depressive features in psychosis being rare in native primitive patients. Lemkau and Crocetti (cited in 161), estimate the range in occurrence of schizophrenia to be conservatively 50-60 per 100,000 per year minimally and 250 per 100,000 maximally. In the U. S., Lemkau, Tietze, and Cooper (163) found that in 1943 there were approximately 290 schizophrenics per 100,000 with 147 of these actually hospitalized. Most present estimates of true incidence cluster about the maximal point of 250 per 100,000 and of hospitalization rate from 160 to 200 per 100,000.

Cultural factors have often been cited in studies first investigated in the U. S. to account for divergent results. For example, Barry and Barry (77) explained the reversal of expected birth order effects due to differently culture-determined parental expectations or attitudes. They felt that the fact that more first-born or early-born siblings were represented in the ranks of the schizophrenic in India (71, 72) could be understood in light of the Indian family constellation, in which these positions were more stressful than later due to the national custom of expecting family responsibilities to be handled by the older children (particularly the male). Caudill (69) made similar comments about his finding the same pattern in Japan, adding that the cultural set-up also placed the youngest daughter in a responsible and dependent role in relation to her father--and so the oldest male and youngest female in the family tended to be overrepresented. These authors also suggested that in tradition-bound families this was especially true. Caudill postulates that this is because modern homes follow Western customs more commonly--and in Western cultures the eldest and youngest both occupy different positions without the added stresses and strains of family responsibility. This added difficulty in sex role was cited in the study by Murphy and Lemieux (121), who investigated three French-Canadian communities notable for their traditionalism in an effort to discover why the incidence of schizophrenia was so high there. They found that the inflated numbers were actually females in these societies and suggested that the ambiguity of their actual vs. nominal sex role accounted for their maladjustment.

The main problem in evaluating cross-cultural studies is that one must be completely versed in the customs involved, often difficult for the observer not of the culture and often impossible for the member observer to fully explain to the outsider. In fact, some of the variables studied by the researcher in one culture may not even be remotely relevant to the second culture; therefore, investigations might yield spurious results and confound rather than clarify understanding. In other words, is it relevant to compare a country like India--where large families are the rule--with England and the U. S.--where they are the exception (except for certain subcultures)--in terms of birth order? Or, for example, when authors cite the more problems accruing to belonging to a traditional culture, are they not ignoring the sociological research which has stressed the crippling difficulties in Western "modern" society like anomiet? In the Japanese study, could not one question the effect of the loss of the greater stability and security of the traditional family or the more conflicts it faces in the changing world, possibly not yet reflected in the statistics? And particularly relevant to physiological factors surrounding pregnancy and birth, the different attitudes and procedures of various cultures have not been investigated to uncover a possible connection in this area between cultural practices and psychosis.

Social Class

Speaking of social factors has been nearly impossible without constantly making reference to social class. In every area covered--race, culture, migration, intelligence--social class has been so completely interrelated that it begins to assume important proportions in a final theory of etiology of schizophrenia. As a confounding variable alone in a huge volume of study it became crucial. For example, Hollingshead and Redlich (132) noted a marked inverse relationship between rates of treated schizophrenics (mostly hospitalized) and social status. Clearly, therefore, the majority of hospitalized patients (on whom the majority of studies are run) are from the lower classes. Von Brauchitsch and Kirk (60) found the same for adult schizophrenics, but the opposite for children. This factor might account for the repeated reference to class variables found in many of the studies cited in this entire paper.

A brief review of the interrelated quality of social class variables and some of these general topics will serve to make this clear. Central studies on birth factors have often postulated a rather direct correlation between pregnancy and birth abnormalities and later neuropsychiatric disorders. However, most of the studies showing this have been conducted using hospitalized subjects, who are usually lower class members. Therefore, it is not surprising that researchers have found neuropsychiatric disorders (134), pregnancy abnormalities and complications (164) (Pasamanick, 1956), and prematurity (41, 59, 165) significantly more common in the lower than upper class. Gruenberg (101) also found that a disproportionately large number of mental retardates came from the relatively small group with the lowest living standards. Differential nutritional standards might also account for some of the birth differences in lower class babies. When Ebbs *et al.* (165) compared three groups of mothers (one poverty group poorly nourished, one poverty group being fed supplemental rations, and one well nourished middle class group) they found that the condition of the babies during the first and second week of life was significantly poorer for the poorly nourished unsupplemented group. They found, furthermore, that the illness record in the first sex months was better for those with better nourished mothers. To their surprise, they found that in some ways the babies whose mothers were fed supplemental vitamins were in better condition and healthier than even the middle class babies, interpreted as suggesting that even the diets of middle class women were sometimes less than perfect. Similar nutritional deficits were used by Baird (41) in explaining why lower class mothers had more premature babies. He suggested that smaller mothers tend to have premature babies--and lower class women poorly nourished from birth themselves tend to be smaller. He found that even the mature babies from the low income group were more feeble as judged by increased incidence of intrauterine death and asphyxia during pregnancy or labor. He also discovered that the cause of half of the mothers in premature labor in his low income group (8.38 per cent of 1019 women) was inexplicable (and therefore deviant) while only 15 per cent of the causes of the high income mothers' prematurity was deviant, the other 85 percent being for the usual medical reasons (5 per cent deviant of 377). Baird also found a higher incidence of stillbirths and neonatal mortality in the lower class group (3:1). Gruenberg (cited in 101) found that the lower class has more brain damage with or without a positive family history, while Masland (cited in 15) suggested that prenatal injury has a less favorable outcome in this class. Schachter (13) compared 35 children with birth trauma and 100 normal children and found that the traumatized group had a history notable for alcoholism (one-third, correlated with later neuropsychiatric disorders), retardation (47 per cent), and neurological manifestations (42 per cent). Since 93 per cent of the traumatized group came from poor homes, this might be yet another finding really correlated with lower class membership.

Seasonal studies have also been linked to social class in many instances. Barry and Barry (131) suggested that membership in the lower class is characteristic of any subpopulation with an elevated birth rate in the first trimester, although Pasamanick, Dinitz, and Knobloch (135) found that both lower and upper classes had fewer births in the winter. Later Pasamanick, Dinitz, and Knobloch (1960) (133) even suggested a dip in the lower classes in the winter with little or no birth variation throughout the year for the upper class. The theory of less protection from bad effects of the hot summer for the lower classes has been suggested to deal with the dip and lower classes' twin rate being less frequent in the winter and most frequent in the spring.

Some of the most striking findings regarding racial differences in the U. S. have been questioned due to the preponderance of Negroes in the lower class. The only study which seems to show a consistent Negro difference which is not flattened by studying social class membership was by Knobloch, Pasamanick, and Lilienfeld (1956). They found that prematurity occurs at the rate of five per cent in the white upper class, 14.6 per cent in the white lower class, and 50.6 per cent in the Negro lower class. While both lower class groups have greater numbers of premature births Negroes clearly outnumber whites; this may, of course, reflect biological differences in race or a lower living standard among Negroes, even when compared to lower class whites.

Regarding social class and sex, Rosenberg (1964) and Kohn (70) both found social class to be extremely relevant when dealing with males and generally irrelevant when dealing with females. This might have reflected the form of measure they used to determine the class membership.

Schooler (70) noted a social class difference in birth order correlations with psychosis; she found that significantly more first-born psychotics were from the lower class and significantly more last-born were from the middle class.

Social class has also entered in the interpretation of why migratory groups apparently have poorer mental health. Both the drift hypothesis and those regarding slum stress, etc., emphasize the lower living standards and class of these migrants and transients, as do theories regarding foreign-born immigrants and their status in their new countries.

When von Brauchitsch and Kirk (60) analyzed 141 hospitalized mentally ill children according to diagnosis, social class, age, sex, race, place of residence, family background, and duration of hospitalization, they noted that most of the variables were either directly or indirectly related to social class. For example, they found that the diagnosis of schizophrenia was more frequent in hospitalized children from the upper socioeconomic classes. These were easier to identify and cases with this diagnosis were usually unanimous since they were often "classic" in symptomatology. Their prognosis was poor and they usually became chronic patients. On the other hand, the rate of schizophrenia decreased as the social standing decreased, so that in lower class children diagnoses were more equivocal with doubts arising among schizophrenia, neurosis, character disorder, and adjustment reaction of childhood. In contrast to adult schizophrenia, there was a positive correlation between social class, family background, and incidence rates of childhood schizophrenia. Bender (1955) also found that non-schizophrenic, lower class children seemed to have a more favorable prognosis and adjusted somehow in adulthood.

Clausen and Kohn (cited in 1) also found some interesting correlations between social class and incidence of mental illness in the Hagerstown, Maryland, study. There was only one significant finding: manic-depressive psychosis occurred three times as often in the upper two strata as in the lower three. Two findings which were not significant were of interest in light of prior research: first, they uncovered no difference in average rates of first hospital admissions for schizophrenia in districts of varying socio-economic status; and second, they found that rates did not vary in occupational groups. Both findings seem to lessen some of the importance of social class relationship membership in psychosis.

When discussing social class, mobility cannot be ignored. The evidence regarding social class change, however, is ambiguous. Before hospitalization, schizophrenics have been found to be upwardly mobile in New Haven (166), downwardly mobile in Chicago (cited in 1) and New Orleans (Liptad, 1957) and neutral in Buffalo (167). This evidence is particularly relevant when evaluating the drift hypothesis; certainly upward mobility casts doubts on its validity.

Several criticisms have been leveled on studies measuring the effect of social class. The statistics presented may be misleading, since they are offered as though they represented an average length of hospitalization for all schizophrenics. However, as more than half of all patients are returned home in less than a year, they represent instead an at least moderately chronic population. These may of course also be the sickest of all schizophrenics. Especially relevant to social class studies is the fact that families must agree to participate in them--particularly if social history is required. The families that agree may in fact be a special group, which is atypical. Investigation of one variable may also result in forgetting about others--for example, everything must be related to a broken home if the investigator is single-mindedly searching this sector to the exclusion of others. Finally, so many variables must be correlated and explained that the task becomes a monumental one, especially if the major source of information is interview and other subjective measures. Many biases also may be interfering with the results, including the bias imposed by the upper or middle class interviewer on the lower class patient (132) and the test items and norms (usually formulated for the middle and upper classes) imposing a negative bias on lower class performance or values.

The bulk of evidence seems to strongly suggest a definite relationship between social class and many variables related to schizophrenia. Perhaps the crucial element will ultimately turn out to be the cluttering effect of this component rather than any true relationship. In other words, if social class can be controlled for and its effects teased out, some clear connections between psychosis and other factors, especially birth factors, may emerge.

SUMMARY

The literature linking birth factors and schizophrenia has some significant and some ambiguous findings to contribute to the study of psychosis.

Birth and pregnancy complications appear to be associated with the occurrence of schizophrenia, while material linking prematurity and birth weight is ambiguous.

Season of birth appears to be correlated with psychosis, although recent methodological inconsistencies throw some question on many previous conclusions.

Order of birth seems to be related to schizophrenia in a sexually differentiated manner, but the present literature has failed to establish reliable correlations.

Sex differences are certainly related to frequency and type of disease category.

Various social factors are definitely interrelated with many of the findings in all birth factor literature. The dependence or independence of such variables is yet to be determined with clarity.

The present state of the literature does not differentiate between crucial and intervening variables, so that the areas under investigation may be the major ones or merely secondary in relationship to a possible new variable or combination of variables as yet untested. These findings may be chance variations or relevant when taken with currently unknown factors or sets of factors. A great deal of further investigation and interpretation is needed to clarify the myriad conclusions which have already been suggested.

REFERENCES

1. Jackson, D. D. *The Etiology of Schizophrenia.* Basic Books, New York, (1960).
2. Maxwell, J. P., Hu, C. H. and Turnbull, H. M. *J. Pathol. Bacteriol. 35,* 419, (1932).
3. Ingalls, T. H. *Amer. J. Dis. Child. 74,* 147, (1947).
4. Preyer, W. *Spezielle Physiologie des Embryo.* Grieben, Leipzig, (1885).
5. Gray, S. H. and Feemster, L. C. *Arch. Pathol. Lab. Med. 1,* 348, (1926).
6. Patterson, W. B. *W. J. Surg. 47,* 273, (1939).
7. Wilkins, L. W., Jones, H. W., Holman, G. H. and Stempful, R. S., Jr. *J. Clin. Endocrinol. 18,* 559, (1958).
8. Taylor, H. M. *Arch. Otolarynx 20,* 790, (1934).
9. Sontag, L. W. and Wallace, R. F. *Amer. J. Obstet. Gynecol. 29,* 77, (1935).
10. Sontag, L. W. and Richards, T. W. *Child Develop. Monogr. 3,* (1938).
11. Plum, P. *Spastic Quart. 11,* 4, (1962).
12. Plum, P. *Dan. Med. Bull. 3,* 99, (1956).
13. Schachter, M. *Amer. J. Ment. Defic. 54,* 456, (1950).
14. Ucko, L. *Develop. Med. Child Neurol. 7,* 643, (1965).
15. Caplan, G. *Prevention of Mental Disorders in Children.* Basic Books, Inc., New York, (1961).
16. Weidon, W. S. *J. Nerv. Ment. Dis. 120,* 1, (1954).
17. Lucas, A. R., Rodin, E. A. and Simson, C. B. *Develop. Med. Child Neurol. 17,* 145, (1965).
18. Pasamanick, B., Rogers, M. E. and Lilienfeld, A. M. *Amer. J. Psychiat. 112,* 613, (1956).
19. Pollack, M. and Woerner, M. G. *J. Child Psychol. Psychiat. 7,* 235, (1966).
20. Whittam, H., Simon, G. B. and Mittler, P. J. *Develop. Med. Child Neurol. 8,* 552, (1966).
21. Gittelman, M. and Birch, H. G. *Arch. Gen. Psychiat. 17,* 16, (1969).
22. Osterkamp, A. and Sands, D. J. *J. Genet. Psychol. 101,* 363, (1962).
23. Bender, L. and Faretra, G. Pregnancy and birth histories of children with psychiatric problems. Reprinted from Proceedings of the Third World Congress of Psychiatry, 1329, (1962).

24. Patterson, V. Block, J., Block, J., and Jackson, D. D. *Psychosom. Med.* 22, 373, (1960).
25. Kanner, L. *Child Psychiatry.* Thomas, Springfield, Ill. (1957).
26. Lotter, V. *Soc. Psychiat. 1,* 163, (1967).
27. Rimland, B. *Infantile Autism.* Appleton Century Crofts, New York, (1964).
28. Terris, M., LaPouse, R. and Monk, M. *Amer. J. Psychiat. 121,* (1964).
29. Pollack, M. *J. Orthopsychiat. 37,* 23, (1967).
30. Pollack, M., Levenstein, S., and Klein, D. F. *Amer. J. Orthopsychiat. 38,* 94, (1968).
31. Pollack, M. and Greenberg, M. *J. Hillside Hosp. 15,* 191, (1966).
32. Stabenau, J. R. and Pollin, W. *Arch. Gen. Psychiat. 17,* 723, (1967).
33. Graham, F. K., Ernhart, C. B., Thurston, D., and Craft, M. *Psychol. Monographs 76,* (1962).
34. Cutler, R. *J. Genet. Psychol. 107,* 261, (1965).
35. Lilienfeld, A. M., Pasamanick, B. and Rogers, M. E. *Amer. J. Public Health 45,* 637, (1955).
36. Lane, E. A. and Albee, G. W. *J. Psychol. 64,* 227, (1966).
37. Keeler, W. R. *Psychiat. Rep. Amer. Psychiat. Ass. 7,* 66, (1957).
38. Rosenthal, D. *The Genain Quadruplets.* Basic Books, New York, (1963).
39. Havelkova, M. *Can. Psychiat. Ass. J. 12,* 363, (1967).
40. Knobloch, H., Rider, R., Harper, P., and Pasamanick, B. *J. Amer. Med. Ass. 161,* 581, (1956).
41. Baird, W. *J. Obstet. Gynecol. 52,* 339, (1945).
42. Ebbs, J. H., Tisdall, F. F., Scott, W. A., Moyle, W. J. and Bell, M. *Can. Med. Ass. J. 46,* (1942).
43. Paffenbarger, R. S., Jr., Steinmetz, C. H., Pooler, B. G. and Hyde, R. T. *J. Chronic Dis. 13,* 161, (1961).
44. Vorster, D. *J. Ment. Sci. 106,* 494, (1960).
45. Knobloch, H. and Pasamanick, B. Etiological factors in early infantile autism and childhood schizophrenia. Paper presented at the International Congress of Pediatrics. Lisbon, Portugal, (1962).
46. Hinton, G. G. *Can. Med. Ass. J. 89,* 1020, (1963).
47. Taft, L. and Goldfarb, W. *Develop. Med. Child Neurol. 6,* 32, (1964).

48. Lane, E. A. and Albee, G. W. Intellectual and perinatal antecedents of adult schizophrenia. Grant M5186 from National Institute of Mental Health. Read at Conference on Life History Studies in Psychopathology, (1967).

49. Pollin, W., Stabenau, J. R., Mosher, L. and Tupin, J. Life history differences in identical twins discordant for schizophrenia. Presented at the 42nd annual meeting of the American Orthopsychiatric Association, New York, (1965).

50. Simon, G. B. and Gillies, S. M. *Brit. J. Psychiat.* *110,* 104, (1964).

51. Elasser, G. and Subke, H. *Arch. Psychiat. Nervenkr.* *14,* 561, (1954).

52. Fish, B. and Alpert, M. *Amer. J. Psychiat.* *119,* 439, (1962).

53. Caplan, G. *Emotional Problems of Early Childhood.* Basic Books, Inc., New York, (1955).

54. Pollack, M. and Gittelman, R. K. *Amer. J. Orthopsychiat.* *34,* (1964).

55. Brackbill, G. A. and Fine, H. J. *J. Abnormal Soc. Psychol.* *52,* 310, (1956).

56. Rosenthal, D. *J. Psychiat. Res.* *1,* 116, (1963).

57. Wenar, C. *Psychosom. Med.* *25,* 505, (1963).

58. Robbins, L. C. *J. Abnormal Soc. Psychol.* *66,* 261, (1963).

59. Pasamanick, B., Knobloch, H., and Lilienfeld, A. M. *Amer. J. Orthopsychiat.* *26,* 594, (1956).

60. von Brauchitsch, H. K. and Kirk, W. E. *Amer. J. Orthopsychiat.* *37,* 400, (1967).

61. Schachter, S. *The Psychology of Affiliation.* Stanford University Press, Stanford, Calif., (1959).

62. Bakan, D. *Quart. J. Stud. Alc.* *10,* 434, (1949).

63. Sletto, R. F. *Amer. J. Sociol.* *39,* 657, (1934).

64. Burt, C. *The Young Delinquent.* Appleton, New York, (1925).

65. Baker, H. J., Decker, F. J. and Hill, A. S. *J. Educ. Res.* *20,* 81, (1929).

66. Slawson, J. *The Delinquent Boy.* Gorham Press, Boston, (1926).

67. Rosenow, C. and Whyte, A. H. *Amer. J. Orthopsychiat.* *1,* 430, (1931).

68. Arieti, S. *American Handbook of Psychiatry.* Volumes I, II. Basic Books, Inc., New York, (1959).

69. Caudill, W. Sibling rank and style of life among Japanese psychiatric patients. Proceedings of the Joint Meeting of the Japanese Society of Psychiatry and Neurology and the American Psychiatric Association, May, 1963, Tokyo, Japan. Supplement of *Psychiat. Neurol. Jap.* 35.
70. Schooler, C. *J. Abnormal Soc. Psychol. 69*, 574, (1964).
71. Rao, B. S. *J. Nerv. Ment. Dis. 138*, 87, (1964).
72. Sundararaj, N. and Rao, B. S. *Brit. J. Psychiat. 112*, 1127, (1966).
73. Wahl, C. W. *Amer. J. Psychiat. 110*, 668, (1954).
74. Wahl, C. W. *Amer. J. Psychiat. 113*, 201, (1956).
75. Granville-Grossman, K. L. *Brit. J. Psychiat. 112*, 1119, (1966).
76. Nowicki, S., Jr. *Psychol. Rep. 21*, 265, (1967).
77. Barry, H. and Barry, H., Jr. *Arch. Gen. Psychiat. 17*, 435, (1967).
78. Solomon, L. and Nuttall, R. *J. Nerv. Ment. Dis. 144*, 37, (1967).
79. Farina, A., Barry, H. and Garmezy, N. *Arch. Gen. Psychiat. 9*, 224, (1963).
80. Paffenbarger, R. S., Jr. *Brit. J. Prev. Soc. Med. 18*, 189, (1964).
81. Schooler, C. *Arch. Gen. Psychiat. 4*, 91, (1961).
82. Smith, C. M. and McIntyre, S. *Can. Psychiat. Ass. J. 8*, 244, (1963).
83. Schooler, C. and Scarr, S. *J. Personality 30*, 178, (1962).
84. Phillips, E. E. *J. Psychol. 43*, 117, (1957).
85. Grosz, H. J. and Miller, I. *Science, 128*, 30, (1958).
86. MacMahon, B. and Sowa, J. M. *Physical Damage to the Fetus in Causes of Mental Disorders: A Review of Epidemiology and Knowledge.* Milbank Memorial Fund, New York, (1961).
87. Pasamanick, B. and Knobloch, H. *J. Obstet. Gynecol. 12*, 110, (1958).
88. Dennegy, C. M. *Brit. J. Psychiat. 112*, 1049, (1966).
89. Granville-Grossman, K. L. *Brit. J. Psychiat. 112*, 899, (1966).
90. Rosenbaum, C. P. *J. Nerv. Ment. Dis. 146*, 103, (1968).
91. Heston, L. L. *Brit. J. Psychiat. 112*, 819, (1966).
92. Huntington, E. *Season of Birth: Its Relation to Human Abilities.* John Wiley and Sons, New York, (1938).

93. Goldfarb, C. and Erlenmeyer-Kimling, L. Mating and fertility trends in schizophrenia. In *Expanding Goals of Genetics in Psychiatry*. Edited by Kallman, F. J. Grune and Stratton, New York, (1962).

94. Creak, M. and Ini, S. *J. Child Psychol. Psychiat. 1*, 156, (1960).

95. Bender, L. and Grugett, A. E. *Amer. J. Orthopsychiat. 26*, 131, (1956).

96. Lowe, L. H. *Arch. Gen. Psychiat. 14*, 26, (1966).

97. Levine, M. and Olson, R. P. *J. Abnormal Psychol. 73*, 215, (1968).

98. Schooler, C. and Parkel, D. The overt behavior of chronic schizophrenics and its relationship to their internal state of personal history. Reprinted with permission by the U. S. Department of Health, Education, and Welfare, Public Health Service (1963).

99. Abe, K. *Psychiat. Neurol. 151*, 276, (1966).

100. Boyd, W. The influence of sex. In *A Textbook of Pathology*. Lea and Febiger, Philadelphia, (1961).

101. Birch, H. G. *Brain Damage in Children*. Williams and Wilkins Co, New York, (1964).

102. May, J. M. *Amer. J. Orthopsychiat. 26*, 144, (1956).

103. Lilienfeld, A. M. and Pasamanick, B. *J. Hum. Genet. 7*, 401, (1955).

104. Asher, P. and Schonell, R. E. *Arch. Dis. Child. 25*, 360, (1950).

105. Lilienfeld, A. M and Pasamanick, B. *J. Amer. Med. Ass. 155*, 719, (1954).

106. Pasamanick, B. and Lilienfeld, A. M. *J. Amer. Med. Ass. 159*, 155, (1955).

107. Kawi, A. and Pasamanick, B. *J. Amer. Med. Ass. 166*, 1420, (1958).

108. Dublin, L. I. *Suicide*. Ronald Press, New York, (1963).

109. Rutter, M. and Lockyer, L. *Brit. J. Psychiat. 113*, 1169, (1967).

110. Jaco, E. G. *The Social Epidemiology of Mental Disorders: A Psychiatric Survey of Texas*. Russell Sage Foundation, New York, (1960).

111. Pugh, T. F. and MacMahon, B. *Epidemiologic Findings in U. S. Mental Hospital Data*. Little, Brown, Boston, (1962).

112. Hoch, H. and Zubin, J. *Psychopathology of Schizophrenia.* Grune and Stratton, New York, (1966).
113. Rosenthal, D. *Psychol. Bull. 59,* 401, (1962).
114. Malzberg, B. *Proc. Ass. Phil. Soc. 99,* 176, (1955).
115. Record, R. G. and Smith, A. *Brit. J. Prev. Soc. Med. 9,* 10, (1955).
116. Shearer, M. L., Davidson, R. T. and Finch, S. M. *J. Psychiat. Res. 5,* 349, (1967).
117. Gardner, G. G. *J. Consult. Psychol. 31,* 411, (1967).
118. Schooler, C. and Long, J. *J. Nerv. Ment. Dis. 137,* 173, (1963).
119. Schooler, C. *J. Nerv. Ment. Dis. 137,* 438, (1963).
120. McClelland, D. C. and Watt, N. F. *J. Abnormal Psychol. 73,* 226, (1968).
121. Murphy, H. B. and Lemieux, M. *Can. Psychiat. Ass. J. 12,* 71, (1967).
122. Costello, A. J., Gunn, J. C. and Dominian, J. *Brit. J. Psychiat. 114,* 433, (1968).
123. Bowlby, J. *Maternal Care and Mental Health.* Schocken Books, New York, (1951).
124. Rutstein, D. D., Nickerson, R. J. and Heald, F. P. *Amer. J. Dis. Child. 84,* 199, (1952).
125. Barry, H. and Barry, H., Jr. *Arch. Gen. Psychiat. 5,* 292, (1961).
126. Knobloch, H. and Pasamanick, B. *Amer. J. Public Health, 48,* 1201, (1958).
127. Orme, J. E. *Brit. J. Med. Psychol. 35,* 233, (1962).
128. Orme, J. E. *Dis. Nerv. Syst. 24,* 489, (1963).
129. Petersen, W. F. The Patient and the Weather. In *Mental and Nervous Diseases, Vol. 3.* Edwards Bros. Ann Arbor, Michigan, (1934).
130. Norris, A. S. and Chowning, J. R. *Arch. Gen. Psychiat. 7,* 206, (1962).
131. Barry, H. and Barry, H., Jr. *Arch. Gen. Psychiat. 7,* 385, (1963).
132. Hollingshead, A. B. and Redlich, F. C. *Social Class and Mental Illness: A Community Study.* Wiley, New York, (1958).
133. Pasamanick, B., Dinitz, S., and Knobloch, H. *Millbank Mem. Fund Quart. 38,* 348, (1960).

134. Pasamanick, B. and Knobloch, H. *J. Nat. Med. Ass. 49*, 372, (1957).
135. Pasamanick, B., Dinitz, S., and Knobloch, H. *Public Health Rep. 74*, 285, (1959).
136. Pasamanick, B. *J. Genet. Psychol. 59*, 3, (1946).
137. Lilienfeld, A. M. and Pasamanick, B. *Amer. J. Ment. Defic. 60*, 557, (1956).
138. Malzberg, B. *Mental Hygiene 37*, 450, (1953).
139. Lane, E. A. *J. Psychol. 68*, 15, (1968).
140. Kardiner, A. and Ovesey, L. The Mark of Oppression: *A Psychosocial Study of the American Negro.* W. W. Norton, New York, (1951).
141. Chapman, L. J. and Baxter, J. C. *J. Nerv. Ment. Dis. 136*, 352, (1963).
142. Kohn, M. L. and Clausen, J. A. *Amer. J. Orthopsychiat. 26*, 297, (1956).
143. Malzberg, B. *Hum. Biol. 28*, 350, (1956).
144. de Hoyos, A. and de Hoyos, G. *Int. J. Soc. Psychiat. 11*, 245, (1965).
145. Tietze, C., Lemkau, P. and Cooper, M. *Amer. J. Sociol. 48*, 29, (1942).
146. Malzberg, B. *Amer. J. Psychiat. 93*, 127, (1936).
147. Odegaard, S. *Acta Psychiat. Scand.* Supplement 4, (1932).
148. Wedge, B. *Amer. J. Psychiat. 109*, 255, (1952).
149. Faris, R. E. L. and Dunham, H. W. *Mental Disorders in Urban Areas.* Chicago University Press, Chicago, (1939).
150. Dunham, H. W. *Soc. Focus 25*, 321, (1947).
151. Clausen, J. A. and Kohn, M. L. *Amer. J. Soc. 60*, 140, (1947).
152. Malzberg, B. *Acta Psychiat. Scand. 38*, 48, (1962).
153. Opler, M. K. and Singer, J. *Int. J. Soc. Psychiat. 2*, 11, (1956).
154. Braatoy, C. *Acta Psychiat. Scand. 12*, 109, (1937).
155. Roe, A. and Shakow, D. *Ann. N. Y. Acad. Sci. 42*, 361, (1942).
156. Kendig, I. and Richmond, W. V. *Psychological Studies in Dementia Praecox.* Edwards, Ann Arbor, (1940).
157. Shakow, D. *Nerv. Ment. Dis. Monogr. 70*, (1946).
158. Harper, A. E., Jr. *J. Consult. Psychol. 14*, 290, (1950).
159. Mason, C. F. *J. Consult. Psychol. 20*, 297, (1956).

160. Miner, J. B. and Anderson, J. K. *J. Abnormal Soc. Psychol. 56*, 75, (1958).
161. Bellak, L. *Schizophrenia: A Review of the Syndrome.* Logos Press, New York, (1958).
162. Benedict, P. K. and Jacks, G. *Psychiatry 17*, 377, (1954).
163. Lemkau, P. V., Tietze, C. and Cooper, M. *Public Health Rep. 57*, 1909, (1943).
164. Knobloch, H. and Pasamanick, B. A developmental questionnaire for infants 40 weeks of age: An evaluation. In *Monograph 61, Society of Research in Child Development* Antioch Press, Yellow Springs, (1956).
165. Barcroft, J. *Researchers on Prenatal Life,* Vol. I. Charles C. Thomas, Springfield, Ill., (1947).
166. Hollingshead, A. B. *Amer. Sociol. Rev. 19*, 577, (1954).
167. La Pouse, R. *Amer. J. Public Health 46*, 978, (1956).

MENTAL HEALTH IN CHILDREN, Volume I
Edited By D. V. Siva Sankar
Copyright © 1975 by
PJD Publications Ltd., Westbury, N.Y.

FERAL AND ISOLATED CHILDREN

Armando R. Favazza
Department of Psychiatry
University of Missouri--Columbia

Greek and Roman folk-lore contains multiple references to children nutured by animals. McCartney (1) extensively reviewed this literature. According to sources such as Homer, Aratus, Ovid, Strabo, and Minucius Felix, Zeus, in the absence of his mother, was supposedly fed and nursed by bees, doves, an eagle, a goat, a sow and a cow.

The best known ancient tale of feral children is that of Romulus and Remus, the founders of Rome. The newborn twins were set adrift in the Tiber River because their uncle desired to eliminate the potential heirs to the kingdom. They floated to the bank of a river where a wolf, who had descended from the hills to drink, discovered and suckled them. Ovid and Plutarch relate that a woodpecker, the bird sacred to Mars, brought them food to eat. They were then found and reared by a shepherd and his wife. Lewis (1885) has recorded 24 different versions of the founding of Rome (2). Among other famous figures reportedly suckled by animals are Atlanta (by a bear), Aesculapius (by a dog), Daphnis (by a goat) and Chloe (by a

ewe). There are about forty instances in Greek and Roman folk-
lore of children suckled or protected by animals. In addition to
the animals already noted the list includes panthers, bears,
lions, sheep and horses. Even fish (Arion), ants (Minerva) and
snakes (Thoas) have been mentioned!

The historian Procopius (6th century A.D.) in *De Bello
Gothico* recounted a story which evidently was treated with
some credence by scholars. The Goths invaded Urbs Salvia in
Picenum (Italy). One woman, in her rush to escape being
captured, left her newborn child behind. A goat, which had also
just given birth, heard the child's cries, suckled it and protected
it from dogs and other animals. Some weeks later, when the
situation had calmed, the Roman townswomen returned and
found the healthy child. The child refused human milk so the
women allowed the goat to continue nursing and guarding the
child. The child was given the name Aegisthus, a name whose
Greek root refers to a goat. References to similar stories can be
found in the anthropologist Frazer's notes on Pausanias
(Vol. III) and E.B. Tylor's *Primitive Culture* (1920) and
Wild-Men and Beast Children (1863).

Homo Ferus:

The concept of feral man achieved scientific respectability
in 1758 when Carl Linnaeus (1707-1778), the great classifier of
science, published the tenth edition of his *Systema Naturae*. In
it he classified man as being either *homo sapiens* or *homo ferus*.
He classified *homo ferus* as *tetrapus* (moved on four feet),
mutus (mute), and *hirsutus* (hairy). The following is a brief
discussion of the cases which Linnaeus listed in order only by
name and which formed the basis for his classification in the
tenth through thirteenth editions of his opus.
1. The Lithuanian bear-boys (1661). Some Lithuanian
hunters discovered a group of bears in the woods. They also
noticed two little boys which had human forms. After a
ferocious struggle, they captured one of the children and
brought him to Warsaw where he was presented before the
king, queen, and highest nobility of Poland. The child was
judged to be about nine years old. Even though he was devoid
of reason and intelligence and had animal-like senses he was

recognized as a human being and was baptised by the Bishop of Posen. He was given to a Polish nobleman to live with servants. He never learned to speak and disliked clothes and shoes. Once a killer bear approached him and caressed him. The time spent on his education was not entirely lost for if one called the name of the Lord, he raised his hands and eyes to the sky.

2. The Hessian wolf-boy (1344). Actually there are reports of two wild children captured in 1344. A sketchy case reports that one boy was taken by wolves in Hesse when he was three years old. They fed and protected him and taught him to run on all fours. He was captured four years later by humans with whom he lived although he preferred association with wolves. In another case a young boy was taken by wolves in Wetterau. He lived with the animals for twelve years until he was captured by a noble's hunting party. The boy lived until he was 80 years old. Jean-Jacques Rousseau in his work, "Discourse on the Origin and Foundations of Inequality Among Men," (1754) cited the Hessian wolf-boy stories with approval and belief.

3. The Irish sheep-boy (1672). Dr. Nikolas Tulp--the physician depicted in Rembrant's "The Anatomy Lesson"-- reported this case in 1672. From earliest infancy an Irish youth who had escaped from his parents lived among sheep and took over their nature. He bleated like a sheep and ate only hay and grass. His actions and looks were those of an animal.

4. The Bamberger cattle-boy. The child involved supposedly had grown up among cattle and was able to run and jump on all fours with amazing nimbleness. Eventually he took over orderly behavior and even married.

5. Wild Peter of Hanover (1724). The best material on this best known of Linnaeus' cases comes from Blumenbach's study (1811). Blumenbach was a German physician, an influential university professor and the "Father of Physical Anthropology." According to his report a farmer from Hameln found a naked, brownish, black-haired creature about twelve years of age running in the field. He was captured and brought to town where street boys named him Peter. He was placed in safe custody at the Hospital of the Holy Ghost by order of the burgomaster. Peter was brutish at first but eventually grew

tamer and cleaner. The next year King George I sent for him and he was brought from Hanover to London.

Peter became a celebrity and scholars discussed this "specimen of man in a state of nature" especially in regard to the origin of mankind and the concept of innate ideas. The physician in charge of the case, Dr. Arbuthnot, declared, however, that "no instructive discoveries in psychology or anthropology were to be expected from this imbecile boy." At the doctor's request Peter received a pension and was sent to live on a farm in Hertfordshire "where at last he ended his vegetory existence as a kind of very old child in February, 1785." In his old age Peter liked brandy and fire, but was indifferent to money and--"an example of his more brutish and invincible stupidity"--had just as complete an indifference for the other sex. He never learned to speak properly and was never seen to laugh.

6. The Pyranees Boys (1717). One source simply notes that two wild boys were found in the Pyranees in 1717 and that they walked on all fours and jumped from one rock to another as easily as a pair of chamois.

7. The girl of Cranenburg (1717). A major source for this case reports that a thousand peasants successfully trapped an eighteen year old wild girl on a mountain in the Netherlands in 1717. Supposedly she originally was kidnapped at age sixteen months from Antwerp. When she was found her mother came to reclaim her. She recognized the child as her lost daughter because of certain bodily marks. The girl was monstrous looking and her hair was like straw. Her hard brown skin fell off after being captured and she grew a new one. She never learned to talk but she accepted her new position in life with ease. She developed a reputation of being kind, good natured and prone to laughter.

8. The Sogny girl from Champagne (1731). Two ten year old girls quarreled when one of them found a rosary on the ground. The victorious one was shot at by a hunter who thought she was a water-bird. She escaped and wandered into the village of Sogny barefoot, her body covered with rags and animal skins. She carried a club in her hands and killed a dog which someone set on her. She was finally captured and for two years she did such things as eating live frogs and fish, and catching wild

game on the run. She muttered a few words and sometimes struck out at people. She became very ill and, as she slowly recovered a great change occured in her. She was taken to a convent, learned the French language, acquired manners, celebrated her communion and confirmation and went on to become a nun. She could not remember her life before her capture except for memories of climbing trees and hunting for animals. She believed that the trees and the earth had produced her and that she had twice passed over the ocean (leading some to believe that she was really an Eskimo). This is one of the few cases in which the wild child reportedly was taught to speak distinctly.

9. Jean of Liege. Very little information is available on this case. Apparently Jean at age five years disappeared in the woods and lived there for sixteen years alone. His sense of smell became quite acute and he could recognize his female guard by her odor after he was returned to human society. For an inapparent reason the great physician Boerhaeve was known to have mentioned this case in his lectures to medical students.

The Wild Boy of Aveyron:

Possibly the most famous case of a "wild boy" is that reported in 1799 by Jean-Marc Itard, an otologist who, because of his devoted work with the "wild-boy" is frequently regarded as the first modern child psychiatrist.

On the 19 Thermidor of the year 8 of the Republic a naked child was seen eating acorns and roots in the woods of Caunes (Department of Tarn). He was seen again and captured by hunters fifteen months later. He was given to a widow *en pension* for safe keeping but easily escaped and spent six months in the forest alone exposed to the cold of one of the coldest winters. In the spring he entered the house of a dyer where he warmed himself and ate half cooked potatoes. He was brought to the Hospiz Saint-Affrique where a physician found him to be dumb. In two weeks he began to shriek and tear off his clothes. He was then placed in the care of the naturalist Bonnaterre in Rodez where he grew considerably and his body strengthened. Bonnaterre wrote the first scientific report about him. He was ten to twelve years old and it was noted that if denied anything he would become angry, bite, scratch, cry and yell. He hated children. He could not speak except for a few inarticulate sounds. The only thing which tamed him was an abundance of food. To express his content while eating he would rock himself from side to side, uttering a continuous murmur. Rather than being grateful he was indifferent to whomever prepared his food. He was quite skilled in stealing although he did not know the value of jewels, money or gold.

The Minister of the Interior ordered him to Paris and Itard took him to the Institution Imperiale des Sourds-Muets (Institute for Deaf-Mute Children). Itard was 25 years old at the time and he lived and worked at the Institute where he was appointed chief physician. He spent five and a half years attempting to re-educate the wild-boy. His first report on his attempts was published in 1801. His second report was written in 1806 and was published a year later by government order.

In the preface to his first report Itard wrote that man, without the aid of civilization, was one of the most feeble and least intelligent of animals. He felt that previous attempts at educating children who had been abandoned at a tender age had failed because these attempts followed the ordinary system of education, whereas these special cases merited special techniques. He noted that it was his duty to prove, by the success of his experiments, that the child with whom he labored was not a hopeless idiot but was rather a highly interesting being who deserved the attention of observers and the assiduities which were devoted to him by an enlightened and philanthropic administration.

The great psychiatrist Philippe Pinel examined the wild-boy but his original report is lost. Itard commented that "Citizen Pinel" found the unfortunate youth to be inferior to a domestic animal. Pinel, who was Itard's teacher, evidently felt that the wild-boy was an incurable idiot and incapable of instruction. Itard did not agree with this unfavorable opinion. He felt that the wild-boy's condition was not congenital but rather was based on the fact that he had been deprived from infancy of all education and had lived entirely separated from other humans. He persisted in his belief that the child was not organically defective despite such strange behavior as sometimes devouring small dead animals, a propensity to sway with a tiresome monotony, and episodes of frantic rage when he would gnash his teeth and become dangerous to those who were near him.

Itard discerned five principle objects in his "moral treatment or education of the savage of Aveyron." His first object was *to attach him to social life, by rendering it more pleasant to him than that which he was then leading, and, above all, more analogous to the mode of existence that he was about to quit.* He noted that the young child, like some savages in a warmer climate, was acquainted with only four circumstances; to sleep, to eat, to do nothing, and to run about in the fields. Itard attempted to make the child happy by putting him to bed at the close of the day, by furnishing him abundantly with food adapted to his taste, by bearing with his indolence, and by accompanying him in his walks and races in the open air whenever he pleased. He noted that it would have been useless as well as inhuman to oppose these habits. He therefore endeavored, and was gradually successful in his attempts, to render the young boy's excursions less frequent, his meals less copious, the time spent in bed much shorter, and his exercise more subservient to his instruction.

Itard's second object was *to awaken the nervous sensitivity by the most powerful stimulants, and sometimes by lively affections of the mind.* He attempted to lead the child's mind to a habit of attention by exposing his senses to "lively impressions." By putting the young child in a hot bath for two or three hours every day he taught him to appreciate the difference between warmth and cold. Itard toilet-trained the young child simply: "The certainty of passing the night in a cold and wet bed induced the necessity of his rising in order to satisfy his natural wants." Itard also thought it right to waken the experience of anger in the young child and did so in various ways e.g., he let him experience a trifling shock from a Leyden phial. Itard also reports that he did not miss a single opportunity to afford the child enjoyment. The child responded well and came to appreciate palatable food rather than the "shockingly disgusting" food which he previously desired. As a mark of civilization the young child even developed the inevitable diseases of civilization, such as a violent cold.

Itard's third object was *to extend the sphere of his ideas, by giving him new wants, and multiplying his relations and connections with surrounding objects.* He found out what was pleasurable for the child and only had to repeat it a few times in order to convert the pleasure into a want. As an example he often took the child to dine with him in the city. The child enjoyed these excursions and Itard took care that these excursions were always preceded by certain preliminaries. Very soon these preparations were considered as the signal of departure. He also noted that the child enjoyed travelling in a carriage. This pleasure, in a short time, became a real want.

The fourth object was *to lead him to the use of speech by subjecting him to the necessity of imitation.* He noted that the child's ear was simply an instrument of self-preservation which informed him of the approach of a dangerous animal or the fall of some wild fruit rather than being an organ which descriminates the various articulate modifications of the human voice. He attributed this to the fact that the child had been raised in the forest far from the society of rational beings.

One day he noticed that the child suddenly turned his head whenever he heard the exclamation, "Oh!" This preference for the sound o induced Itard to name the child Victor.

Itard was greatly encouraged when Victor seemed to pronounce, rather harshly, the word milk (*lait*). He discovered, however, that the word pronounced, instead of being a sign of a want, appeared from the time it had been first articulated to be merely an exclamation of joy. He then "abandoned the organ of voice to the influence of imitation, which, although weak, is not, however, altogether extinct, as appears from some little advancements that he has since made."

He noted that Victor was able to express the small number of his wants through methods other than speech. For example, when the hour for walking had arrived he presented himself repeatedly before the window and door of his chamber. If he was impatient to dine, he placed the cloth upon the table and presented his gouvernante with plates in order that she might go into the kitchen to fill them. When Victor became fatigued with the length of visits by curious individuals he presented to each of them their cane, gloves and hat, pushed them gently towards the door, and afterwards violently shut the door upon them.

Itard's fifth object was *to exercise, drawing some time, on those things which were connected with his physical wants, the most simple operations of his understanding; and afterwards to direct the application of them to matters of instruction.* He attempted to place between Victor and his wants obstacles that were continually increasing and continually changing in their nature, and which he could not surmount without perpetually exercising his attention, his memory, his judgement, and all the functions of his senses. He noted, for example, Victor's remarkable taste for order, especially with regard to those things which were suspended on the wall. Itard exercised Victor's attention by suspending from a nail objects below a figure which represented them. Itard would then leave them hanging for some time. He afterward took them away and gave them to Victor. Victor immediately replaced them in their proper order. In order to prove that Victor's actions were not simply due to memory Itard experimented with the respective positions of the figures and Victor performed admirably. Itard presented Victor with increasingly difficult tasks, utilizing colors which had only a slight shade of difference between them and objects in the shape of a parallelogram and circle and triangle. Victor tried his best, but when frustrated would gnaw his bedclothes and the mantlepiece, throwing about his chamber the fire-irons, the cinders and the burning coals, and concluding the scene by falling into convulsions "which seemed to be of a nature somewhat analogous to those of epilepsy, a complete suspension of the sensorial functions." Itard feared that Victor was epileptic, "a malady which is one of the most terrible and least curable in the catalogue of human diseases." Itard took a calculated chance by treating this symptom with a method that "awakened horror." He noted that Victor was terrified of heights. During one of Victor's most violent fits of passion, Itard picked him up and suspended him outside the upper window of the four story building. "When, after some seconds, I withdrew him from the situation, he appeared pale, covered with a cold sweat; his eyes moistened with tears, and still agitated with a slight trembling which I attributed to the affects of fear: I then took him again to his boards; I made him gather up his

scattered papers, and insisted that they should all be replaced...
This was the first time, at least to the best of my knowledge
that he shed tears." Victor ceased having these convulsive-like
spells and when frustrated went no further than to express
ennui impatience or to utter a plaintive murmur which in
general, terminated in a flood of tears.

Itard concluded his first report by noting that the savage
of Aveyron was endowed with the free exercise of all his
senses and that he gave continual proofs of attention, reflection
and memory. He felt that Victor was able to compare, discern
and judge, and to apply in short, all the faculties of his
understanding to the objects which were connected with his
instruction. He was especially encouraged that these happy
changes had been produced in the short space of nine months.

In his second report Itard wrote of his work on the
development of the functions of Victor's senses, intellectual
functions, and emotional faculties. In order to make Victor not
only hear, but listen, he placed a thick blindfold over his eyes
and then subjected his ears to the loudest and most dissimilar
sounds. At first Victor had only to distinguish between the
sound of a bell and that of a drum. Progressively difficult
discriminatory experiments were tried and Victor eventually
learned to appreciate the different intonations of the human
larynx. Itard tapped Victor on the fingers with a drumstick
every time he made a mistake. A feeling of fear overcame
Victor, however, and exercises became difficult to perform.
This feeling of fear became a great obstacle and Itard wrote,
"Vain hopes--everything was useless. Thus I saw the end of
the brilliant hopes I had founded, not without reason, on an
uninterrupted chain of useful and interesting experiments."

Saddened, rather than discouraged, by his lack of success
achieved with the sense of hearing, Itard devoted great efforts
to the development of Victor's sense of sight. Within a few
months Victor could read and write passably a series of words
sufficiently similar in appearance for an inattentive eye
to misjudge them. It was however only an intuitive reading
since Victor read the words without pronouncing them and
without knowing their meaning.

In another experiment Itard placed various objects at the
bottom of a vase whose mouth was just big enough to permit

the entry of a hand. Victor was able to distinguish through touch various objects such as an apple, a nut, small pebbles and metal letters, even such similar ones as B and R, I and J, and C and G.

Itard noted that Victor had an aversion for alcoholic spirits, but eventually grew to like wine. Victor's preference, however, was always for water. "He drinks his water standing at the window, eyes turned towards the countryside as if in this moment of sheer delight this child of nature seeks to unite the only two things which remain from his lost freedom, a drink of clear water and the sight of the sun on the countryside."

Itard felt that these exercises were of great value for Victor and that they prepared him for the great task of the communication of ideas. Victor, however, did not progress well in these experiments. For example Itard noted that the word "lait" meant for Victor many things, the drink itself, the vessel containing it, and the desire of which it was the object. Disheartened by his lack of progress with Victor, Itard wrote: "Unhappy creature, since my labors are wasted and your efforts fruitless, go back to your forests and the wild life of yore; or if your new needs now leave you dependent on a society which you cannot serve, then go and die of poverty and boredom at Bicetre."

Itard persisted in his work, however, and after a few months Victor learned to copy words whose meaning he already knew and very soon afterwards he could reproduce them from memory. He finally could make use of his writing, shapeless as it was, to express his needs and to ask for the wherewithal to satisfy them.

Itard's greatest hope was that he could reach Victor to speak. His hopes were entirely deceived however, since Victor could only pronounce meaningless monosyllables, sometimes shrill, sometimes deep, and much less clear than those which he had pronounced in the early experiments. Itard wrote, "I resign myself to giving up my experiments with speech and abandon my pupil to a life of incurable dumbness."

Itard felt that Victor's emotional faculties had developed. They were first aroused by the feeling of need inspired by an instinct of self-preservation. They were then stirred by less selfish feelings and by more generous impulses. He finally felt that Victor had achieved some of those noble feelings which are the happiness and glory of the human heart. He noted for example that it was Victor's job to set a place at the table for the husband of his gouvernante, Madame Guerin. Her husband died, and Victor set his place at the table as usual. This action had a distressing effect on Madame Guerin. Victor, witnessing the sad scene, understood that he was the cause, and he never set the place again. "This was a moment of saddness, an emotion belonging entirely to civilized man."

Just as civilization increased Victor's moments of sadness, it also increased his moments of pleasure. Itard noted the civilized zeal Victor showed and the pleasure he found in helping the people he loved and even in anticipating their needs, as well as in performing small services which were within his scope.

Itard conducted an experiment which led to "incontestable proof" that the ideal of justice and injustice, the permanent basis of social order, was no longer foreign to Victor's mind. Victor had been performing his duties very well when Itard offered him no rewards or demonstrations of pleasure. Instead Itard put on a severe and threatening expression, seized Victor by the arm and dragged him roughly towards a little dark room which had sometimes served him as a prison when he first came to Paris. Victor resisted and beside himself with indignation and scarlet with rage he threw himself upon Itard's hand and bit it long and hard. "At that moment I would have given anything to make my pupil understand my act and to tell him that the very pain of his bit filled me with satisfaction and more than rewarded me for my pains! It could only delight me, for the bite was a legitimate act of vengence...I had raised savage man to the full stature of moral man to the most striking of his characteristics and the most noble of his powers."

Despite some successes Itard's conclusion to his report was pessimistic. He wrote that Victor's education was still, and always would be, incomplete. He was discouraged by the fact that the most forceful methods had only obtained slight results and he lamented the fact that Victor's emotions were subordinated in the application to the deep feeling of selfishness. Itard was very astonished by a fact that defied all explanation: Victor's indifference to women.

Thus, disheartened, Itard ceased his therapy with Victor after five and a half years. The Minister of the Interior provided a pension to Madame Guerin for her care and attention in looking after the wild boy of Aveyron. Victor went to live in an annex of the Institution Imperiale des Sourds-Muets and remained there until his death at the age of forty in 1828.

Kaspar Hauser:

Undoubtedly the single case which has caused the greatest commentary is that of Kaspar Hauser. Over one thousand articles and books have been written about the case. One of the finest contemporary sources is the lengthy account written by the great jurist, Anselm Ritter von Feuerbach, entitled *Kaspar Hauser, An account of an individual kept in a dungeon, separated from all communication with the world, from early childhood to about the age of 17* (1832).

In 1828 in Nuremberg a young man in peasant dress was found by a citizen. This young man was in distress. His language consisted mostly of tears, moans and some nonsense sounds. He held out a letter to the citizen, directed to a local military captain. He was brought to the military quarters and it was noted that his conduct and demeanor seemed to be that of a child scarcely two or three years old. To everyone's surprise, after being handed a pen and paper he legibly wrote the name Kaspar Hauser. He was delivered over to the police and slept soundly in a small cell even though he had great difficulty walking to the police station, groaning and sinking down at every step.

The letter which accompanied Hauser was unsigned. The letter writer, supposedly a poor laborer, noted that Hauser's mother gave him up for adoption in 1812 and that his father was dead. The laborer did not know the identity of Hauser's mother. He said that he raised Hauser as a Christian and taught him to write. He also said: "Since 1812 I have never suffered him to take a single step out of my house, so that no one knows where he was brought up, nor does he know either the name of my house or where it is."

Kaspar was examined medically and it was noted that his arms showed the scars of innoculation and that his legs were strangely deformed. He scarcely knew at all how to use his arms and fingers. Rather than walk he waddled and tottered. He was destitute of words and of conceptions and was totally unacquainted with the most common objects and daily occurences of nature. The only food he would eat was dry bread and water. He was astonished by music and he was thrown into convulsions at the first sounds of a great regimental drum during a military parade. His most frequently uttered sound was the word "Ross" (German for horse) which he applied to all quadrupeds. He loved horses and was given two plaster rocking horses to play with. His demeanor, in the words of his prison-keeper, was "a perfect mirror of child like innocence."

The burgomaster, Mr. Blinder, befriended Kaspar and by frequently questioning him was able to gather his astonishing history in two months time. The history had been criticized by some as being made up of conjectures, since Kaspar could not reasonably have been expected to produce such details. One year later, however, Kaspar wrote his own memoir which agreed with the official promulgation, and over the years related this same history to others.

The essentials of his history are that he recollected always living in a cage or a hole where he never saw any daylight, never heard a sound, and where he sat on the ground all the time. When he awoke from sleep he found a loaf of bread and a pitcher of water at his side. Sometimes the water had a funny taste and when he drank it he felt compelled to sleep (probably the effect of opium). When he awoke from such a sleep he found that his nails were cut and that he would be wearing a clean shirt. He never saw the face of the man who brought him his food. His only playmates were two wooden horses and several ribbons. Living thus he never felt the want of anything and was happier there than in the world, where he was obliged to suffer so much. His prison keeper taught him to write his name and also tried to teach him to stand. When this was accomplished he bound Kaspar and carried him to Nuremberg.

Kaspar became a celebrity rapidly and every person who wished to see him was admitted to his house. In Feuerbach's words "Kaspar attracted scarcely fewer visitors than the kangaroos, or the tame hyena, in the celebrated menagerie of M. von Aken." He became busily engaged in his education and he learned rapidly to write and to draw. Most people were astounded at his curiosity, thirst for knowledge, and the inflexible perseverance with which he fixed his attention to anything he was determined to learn or comprehend.

He repeatedly expressed his desire to go back to "the man with whom he had always been." When Feuerbach expressed his surprise that Kaspar would want to return to that abominably bad man Kaspar indignantly said, "Man not bad, man me no bad done."

Kaspar's memory was a marvel. He was able to remember, for example, all the types of flowers in a nosegay when asked to name the flowers several days later.

When he became ill the city fathers sent a physician, Dr. Osterhausen, to examine him. The physician's report notes that Kaspar was melancholy, very much dejected and greatly enfeebled. His nervous excitability was morbidly elevated, e.g. his facial muscles frequently went into spasm, his hands trembled, he was extremely sensitive to noise and to light, was anorexic and complained of an unpleasantness in his abdomen. The physician felt that these symptoms were the result of overstimulation. After being buried alive in a dungeon for so many years Kaspar's system simply was succumbing to multifarious and heterogeneous impressions such as free air, light, objects, the awakening of his mental individuality and his intense desire for learning and knowing.

At the physician's request Kaspar was removed from the tower and committed to the care of a Professor Daumer. This man was very kind and took Kaspar into his family as a member. He was given a real bed instead of a straw mat and was greatly pleased. After sleeping in the bed he began to have dreams, although he was initially unable to distinguish between a dream and a real event. He learned regularly to eat meat and grew more than two inches in height in several weeks. The professor noted however that, "After he learned regularly to eat meat, his mental ability was diminished; his eyes lost their brilliancy and expression; his vivid propensity to constant activity was subdued; the intense application of his mind gave way to absence and indifference; and the quickness of his apprehension was also considerably lessened."

His education progressed, however, and with great patience he was taught such basics as discriminating between animate and inanimate objects. If a sheet of paper was blown down by the wind he thought that it was running away from the table. He had little interest in the beauty of nature. But one summer night his instructor showed him a star serried sky and Hauser exclaimed, "This is indeed the most beautiful sight that I have ever seen in the world. But who has placed all these numerous beautiful candles there? Who lights them? Who puts them out?"

He developed great skill as an equestrian and he truly seemed to love horses. It was also noticed that his vision was perfect, especially at night, e.g. one night he read the number of a house at a distance of 180 paces which, in daylight, he was not able to distinguish. His sense of hearing and of smell was likewise extremely acute. In fact, the most delicate odor of a rose was perceived by him as an insupportable stench. He reacted strongly, e.g. with shuddering or sweating, to the presence of metal. These reactions disappeared over time.

Attempts were made to awaken religious ideas in his mind but he complained to Professor Daumer that he could not comprehend what the clergymen were telling him. He grew to have a marked aversion to clergymen and physicians. He disliked phyicians because of the abominable medicines they prescribed and with which they made people sick. He disliked clergymen because they frightened people with their incomprehensible arguments.

Kaspar, in 1829, set to writing his life story. Word of this spread throughout Europe for he had become quite famous and was the object of universal public attention. Then, all Europe was shocked when it was reported that an unknown person attempted to assassinate Kaspar by cutting his throat. The assassin managed to slash only his forehead, however, and Kaspar survived. There was speculation that Kaspar was really the royal heir to the throne of Baden and that the assassination attempt was politically motivated. The complicated reasons behind such speculation can be found in the works of Evans (1892) (3) and Bartnig (1930, in German)(4).

He continued his education and was sent to class with other students. He suffered through the study of Latin and eventually came to be like his peers. He was transferred to the care and protection of the English Lord, the fifth Earl of Stanhope, and was moved from Nuremberg to Ansbach. In December of 1833 Kaspar was told by a stranger that he had news of his mother. Kaspar followed the stranger into the little Hofgarten of Ansbach and there he was stabbed in the chest. Within three days he died.

There was immediate and sustained controversy about Kaspar's death. Some accused him of suicide. Interest and suspicion remained so great that 42 years later the German Emperor William I, had the official reports of the post-mortem and burial of the hereditary prince of Baden published in the newspapers. Official papers relating to the case of Kaspar Hauser fill 49 folio volumes in the Munich public records office. Literature on the case is abundant, most of it in German. Novels about Hauser have been written by Jacob Wasserman (1908), Sophie Hoechstetter (1925) and Otto Flake (1950). Paul Verlaine wrote a poem in *Sagesse* (1881) about the case, and Erich Ebermeyer wrote a play about it (1928).

THE WOLF-CHILDREN OF MIDNAPORE:

In 1942 Reverand J.A.L. Singh published *The Diary of the Wolf-Children of Midnapore* (India), undoubtedly the most provocative twentieth century case of feral man (5). Four different "experts" wrote positive forewords for the work. Professor Ruggles Gate of the University of London and Chairman of the Human Heredity Bureau noted that he first learned of the wolf-children in 1926 from a newspaper article. He exchanged letters with Reverand Singh. Of the *Diary* Gates wrote: "The account bears the unmistakable marks of truth, and although one may not agree with all the interpretations of the Reverand Mr. Singh, the facts speak for themselves, and are of unique interest."

Professor Arnold Gesell, Director of the Child Development Clinic at Yale University, wrote: "There can be no doubt whatever that Amala and Kamala early in life were adopted by a nursing wolf...the *Diary* covers a period of nine years, and fortunately the observations are dated. This enables us to interpret Kamala's mental development in terms of time. The ancient antithesis of heredity and environment prove barren. We are not dealing with the utter incapacity of true amentia, but with the suppression and the liberation of latent maturation."

The third foreword was written by Francis Maxfield, a professor of psychology at Ohio State University. He felt that Singh's *Diary* "carried its own internal evidence of significance," and likened the wolf-children to Itard's Victor.

Kingsley Davis, a sociologist at Pennsylvania State University, wrote the fourth foreword. He praised Singh's *Diary* and predicted that it would become a classic on a par with Itard's story of Victor, and Feuerbach's account of Kaspar Hauser. He felt that the results of studies of feral or isolated children prove that Aristotle was wrong: Man is not by nature a social animal; he is social because he is made social.

Singh's *Diary* itself runs for 125 printed pages. He noted that he received his vocation for the ministry in 1910 and that he "was fired with a zeal to explore human habitations in the jungle area...it was a search for the aboriginals." Between 1907 and 1920 he converted 700 souls. He kept two or three families at a time housed at his Midnapore residence and catechumens "and after their conversion they were allowed to go to their native homes."

In 1920 while on a jungle missionary tour he was told by the natives of a *Manush-Bagha* (man-ghost). He staked out the tunnels near a white-ant mound as high as a two story building. At dusk three grown wolves (probably *Canis Pallipes*, an animal intermediate between a jackal and a wolf) emerged from a tunnel. Then came several wolf cubs, then two "ghosts." Singh decided that they were human beings even though their eyes were bright and piercing "unlike human eyes," and their heads were big balls of matted hair, hideous to behold. He arranged to dig into the wolves den. The "mother" wolf was killed by the natives. The two cubs and the two hideous human children were separated and Singh left them in a small barricaded area of a friend's courtyard. He returned five days later and discovered that the children were severly ill from neglect and lack of food and water. The villagers had panicked at the children's presence and the village was depopulated. Singh finally managed to bring the children safely to his orphanage.

He judged the older child to be about eight years old and the younger one to be about one and a half. He named the elder Kamala and the younger Amala. Their health improved on a diet of raw milk and vegetables. "We could not give them anything else through fear lest they should get ferocious and become unmanageable." The children disliked "everything human" at first, and were meditative and morose because "they could not prowl about with the wolves."

Physically, the children had abnormally long and pointed canine teeth, and the color of the inside of the mouth was "blood-red, not naturally found among men." Their eyes were half shut during the day, but were wide open at night and had a peculiar blue glare. The children could see perfectly in the darkest place "when and where human sight fails completely." They could smell meat at a great distance and possessed a strong power of hearing. They ate and drank like dogs, and they slept like "little pigs or dog pups, overlapping one another." They never laughed. Kamala shed one tear from each eye only when Amala died in 1921.

Reverend and Mrs. Singh accepted the children and dealt with them as if they were at the age of one year, and less than a year, respectively. They had no language, and "had cultivated the animal nature and condition of life almost to perfection in the animal world." The Singhs, therefore, attempted to humanize them through behavioral techniques.

Mrs. Singh fed them biscuits by hand and eventually trained them to point to a desired food or drink. She massaged them gently with oil and spoke affectionately to them at the same time. Then, in 1921 Amala became very ill with dysentery secondary to an infestation of round worms. She developed a high fever, became emaciated and finally died, despite medical attention.

Kamala, after several days of sitting alone, commenced crawling towards the other children in the orphanage and tried to utter words to them. She enjoyed especially following chickens and imitated them. She then became so attached to a hyena cub that the Singhs felt obliged to remove the cub from the orphanage. She received extra massages to soothe her.

The Singhs devised several plans to encourage Kamala to stand. They made her sit on a high stool, and they supplied her with pillows to support her back when standing. Slowly she began to stand on her knees and to walk on her knees for a short distance. When tired, she would revert to walking on all fours. The Singhs also built special wall brackets to help Kamala lift herself up to a hanging plate of food. She ate carion, and even fought the vultures and crows for a dead carcass in the fields. She eventually learned to stand on two legs.

Kamala disliked bathing at first but finally, in 1926 "became somewhat tame at the time of bathing." In the same year the Singhs felt that she had begun to understand language and could communicate with facial expressions. She seemed to like Mrs. Singh especially. After several years she also seemed to enjoy being with other children and no longer attacked them. She developed a forty word vocabulary.

In 1928 Kamala "went on learning and practicing...and grew in mind and human character." In 1929 she became seriously ill and died. Her death certificate, signed by her attending physician notes the cause of death to be uremia. Prior to her death Reverend Singh had received an invitation from the Psychological Society of New York to bring Kamala to America, to present her before the public and to describe with photos her rescue and her life in the orphanage.

Reverand Singh at first tried to keep the story of the two girls a secret. He thought that it would be difficult for them to marry if their backgrounds were known, and he was afraid that he would be overwhelmed with time-consuming visits and queries from interested and curious individuals. The secret became public, however, when the physician treating Amala rapidly made it common knowledge, much to Singh's displeasure.

Newspapers and journals published stories of the wolf-children "which at times were at variance with the actual history." The English and American Press was highly interested "from the psychological point of view" and Reverend Singh "promised all the universities of the world who inquired about the wolf-children to publish the Wolf-Children Diary in due course." It was not until 1942, however, that the entire Diary was published. Reverand Singh was assisted by Robert Zingg, an anthropologist at the University of Denver.

Zingg felt that the Diary was accurate and believable. The Diary was published along with Zingg's scholarly study of feral man and cases of extreme isolation of individuals.

The last scholarly report on a new-found case of a feral child was by the sociologist Ogburn (1959) on the wolf-boy of Agra. While in India, Ogburn read a newspaper article about a six year old lost child, Parasram, who had been returned to his parents after being raised by a wolf for four and a half years. Ogburn found the child to be extroverted and curious. In his search he discovered that the child had not been raised by a wolf at all, and concluded that the natives had over-active imaginations. He felt that embellishment of word of mouth tales gave rise to this case.

In 1940 J.H. Hutton published his presidential address entitled "Wolf-Children" to the English Folk-Lore Society (6). In his article Hutton traced the history of reports concerning feral children. He noted that, with only two exceptions, "the capture of a child from the company of carnivorous animals believed to have suckled it has seldom if ever been witnessed by a European, at any rate since the seventeenth century." He also stated that it is remarkable that there have been no such cases reported from the New World. "Cases of wolf-children, if not of bear-children, might be expected from North America, and perhaps of jaguar-children from South America, while in view of the alleged pro-human disposition of the puma, puma-children might be more readily expected than either." Hutton was unable to conclude with a note of finality, however, because he felt that evidence from India of wolf and leopard-children and from Africa of a baboon-child "seem on the whole to support the thesis that the belief is founded on observable facts."

Isolated American Children:

In 1938 the sociologist Kingsley Davis read a paper at the annual meeting of the American Sociological Society. The paper, in condensed version, was published in 1940 and was entitled "Extreme Social Isolation of a Child." The child, born and raised in rural Pennsylvania, was named Anna and she was illegitimate. Her mother tried to bring Anna home to live but mother's father was so antagonistic that Anna was given out to a local minister for adoption. The minister returned the child, however, when he discovered that she had vaginitis. She was given to an agency at age three weeks but was not regarded a likely subject for adoption. For five months she was shuffled from agency to foster home and back again until finally mother took Anna to live with her. Mother placed Anna in an attic-like room from which the child never emerged for more than five years. The child's grandfather was so angry that he refused to allow her to come into his presence during all the years of her captivity.

Mother fed Anna a milk diet until age five when she added oatmeal. She supposedly neither bathed, trained, supervised or caressed the child. Mother and her first child, an illegitimate son, slept together in the same dirty room with Anna. Anna slept in a small broken chair. She became so weak and apathetic that mother tied her so she would not fall out of the chair. *The New York Times* article of February 6, 1938, noted: "(She) was wedged into the chair, which was tilted backwards to rest on a coal bucket, her spindly arms tied above her head. She was unable to talk or move...'The child was dressed in a dirty shirt and napkin,' the officers said. 'Her hands, arms and legs were just bones with skin drawn over them, so frail she couldn't use them. She never had enough nourishment, she never grew normally and the chair on which she lay, half reclining and half sitting, was so small the child had to double her legs partly under her'."

The child was placed by the authorities in the "county home" in March for nine months. Most of the 324 residents of the county home were infirm or mentally defective adults who were looked after by one nurse. Davis first saw Anna three days after her arrival. He noted that she would sit up if placed in a sitting position and seemed to respond well to her high vitamin diet, massages and attention. She neither smiled nor cried and was usually expressionless. She did not play with toys, but merely handled them in a distracted manner.

After two weeks in the home Anna showed some improvement. She preferred one food to another, a green pencil to a yellow one. She began to smile and to sit on the edge of the bed. "The doctor claimed that she had a new trick every day." Several months later she had gained five pounds, was more energetic, laughed a good deal and made a sound like "da."In June she ranked below a one year old child according to items of the Gesell schedule. She was removed to a foster home in November and at that time she had not learned to chew, drink from a glass or crawl. During her stay at the county home "she remained in much the same animal-like stage except that she did not have the animal's inherently organized structure, and hence remained in a more passive, inadequate state."

A "remarkable transformation" occurred after Anna was in the foster home for only a week. She learned to drink from a glass, feed herself with a spoon, and take a step or two while holding onto something. "Her new guardian was using the same common sense methods by which mothers from time immemorial have socialized their infants--unremitting attention, repetitive correction, and countless small rewards and punishments, mixed always with sympathetic interest and hovering physical presence."

In August 1939 Anna was moved to a small private home for retarded children. She was twenty pounds overweight, understood the procedure of proper toilet habits, and comprehended verbal instructions although she could not speak.

Davis concluded that Anna's difficulties were the result of social isolation and not congenital deficiency. He compared her to other cases of isolated children and noted interesting parallels; the almost universal failure to learn to talk with any facility and the presence of sensory abnormalities. He felt, citing Freeman's volume on individual differences (1934) that Itard's Victor was not biologically damaged, but rather was a victim of social isolation like Anna. He agreed with the Cooley-Mead-Dewey-Faris theory of personality which stated that "human nature is determined by the child's communicative social contacts as much as by his organic equipment."

In 1947 Davis published a "Final Note" on Anna (7). She was evaluated in November, 1939, and it was noted that she walked about aimlessly, made rhythmic motions with her hands and made gutteral and sucking noises. She was evaluated by a psychologist in April, 1940, and on the Vineland social maturity scale she made a score of 23 months. In July, 1941, she was regarded as feeble-minded, probably congenital in type. She began to develop speech and could call attendants by name. She died, in 1942, of hemorrhagic jaundice.

In 1942 Marie Mason, an assistant professor of speech and visual hearing at Ohio State University, published the case of Isabelle entitled "Learning to Speak After Six and One Half Years of Silence." Isabelle's mother was injured as a child and could neither see out of one eye nor develop speech (presumably due to a cortical lesion in Broca's area). She could neither talk, read nor write. Communication with her family was via crude gestures. She was not allowed to leave the family home unaccompanied. At age 22, much to everyone's surprise, she became pregnant and gave birth to Isabelle.

For six and one half years both mother and child were "locked in a room behind drawn shades." Mother finally "escaped" with Isabelle who was so rachitic that she could not walk. State authorities placed the child in Children's Hospital, Columbus, Ohio, for orthopedic surgery and physiotherapy.

Dr. Mason was called in to help teach Isabelle to speak. Audiometric testing showed that Isabelle could hear, thereby eliminating deafness, auditory aphasia or word deafness as a cause of her speechlessness. A general impression was that she was feeble minded, wholly uneducable, and that "any attempt to teach her to speak, after so large a period of silence, would meet with failure." Mason, however, decided to try to work with her.

Recognizing that gesture was Isabelle's only mode of expression, Mason adopted "an educational approach combining gesture, facial expression, pantomime, dramatization and imitation." After one year of effort Isabelle made remarkable progress. She could identify the printed forms of many words and sentences, could speak (although her words often ran together), could write clearly, could count to twenty, and could listen attentively to a story. After a year and a half of training Isabelle had acquired a vocabulary of between 1,500 and 2,000 words and asked penetrating questions. She communicated readily and clearly with others and developed an excellent sense of humor.

Conclusion:

What are we to make of the old myths and folk-tales? Many ancient scholars doubted, and even ridiculed the tales of children suckled and protected by animals. Athenaeus felt that the "doves" which supposedly fed Zeus were really the daughters of Atlas, metamorphosed into the Pleiades constellation, a combination which may be linked etymologically with doves. Some scholars debunked the Romulus and Remus story by providing a more earthy explanation. The *lupa*, or wolf of the story, may have referred to the wife (Acca Larentia) of the shepherd who rescued them. *Lupa* was also one Roman term for prostitute. Some Greek and Persian scholars provided a similar argument to debunk the legend that Cyrus was raised by a dog, noting that the shepherd's wife who found him was named Spako, a bitch. Some authors, such as Lactantius, felt that Aesculapius kept dogs in his temple because he himself had been suckled by a dog. Others felt that dogs were kept in the temple for therapeutic reasons, i.e. they helped to promote the healing of wounds by their licking.

It is difficult to understand why Linnaeus, on the basis of rather meager evidence, formulated his category of *homo ferus*. It is easy to speculate that he simply became overzealous in his desire to classify *everything* and decided to include *homo ferus* in an effort to be absolutely complete. He was not alone, however, in his belief that *homo ferus* was an entity. The Irish sheepboy, for example, was reported first by a respected physician, Dr. Tulp. In France Jean-Jacques Rousseau and romantic authors, such as Chateaubriand, reveled in the concept of the noble savage, and it was only a brief jump from a belief in a noble savage to a belief in the possibility of feral man. Lord Monboddo, in 1774, declared that the discovery of Wild Peter was more remarkable than the discovery of the planet Uranus.

There were early critics of the feral man concept though. Concerning Wild Peter, Blumenbach wrote in 1811: "This pretended ideal of pure human nature, to which later sophists have elevated the Wild Peter, was altogether nothing more than a dumb imbecile idiot." (For a more lengthy commentary on this case see Tennant's book, *Peter the Wild Boy*, published in 1937) (8).

Schreber, a scholar interested in feral data, thought the case of the Hessian wolf-boy to be akin to a fairy tale (1826) (9). E.B. Tylor, one of the founders of cultural anthropology, in

1864 referred to Tulp's Irish sheep-boy as "a poor dumb idiot
and about as much a wild boy as the wretched malformed Red
Indian children that drew crowds of sightseers in London, not
long ago, were 'Aztec Children of the Sun.' " Tylor concluded
his study by writing:

> The whole evidence in the matter comes to this. First,
> that in different parts of the world children have been
> found in a state of brutalization, due to want of educa-
> tion or to congenital idiocy, or to both; and secondly,
> that people often believe that these children have been
> caught living among wild beasts, a supposition which
> accounts for their beast-like nature...I cannot see that
> the whole evidence on the subject proves anything
> whatever, except the existence of the stories, and the
> fact that there have been and still are people who
> believe them.

Itards' work with the Savage of Aveyron is in a different
class from all other reports and its brilliance has not dimmed
over the centuries. In the long run Pinel was pretty much
correct in his pessimistic evaluation of Victor's status but
Itard's gentleness, optimism and ingenuity are not to be
denied. Rather than leaving Victor to waste away in an
asylum--the fate which faced many young children suspected
of being congenital idiots--Itard was driven and sustained by
his almost delusional belief in Victor's past. His tenderness
in dealing with the young "savage" provided a distinct
contrast to the neglect, sometimes benign, sometimes malig-
nant, practiced by contemporary psychiatrists. Edouard
Seguin, author of *Traitement Moral, Hygiene, et Education des
Idiots* (1846), applied and modified the techniques of his
"illustrious master," Itard. Seguin, "The Apostle of Idiots,"
emigrated to the United States and was instrumental in
founding a number of institutions for the mentally retarded
which were based on Itard's concepts. Maria Montessori
admitted to being "guided" by the works of Itard and Seguin.
Itard's experiments might be regarded as a direct precursor to
behavioral therapy. Certainly the modern concept of mental
retardation due to socio-environmental causes may be seen to

have originated in Itard's work. In an article appearing in the first volume of the *Journal of the American Academy of Child Psychiatry* (1962) Silberstein and Irwin wrote that Spitz's work on anaclitic depression and Levy's work on primary affect hunger "seem to be a direct continuation of theories advanced by Jean-Marc Itard " (10).

The revival of interest in feral man in the twentieth century was due in great part to the influence of the anthropologist, Robert Zingg. Through his persistent efforts the cases of Amala and Kamala were published. Singh's *Diary* was favorably received partly because of Zingg's scholarly contributions. Zingg's lengthy and well researched report on the history of cases of feral and isolated children was published as the second part of the book which contained Singh's *Diary*. Zingg's scholarship made the cases of Amala and Kamala seem more credible. From a publisher's point of view I suppose it makes sense to have favorable commentary about a book's contents in the foreword. Zingg stacked the cards in his favor, however, by finding *four* "experts" who were favorable to Singh's *Diary*. From a scholarly point of view one might argue that science would have been better served had the book also contained commentary by "experts" who were skeptical about the *Diary* and who might have raised pertinent questions.

Before the publication of the *Diary* several brief articles on Amala and Kamala had appeared in the scientific literature. (Squires, 1927; Zingg, 1940). Zingg's article in *Scientific American* was prefaced by the editor as follows:

> As the accompanying account of two human infants reared by wolves is extraordinary, the reader is entitled to know just how much scientific backing was required before it was accepted for publication. He may recall the unfortunate instance last year in which a psychologist rushed into print with poorly invest-igated claims concerning a South African boy nurtured by baboons; then was forced to retract his story with an admission that he had been mis-taken (11).

The case to which the editor referred was that of Lucas, the baboon-boy. Evidently references to a Negro boy raised by baboons were published periodically in South African newspapers starting in 1927. Two mounted Cape police officers supposedly found the boy, judged to be about thirteen years old, frolicking with a troop of baboons in a remote area in 1903. He was taken to a mental hospital. He stayed there for a month and then was eventually given to a "kind master" to serve as a farmhand. In 1931 his master noted that Lucas was a good, hard worker and a great help to him. In 1939 a United Press dispatch reported an account of the case given originally by Raymond Dart, an anatomy professor at the University of the Witwatersrand in Johannesburg. An American psychologist at George Washington University, John Foley, communicated with Dr. Dart, gathered various documents and hurriedly published his report. He noted that Lucas "mimicked like a baboon...was full of monkey tricks...chattered like an ape." He felt that the case was "reasonably authenticated" and "appeared to be the first case of a human child adopted and reared by infrahuman primates." In 1940 Zingg reported that the case was a fiction (12). His article included recent communications from a host of South African authorities.

In 1940 Arnold Gesell of Yale published a highly romanticised account of Kamala's life history based on the *Diary* (13). Gesell, a highly reputable and famous researcher, did little to enhance his reputation with this book. He was quite impressed with Kamala's "slow but orderly and sequential recovery of obstructed mental growth." He even produced a chart depicting the mental growth trends of Amala, Kamala, Itard's Victor, Kaspar Hauser and Dina Sanichar (an Indian wolf-child, reported first by Ball in 1880).

Gesell's book was reviewed extensively in the *Psychological Bulletin* (1941) by Wayne Dennis (14). He took Gesell to task for publishing his account of the wolf-children before the complete diary had been published. He noted that writers had commented on the willingness of Hindus to allow missionaries to care for idiots and other defectives. He challenged Gesell's interpretation of the case on many points, e.g. why should Kamala's quadrupedal locomotion be attributed to her association with wolves when orthopedic causes were apparent? Dennis concluded by offering an alternative hypotheses to that of Gesell's: Perhaps Kamala was a "mistreated idiot foisted upon a kindly, but gullible, missionary through a native strategem."

In the *American Journal of Psychology* (1941) Dennis also published a discussion of the significance of feral man (15). He noted his concern that several sociological texts seemed to accept data on feral man as proofs for certain theories of human nature. He attempted to point out the weaknesses in original documents on cases of feral man. He wrote: "So far as I can determine not a single account has been written by an eye-witness of the fact that the child was captured in an animal den or in close company with an animal." He noted that in nineteenth century India, when a large number of wolf-children were reported, there were no institutions for the mentally abnormal and that idiots wandered freely about. "To the naive it is obvious that a child who eats raw meat had eaten with animals...This interpretation, of course, would occur more readily to the vegetarian Hindu than to us."

Zingg published a reply to Dennis in which he claimed that the new evidence from Singh's *Diary* refuted Dennis' arguments (16). He claimed, for example, that Singh was an eye-witness to the capture of Amala and Kamala in a wolf's den. Zingg did *not* note that the existence of a wolf's den in an ant hill was very rare. In his *Diary* Singh himself admitted that he had never before heard of such an occurance. Zingg also did *not* mention the fact that Singh's discovery took place at dusk, a time which is not too reliable for accurate visual reporting.

Dennis published a further analysis of reports of wild children in *Child Development* (1951) (17). In this brief article he concluded: "...taken at their face value, these data show two things: that the socialization which ordinarily takes place during the early years is readily lost upon close contact with animals; that animal influences are relatively permanent. Rather than accept these conclusions, it seems better not to attempt to draw generalizations concerning childhood from data so tenuous as the reports on alledged animal-reared children."

Undoubtedly the finest critique of the feral child concept is that by the psychologist Bruno Bettleheim (18). He is famous as the director of the Sonia Shankman Orthogenic School--a laboratory school at the University of Chicago devoted to the education and treatment of severely disturbed children. After reading Ogburn's story, he wrote, "Suddenly the blinders fell from my eyes." If Parasram was not really found in the company of wolves, then there is reason to doubt that Kamala and Amala were found living with wolves.

Bettleheim felt that Reverend Singh was sincere but that his interpretations were false. "He was carried away by his imagination about that one event which makes or breaks his interpretation, namely the way in which the children were found." Singh's story was likened by Bettleheim in his own fantasies about the past of the autistic children he treated when he first met them. He came to recognize that his speculations originated first in his narcissistic unwillingness to admit that these animal-like creatures could have had pasts at all similar to ours, and second, in his need to understand, to explain and "to find emotionally acceptable explanations for the nearly inexplicable and wholly unmanageably behavior of these children."

Almost item by item Bettleheim pointed out details in Singh's *Diary* which could be explained on the basis of child-hood autism. He presented cases of autistic children and noted the following:

> "Even after years with us the well-groomed hair of one of our autistic girls could, within hours, turn into a 'hideous ball of matted hair,' glued into a mass by saliva, reminants of food, dirt, and whatnot.
>
> "The parents managed to disengage themselves from them (autistic children) by placing them in an institution, or by setting them out to fend for themselves in the wilderness, or, the most likely explanation, by not pursuing them when they run away.
>
> "The children regularly bare their teeth when annoyed or angry...Reminiscent of animals is their prowling around at night, in marked contrast to their quiet withdrawal into a corner during the day.

"Then there is their great preference for raw food...
others lick salt for hours, but only from their hands.

"Others, again, build themselves dens in dark
corners or closets, sleep nowhere else, and prefer
spending all day and all night there.

"Some of these children, on seeing animals, respond
as though they had found a dear long-lost friend.

"Schizophrenic children often behave as though
they were totally insensitive to heat and cold.

"Sensitivity to pain in psychotic children is unlike
that of normal children and has to do with the nature
of the disturbance and not with a feral past.

"Hardly anyone who has worked with psychotic
children and has reported on them in any detail has
failed to remark on their strange hypersensitivity to
sensations of smell and touch.

"The inability to laugh, too, is quite characteristic
for most, if not all, autistic children."

Only one item puzzled Bettleheim because it did not have
a parallel among autistic children--Amala and Kamala's
inability to walk erect when they were first found. He thought
this might be explained by the initial confinement of the
children in a narrow barricade after being first found by
Singh. It should also be pointed out that in 1931 that most
eccentric of anthropologists, A. Hrdlicka, collected data on 387
cases of children who ran on all fours. These were mostly
white children of civilized parents.

Bettleheim espoused a primary psychological etiology of
autism. "Feral children seem to be produced not when wolves
behave like mothers, but when mothers behave like non-
humans. The conclusion tentatively forced on us is that, while
there are no feral children, there are some very rare examples of
feral mothers--of human beings who become feral to one of their
children."

The last major volume devoted to the study of feral and
isolated children was written by Lucien Malson in 1964 and was
titled *Les Enfants Sauvages* (19). The book was published
in English translation in 1972. The first half of the work
contains an introduction on wolf-children and the problem
of human nature and has chapters on the heredity of the

individual and the inheritance of the species; legendary and historical accounts; and major examples of the three types of wolf-children. The second half of the book contains a new translation of Itard's report on the Wild Boy of Aveyron.

I found Malson's comments to be uneven, at times penetrating, at times pedestrian. He provides interesting references which testify to the peculiar fascination which the cases seem to hold for some French scholars. Among those whom Malson quotes are Levi-Strauss, Merleau-Ponty and Sivadon. Although he does provide some interesting references from the French literature on the topic, Malson himself did not make any personal contribution of significance to the field. He noted that the majority of cases should be considered as hoaxes and pointed to the epidemic nature of reports, e.g. fourteen wolf-children were reported in India between 1843 and 1895 and "people named Singh were particularly gifted at finding them." He did not seem to consider that these reports came from that area in northern India where the vast majority of the population is named Singh.

Williams' recent book, *Introduction to Socialization* (1972), devotes an entire chapter to studies of isolated children and twins (20). As part of his conclusion he states: "Data from studies of isolated and autistic children and twin studies demonstrate the fact that, without regulative communicative contact with parents and other agents of socialization, the process of transmitting and acquiting culture is modified or alterred in significant ways. Such studies provide evidences that, without a socialization process there is little that can be recognized in the everyday sense of the term *human being*... Data of the consequences of extreme situational isolation, while far from complete, tend to show that the socialization process is capable of being reversed, even after a long period of time."

The cases of feral children all do appear to be hoaxes although certainly one cannot question the integrity of many reporters. Reverend Singh's *Diary* appears to be the sincere work of a man who falsely interpreted events because he approached these events with a strong bias. Once he convinced himself that Amala and Kamala were wolf-children he could interpret their behavior accordingly.

We should not deal harshly with individuals such as Reverend Singh. Biologically we are descended from and irretrievably linked to, animals. Scientists tell us that we can learn about human behavior by studying animal behavior and ethology has become a respectable behavioral science. We are proverbially told that man's best friend is not his mother, or his wife, or his children, but rather an animal, a dog. The majority of us were raised, not on mother's milk, but rather on the milk of a cow. All of us have seen "normal" individuals who appear to have stronger emotional attachments to their pets than to other humans. Scarcely a month goes by when a major news service does not provide newspapers with a cute picture of an animal who has been adopted by another animal of a different species. Much of mankind, in short, is attracted to animals and has a psychological dependence, as well as a physical one, upon them. The clearest examples of how much we have anthropomorphized animals can be seen in advertisements for pet foods.

I think Bettleheim was correct in reasoning that we have a need to distance ourselves from the bizarreness of autistic and mentally retarded children. Our narcissism impels us to believe that these children are so strange that they could not have had pasts similar to ourselves, therefore they must have been raised by animals. Although the thought may be comforting to some and seem logical to others, it must be seen for what it truly is, a rationalization.

LIST OF RECORDED CASES

The following list is adapted, corrected and expanded from that of Malson.

Name of case	Age in Years at Time of Discovery	Date of Discovery	Early Detailed Report
1. Roman child	infant	3rd century A.D.	Procopius, *De Bello Gothico* Lib. II cap. XVII
2. The Hesse wolf-child	7	1344	a) Camerarius, P., *Operae horarum subcisvarum sive meditationes historicae auctiores* (Frankfurt), 1602 b) Rousseau, J.J., "Discourse on the Origin and the Foundations of Inequality Among Men," 1754 c) Tafel, J. *Die Fundamentalphilosophie in genetisher Entwickelung mit besonderer Rucksicht auf die Geschicte jedes einzelnen Problems*, Tubingen, Verlags-Expedition, 1848 d) Rauber, A., *Homo sapiens ferus oder die Zustande der Verwilderten und ihre Bedeutung fur Wissenschaft Politik und Schule*, Zweite Auflage, Leipzig, 1888 Julius Brehfe (Denicke's Verlag)

3. The Wetteravian wolf-child	12	1344	a) Tafel, J. b) Rauber, A.
4. The bear-boy of Denmark	14	ca.1600	*La vie et les sentiments de Lucilio Vanini. A Rotterdam aux Depens de Gaspar Fritsch,* 1717
5. The first Lithuanian bear-child	12	1657	Tylkowski, P. *Historia Naturalis Curiosa Regni Poloniae,* 1721
6. The Irish sheep-child	16	1672	Nicol. Tulpii Amstrelredamensis *Observationes Medicae,* 1672
6. The Bamberger calf-child		1680	Camerarius, 1602

8. The second Lithuanian bear-child	10	1669	Conner, B. *History of Poland* Evangelium Medici, London, 1688
9. The third Lithuanian bear-child	12	1694	Conner, B., 1688
10. The Cranenburg girl	18	1717	*Sammlung von Natur und Medizin wie auch hier zu gehorigen Kunst und Literatur--Geschicte so sich in Sclesien und andern Landern bergeben. Von einigen Breslauischen Medicis.* Winter 1718, pp. 548 ff.
11. The two boys of the Pyra-nees		1719	Rousseau, 1754
12. Wild Peter of Hanover	13	1724	a) Rousseau, 1754 b) Blumenbach, 1811 (Bendysche, T. *Anthropological Treatises of Blumen-bach.* Longman, Roberts and Green, London, 1865)

13. The Sogny girl	10	1731	La Condamine, *Histoire d'une jeune fille sauvage trouvee dans les bois a l'age de dix ans*, Paris, 1755
14. Jean de Liege	21		Digby, *Two treatises, in the one of which the nature of bodies, in the other, the nature of man's soul is looked into*, Paris, 1844, Folio p. 247.
15. Tomko of Zips	15	1767	Wagner, M. *Beytrage zur Philosophischen Anthropologie und den damit verwandten Wissenschaften*. Wien bey J. Stahel und Compagnie, 1794
16. The Karpfen bear-girl	18	1767	Bonnaterre, P. *Notice Historique sur le savage de l'Aveyron et sur quelques autres individus qu'on a trouves dans les forets a different epoques*, Paris, 1800
17. Wild Boy of Kronstat	23	ca.1781	M. Wagner, 1794
18. Victor of Aveyron	11	1799	a) Bonnaterre, P. 1800 b) Itard, J. 1801. (*The Wild Boy of Aveyron* translated by G. and N. Humphrey, Century Co., New York, 1932.)

19. The Wild Man from Tre-bizond	adult	1813	Kinneir, J. Journey to Asia Minor and Koordistan in the Years 1813 and 1814, London, 1818.
20. Kaspar Hauser of nurem-berg	17	1828	Anselm Von Feuerbach. Kaspar Hauser, an Account of an Individual Kept in a Dungeon, Separated from All Communication with the World, from Early Age to about the Age of 17. Translated from the German, Simpkin and Marshall, London, 1833. (Original in German, 1832)
21. The Salzburg sow-child	22	ca.1829	Horn, W. Reise Durch Deutschland, Ungarn, Holland, Italien, Frankreich, Gross-brittanien, und Irland. Verlag von enslin, 1831, Vol I
22. The first Hasun-poor child	9	1841	Sleeman, K. A. Journey Through the Kingdom of Oude, 1849-1850, Richard Bently, London, 1858.
23. The Bondee child	10	1842	Sleeman, 1958

24. The second Hasunpoor child	12	1843	Sleeman, 1858
25. The Ghutkoree Child		1843	Sleeman, 1858
26. The Sultanpoor child		1847	Sleeman, 1858
27. The Chupra child	9	1849	Sleeman, 1858
28. The Lucknow child			Sleeman, 1858
29. Clemens, the Overdyke pig-child			a) *Dusselthal Abbey*. Nisbet, London, 1837 b) Tylor, E.B. "Wild Men and Beast Children," *Anthropological Review*, London, 1863, pp. 31-32, Vol. I

30. The Overdyke wolf-child			Tylor, E.B., 1863
31. The wolf-boy of Shahjehanpur	20	1858	Willock, H. *The Field*, January 11, 1896, No. 2246, pp. 36-37
32. Dina Sanichar of Sekandra	6	1867	Ball, V. *Jungle Life in India*, Thomas de la Rue, London, 1880
33. The second Sekandra child	10	1872	Ball, 1880
34. The Shajampur child	6	1898	Ball, 1880

35. The second Lucknow child		1876	Ball, 1880
36. The Greek sheep-boy	5	1891	Ornstin, B. "Wilden Menchen in Trikkala," *Zeitschrift fur Ethnologie Organ der Berlin Gesellschaft fur Anthropologie*, 23:817-818, 1891
37. The Jalpaiguri bear-child	8	1892	Mitra, S. "On a Wild Boy and a Wild Girl," *Journal of the Anthropological Society of Bombay* III:3-4, 1892
38. The Batzipur child	14	1893	a) Frazer, J. *Fasti of Ovid*, MacMillan and Company, London, 1929. b) Mitra, S. 1892
39. The Justedal snow-hen	12		LeRoux, H., *Notes sur la Norvege*, Paris 1895.
40. The Sultanpoor child	4	1895	Ross, H., *The Field*, London, November 9, 1895, No. 2337, p. 786

41. Lucas, the South African baboon-child	13	1903	Foley, J. "The Baboon-Boy of South Africa," *American Journal of Psychology* LIII:128-137, 1940.
42. The Indian panther-child		1920	Demaison, A. *Le Livre des Enfants Sauvages*, Andre Bonne, Paris, 1953
43. Amala of Midnapore	2	1920	Squires, P. "The Wolf-Children of India," *American Jounal of Psychology*, 38:313, 1927
44. Kamala of Midnapore	8	1920	Squires, 1927
45. The first leopard-child	7	1939	Baker, Stuart, "The Power of Scent in Wild Animals," *Journal of Bombay Natural History Society*, XXVII:117-118, July, 1920.

46. The Maiwana child			a) *The Pioneer*, April 5, 1927 b) J Woodward and R. Sutherland *Introduction to Sociology* (Chapter 9) Lippincott, New York, 1937
47. Tarzancito of El Salvador	5	1933	"Mystery of Salvador's Jungle WildBoy," *American Weekly*, October 27, 1935.
48. The Jhansi wolf-child		1933	"The Wolf-Child," *Illustrated Weekly of India*, February 5, 1933, p. 37
49. The Casamance child	16	1930s	Demaison, A., 1953
50. Assicia of Liberia		1930s	Demaison, A., 1953
51. The second leopard-child	8		Zingg, R. "Feral Man and Extreme Cases of Isolation," *American Journal of Psychology*, 53:487-517, 1940

52. The bear-girl of Mt. Olympus	9	1937	Maranz, G. "Raised by a Sheep That Stole Her When a Baby," *The American Weekly*, September 5, 1937.
53. Anna of Pennsylvania	6	1938	Davis, Kingsley, "Extreme Social Isolation of a Child," *American Journal of Sociology*, XVI:554-565, 1940.
54. Isabelle of Ohio		1940	Mason, Marie, "Learning to Speak after Six and One Half Years of Silence," *Journal of Speech Disorders*, 7:295-304, 1942.
55. The Syrian gazelle-child		1946	Demaison, A., 1953
56. Ramu, the New Delhi child	12	1954	Agence France Presse 8 February 1954
57. The wolf-boy of Agra	6	1959	Ogburn, W. "The Wolf-boy of Agra," *American Journal of Sociology*, 64:449-454, 1959.

58. The Mauritanian gazelle-child		22 Sept. 1960	Auger, J. "Un Enfant-Gazelle au Sahara Occidental," *Notes Africaines*, 98: 58-61, 1963
59. The Teheran ape-child	14	1961	Agence France Presse, 28 Sept. 1961
60. The Czech twins	7	1967	Koluchkova, J. "Severe Deprivation in Twins," *J. Child Psychol. Psychiatry* 13:107-114, 1972.

ADDITIONAL BIBLIOGRAPHY

1. McCartney, E. *Papers Mich. Acad. Sci. Arts Letters, 4,* 15, (1924).

2. Lewis, G. *An Inquiry into the Credibility of the Early Roman History,* London, (1885).

3. Evans, E. *The Story of Kaspar Hauser from Authentic Records,* Swan Sonnenschein, London, (1892).

4. Bartnig, L. *Altes und Neues zur Kasper Hauser,* Brugel and Sohn, Ansback, (1930).

5. Singh, J. and Zingg, R. *Wolf-Children and Feral Man,* Harper and Brothers, New York, (1942).

6. Hutton, J. *Folklore LI,* 9, (1940).

7. Davis, K. *Amer. J. Soc. 52,* 432, (1947).

8. Tennant, C. *Peter the Wild Boy,* Clarke, London, (1937).

9. Schreber, J. *Die Saugetheire, in Abbildung nach der Natur.* Erlangen, (1775).

10. Silberstein, R. and Irwin, H. *J. Amer. Acad. Child Psychiat. 1,* 314, (1962).

11. Zingg, R. *Sci. Amer. 164,* 135, (1941).

12. Zingg, R. *Amer. J. Psychol., 53,* 455, (1940).

13. Gesell, A. *Wolf-Child and Human-Child,* Harper and Brothers, New York, (1940).

14. Dennis, W., *Psychol. Bull. 38,* 889, (1941).

15. Dennis, W. *Amer. J. Psychol. 54,* 425, (1941).

16. Zingg, R. *Amer. J. Psychol. 54*, 432, (1941).

17. Dennis, W. *Child Development, 22*, 153, (1951).

18. Bettleheim, B. *Amer. J. Soc., 64*, 455, (1959).

19. Malson, L. Wolf-Children, original in French, 1964, *Monthly Rev. Press*, New York, (1972).

20. Williams, T. *Introduction to Socialization.* Mosby, St. Louis, (1972).

CHILD PSYCHIATRY
IN THE EUROPEAN SOCIALIST COUNTRIES

Christo Christozov
Medical Academy, Sofia, Bulgaria

Child psychiatry arose as a separate discipline at the end of the last century. In the first steps of its development the children's and the teenager's psychic troubles were studied from the standpoint of adult psychology. It wasn't until later that an evolutionary - psychological and biographical - dynamical approach was suggested for further study of the phenomena. All of the developed countries contributed to the marked progress in this field, each according to the level of their social, economical and cultural development. The East European countries taking an active part in this process developed many new and progressive tendencies and conceptions related to the social structural reforms passed during their socialist development. This invests original characteristics to the process in all its details and organizational aspects. All these characteristics cause us to believe that a deeper study of the aspects of psychology by the socialist countries will be beneficial for everyone.

In this article, the history, organization of medical help, scientific research and perspectives for the development of child psychiatry in a number of countries will be discussed, beginning with Bulgaria.

BULGARIA

It was not long ago that organized help for mentally ill and retarded children in Bulgaria became available. The first medical, professional school was founded in 1921. Under its initiative 3 classes were formed for retarded children and another 3 for stammering children. Sixteen years later the Developmental Institute, which was founded in the outskirts of Sofia, offered five classes and a boarding house for underdeveloped children. These were the only resources available for medical and educational aid to underdeveloped and stammering children until September 9, 1944, when Bulgaria became a Socialist country.

The period from 1944 until now is remarkable for the noticable progress in all branches of science and psychiatry. Until 1949 a number of classes in each public school were specially designed for retarded children. That year the first school for retarded children was opened in the capital. Later a dense network of similar schools was established across the whole country.

In 1952 the Medical-Educational Institute merged with the Bulgarian Academy of Sciences and formed the Institute for Physical Education and Hygiene in schools. This Institute organized the development of medical-educational institutions around the country and made scientific observations in schools. From the end of World War II till now a dense network of psychoneurological inpatient clinics was created in regional towns, and two were founded in Sofia - one for the town and the other for the region.

In 1949 an asylum for oligophrenic children was opened in Sofia. In 1951 this was transformed into the first children's psychoneurological hospital. Those admitted as patients were children and teenagers from 4 to 16 years old with acute psychic disorders, chronic forms of psychic diseases as in the case of exacerbation, epilepsy with psychopathologic syndromes, and children with neuroses. This hospital has a 50 bed capacity and also maintains an outpatient department.

In 1959 this hospital joined the Faculty of Medicine, which then became known as a Medical Academy (an independent University consisting of the previous Medical Faculty to the University) and finally became a Children's Department to the Chair of Psychiatry. This necessitated some changes and accomodation of the surroundings to the new tasks. As criteria for admission of children, the following illnesses were established: acute psychoses, neuroses, psychopathies, and epilepsies with mental troubles. Oligophrenic children were not admitted. The therapeutic arsenal consisted of modern medicines including neuroleptics, insulin-treatment by Sakel, psychotherapies and occupational therapy. The scientific and experimental work was performed in laboratories specially created for this purpose. Investigations on the activity of the nervous system and learning ability were carried out.

These investigations were stimulated by the fact that this work was looked upon with great interest by the leading psychiatrist in the country - Professor G. Usunoff, even before becoming a unit in the University system. He was a clinical consultant and helped solve some of the research problems. His main interest was in the field of childhood schizophrenia and epilepsy. A. Chubavenkova, N. Zaimova, L. Sachatschieva and others have worked in the diverse areas of child psychiatry and their results have been published in a number of scientific journals. The topics include psychoses of varying etiologies in children and their development, the deviant and criminal behavior of juveniles (in collaboration with L. Galabov), the treatment of epileptics and more. Nowadays the study of epilepsy in children is mainly concerned with the blood-brain barrier (through the use of isotopes), some new medicines, some electroencephalographic studies and the relation between epilepsy and tetany. Investigations on childhood schizophrenia, brain damage and other problems of mental health in children continue.

Soon after the creation of the first medical institution for child psychiatry, a second one was created by the founding of the Research Center for Neurology and Psychiatry. These two institutions serve overlapping areas - North and South Bulgaria. A close working relationship was established between them.

Of particular importance in psychiatric care for Bulgarian children are the psychoneurologic inpatient clinics. A dense network of inpatient clinics has been created to care for the mentally ill in this country. Nine outpatient departments for children and adolescents have been added to the inpatient clinics since 1955. Until now, mainly psychiatrists have worked in these outpatient departments, but an increase of basic scientists is planned. Also, a great deal of work has been done towards the release and follow-up studies of the patients. Children from 1 - 3 years of age are examined in these outpatient departments. Statistics show that almost 1/3 of the patients registered in the inpatient clinics are children. This shows how important the inpatient clinics are for children and adolescents. It is well known that a number of diseases appear in early childhood, so the sooner a child is registered at an inpatient clinic, the sooner treatment can begin and thus prevent further complications. The diverse activities of the inpatient clinics facilitates the study of a number of psychic disorders in childhood and adolescence and correlates them with the somatic infectious ones, the study of the development of these disorders, etc. The most frequently treated diseases are: epilepsy (mostly with symptomatic character, as a result of brain damage), oligophrenia (a group quite variable in etiological and nosological aspects, most often connected with infectious and toxic damages to the brain during early childhood, neonatal trauma, etc.), psychopathies, neuroses, and psychoses.

Undoubtedly, the effect of the treatment is dependent on the study of the etiological factors. The regional psychiatrists aid in the post-release treatment by making home visitations.

As can be seen, the activities of the child psychiatrist are quite diverse. Currently they are limited by the outpatient departments but it is hoped that in the future additional clinical services for children and adolescents will be added to the outpatient departments.

A number of schools have been built for mentally retarded children. These institutions have a strong emphasis on development and learning. They include special kindergartens for children aged 3 to 8 years and special schools for children aged 8 to 15 years. Thirty of these schools exist in the whole country. Their residents are children with the milder forms of oligophrenia. These are mainly defective children who are educated by specially trained teachers. For the children with more severe forms of oligophrenia, medical-educational institutions have been created, called "Houses for Social Help for Children and Teenagers with Mental-Physical Damages." Depending on the age of the children, two types of houses are indicated; one for children 3 to 10 years old and one for adolescents 11 to 20 years old. In the first type, where the boys and the girls are put together, there is subdivision. Three of these houses are built for oligophrenic imbecilic children and 3 for idiots. Experience shows that mixing the different stages of oligophrenia has a detrimental effect. That is why special institutions for deficient children, imbeciles and idiots have been created. The houses for teenagers (of which there are 7) are subdivided according to the same principle: 4 for imbeciles and 3 for idiots.   However, unlike the houses for children, there is a sex division; the boys and girls are put in different houses.

These houses are scattered around the country and each covers a definite territory. In addition to medical-social help, occupational therapy is important in the teenage house. The main trend in their educational work is the reasonable and healthy organization of the life of the mentally ill, with its goal as reaching the greatest possible independence and richness in the graduate's behavior. Experience proves that a beneficial effect is produced if the pupils (when at home) are charged with the task of performing some activity properly and in definite order. The following is a list of activities needed for this purpose:

1.   Activities connected with everyday life and the organizing of self-service.

2.   Instructive games and exercises to stimulate good peer relationships.

3.   Vocational training and related activities.

4.   Gymnastics, singing, modelling, drawing, physical exercises and broadening of orientation.

5.   Cultural diversions and rests.

In addition to the above, a specially trained tutor performs special corrective exercises aimed at sharpening and coordinating sensory functions with motor activity, and also gives speech therapy.   Special care is taken in teaching the children how to read and write, and in social studies.

In addition to the above mentioned houses, an establishment exists for handicapped children from 3 to 16 years old. A special enterprise named "Labor" ("Troud") combining both education and work was founded for teenagers and young adults. Usually after graduating from the special schools, people with a diminished ability for work are accepted to these enterprises.

The measures taken to prevent crime among children are the juvenile courts. Teachers, under the supervision of a committee, are usually the ones who contact the children. Also involved are: the mayor, who concurrently is the chairman of the committee, the regional judge, the regional chief of the militia (police), the headmaster of the regional school, an eminent neurologist or psychiatrist or social worker and members of the various social organizations. Along with a psychiatrist they oversee the placement of these children in schools for children with criminal tendencies, of which there are 10 in the country. These schools are under the control of the Ministry of Education. In addition to their schooling, psychiatric help is given to these children. The committees concerned with the juvenile courts work both to prevent alcoholism and to conduct activities.

The state maintains these enterprises. There are no enterprises supported by charity. The functions of all of these combine and mutually complement one another. There is a close working relationship and a coordination among them so as to do their best in helping to treat psychiatrically ill and mentally retarded children.

The main tasks of the childrens' and adolescents' outpatient departments of the psychiatric inpatient clinics, or of the corresponding departments of the regional hospitals are:

a. Organizing the search for possible patients, their examinations in outpatient departments and their treatment, and if necessary, their hospitalization.

b. Organizing, directing and carrying out all possible psychiatric treatments and therapies for the children and teenagers in the region.

c. Organizing and directing the social and educational adaptation and rehabilitation, and the psychiatric help necessary for mentally ill and mentally defective children and teenagers.

d. Methodical directing and supply of additional medical and educational staff qualified in the field of child psychiatry to work in the special schools.

e. Guaranteed availability of medical-educational help for feeble children, or children with psychosocial problems.

f. Insurance of closely specialized consultations to help all of the medical and educative institutions for children and teenagers.

g. Giving help in solving problems, to the best of their ability, to all services, institutions or social organizations in their activity concerning the mental health of children and teenagers.

For the fulfillment of that great number of tasks the child psychiatrists and their co-workers from the various departments should establish a close relationship with a number of services for children and teenagers with psychic deviations:

1. With the special, academic, speech, training and therapeutic schools.

2. With the houses for children and adolescents with mental troubles.

3. With the obstetrical and pediatric departments of the hospitals.

4. With the committees struggling against antisocial deeds.

5. With other institutions and social organizations, dealing with the mental health of children and teenages.

Important research work was done in the study of schizophrenia, and a number of concrete achievements have been reached. The problems concerning the intellectual development in the impaired state, the clinical and evolutionary problems of pfropfschizophrenia, and the characteristics of the games of schizophrenic children (by M. Atschkova); the problems concerning the young autistic child studied from the stand-point of the nosological trend in psychiatry (by C. Christozov and M. Atschkova); fundamental profound studies on the evolution and prognosis of this psychosis (by C. Christozov and M. Atschkova); the initial phenomena of the schizophrenic child (by K. Tzafarov); and the speech disturbances and characteristics of the premorbid personality (by S. Zaimova) are just some of the areas which have been explored.

In the field of manic-depressive psychosis (Cyclophenia), great success has been noted in the clinical determination of atypical characteristics and of atypical dynamics of the manic and depressive phases (by C. Christozov, M. Atschkova, M. Galabova and N. Dachinova). It is believed that after the age of 10 this psychosis can be expressed in the usual clinical manner.

Epilepsy is studied both in its clinical manifestations - psychotic episodes and febrile convulsion (by C. Christozov and M. Atschkova), and in its therapeutical aspects - treatment with Tegretol, and also a lay lasting treating of the picnolepsie with Zarontine (by M. Atschkova and D. Dascalov).

Work has been done on the relation between neuropathy and the neuropathic constitution (N. Daschinova). A broad and profound clinical-statistical study has been carried out on the postencephalitic state in relation to the psychiatric aspects concerning children and teenagers. A profound work has been carried out on the neuroses. Here we should mention the works of C. Christozov on the basic clinical characteristics, classification, treatment, rehabilitation (especially the type connected with educational influences), psychologic profile and the role of the family factors. The neuroses in school age children are studied together with epidemiological research by V. Jontschev.

Alcohol intoxication, alcohol encephalopathy and the alcohol psychoses are studied by G. Usunoff, M. Gagabov and S. Zaimova. Suicides among children and teenagers are studied by M. Galabova, C. Dimitrov and K. Tzafarov.

Other studies cover such topics as: the psychiatric problems of being an only child (M. Boyadjieva), sexual development and puberty (G. Usunoff), the pathological picture of Heller's disease (G. Usunoff and T. Gentschev), the clinical and epidemiological characteristics of oligophrenia (L. Timtschev) and hysteria among children (N. Schipkovensky).

The prophylactic-hygienic and organizational activities in the field of child psychiatry are being studied systematically, according to the progressive concepts of the socialist health system (C. Christozov, T. Taschev and S. Dobreva).

Special attention is paid to the testing and application of foreign treatments and methods of clinical work (C. Christozov, R. Penuschlieva, A. Kokoschkarova and K. Metschkov).

A number of national conferences have been dedicated to the problems of child psychiatry, and in 1973 the Third International Symposium of Child Psychiatrists from the socialist countries was held in Sofia, with the main theme being "The Child and the School."

SOVIET UNION

Child psychiatry in the Soviet Union developed as a branch of general psychiatry only after the October Revolution. Research in this field was determined by the problems of practical psychiatric care for children.

In 1918 a Department of Child Psychiatry was set up at the Ministry of Health. Under Soviet power a number of special institutions, schools and homes were built for the education and treatment of children with mental retardation and behavior problems. The Institute for Handicapped Children in Moscow and the Child Research Institute in Leningrad developed extended studies concerning the theoretical and organizational problems of child psychiatric care under the guidance of M. O. Gurevitch, T. I. Judin, A. S. Grobpedov, etc. Congresses and conferences were held and detailed programs were drafted.

Many specialists were educated in the new child psychiatric hospitals built under Soviet power. It was for this purpose that the Children's Department of Don's Psychiatric Hospital was organized in 1920 by V. A. Gilliarovskij, A. I. Vinokurova and T. P. Simson.

At the same time a children's psychiatric hospital containing 200 beds was built in Moscow, and a children's department for epileptic children was organized at the 3rd pyschiatric hospital built in Leningrad.

Children's departments were organized at the psychiatric hospitals in many other towns, headed well known specialists in child psychiatry, like S. S. Mnukhin, N. I. Ozeretskij, E. A. Ossipova, T. P. Simson, and G. E. Suchareva.

The preventive tendencies of Soviet medicine were further developed when in the 1920's the system of psychiatric inpatient clinics was built up. In 1925 the Moscow State Psychiatric Clinic was organized and a department of child psychiatry was attached.

The struggle against infectious diseases was a major problem of public health services in the Soviet Union. It explains the great attention and efforts of child psychiatrists in studying mental disturbances during the acute and chronic phases of general and brain infections. Clinical studies were done concerning the mental symptoms of grippe in children, of acute child infections, of pulmonary tuberculosis, of congenital lues, etc. (by E. A. Ossipova, E. I. Gorelik, K. G. Rabinovitch and D. L. Eingorn).

A major problem of child psychiatry in the 1930's was the residual symptoms of encephalitis and meningoencephalitis of different origins (by A. A. Volianskij, M. O. Gurevitch, K. M. Kandaratskaja, N. I. Ozeretzkij, A. B. Amirdjanian, M. S. Pevzner, T. P. Simson, and L. S. Jussevitch). Considerable attention is also paid to the neurological and psychiatric symptoms of brain trauma in the acute and residual stages (by K. A. Novlianskaja, M. V. Soloveva, O. G. Jurova, and G. E. Suchareva).

Children with behavior problems was another field of clinical investigation in the 30's and 40's. The psychopathology, classification and correction of psychopaths through education was the subject of many discussions. In Soviet child psychiatry, the psychopathic constitution is a concept of much narrower range when compared to the classical view of E. Kretschmer and K. Schneider. The psychopathic traits due to organic brain lesions and the psychopathic-like states closely related to them were studied intensively by A. A. Parchomenko and V. P. Kudriavzeva. The well established role of a number of exogenous factors - whether prenatal or operating at the time of delivery or in early childhood - contributed to the prevention of the so-called border-line cases.

A number of works are concerned with the causes of "nervousness" in children (E. A. Ossipova, O. F. Ijboldina, and G. E. Suchareva), the personaltiy traits of children with neuroses (V. N. Miassishtschev), the clinical features of neuroses and reactive states in children (E. A. Bley, A. I. Ploticher, T. P. Simson and E. E. Scanavi), and the psychopathic development of children (I. S. Iskovleva-Shnirman).

Neurophysiological findings were widely applied to the explanation of reactive states and neurotic reactions in particular. This approach differed essentially from the psychoanalytic interpretations popular at the time among western investigators.

Schizophrenia in childhood and adolescence was another field of intensive work in the pre-war years. A number of studies investigated the clinical features and course of psychopathology in childhood (P. D. Brill, N. I. Ozeretzkij, I. V. Shur, M. S.

Pevzner, K. G. Rabinovitch and S. S. Perskaja); the role of premorbid personality traits (K. A. Novlianskaja); and the treatment of schizophrenia in children (N. N. Bodnianskaja, V. J. Deianov, F. J. Kaznelson, D. L. Eingorn, L. I. Gelina and O. G. Jurova).

Soviet child psychiatrists proved that schizophrenia could be an illness of early childhood and were among the first to give a detailed description of its clinical features (S. Z. Galatzkaia, E. S. Grebelskaja and others) based on the nosological principle.

Epilepsy in children was given much attention in the prewar years by a number of investigators (S. S. Mnukhin, A. I. Ploticher and M. A. Uspenskaia).

A problem of particular interest in the 40's was the central nervous system activity in children (by A. G. Ivanov-Smolenskij, N. I. Krasnogorskij and others), which was of fundamental importance for theoretical interpretations of psychopathological data. This period is also characterized by intensive work in the field of organization of child psychiatric care (by A. S. Griboedov, V. A. Gilliarovskij, E. A. Ossipova, K. G. Rabinovitch and G. E. Suchareva).

In 1933 a course in child psychiatry (N. I. Ozeretykij), was organized at the First Institute of Medicine in Leningrad and in 1935 a Department of Child Psychiatry was set up (G. E. Suchareva) for postgraduate education at the Central Institute for Specialization of Physicians.

An event of particular significance for child psychiatry in this period was the first scientific Conference on Child Psychiatry and Neurology held in 1934 by the Moscow Society of Neurologists and Psychiatrists.

The first handbooks of child psychiatry were published prior to the Second World War by M. O. Gurevitch, N. I. Ozeretzkij, T. P. Simson, M. M. Model and G. E. Suchareva.

The war caused great damage to the whole system of children's psychiatric institutions and hampered all research.

The first publications after the war were concerned with observations made during the war period such as the clinical features of reactive states in children during the war (I. D. Kossaia, V. P. Kudriavzeva, T. P. Simson, E. E. Skanavi, E. A. Ossipova and others); and the neurological and psychiatric disturbances in general and brain infections, and in cerebral traumas. Many works were published on the specific features of psychoses caused by influenza (F. J. Kaznelson); scarlet fever (V. P. Kudriavzeva); measles (T. P. Simson); malaria (M. A. Uspenskaia); tuberculous meningitis (M. I. Lapides); acute brain lesions (M. V. Soloviova); and encephalitis (Z. A. Kossenko).

A specific form of encephalitis with predominance of sensory symptoms was described in children in the late 40's by M. O. Gurevitch, E. A. Ossipova, T. P. Simson and others.

The great problem of rheumatism in children attracted the attention of many child psychiatrists. Descriptions of acute rheumatic psychoses in children (E. A. Ossipova and T. P. Simson), and other mental disturbances (V. J. Deianov) were published.

A further intensification of research became possible after the effects of the war on the system of child psychiatric care were overcome. Particular emphasis was made on the problems of epilepsy, residual encephalopathy and mental subnormality.

Epilepsy was subjected to particularly detailed studies by child psychiatrists in Leningrad. An original evolutional view in the research of epilepsy in children was introduced by this school (A. I. Barykina, V. N. Bondarev, N. D. Issaev and others). Their contributions include a number of specific features in the course of epilepsy in children and descriptions of new forms of petit mal seizures, as well as proposing a new classification based on clinical and physiological evidence and a number of pathophysiological mechanisms.

Many new ideas and aspects of the clinical picture and course of the epilepsies were brought forward by G. B. Abramovitch in support of the role of compensatory mechanisms in pathogenesis and modern treatment (V. J. Deglin, V. P. Kudriavtzeva, O. P. Jureva, L. J. Visnevskaia, R. V. Ivanova, and K. A. Novlianskaia).

The problem of residual symptoms following organic brain lesions, which is of particular importance in child psychiatry and neurology, was studied further in the past few years. In a number of publications (G. B. Abramovitch, S. S. Mnukhin, M. S. Pevzner, and G. E. Suchareva and coworkers), the pathogenetic role of residual encephalopathy was demonstrated in the epilepsy clinic, along mental subnormality and psychopathic traits of organic origin. The clinical course of these disturbances was studied and methods of pathogenetic treatment were proposed. At this point, mention should be made of investigations on endocrine deficiences (K. S. Lebedinskaia), child cerebral paralysis (E. I. Kirichenko), residual symptoms of encephalitic forms of poliomyelitis (V. M. Galinis) and asphyxia neonatorum (E. M. Mastiukova).

The investigations on residual encephalopathy were summarized at the National Scientific Conference on Child Neurology and Psychiatry in January 1966, where both the theoretical and practical importance of these studies were stressed.

The research on mental subnormality in the last 15 years was mainly concerned with the etiology and pathogenesis of these states. This became possible due to the great progress in the fields of physiology, biochemistry, immunology, embryology, genetics and the allied sciences. Some basic disturbances in the activity of the central nervous system of the mentally subnormal were established (L. B. Gakkel, V. I. Lubovskij, and A. R. Luria). The application of new biological methods made it possible to establish the role of the following in the genesis of mental subnormality: immunological incompatibility (G. B. Abramovitch, A. I. Shapiro, and K. N. Nazarov), insufficiency of enzymic systems (M. G. Blumina, and B. V. Lebedeva), chromosomal abnormalities (E. F. Davidenkova and others) and toxoplasmosis (N. V. Bodnianskaia, R. D. Kogan and others). New classifications of mental abnormalities were proposed based on etiological and pathogenetic principles (G. E. Suchareva, S. S. Mnukhin, and M. S. Pevzner. The clinical features of mental subnormality of different origins are constantly being clarified (S. N. Zinchenko, E. M. Mastiukova, I. A. Iurkova and others). A number of monographs on mental subnormality were published recently (M. S. Pevzner, V. I. Lubovskij, E. N. Pravdina-Vinarskaia, and G. E. Suchareva).

In addition to these fundamental fields of investigation, a lot of work has been done on the problems of border-line states (V. V. Kovaliov, M. I. Lapides, I. A. Iurkova, E. E. Skanavi, G. E. Suchareva and O. A. Trifonov), schizophrenia (M. S. Vrono, V. N. Mamtzeva, O. D. Sosiukalo, G. E. Suchareva, G. K. Ushakov and others), and mental disturbances of somatic origin (V. P. Belov and V. V. Kovaliov).

This short historical review of Soviet child psychiatry proves that this relatively new branch of psychiatry has been developed on the principles of clinical nosology, in accordance with the practical need of child psychiatric care and in close relation with general clinical psychiatry and pediatrics.

CZECHOSLOVAKIA

Child psychiatric care in Czechoslovakia, as in the other European countries, began in the second half of the 19th century.   In the beginning, this care was directed towards mentally deficient children, and its emphasis was mainly educational, not medical.   Interest in the psychological and educational problems, and in psychological disturbances was revived by the famous pediatrician Czerny.   He stressed the need of educational work with neuropathic children.   His lectures made him very popular.   He maintained the concept that the pediatrician ought to be not only a physician, but also a teacher of suffering children.

The development of child psychiatry in Czechoslovakia (CSSR) was connected with the collaboration between the medical and educational professions.   Dr. Slavoj Amerling was both a physician and an educator at the same time.   This collaboration is still current.

After the First World War, child psychiatry was in an educational period.   There were local outpatient clinics for young people and after the Second World War the social institutions became interested in the so-called deviant, defective and abnormal children.   At this time, the authorities had the opinion that the mental life of children is determined by biological and social factors, heredity and environment, which was believed to be immutable.   The educators tried to prove that the class origin of the children also had a biological basis.

Two groups of abnormal children were distinguished: intellectually deficient (mentally retarded) and morally defective (juvenile delinquents).   Methods for diagnosis were individual and collective tests, and IQ tests.   The mental and moral defects were considered to be lasting states, inborn or inherited.   The educators founded institutions for the care of these children; these were mainly educational institutions.   For juvenile delinquents there were reform schools, which in the popular mind still serve as a menace for unobedient children. With the foundation of organized child psychiatrics care, the educational era in the history of child psychiatry was ended. At present, rehabilitation is a well-defined specialty whose central problem is the education of children with organic cerebral lesions. At the same time, child psychiatry works in close collaboration with the rehabilitationists. (Hádlik, J. Paediatric Psychiatry, Its Concept, Content and Approach, *Csl. Pediat.* XII, *12, 861,* 1957).

The first regular institute for mentally retarded children was founded in Prague in 1871 under the direction of Karl Slavoj Amerling. In the literature, this institute is known as "Ernestinum." In 1902 Amerling was replaced by Karel Herfort, professor of psychiatry and founder of child psychiatry in Czechoslovakia (Vondrácek, V. Lékarská psychologie a vseobcná psychiatrie. Státni pedagogicke nakladatelstvi, Praha, 1960).

The year 1902 is considered by Professor J. Fischer (Detska psychiatri. Státni zdravotnické nakladatelstvi, Praha, 1963) as the beginning of the scientific period of child psychiatry in the CSSR. Since 1914, K. Herfort, together with Prof. Matejk and Prof. Cad, worked at the newly built educational institute in Prague. There Herfort organized an out-patient clinic for child psychopathology. In "Ernestinum," which was moved to Budenická, he created an experimental eugenic station and gave lectures to students in medicine and education. His collaboration with inspector Zeman once again proves the unity of education and child psychiatry is Czechoslovakian psychiatry.

Another supporter of child psychiatry in this country was the physician and Doctor of Philosophy, Josef Apetaur. His dissertation at the philosophic faculty was "Psychological and Other Studies of Puberty, with Regard to Czech Children." In 1924 he began working at the Youth Institute with Prof. Herfort, in 1936 he worked in the Psychiatric Clinic with Prof. Mislivecek, and in 1939 he became the Director of the Psychiatric Department at the Institute of Learning, which in 1946 became the Psychiatric Out-Patient Clinic for Children and Adolescents at the Institute of Mental Health in Prague.

Apetaur took part in the development and reorganization of the reformatory schools and the educational institutions for mentally and morally abnormal adolescents. He was a consultant to the Ministry of Education and the Ministry of Health. In 1947, Apetaur began conducting studies on the problem "Innocence in Puberty" at the Faculty of Medicine. In 1945 he returned to the Psychiatric Clinic of Karlow University directed by Prof. Milivecek and there he founded and headed the first child psychiatric department at this clinic. He had many clinical and research activities and was an expert in Forensic Psychiatry, especially for the adolescent. His untimely death was in 1955.

J. Apetaur was replaced by Prof. Fischer, Doctor of Medical Sciences, who is currently the Director of the Child Psychiatric Clinic at the Pediatric Faculty in Motol, which has functioned since 1971, after the foundation of the new University Hospital in Motol. The Child Psychiatric Clinic used to be the educational ward of the first pediatric clinic, whose director - Prof. Schweizer, a Doctor of Medical Sciences and a pediatrician, is currently working at the Institute of Post-graduate Pediatric Specialization in Prague - Krc, developing child psychiatric care. The chief of the educational ward was a teacher of 20 years practice, who later finished his education at the Faculty of Medicine and dedicated his life to the problems of education, rehabilitation and prophylaxis. From this ward Dr. Z. Valkova, who successfully defended her dissertation "The Course and Clinical Aspects of Enuresis", came to the first psychiatric clinic of the Pediatric Faculty in 1973.

The pedopsychiatric clinic currently has 25 beds for children with psychoses, severe neurotic troubles and other diagnostic problems. This clinic is for training of students from the Pediatric Faculty and for pediatricians and psychiatrists preparing for their specialty examinations.

Child psychiatry was legalized in the 60's and the first specialty examination was given on Feb. 8, 1961. The first approved specialists were Dr. Cerny, D. Z. Válková and Dr. V. Valencik. There are 70 child psychiatrists now.

The organization of child psychiatric care in CSSR was legalized by an act of the Ministry of Health in 1953. Dr. Kucera wrote about this act in 1954 in the pedopsychiatric journals. Dr. Otakar Kucera (physician ana lawyer) was a specialist in light organic lesions in children. He also worked with juvenile delinquents, and had written some papers concerning infantile and adolescent crimes. Because of his psychoanalytical orientation, he was the first to translate some papers of Freud and his pupils for CSSR psychiatric literature.

In the CSSR there now exists a wide network of pedopsychiatric and psychiatric hospitals, as well as the so-called pedagogic-educational psychologo-educational and other in-patient and out-patient departments. There are some differences between Czek and Slovakia in the organization of child psychiatry, since the tradition of Slovakia (according to the opinion of Bajan, Dr. of Philosophy) is that these in-patient and out-patient clinics are to be directed by psychologists. There are articles concerning these problems in "Czechoslovenska Psychologia."

One of the biggest psychiatric hospitals has been in existence for 80 years and is situated in South Chekia. For a long period of time it was directed by Dr. Voyta who is now the chief of the psychiatric ward for adolescents in Bohnice.

Dr. Vrzal, chief of the out-patient clinic at the Children's Hospital in Brno, has written several articles on adolescent psychiatry. Dr. Vyborova is the chief of the children's psychiatric ward in the Psychiatric Clinic and Dr. Jan Cerny is the chief of the children's psychiatric ward in the Psychiatric Hospital in Brno. He is the author of many special pedopsychiatric papers and of the chapter on oligophrenias (1961). Dr Ludek Cerny, chief of the psychiatric ward in the hospital in Dolni Pocernice, was the originator of the "telephone call of faith" for youth in Prague. He has written some papers and monographs about suicides in children, and together with his co-workers, has treated dysleptic children. (Telephonische Beratungstelle fur Kinder und Jugendliche, Leitung des Vertrauens; *Acta Paedopsychiatrica*, *35*: 274, 1968; Suicide in Children and Adolescents, Measures of Prevention; Avicenum, Praha, 1970).

Dr. Vodák, together with the educator Sulc, has worked on the problem of deviant behavior in children. He wrote the monograph entitled "Poruchy a závady chóvani a se spolupracovniky problemy osvojeni deti", Stat. zdravot. naklad., Praha, 1967.

At present Dr. L. Richterova is the only honored pedo-psychiatrist. She is the chief editor of *Ceskoslovenski Psychiatria*, and is very active in out-patient work connected with academic, E. E. N. T. and speech institutions, and with legal and other institutions.

Detailed information about child practitioners is given by Dr. M. Fibihova, who is the chief of the child psychiatric ward in the Psychiatric Hospital in Bohnice, Prague. (The Beginnings of Child Psychiatric Activity in Sternberk, Csl. Psychiat. 4: 247, 1956). The chief of psychiatric consultants for the district of Prague is Dr. R. Nesnidalová. An experienced psychiatrist, she has written many publications in *Ceskoslovenská Psychiatria*, and has published the very interesting monograph entitled 'Extreme Solitude' (Avicenum, Praha, 1973). p.480

GERMAN DEMOCRATIC REPUBLIC (DDR)

In the German (Deutsche) Democratic Republic, there is no differentiation between neurology and psychiatry either in private practice (consultations) or in the majority of specialized hospitals. In view of this, the development of neurology and psychiatry of children and adolescents, is significant indeed. The official name of this speciality is, "Child Neuropsychiatry" and includes children and adolescents from age one year to eighteen years. There is no tendency, as may be noticed in many other countries, to combine child neurology with pediatrics and child psychiatry with adult psychiatry. Our investigations show that almost all of the neurotic diseases of childhood influence the child's development to varying extents.Supplementary psychic and/or psychopathologic symptoms are also found as a rule. Further, entirely psychic or psychopathologic disturbances in these children and adolescents are caused to a major extent by body injuries, or, more precisely, organic brain injuries or precedent acute disease. When making these diagnostic findings, it is important to note that the departments of child neuropathology and child psychiatry are always attached to the great clinical departments of neurology, psychiatry or pediatrics. This environment possess a typical hospital atmosphere and thus hampers the creation of a stimulating and active environmental milieu.

The departments of child psychiatry, which are attached to the specialized hospitals of neurology and psychiatry or to the University Clinics, possess usually a consultation of their own, beds and/or territory for the expansion and enlarging of

---

Part of this material has been prepared in collaboration with other colleagues as shown below:

Prof. Dr.sc.med. Gerhard Göllnitz (*GDR*)
Dr. Zofia Szymanska (*Poland*)
Dr. Jozsef Szenasy (*Hungary*)

the correspondent class rooms, occupational therapy, psychotherapy, rehabilitation (re-education), music and gymnastic
rooms. Together with the medical staff - doctors, nurses, and
methodologists for healing physical culture (physical therapists
and orthopedists, there are also clinical psychologists and the
teachers associated with the special schools at the hospital.
Music therapy of different kinds is applied for the correction of
disorders in behavior and mental development. Music therapy
presents a most effective factor, able to vary according to the
treatment goals and the individuality of each child. When it is
applied as a group therapy, it facilitates the child's
accomodation to his environment and early release to the
family.

A section of Child Psychiatry was organized as a component of the Society of Neurology and Psychiatry. This section
united all the professionals interested in Neurology,
Pediatrics,Clinical Psychology, Special Education etc., in respect to their association with departments of child psychiatry.
The section of Child Neurology in DDR is a member of the International Federation of Child Psychiatry and the allied
disciplines, of the European Union of Child Psychiatrists. It is
also a founder of, and works closely with, the Working Group of
Child Psychiatry of the socialist countries.

The first Chair of Child Neuropsychiatry was founded in
1952 at the University of Rostock. It had a Polyclinic, clinical
departments and scientific experimental laboratories of its own.
A number of clinical and polyclinical departments were added
to the Universities at Leipzig and Berlin, and included Chairs of
Speciality as well. There are also departments and hospitals,
headed by physician specialists, attached to other medical Universities and to the Medical Academy as well.

A large number of specialized hospitals of Neurology and
Psychiatry have also excellent departments of Child Neuro-
psychiatry. Hospitals for Child-Adolescent Neuropsychiatry
were created for them, as for example, those in Brandenburg,
Nordhausen, Uchtspringe, Ueckermunde, Leipzig-Dosen and
Berlin-Herzberge.

The students receive their special education about the
bases of the child Neuropsychiatry during the 4th or 5th year of
their educational course, by the lecture-course (complex) of

Neurology and Psychiatry. The number of hours is defined and varies according the organization from 16 to 20 hours during the semester. This complex is a separate part from the state examination in medicine. For the students, beginning their education in child Neuropsychiatry and the doctors interested in the matter, a textbook was created (G. Gollnitz, Iena), which will appear in its third edition in 1975. In addition to this there is a sufficient number of monographs in Neurology, Psychopathology, Developmental Psychology, Psychodiagnostics, Special Education, which deal with some specialized problems in the matter. In the medical journal for this subject "Psychiatrie, Neurologie und medizinische Psychologie" (Leipzig) special attention is paid to child Neuropsychiatry and is headed by an editor of its own.

After the section of child Psychiatry was created as a programme for specialization, which was approved by the Ministry of Health of GDR and the Academy of GDR for specialization of doctors, child neuropsychiatrists were educated according to this standard in the past 4 years. With the instruction Nr.2 from 23.V. 1974 a legal basis was created for the subspecialization of the doctors, stating that the child psychiatrists could specialize complementary according to the established standard. A subspecialization is allowed for specialists in Neurology and Psychiatry, and specialists in Pediatrics, as well. The specialization in Child Neuropsychiatry lasts 2 years. During another, i.e. third year, the corresponding standard of training becomes available to the pediatricians and the neurologists, so that the future neuropsychiatrists, no matter of their study in the Pediatrics or Neurology, achieve the same knowledge and training. This system excludes the negative opposing of Pediatrics and child Psychiatry which exists in some countries. For the benefit of the children and adolescents, a common complex of developmental Neurology, developmental Psychology and developmental Psychopathology is held valid. A larger number of child neuropsychiatrists work in clinics. Nowadays there is one Neuropsychiatrist for 100,000 people and the tendency in the following year is to reach 1 per 75,000. Each district should have at least one child neuropsychiatrist and every region at least one hospital of child neuropsychiatry. In the regional ambulatories a close co-operation exists among the pediatricians, the specialists for women, the neurologists, the education-school and the specialists on educational problems. Psychotherapy in the child and adolescent is developed especially well in terms of the specialization and subspecialization in child Neuropsychiatry, so that it is not necessary for a special group to be created for these important therapeutical methods. It should be noticed, that the child neuropsychiatric clinics and hospitals work in closes relation with the clinical psychologists and specialized educators, aiming thus to attain the widest possible diagnosis and treatment. By means of the clinics a close relation is established with the psychiatrists, orthopedists, ophtalmologists, otorhinolaryngologists, stomatologists and others. The specialization and perfection is carried through by Academy for specialization in GDR, which organizes every year a course for child neuropsychiatrists. In addition to this every year there is a change from one initial course for medical specialists interested in the matter and one for certification especially for child neuropsychiatrists.

From 1969 a state plan was created for investigations, dealing especially with the health of the young generation. It directs the attention mainly towards the early identification of the genetic disorders, perinatal problems, the evolution of "menaced" children, reeducation of the retarded and children with brain injuries, the epileptics, and children and adolescents with disturbances in behaviour and disorders of development. These problems establish an indirect link with the pedagogical and defectological problems and with the psychic reactive disturbances of the adolescents as well. By this comprehensive programme, conditions will be created for the development of the diagnosis, the therapy and the long term reeducation and rehabilitation. Special attention is paid to the prevention of brain injuries and disturbances of brain development. Thus the problems of the child Neuropsychiatry are given opportunity to develop and are included in a favourable medical policy in GDR, enjoying a careful attitude and attention from the part of the State and the Party.

CHILD PSYCHIATRY IN POLAND

There are three periods in the development of the Polish psychiatry-the first was before the war in 1939; the second was during the occupation and the years after the war to 1948, and the third - from 1949 to the present time.

Greater interests in the field of child psychiatry and psychology arose in the first ten years of our century, but several articles treating similar problems appeared in the second half of the 19th century.

During 1923 a new society was organized in Warsaw from the society "Friends of the children". This is the first therapeutical-pedagogical out-patient clinic, called "Pedagogical Polyclinic", which became very popular. There and then was created the principle of close collaboration between doctor, psychologist and social worker (trustee), which in our contemporary understanding is a team.

Ancilliary child centers (similar to child-guidance clinics) were affiliated to the municipal health institutions and other specialized groups.

In 1932 were created the first child neuropsychiatric depertments in the general hospitals in Warszawa and in the psychiatric hospitals in Swiecie n. Wisla, Gniezno-Dziekanka, Tworki, Rybnik, especially for mentally retarded children.

In 1935 appeared the Insitute for Mental Hygiene (under the direction of Dabrowsky) with a polyclinic for children suffering from neurotic and psychotic disorders, epilepsy, stuttering and which developed a large educational program publishing monographs, journals, etc.

The State Insitute for special educators which trained teachers educating mentally retarded children in child neuropsychiatric departments, was established in 1923.

The war destroyed almost everything, but the Insitute of Mental Hygiene continued its activities even with a reduced capacity. After the war (from 1945 to 1948) were organized 12 filials in different towns, and also child wards for neurotic and other children in Warszawa, Krakòw, Wroclaw.

During 1948 there were significant changes in the organization and the structure of psychiatric care. The Insitute of Mental Hygiene was transformed into Central Polyclinic for Mental Health. Child psychiatry development was directed by the Section of Mental Health in the Ministry of Public Health.

At present child psychiatric care consists of open and closed therapeutical insitutions. Open psychiatric polyclinics exist in all districts, countries, towns and villages. Hospital care is delivered by clinical, hospital and sanatorial child psyciatric wards, through a staff of competent child-psychiatrists and other specialists. The psychologists use tests and special techniques and are functioning at the same time as social workers. The medical examination is comprehensive (somatical, neurological, psychologic and psychiatric) and the necessary consultations with other specialists are regularly made.

In Warszawa functions the best organized polyclinic which has a central and five periferal flilals (Warszawa - Praga Potnoc, Warszawa - Żolibórz, Warszawa - Ochota and ul. Jasna). There are several out patient clinics for school hygiene situated in community polyclinics and the Institute for Mental Hygiene and Special Pedagogy. The hospital care in Poland includes 5 clinical wards, 7 departments in psychiatric hospitals and about 1800 beds in 5 child sanatorial insitutions. In Wroclaw exists an ward for observation of border-line cases.

There are two clinical wards in Warszawa - one is in the Psychiatric clinic of the Medical Academy and the other in the Pediatric clinic, with a total of 46 beds.

Clinical wards exist in the psychiatric departments in Choroszez k. Bialegostoku, Gdansk, Krakow, and other towns with a number of 270 beds. In Lublinec functions a special ward for adolescents with 150 beds. There are child wards at the psychiatric hospitals in Gniezno-Dziekanka, Kraków 18-Kobierzyn, Gdañsk, Swiecie N. Wisla and Morawica k. Kielc.

Sanatoria which could be with one or more profiles have a special role for the child neuropsychiatric care. The sanatorium in Krosnice, pow. Milicz Wojewodztwo wroclawkie has 500 beds and many divisions for children of preschool age, and older ones with neuroses, encephalopathies, intellectually normal or subnormal, and for psychotics for reeducation etc. There are observation wards, somatic wards and well organized schools. In Nowe Czarnowo Województwo szczeciñskie the sanatorium of 350 beds has two wards for children with organic cerebral lesions, neurotic ward, and the only logopedic ward in Poland, as well as a ward for special diagnostics and a ward for enuretic children. Specialized sanatoria are situated in Garwolin, in Warszawa county, with wards for children who suffered from poliomyelitis, and neurotic ward, in Józefów k. Otwocka with 50 beds, in Cichowo for boys and girls with 120 beds and one for boys in Rybienko n. Bugiem. (next to Warszawa) with 75 beds.

For epileptic children there are sanatoria in Zary k. Zagania Wojewodztwo zielonogorskie with 250 beds and normal and special school, in Bliszczyce Wojewodztwo opolskie for boys (professional orientation), in Brwinow Wojewodztwo warszawskie for boys and girls in school age and in Wojsce for 10-12 years old boys.

According to the provision of Law, from 1949 the care for children between 1-3 years of age was handled by the Ministry of Health and the care for adolescents between 4-18 years of age - by the Ministry of Education. In 1950 the Ministry of Education handed over all institutions for severely mentally retarded children who were unable to be reeducated, to the Ministry of Health as needing medical treatment.

At present, the Section of Social aid to the Ministry of Public Health has 7000 beds for mentally retarded children. Very important for them are the so-called "life-schools".

The need for specially trained and educated people in the field of child neuropsychiatry is great. From 1958 psychiatrists and pediatrists could performs first degree specialization after three years practice in child neuropsychiatry.

As opposed to adult psychiatry, child psychiatry deals more often with border-line cases - child nervousness, deviant behaviour, etc.

HUNGARY

During the first half of the century child psychiatry was practiced both by pediatricians and neuropsychiatrists. As far as psychiatrists are concerned this field of medicine was popular among such followers as Pál Ranschburg from the University Clinic at Margit Révész, László Focher and Janos Schnell. In 1926 Janos Schnell set up a Consulting Center on the problems of upbringing and education and in 1934 he founded the Insitut of Child Psychology where he guided the efforts of a number of pediatricians, neuropsychiatrists, pedagogues, psychologists and social workers.

Long before World War II, Pál Gegesi Kiss organized a Consulting Center on problems of development and education at the Budapest Child Clinic where modern methods of investigation were applied to neurological cases.

Twenty five years ago a Child ward was set up at the Budapest neuropsychiatric hospital due to the efforts of Simon, Blanka Loránd. Cases of severe agression, epilepsy, hysteria, poriomania and asocial behaviour are treated there. Numerous other conditions are also treated: mental disturbances of early age, leading to a social behavious, along with various cases traditionally considered to be of exogenous or hereditary origin which lately, due to modern diagnostic methods, were identified as resulting from specific lesions of the nervous system: genetic abnormalities, enzyme deficiencies etc. 25% of the patients treated in this ward are epileptics.

At the Budapest Child Hospital, Heim Pál another neurological ward for children has been functioning for 25 years now, confined mainly to organic neurological conditions.

In 1954 at the Institute of Neurosurgery in Budapest, a child ward of 20 beds was set up. In 1975 the number of beds increased to 9, equiped for intensive therapy and neurosurgery for infants.

At one of the district child hospitals in Budapest a ward for child neuroses is functioning for 5 years now.

Each of the wards mentioned above is supplemented with an outpatient service. Continuity of care is thus secured for the chronic conditions requiring follow-up after discharge.

At the child clinics in Pécs and Debrecen psychiatric and neurological wards are functioning with several beds each. A year ago such a ward was set up at the Clinic in Oroshaza.

Since 1958 in Budapest a Child Neurologic outpatient service is functioning having one central and four district stations. Children with epilepsy are treated at the Central station.

From 1958 onwards, a number of psychoneurological outpatient services were set-up in many of the bigger cities of the country - 15 in all apart from those in Budapest. Services there are rendered by pediatricians, who have either specialized in neuropsychiatry or practiced long enough in this field.

Just like in neighbouring countries, Child neuropsychiatrists in Hungary differentiate depending on their basic specialty of pediatrics or neuropsychiatry. What is more important is the child neuropsychiatrist to be willing to learn the skills he lacks - pediatrics if he is a former neuropsychiatrist or neuropsychiatry if he is a former pediatrist.

In 1974 the Society of child neurology, psychiatry and neurosurgery was founded whose members are former participants of one of 3 societies that of pediatrists, that of neurologists and psychiatrists and that of neurosurgeons. This gives grounds to believe that in Hungary a unified approach to child neuropsychiatry will be achieved.

MENTAL HEALTH IN CHILDREN, Volume I
Edited By D. V. Siva Sankar
Copyright © 1975 by
PJD Publications Ltd., Westbury, N.Y.

CHILD PSYCHIATRY
(INDIAN SCENE)

Brij B. Sethi and Narottam Lal
King George's Medical College, Lucknow, India

It is well recognised that psychiatric services in India are far from adequate. Not only is there an acute shortage of psychiatrists but auxillary personnel, such as social workers, trained nurses, psychologists, child counsellors etc. are also to be had after a hectic search. For a long time psychiatry consisted of some widely scattered state mental hospitals where a traditional hospital superintendent was expected to look after therapeutic and other needs of hundreds of patients. Such was the exposure that a medical student had for a period of 7-10 days during his entire 5 years of training; he spent most of his time in the pursuit of pleasure rather than examining the patient or learning psychiatry. Similarly, psychiatry was never an independent subject in the curricula of medical schools and if at all any teaching was done, a teacher in medicine or a teacher in neurology with or without training in psychiatry, would deliver a few lectures in a casual manner to a sparsely attended class. The position of academic psychiatry has of late changed. Of the 105 medical schools in this country, at least 50% have established psychiatric units with a skeletal but a trained staff to look after service programs mainly consisting of an out-patient department, perhaps a child guidance clinic in some instances, and 10 to 20 beds in still fewer instances. Twenty-five percent of the medical schools have, however, established independent departments of psychiatry with a reasonbly sized inpatient unit, largely attended out-patient clinic, and some para-psychiatric staff. More than half of these are now offering post-graduate training programs in psychiatry leading to a post-graduate degree and carrying the distinction of being categorised as a specialist. It is accordingly not difficult to appreciate that whereas the extent of growth in adult psychiatry has been a relatively recent one as well as a slow one, the number of places where child psychiatric facilities might assume a respectable proportion are fewer still and the establishment or expansion of these centers have proceeded at an exceedingly sluggish rate.

From time to time the importance of the child has been made known to our policy planners with a result that almost all medical schools now boast of possessing independent departments of pediatrics. At a number of places, newly established child guidance clinics consist of a psychologist, one or two social workers, one statistician and an office assistant. The psychiatrists have not yet assumed full charge of these clinics partly because of the fact that trained child psychiatrists are not available, and partly on account of their preference to opt adult psychiatry, which is more expedient to practice and positively more rewarding. Separate in-patient facilities for children are hardly present at all in this country. Efforts are being made by a number of centers, including Lucknow, to obtain necessary funds from the state Governments for setting up such units. A large number of places where adult psychiatric facilities exist, the bed strength is so small that every attempt is made to enhance the adult beds, thereby completely ignoring the needs of children. It may not always be necessary to hospitalize the child. That the whole emphasis is being directed towards adult psychiatry is no longer a question, but it results in step-motherly treatment for child psychiatry.

Any attempt directed towards a study of mental health in a child or in an adult in a country, such as India, must take into account some of the contemporary cultural as well as ancient philosophical formulations. We have pointed out in the past that India has been witnessing a rapid change in terms of social, cultural, community, familial and religious beliefs, and individual as well as group behaviour has accordingly gone through a transformation (1). The changing patterns of culture as they relate to modern India must of necessity influence the growth, development, upbringing and the formation of adaptative or a maladaptative behaviour.

It may be well to mention at the out-set about some of our age old concepts. Indian philosophers have been aware of the nature and functions of mind and have made significant contributions towards the promotion and preservation of mental health (1). According to Ayurveda (2), the Indian system of medicine, *Swasthya* (a) is a condition where there is an equilibrium in *doshas* (b) and *dhatus* (c) with normal digestive as well as excretary functions with *prasannata* (d) of *indriyas* (e) *atma* (f) and *manas* (g). Such an understanding would indicate that freedom from physical illness alone is not to be considered as health. We are aware of an almost similar definition as provided by the World Health Organization in the late 20th century. The "upanishads" (1200 B.C. to 500 B.C.) are the first recorded attempts of Hindus at systematic philosophizing, and were the products of the highest wisdom (3). Fearlessness and renunciation of hatred were major teachings of "upanishads" which were to contribute heavily towards the development of an integrated personality (1). Similarly illuminating references to the levels of consciousness and in particular to dreams, are also found in these ancient documents. Accordingly, fantasy finds an important place in the motivation of dreams. "He who desires, dreams; he who does not desire, does not dream" (4). It was also emphasized by Lord Buddha (5) that desire is the root of all evil. "Bhagvat Gita" has also laid stress on the deterioration of personality in cases where temptations go unchecked. A quotation from Gita reads "A man thinking of subjects of senses becomes attached to them; attachment causes longing; from longing grows anger; from anger arises delusions; from

a = *Health*   b = *Disturbance of Body Humor*   c = *Body Humor*   d = *Pleasure* e = *Senses*   f = *Soul*   g = *Mind* delusions arise loss of memory; from the loss of memory arises a ruin of discrimination and from the loss of discrimination, he ultimately perishes. Bhagvat Gita's role, as an important tool of psychotherapy, is exemplified by (5):

"When a man puts away all the desires of his mind and when his spirit is content in itself, then he is called stable in intelligence. He, whose mind is untroubled in the midst of sorrows and is free from eager desire amidst pleasure, he, from whom passion, fear, and rage have passed away, he is called a Sage of settled intelligence".

A little later sufficient evidence is recorded that showed existence of a highly developed civilization in India during the period 3000 to 2000 B.C. We are also aware of the existence of different theories of perception, illusions and differentiation of mind into different layers about 1000 B.C. (5). The theme indicates that prevention of mental disturbances depended on how well the control of desires was encouraged, if meaningful, the attainment of tranquility was not an impossible task.

Further down the historical avenue in Ayurveda, a broad term *unmad* which is generally employed for mental illness, has been employed (3). Bhela also freely uses *unmad* and advances the familiar *dosha-disturbance* theory, as a sort of blanket explanation as aetiological factors in mental ill health (3). He holds that *doshas* (a) situated between the "head and the palate" are disturbed. As a result of these imbalances, the mind gets at once imitated with a manifestation directly reflected in consciousness being impaired, subsequently *buddhi* (b) is ruined, and the individual is confused. Bhela distinquished between mada (c) intoxication, and mild insanity and unmada (d). Further, when the mind is distressed by sorrow, anger, joy or loss of wealth, *mada* (c) sets in with *unmad* (d) being reached after the manifestations are excessively exaggerated. As a treatment measure, Bhela recommended various means of shocking the patient, like canning, whipping, confronting him with elephants and snakes, etc. Some such methods are still being practised by "witch doctors" in many primitive societies. Bhela, in addition, provided a list of drug prescriptions as well.

a = *disturbance of body humor*   b = *insight*   c = *intoxication and mild insanity*   d = *more morbid insanity*

There is a concept in classical Ayurveda about the *sattvavajaya* (e). It is aimed at protecting the mind from harmful influences. A fear experimentally instituted to counteract another fear, or an anxiety therapeutically produced, serves to root out another source of anxiety, and it is a familiar practice in *tantric* (f) cults.

e = *conquest of mind*   f = *shamonac*

Desire is a normal quality of the mind but when its limitations are exceeded, desire and others like *rage* (a), *lobha* (b), *moha* (c), *mada* (d), *krodha* (e) and *matsarya* (f) (generally termed as passion) contribute for a variety of mental disorders and diseases. It is for this reason that Ayurveda laid stress on these factors relating to maintenance and preservation of health (6). It may be seen that Indian philosophy, as contained in *upanishads* (g), Bhagwat Gita (h) and *dharma sastras* (i), emphasizes the ultimate goal as *samadhi* (j) (5).   Modern psychiatry, too, has a somewhat similar goal.

Philosophical literature of India is rich in metaphysics, psychology, logic, ethics, etc. The Hindu mind is essentially synthetic. It analyses the problem in its various aspects and considers their synthetic relationship to one another at an intensive level. Indian psychology is based on metaphysics, and the relevant theories were described earlier than 1,000 B.C. Sufficient guidelines at maintenance of equilibrium and tranquility during day to day stress of living are also provided (5).

Even though the systematic and some-what scientific understanding into the causation and prevention of mental illness had been provided by our earliest monographs, somewhere along the line transmission of a clear and somewhat consistent message got disrupted.   For a very long time people in general and masses in particular have looked upon mental illness as arising from unnatural factors, such as evil influences of spirits, supernatural phenomenona, existence of being haunted by a dead spirit or ghost and occasionally by feeling that the individual is being punished for his sinful deeds

a = *lust*   b = *greed*   c = *infatuation*   d = *arrogance*
e = *anger*   f = *jealousy*   g = *sacred book*   h = *sacred book*
i = *sacred book*   j = *tranquility*

in the present or past birth. Many of these beliefs have continued to prevail in large segments of our population irrespective of religion, social structures, or educational attainments. Since such worthy beliefs widely prevailed, the practices aimed at providing a person with the state of well being actively took into account theraeputic measures, such as beating, shocking, burning, threatening, and producing pain, or physical discomfort by a variety of means.   Interestingly, the historical perspectives advanced so far made no attempt to differentiate between a child psychiatric disorder from that of an adult. Accordingly, if a child was found to be indulging in unacceptable social practices such as quarreling, running away from school or home, manifesting behaviour exemplified by thumb sucking, nail biting or bed wetting he received a similar therapeutic approach as outlined above for adults.

Now as a result of awareness and acceptance of mental illness, even though at a limited scale, a vast majority of Indians, regardless of their religion or social class look upon mental illness as something different from physical illness. Superstitions are less prevalent than a few decades ago, and their effects have been diluted by inroads of modern civilization.   Only a few decades ago it was uncommon to find a villager rushing to a modern medical man for treatment of his sick child, without having first tried some of the traditional modes of relief. Today the average Indian readily accepts the role and usefulness of modern treatment but at the same time attempts to please the "displeased Gods" (7). Yet another reason is improvement in their economic condition. Now, an average villager, or even people from tribal regions offer no great resistance in accepting the fact that mental illness can be treated and people do get well. It does not matter whether they view illness in terms of constitutional, hereditary or physical factors, or in a more dynamic manner so long as they cooperate in treatment outlined for them. Obviously, some of the major changes noticed in India during the past three decades are to be witnessed in greater urbanization, industrialization, availability of millions of more jobs, breaking up of the joint family set up, changes in the rules concerning arranged marriages, ever increasing rates of literacy, and the pride at being an independent and now a relatively self-sufficient nation (7).

Natural disasters are many, dependency on 'rain Gods' plenty, health and hygiene measures still being inadequate, the catastrophy of starvation still being tossed around, does create an occasional sense of doom, which threatens the very survival of the nation (8, 9).

It would, however, be a great mistake to view that all Indians have changed their "outlook" regarding mental sickness or even those who seem to have developed such a view have given up their historical and cultural legacy. The fact is that most of the families would like to feel that mental illness will not strike their family; if it has, it should be ignored or at least hiddent from society. Treatment, if being contemplated should be a strictly confidential one, for the fear that a young man, if so identified, may find it difficult to obtain a job or a suitable matrimonial alliance. Similarly hell would break lose if a young unmarried girl were to get ill and may thereafter lose a chance of settlement in life for good. But then, it is our impression that similar concern prevails in other societies as well, perhaps in a less exaggerated form.

CULTURAL FACTORS EFFECTING DEVELOPMENT OF PERSONALITY IN A CHILD

As has been reported elsewhere (1), India is a country which has multiple religions, divergent sub-cultures and as many as 14 languages with more than 200 dialects (10). Hinduism is the flow of Indian life because a vast majority of the population are Hindus. There were rich spiritual and moral values which have stood the test of time. A distinguished feature of the culture is its continuity in the sense that the values which were evolved several thousand years ago still persist. India has been rightly called a sea-shore of humanity. The vast size of continental India gave shelter to several races. Dravidians, Indo-Aryans, Arabs, Polynensians, Mughals and Britishers settled in this land at one time or another. Some of the earliest communities which exist until today still preserve their own religious beliefs, languages and social customs.

Rural Verus Urban India

More than 82% of the total population of this country resides in approximately 600,000 villages (11). The rural population mainly consists of peasants who have a family tradition of cultivation. The other class of people in villages are: gold-smiths, carpenters, barbers, weavers, washermen, and untouchables. A village in the good old days used to be a self-sufficient unit. They were mutually dependent on each other, they had very little contact with the world outside, and village people used to go out of the village only on special occasions. Although the pattern of village life has undergone rapid change in the post-independent era, the basic features are still the same. Their children still have to follow the family occupation, even though education is now readily and freely available. Inspite of the fact that large scale industrialization has resulted in considerable migration, the unemployed amount to 8 million. Besides, the family contact, if not maintained, may result in perpetual tension often leading to a massive guilt.

CASTE SYSTEM

It is the all pervasive caste system which is one of the major characteristics of India. Nowhere else does caste form such a strong component of social life. The caste system has divided the Hindu community into a multitude of hierarchically graded sealed groups based on birth. It is more ancient than the Vedas. Originally the Hindu society seems to have been differentiated into 4 castes, i.e. Brahmin, Kshatriya, Vaisha, and Shudra. With the growth of racial admixture, geographical expansion and development of craft industries, the original castes broke up into various smaller castes and sub-castes. Hindus became socially distinguished with the ever increasing number of groups and sub-groups. In all vital social matters such as marriages, vocations and family ceremonies, each sub-group was an exclusive unit. Yet, there are certain beliefs held by almost all Hindus and it is these that have provided a con-crete reinforcement to the caste system. *Karma* (a) and *Dharma* (b) are the twin essentials of Hindu religion. Karma proclaims that an individual is born with a particular caste because of his deeds in preivous life, and Dharma demands that he should accept his condition without protest and perform the functions most sincerely (13).

The caste system was not only an undemocratic one but authoritarian as well. Each caste was considered inferior to those above it and superior to those below it. The status of a

a = *Philosophy of deeds and action*   b = *Philosophy of religion* man born in a particular caste was determined by the rank of that caste and his status was immutable. The caste predetermined his vocation, marriage and social life. He had no choice but to accept a predetermined life and its goals. A person belonging to one caste could not marry into another one. Caste did have some advantages. It neatly placed each person in his position and conflicts were "avoided". Furthermore, each caste and community was provided with their own schools and hospitals, etc. The hierarchical classification of caste was based on social inequalities. For example, at the apex of this social pyramid stood the caste of Brahmins who had the right to officiate as priests with exclusive access to all higher religious learnings and were therefore called upon to bless the high and the low. At the base of it were found a mass of Shudras and untouchables who were assigned the duties of serving all other castes and were subjected to severest penalty. Such "low" groups included vocations as those of scavengers and tanners. Social inequalities were prevalent to such an extent that even in matters of residence the lower castes were segregated from the higher ones and were assigned separate quarters away from the mainstream. The lower castes were not to make use of public wells and were denied entry into temples. The citadel of social oppression was to be seen in the Brahmins who felt contaminated at the mere sight of an untouchable (1).

There are many castes and sub-castes, but the broad division is into upper caste, intermediate caste and lower caste. A group of people, now put broadly under the group of schedule castes, are considered as untouchables. They have to do the worst and poorer job, and have little opening for progress. Their children were not allowed to go to schools, could not mix and play with children belonging to higher castes and usually had to shoulder the responsibility of the family from a very early age. These children were "bound" to follow the family profession. Such children always entertained feelings of inferiority, suffered from lack of confidence and never did get a chance to learn or to live well. They belonged to the poorest economic strata and usually had a large number of siblings. Although legislation has now been provided which is expected to bring about a change in their sad plight, the allegations of injustice, cruelty, and social boycott are as frequent as before. It has, however, resulted in their attaining admission to schools, colleges, and competitive examinations. As such, there are possibly more employment opportunities with a greater rate of literacy existing in the group as a whole. The poverty is as rampant as ever, the availability of adequate needs is still a big question mark, the rate of diseases is higher with the malnutrition claiming the highest toll. Consequently it is our clinical experience as well as objective observations, on the basis of our clinical and field studies (13), that highest number of mentally retarded children exist in such a group. Yet another group of people belonging to the same category are freely mobile. They change their place of residence so frequently that they may be considered equivalent to gypsies. The reason for transfer of residences may have something to do with their inability to remain at one place, or hope to make a better living at another place, or they may try to get away from the law enforcing authorities since their involvement in crimes is often a solid one. Not only do they move themselves, but they take their negligible belongings along. The most devastating aspect is the sad plight of their children who never have a home, seldom see a school even from the outside, lack identification with important figures, but do get excellent training in destructive and sociopathic aspects of behavioral maladaption.

FAMILY UNIT

The joint family system has been the chief characteristic of Indian culture. For generations, life in India has centered around the joint family constellation. In such a family unit more than two generations often lived together. Usually a joint family consisted of parents, grand-parents, uncles, aunts, children and of course grand-children. All of them lived together in a single house which was usually a large one. Often no individual accounts were maintained and every one's needs were taken care of by the head of the family. The oldest member of the family, usually a male, was recognised as head. He made all decisions regarding marriage, purchase of property, expenditure of the family, and future of the children. It is the head of the family who would decide the type of school, education for the children, and choice of a job for the children for which the parents may not have much of say. Similarly, the old lady of the house, usually the mother-in-law, would take over the responsibility of deciding what is good or bad for the child.

They would guide the mother about the manner or extent of feeding, toilet training, dress to be worn and would be sole judge for assessing whether the performance of the child is worthy of award or punishment. The mother would have very little discretion in such matters and expectedly would render such a "service" with protest and resentment. Similarly, while the child is growing up, he is apt to recognize the authority of the grandmother, which a little later would make him a focus of all conflicts within the family set-up. The mother in addition, would be burdened with carrying out the obligations of a housewife. She is expected to prepare and serve food to every member of the family, thereby reducing further the chance of her spending some time with her small and growing child during critical phases of psychosexual development. The child has obviously little scope of developing positive identification with his mother. With lack of an identification a series of adaptive measures may be brought into play. He may resent being brought up by a mother substitute while his mother is still around. He may express resentment in the form of irritability, withdrawal, thumb sucking, bed wetting, temper tantrums, delay in attaining control over toilet training, or may manifest behavioural disorders of a varying nature.

Similarly, if a child has developed some physical disability or crippledom with or without low intelligence, it would also induce feelings of inferiority leading to infantile neurosis, psychosexual development of the child would be impaired.

The joint family set up was under heavy fire in the recent past. Many investigators started blaming the joint family set up for a variety of emotional ills. Because of urbanization, change in social outlook, and migration, the joint family system started getting replaced by a unitary family system. It is, however, our clinical and experimental observation that the frequency of illness is no less in members drawn from a unitary family as compared to a joint family (14).

Whereas the joint family had provided a sense of security, a sense of belonging, identification and was a source of strength particularly when one was confronted with rituals of death or a serious illness or any other major calamity, the unitary family offered no such support. As a matter of fact, in a unitary family, more so in one which has come into being as a result of

disagreeable disassociation from the joint family, the effort to
make a go of it, to reestablish new and lasting conventions, as
to be able to exist without looking for a dependent support, is a
formidable one. Time and experience will, however, offer more
information in regard to particular advantages or reversal in
the trend or disadvantages, more so as the unitary family
accepts its obligations towards children or unfolds its displeasure in an inability to function in such a manner.

The advantage of a large set up offered the child an early
experience of co-existing in a competitive set up. Feelings of
jealousy, inferiority, inadequacy, lack of confidence, resentment with a resultant aggression, or aloofness may be an
essential part of such living. Personality under the circumstances will develop some scars with overt manifestations of
personality disorder later in life.

IMPORTANCE OF THE MALE CHILD

An important feature of Indian culture is a higher premium on the male child and his responsibilities in the family
structure. Male children are considered more valuable than the
female siblings. A family is considered grossly incomplete
unless it has been blessed with a male child. It may be so
because of the traditional economic cushion that the male child
offers or a feeling that only through sons does the progeny survive. As such, most of the parents in this society wish to have a
greater number of male children compared to females. It is,
therefore, not rare to witness families who have had 7, 8 or 9
girls in anticipation of a male child. One can imagine the
responsibilities that a male child would carry in that family
(15). In order to meet family expectations he starts sharing the
burden of his father at a much earlier age. He is trained to
think in terms of providing education, occupation and settling
the marriages of his siblings. The eldest male child may have to
compromise in his personal goals and ambitions in order to
satisfy the Jonses and keep the social prestige of the family intact. He can not, therefore, think in terms of independence as is
to be observed in the West. He has not only to support the
younger siblings for a very long time but most stand by during
their stressful moments of life. Moreover, the responsibilities
of the older sibling would be determined by the family size. The

larger the number of siblings the greater the responsibility and the burden. A large number of couples become parents at an age when they are emotionally immature and financially ill-equipped. In addition, a large number of rural folk measure their good fortune by the number of male children they have been blessed with, even if the economic resources may not stand the strain of raising a large family. Like the eldest son, the eldest daughter is also expected to pitch in and share the responsibilities of her mother. The sex is a major determinant in behavioural disorders. There are series of reports by Indian workers indicating that a majority of children diagnosed as mentally retarded (14, 16, 17), or suffering from disorders of speech (18, 19), delinquent behaviour, bed wetting and other neurotic disorders (20) are males. Thus, a male child in Indian families is usually under greater stress with a greater likelihood of a breakdown. Kishore et al. (21) have observed that purely aggressive behaviour, the mixed aggressive-regressive behaviour and unsocialized aggression have been found predominantly in male children only, whereas the regressive and monosymptomatic anxiety reactions which are usually overloaded with neurotic symptomatology, were seen most commonly in female children. This is so because of the difference in the patterns of upbringing of boys and girls in our culture. In the upbringing of girls the atmosphere seems to be more restrictive than for boys. In the social behaviour of girls a high premium is based on modesty, social reservedness, conservation in dress and habits, non-assertiveness, and a restrain in emotional expressiveness with particular reference to negative emotions (22). On the other hand the birth of a son, particularly the first born, is hailed as a great event in a vast majority of Indian families. This is so because he would be the bread earner of the family and would carry on with the name and tradition of his family. Moreover, if a son is born the responsibilities of offering a substantial dowry do not befall on his parents. The result of this cultural attitude is that male children are usually pampered and overprotected in an indulgent manner, which may result in aggressive traits and aggressive behavioural disorders. Secondary position of a female child in the family forces her to utilize other means to compete with male siblings in order to obtain a warm relationship with her parents. Thus, either she tries to excel in on studies or demonstrates mastery over a series of domestic assignments; she may exhibit extra-ordinary qualities in music, dance or art. In case of failure, these girls are more likely to utilize one of the neurotic defense mechanisms and develop illnesses like hysteria with a very obvious secondary gain.

Age may appear another important variable for emotional disturbances in children. It may be interesting to note that in our psychiatric clinics children above the age of 5 are seen more frequently, especially for subnormality and unsocialized behaviour. This is so because of the over protective attitude on the part of parents, especially in the case of the only child and a prevailing attitude on the part of these parents to overlook the activities and abnormal behaviour in early years. Kishore *et al.* (21) emphasized that the monosymptomatic anxious reactions and the unsocialized aggressive reactions are first seen between the ages of 9 and 15 whereas aggressive and regressive reactions are usually first seen between the ages of 3 and 9, and more so between 6 and 9. Such a pattern of age distribution has been explained by them on the basis of "psychoanalytical approach." In children with unsocialized aggressive reactions, the ego is weak and superego fails to develop. Further, these reactions are manifested in our children for the first time at or after 9 years of age. Since the boys are confined at home and remain under direct supervision of parents, they experience pleasure at home as a result of dependency needs being fully met. Later, permission to avail the joys of the outside world and greater social contacts with wider interests may lead to a relatively greater pleasure outside the home. Because of the immature ego which is developed as a result of the first contact with such an environment, he develops a new outlook and belief of his own which are often contrary to his family and social norms (23). The situation in this stage of adolescence is that his sphere of activities is circumscribed, his efforts to assert himself are suppressed, his possessions are definitely limited, his economic independence is not tolerated, his status as an adult is unrecognized and many of the restrictions of childhood remain in force. The child is, therefore, frustrated and the conflicts lead to a rebellion and unsocialized aggressive behaviour. In children with aggressive or regressive behaviour, the superego is still weak and the conflict between id and ego is manifested at an earlier age. Depending on the sex and personality pattern the child develops a neurotic reaction.

A review of the literature indicates that a host of investigators have reported that the first or early born sib has a greater risk for developing an emotional illness (15, 24, 25, 26, 27). Some of the explanations offered have also been reviewed. In India the first born are offsprings of immature parents with limited knowledge of child rearing and nursing (24). Rao (25) and Teja (27) felt that this relationship may reflect the stress that characterises the personality development of the earlier born in the sib group. The older childen become dependent because of all the love and affection which they enjoy. Later when they are called upon to shoulder the responsibility of demonstrating maturity, they develop a clash with their basic dependent needs. Kishore *et al.* (21) in their studies have found that the only child, the eldest child and the youngest child comprised 72% of the behavioural problem children seen by them. It has been observed that a special position of the child in the family is a very significant determinant since it leads to a special relationship with the parents' possibility of undesirable attitudes being developed including pampering, over protection, inconsistency in maintaining discipline, and greater tolerance towards unacceptable traits of the child. It is quite well to expect that such a pattern may well be etiopathogenic in nature. In some of the illnesses, it is usually the third or the later sib who is prone toward developing emotional disorders like unsocialized behavior.

It has been pointed out (21) that these children belong to families with poor socio-economic status; whereas the first born is most welcome, the second may be accepted but the third and subsequent may be neglected. Sethi and Gupta (15) on the basis of analysis of 1000 psychiatric patients concluded that the eldest or early born are effected to a significantly greater extent. It has been pointed out (15) that in Indian families there are heavy responsibilities on the eldest or early born sibs because of our family pattern, hence these children are always under stress.

MARRIAGE

Until the early 20th Century child marriages were frequent in India. Marriages were arranged during infancy or

early childhood although consummation did not take place
until puberty.   It was only in 1929 that a child marriage
restraint act was passed in which the marriages age of boys and
girls was raised to 18 and 14, respectively, which was further
raised to 21 and 18.   Nevertheless, most of the marriages are
still contracted in adolescence and all but a very few of them are
arranged by the parents.   The prospective bride and bride-
groom must be of the same caste.   Moreover, an arranged
marriage is more of a financial transaction since a girl's dowry
is usually more "important" than her appearance or ability. The
financial burden of the dowry on the bride's family is crushing.
Marriages are arranged not according to the merits of the partners but rather the two families are matched in their socio-
economic status. The Indian girls and boys are not expected to
fall in love and then marry but to marry and then fall in love.
The arranged marriage, a union between two strangers, may
become a source of discontentment, frustration and depression
(7). Both partners are expected to treat marriage as a measure
of their fate and suppress their feelings.   Few parents would
appreciate even a casual friendship between a young boy and
girl.   Such associations produce only fear and hostility.

During recent times the institution of marriage is undergoing a change.   As girls procure better education, the dowry
system is being shaken at its roots.   Many a man would now
want a woman to be an intellectual companion as well as a wife.
It is no longer news when love marriages are announced, or
intercaste or interreligious marriages take place.   The least
frequent and most frowned upon is the interreligious marriage.

SUPERSTITIONS

Superstitions are now less prevalent in India perhaps due
to rising literacy and improved means of communication.
Previously, a variety of illnesses were considered as punishment for evil deeds.   Even now birth, illness, marriage and
death - the so called crises of life - are recognised to be beyond
human control.   There is a deep-rooted belief that every living
creature on this earth is allocated a particular period of existence.   The birth and the death are therefore by and large
predestined.   In India beliefs in magico-religious causes of

disease have their roots in cultural history. A study of Vedic records of early medicine reveals that Hindus did not recognize the difference between some of the diseases and spirits. For example, small-pox has been known as an indication of the presence of a Goddess and therefore no treatment was given to the patient. Similarly, evil spirits are often recognized to be responsible for producing serious illnesses in our children. Emotional disorders were invariably viewed arising from malevolent influences exercised by God or a "supernatural being" or by another human being, alive or dead. This view is still held by a vast majority of Indians. A number of methods are still employed by people for the control of evil spirits. For instance, at the time of child birth mother is shifted to the inner most room of the house where very little of the sun and fresh air is available. None except the immediate family are permitted to go into that room. Moreover a small knife, a skull of a monkey and a burning piece of wood may be kept nearby to ward off evil spirits.

When there is repeated infant mortality in a family and no child survives, some radical measures may have to be thought of to please the spirits. One such step may involve sacrifice of a human child or an animal. Another common belief, particularly in the villages, is the presence of an evil spirit in a specific house. In case of repeated deaths in a family it is believed that the house is a haunted one. The ideal remedy is to desert the house. It is commonly held that the soul of a person which does not find peace may become a ghost and haunt the house, and may thus appear in "unnatural stances" in that family. These superstitions are now mostly limited to illiterate and backward families. The presence of such beliefs in the family is quite detrimental for the growing child. Not uncommonly, such children may carry these beliefs over.

It may be well to summarize some of the more prevalent phenomena which are increasingly observed in this country. The pregnancy is, by and large, for a vast majority of people, a natural one. It is expected that an Indian woman will quickly get   pregnant. Failure of pregnancy within a reasonable time of the marriage is a source of ridicule. A large body of women, particularly those who reside in classical Indian homes, are ignorant about the methods of birth control. The question of

regulated or a controlled pregnancy is obviously out of question, so much so that our gyneacologists have a hard time
explaining to them the safe periods, the rythm, or more recent
family planning devices. It is, therefore, legitimate to infer
that pregnancy is almost always a chanced one. The discovery
of pregnancy is further inferred by missing a period, which
could be a false alarm, or by onset of psychophysiological con-
commitants, i.e. nausea, vomitting, or a particular desire to eat
unusual foods. For many women, a consultation with a
gynaecologist never takes place. The possibility of identifying
any other mild to moderate complications of intra-uterine life
pertaining to the foetus or having a bearing on the mother does
not exist. Only if life threatening adverse reactions set in do
these women head for a hospital. The stresses or strains which
are concommitant part of any pregnancy are not expected to
be experienced. If experienced, not to be expressed; if expressed, should be immediately suppressed. It is not fashion-
able or socially acceptable for the woman to report any subjective sensation of discomfort, anxiety, fear or other related
feeling states. That may be the reason why there are few
reports by Indian workers on the subject. Although it has been
well accepted by our ancestors that emotional states of the
mother, her relationship with the family, comfort or conflict
during pregnancy and other such factors do have a bearing on
the emotional health and physical well being of the forthcoming
child. Marfatia (17) failed to find any such factor on the study
of Mental Retardation. At times it is difficult to elicit such
information retrospectively in our clinical practice.

In a report from our child guidance clinic (28), we have
observed that information in available only in 299 of a total of
722 cases. Only 4% of the mothers reported emotional stress
in the form of an unwanted pregnancy or fear of having a female
baby while she would want a male child. Marital disharmony,
family conflicts and economic difficulties were the other
reported stresses. Similarly, in a field study (29) we attempted
to elicit the information which is tabulated in Tables 1 and 2.

Thus, mothers in 34. 1% of the pregnancies did experience
emotional stress. The most prominent stress was the dreaded
possibility of a girl being born. Such types of stress were
most evident either during the first pregnancy or during the

subsequent pregnancies if the first born was already a female child. It should be noted that only 10% of the children who were products of such pregnancies gave positive evidence of an emotional illness at one time or another.

Since physical illness, related or unrelated to pregnancy, is an important precursor for the subsequent development of mal-formation of the foetus, attempts were made to collect information from our child guidance clinic (28) as well as in our field study (29). Hardly 3% of the children had a positive history of such factors in the child guidance clinic; only 1.2% of pregnancies in our field survey were reported to be accompanied by physical stresses (Table 3). All the cases of the child guidance clinic with a positive history were suffering from varying degrees of mental retardation whereas no child born of a similar preg-nancy in a field survey was ill.

Many physical, chemical, and biological factors have been incriminated in the literature. Evidence implicating such agents has been fairly strong in some instances, but in others merely by association of events rather than an experimental observation (17). Marfatia (17) has reported such factors only in nine cases from (Table 4) a sample of 100.

If events leading to pregnancy and progress towards a natural termination have been of some interest, the process of child birth is no less breath taking an exercise in this country. For a vast segment of Indian women a well equipped maternity centers, trained gynaecologists or qualified nurses are still asking for the moon. Most deliveries are conducted by 'Dais' (unqualified and untrained personnel) not only in villages but also in some cities. Indian mothers still prefer home deliveries rather than going to a hospital (Table 5) a fact very clearly brought out in a study conducted at Delhi (30). Factors forcing the mothers to have hospital delivery have been listed as lack of space at home, no one to look after them at home, expected complications during confinement, and belief that a change in locale may help in having a boy (30).

In villages local "Dai" (an unqualified and untrained local lady) performs the task of a gynaecologist. The damage to the mother, including the possibilities of severe infection to the mother or the child, may be a massive one. Similarly, the infant receives little care; injuries and infections of varying degrees

Table 1

EMOTIONAL STRESSES DURING PREGNANCY
(Total No. of pregnancy = 270)*

Replies given by mother	No.	Percentage
Does not recollect	102	37.8
Denied any stress	76	28.1
Positive history of emotional stresses	92	34.1

* Out of 272, two children were dropped as they were adopted children.

Table 2

NATURE OF STRESSES DURING PREGNANCY
(N=92)

Nature of stresses*	No.	Percentage
Family maladjustment	23	25.0
Marital disharmony	3	3.3
Death in the family	7	7.6
Death of husband	1	1.1
Fear of having female child	33	35.8
Unwanted pregnancy	16	17.4
Miscellaneous	9	9.8

* There were more than one stresses during 11 pregnancies but most prominent one as perceived by the mother has been tabulated.

Table 3

HISTORY OF PHYSICAL ILLNESSES DURING PREGNANCY

Physical factors	Child-guidance clinic (N=722)		Survey (N=270)	
	No.	Percent-age	No.	Percent-age
Drugs	3	0.4	1	0.4
Threatened abortion	5	0.7	-	-
Toxemia of pregnancy	2	0.3	-	-
Prematurity	3	0.4	1	0.4
Anti-partum haemor-rhage	4	0.6	1	0.4
Other physical illnesses (Tuberculosis, measels, pyrexia).	5	0.7	-	-
Total	22	3.0	3	1.2

Table 4

GESTATIONAL DISORDERS RESULTING IN MENTAL RETARDATION*
(N=100)

(a) Drugs: Progesterone	1.0%
Unknown drug used for abortion	1.0%
(b) Threatened abortion	3.0%
(c) Toxemia of pregnancy	1.0%
(d) Prematurity	3.0%
(e) Ante Partum Haemorrhage	1.0%
Total	9.0%

*Marfatia (17)

Table 5

*PLACE OF BIRTH AND ATTENDANT AT DELIVERY**

Place of birth	Attendant at Delivery							Total	
	None	Relative	Untrained dai	Trained dai	Mid wife/ Nurse	Health visitor	Doctor	N	%
Home	3	2	35	91	9	-	4	144	56.2
Maternity home	-	-	-	-	2	-	3	5	2.0
Hospital	-	-	-	-	5	-	101	106	41.4
Nursing home	-	-	-	-	-	-	1	1	0.4
Total No.	3	2	35	91	16	-	109	256	100.0
Percentage	1.2	0.8	13.7	35.5	6.2	-	42.6		

* Malhotra (30)

are frequently observed. Singhal (31), in a village field study on morbidity in children, observed that 32.6% of the babies had complications in the neonatal period. Such complications were more frequent in cases where delivery was conducted by a relative or untrained Dai (Table 6).

Table 6

*NUMBER OF COMPLICATIONS AND AGENCY OF DELIVERY**

| Agency of delivery | Complications | |
	No.	Percentage
Relative	13	18.57
Untrained Dai	44	62.86
Trained Personnel	13	18.57

*Singhal (31)

Deliveries conducted by untrained personnel had maximum complications (81.43%). In the same study, it was also observed that all neonatal complications in the infant were greater in cases delivered by untrained personnel, except diarrhoea which was found occurring equally in cases delivered by trained and untrained personnel. Cord infection was present in all the cases of an infant being attended by untrained personnel.

The importance of premature births lies in the fact that half of the neonatal deaths and more than half of the still births are derived from 8-10% of the premature infants (32). Premature infants who survive have a greater than average chance of being physically or mentally handicapped despite the highest standard of pediatric care (32). The prematurity rates for Indian male and female infants have been worked out as 22.5% and 26.7% (33). Venkatacholam (34) reported a prematurity rate of 13.8% in high and 29.2% in low socio-economic groups of South Indian women. Mukherjee and Mukherjee (32) observed a prematurity rate of 8.73% for North Indian high altitude areas. The observations lack confirmation regarding the mental health of premature children in our country. Marfatia (17) found 3 cases of mental retardation out of 100 who had a premature birth. In our field study of 272 children (29) the history of premature delivery was available for 6 children out of which only one male was mentally retarded and the other male had enuresis.

Since the children are considered as blessings of God, there is a great desire to have as many children as may be given by God. In the case of death, every attempt is made to replace the lost child as quickly as possible. The mother is, thus, subjected to a similar ritual once again. That may probably explain the observation in a study conducted at Delhi that 73.1% of the subjects were six para birth (30). Further, the wish of having many children, and at an early age, is exemplified by the observation that 52.4% of women with children in ages ranging from 19-24 months were found pregnant again; 6.5% of women who had a child aged 7-12 months were again in stages of advanced pregnancy (30). Sen (35) has observed that still births and neonatal deaths are higher in those mothers where spacing between pregnancies is short.

Repeated pregnancies produce a physical state of ill health (35) in mothers. Malnutrition sets in with deteriorating physical and emotional health which takes a heavy toll of the child in terms of neglect or deprivation.

A major problem of present day India is poverty and poor nutrition. India is a poor country where a large family is usually the order of the day. Repeated and intensive family planning programs have yet not started; the so called green revolution is already looking like a transient dream, which was good while it lasted. Essential foods are in short supply. The availability of daily bread is posing difficulty even for the rich, but for the poor it is an himalayan effort to procure supplies. The prices of essential commodities have gone up 100% during the last two years. Unemployment is close to 8 million. The nation is going through an upheaval the likes of which have never been witnessed in the recorded past. There is a rapid breakdown of law and order. Insecurity and panic often grip large communities, and hoarding in one form or another is the hall mark of contemporary India.

Malnutrition is one of the greatest problems in the practice of pediatrics in this country. The child suffers mainly because of the lower per capita income, and lack of parental knowledge regarding the feeding schedule of infants. Other

Table 7

NUTRITIONAL STATUS AND PSYCHIATRIC DISORDERS*

Nutritional status	Psychiatric disorders			Mental Subnormality			No Disorder	Total
	Behavioural	Childhood psychosis	Epilepsy	Mild	Moderate	Severe		
Experimental group								
Mild deficiency	2 6.3%	-	1 3.1%	4 12.5%	3 9.4%	1 3.1%	-	11 34.4%
Moderate deficiency	-	1 3.1%	-	6 18.7%	4 12.5%	2 63%	-	13 40.6%
Severe deficiency	-	-	-	1 3.1%	4 12.5%	3 9.4%	-	8 25.0%
Total	2 6.3%	1 3.1%	1 3.1%	11 34.4%	11 34.4%	6 18.7%	-	32 100.0
Control group								
Adequate or Normal	1 3.1%	-	-	5 16.6%	2 6.3%	-	22 68.7%	32 100.0

*Sharma (43) The number of neurotic cases in control group was 2 (or 43%)

reasons are poor physical states of the mother, a large number of conceptions, and underweight and premature deliveries. The commonest deficiency met with is of "proteins", followed by vitamin deficiency. Faulty feeding may lead to infantile diarrhoea, poor reabsorption and malnutrition. Koshi *et al.* (36) found that diets of urban school children were adequate in proteins and iron only. Lesser amounts of the remaining items were consumed than recommended by the nutrition expert group (37). It has also been noted in this study that although proteins were adequate only 52.7% of the boys and 56.7% of the girls had a good physique, which shows that proteins must have been used to make up for the deficiency in the caloric intake. Recent nutrition surveys have demonstrated that both proteins and calories are lacking in the diets eaten by the pre-school population (38). In a nationwide survey in India among pre-school children, their diet was found deficient in all essential items. The incidence of nutritional deficiency is high among South Indian children for almost all the nutrients (39, 40). In North India, the average intake of calories among males in various age groups was: 1 year - 701 calories; 2 years - 496 calories; 3 years - 1037 calories; and 4 years - 1232 calories. These reports emphasize the grave deficiency of both proteins and calories in the average child population ages 1-5 years. Thus, in both kwashiorkar and marasmus, which are very common in our young children, the diet is often wanting in all the nutrients. The incidence of marasmic-kwashiorkar in North Indian pre-school children (41) is observed as 1.1% with the peak age period of 18-24 months. In another survey conducted in 4 South Indian states with a population of 100 million, the incidence of protein caloric malnutrition in the form of kwashiorkar and marasmus was reported to be 1-2% among children in the age group 1-5 years (42).

The effects of malnutrition as a cause of physical and mental devastation in children has been demonstrated in several studies (43). MacGregor (44) has quoted the findings, presented at the 18th International Congress of Nutrition, that direct relationship between severe malnutrition and brain damage has been found.

The state of malnutrition has a great significance for our children. Sethi *et al.* (14) in a comprehensive field study observed that all mentally retarded developed retardation in the first decade of life; most of them had mild or moderate degrees of retardation. If nutritional deficiencies could be made up, the intellectual retardation may sharply decrease.

Sharma (43), in a controlled study of malnourished and normally nourished children, observed that malnourished children showed noticeable deficiencies in the intellectual sphere. The severity of malnutrition was found to be positively related to the level of deterioration. An analysis of the relationship between the nutritional status and mental health in the same study brought forward some interesting results (Table 7). A relatively high percentage of the occurrence of psychiatric disorders among the malnourished group of children indicates that nutrition had a significant influence on the optimal development of the mental health of the children.

In a field study of 272 children (29) at this center, the nutritional status of children was assessed: (a) On the basis of age, height, and weight records in relation to the all India mean (45); (b) On the basis of clinical evaluation and signs of deficiency diseases.

The results are presented in Table 8.

Table 8

MALNUTRITION ON THE BASIS OF

CLINICAL EXAMINATION

Total Sample	Nutritional deficiency (clinically)		Sick Children Subnormality N = 58		Enuresis N = 7		Neurotic symptoms N = 30	
	N	%	N	%	N	%	N	%
Present	28	10.3	10	20.8	1	16.6	1	3.3
Absent	244	89.7	48	79.2	6	83.4	29	96.7

On the basis of height, 2 male children and 12 female children were less than 2 S.D. (Standard Deviation) units from the all India means for all age groups put together, of which 2 males and 3 females were sick. On the basis of weight, 6 males and 3 females were less than 2 S.D. units from the all India mean for all weight groups put together, of which 2 males and 3 females were in the sick group. Clinically 28 children (10.3%) were found having signs of nutritional deficiency, of which 12 children (4.4%) were found psychiatrically ill.

PHYSICAL GROWTH AND NUTRITION

A steadily progressive trend in the pattern of growth of a child is his height and weight of a particular age. This is a reliable index of the state of his health. A close parallelism between the health of the child and the graph of his general appearance and weight gain is strongly ingrained in the minds of the parent. It is usually the general physical appearance which is taken into account by Indian parents in assessing the growth and nutrition of their child. Studies in physical growth have been conducted in all parts of India; standardized all India norms have been worked out by I.C.M.R. (45). In a study in North India in school going urban children, Koshi et al. (36) found 52.7% of the boys and 56.7% of the girls of good physique. The mean birth weight of full term normal babies has been found to be above 5 lbs. in many studies reported from India (46-53). All the above studies were unanimous in reporting that female babies weighed less than males. The birth weight of Indian babies has been found to be towards the lower side (52) than those reported by western workers. However, difference in mean birth weight of male and female babies have been found universally (52).

DEVELOPMENTAL MILE STONES

Studies available from different regions of the country indicate the superiority of Indian subjects in attaining motor development (54,55,56). It has been observed that Indian children show superiority over western ones in terms of Gasell's rating (57). Boys have been found to be ahead in achieving motor and adaptive mile stones, while girls showed superiority in language and social fields (57). There are difficulties in establishing a norm for "developmental milestones" for such a divergent group of population as exists in India, and as such, it has been suggested to establish norms for every population (57). Developmental milestones have been of greater importance especially in cases of mental retardation, where several investigators have reported delayed milestones in these children. The importance of association of delayed milestones have been emphasized repeatedly in almost all the psychiatric text books, and it is our day to day experience in this country that mentally retarded children do present histories of one or more delayed milestones in early developmental stages.   At times it is a problem to elicit the exact developmental landmarks retrospectively, but if a particular child had an abnormality it is usually remembered by Indian mothers.

Marfatia (17), in his clinical investigation of 100 cases, found evidence of delayed milestones when parents could recognize the retardation even in the first year of age on the basis of delayed developmental land marks. In our field study (29), we found only 38 cases of delayed milestones from a sample of 272 children. Eleven cases were mentally retarded, 4 moderate, 2 mild and 5 borderline. All but one case of enuresis had delayed milestones; usually bladder control was delayed and could not be achieved till the time of study. A history of delayed milestones could be elicited only in 3 other children who were sick. Thus, the remaining 50% of the cases in whom parents observed delayed land marks in early childhood were found clinically normal at the time of study. In a clinical study of 51 cases of mental retardation, Sethi et al. (58) found histories of delayed milestones in 82.35% of the cases. It should be noted that these cases had I.Q.s less than 55. Our records from child guidance clinic (28) also show that more than three fourths of the mentally retarded children had a history of delayed milestones which was not so in other childhood disorders. Teja et al. (59) found a high correlation between delayed motor milestones, impairment of social functioning and measured levels of intelligence, which have been found to hold good for profound, severe and moderate retardation only. In the mildly retarded group, these impairments do not correlate well with each other.

PSYCHIATRIC ILLNESS IN CHILDREN

We have already pointed out that the attention paid to the treatment of childhood psychiatric disorders has been of a most inadequate nature. Furthermore, the extent of mental illness relating to an adult is still not fully known, but fortunately in the past decade a number of epidemiological studies have been conducted and several reports have appeared in the literature (13, 16, 60-67). Keeping in mind observations we have made in the earlier part of this paper, a similar trend exists in so far as estimation of morbidity in children in this country is concerned. The literature is rather scanty and we do not even have a rough idea about the number of children who require professional help, or the type of diseases that these children may be suffering from. No large scale survey has been reported in journals from this country which may focus on this issue and may provide some meaningful information.

We conducted several field studies at this center between 1967 and 1974 in which attempts were made to screen the population in rural and urban areas in a limited manner.

The first such survey, conducted during 1967-69 (16), included the study of all rural families of four villages near Lucknow. There were a total of 500 families in these villages and 85 (17.0%) of them were found having one or more psychiatrically ill patients. Of a total of 2691, 106 individuals were found sick. Thus, a morbidity rate of 39 per 1000 was estimated. Children less than 10 years of age were classified as: 88.2% cases of mental retardation, 11.1% cases of psychoneurosis, 83.3% cases of epilepsy and 57.1% cases of the miscellaneous group. Table 9A shows the diagnostic break-up of the total cases and their distribution according to age. In the total sick population, 67.0% were below 10 years of age.

Similarly in an urban survey (14) conducted in Lucknow city during the years 1969-71, a three stage random sampling was employed and 850 families were evaluated by door to door visits. Of the families sampled, 28.4% were identified as having one or more psychiatrically sick individual. Three hundred patients could be screened out of a total population of 4481 thereby suggesting a period prevalence of 67 per 1000. Out of this population, 24.0% of the sick individuals were in the age range 5 - 10 years.

Table 9A

DIAGNOSIS AND AGE DISTRIBUTION*

	0-10 yrs.	11-20 yrs.	21-40 yrs.	Above 41
Subnormality N=68 - 64.2%	60 (88.2%)	7 (10.3%)	1 (1.5%)	-
Psychoneuroses N=16 - 17.0%	2 (11.1%)	3 (16.7%)	8 (44.4%)	5 (27.8%)
Epilepsy N= 6 - 5.7%	5 (83.3%)	-	-	1 (16.7%)
Schizophrenia N= 3 - 2.8%	-	-	2 (66.7%)	1 (33.3%)
Personality Disorder N= 4 - 3.8%	-	-	4 (100.0%)	-
Miscellaneous N = 7 - 6.1%	4 (57.1%)	-	2 (28.6%)	1 (14.3%)

* Sethi, B.B., Gupta, S.C., Kumar, R. and Kumari, P. (16).

Table 9B

AGE BREAK UP

Age (in yrs.)	Neuroses %	Affect. Dis. %	Mentally Retd. %	Schizo. %	O. B. S. %	Misc. %	Total %
5 - 10	0.8	-	42.6	-	19.0	75.0	24.4
11 - 20	9.8	2.9	49.0	27.3	14.3	18.8	18.0
21 - 30	16.4	11.4	4.2	18.1	14.3	-	10.3
31 - 40	34.5	11.4	-	27.3	14.3	3.1	18.0
41 - 50	24.6	34.3	4.2	9.1	14.3	3.1	16.7
51 - 60	9.8	17.1	-	9.1	-	-	6.3
61 and above	4.1	22.9	-	9.1	23.8	-	6.3

Further, the detailed analysis of the data for different diagnosis groups of the total population according to the age (Table 9B) revealed 95 children below 14 years of age; mental retardation (42.6%) was most frequent in these children. The lowest income group had 70.2% of retarded children; male children out numbered the female children. In the miscellaneous group, enuresis was the major category; in the organic brain syndrome, epilepsy was the major diagnosis.

Further, the detailed analysis of the study revealed that the majority of these children were diagnosed as mentally retarded, 42.6%; organic brain syndrome (including epilepsy), 19.0%; enuresis and speech disturbances, 7.5%.

Further, we surveyed 109 families during 1974 in an area adjoining our hospital to find out the extent and nature of psychiatric morbidity in children. It was observed that 55% of the families had one or more sick child up to the age of 12 years: 35.4% of the total children in these families were found emotionally disturbed (29). The diagnostic break up is given in Table 10.

Table 10

DIAGNOSTIC BREAK UP AND SEX (N=272)

Diagnosis	Number	Percentage
Subnormality	43	15.8
Subnormality with neurotic behaviour	14	5.1
Subnormality with organic Brain Psychosis	1	0.3
Neurotic Disorders	30	11.0
Enuresis	7	2.5
Anti-social Personality	2	0.7
No Psychiatric Illness	175	64.6
Total	272	100.0

Of the total sample in the same study, 15.8% were suffering from mental retardation; 5.0% of the cases had behaviour disturbances in addition to subnormalities which were enuresis (1.8%), somnambulism (0.7%), aggressive behavior (1.1%) and neurotic behaviour (1.5%). Only one case (0.3%) of subnormality had psychotic features; evidence indicated that the patient was suffering from a postinfective organic brain syndrome. The majory of sick children were males (53.7%), were middle siblings (48.5%), belonged to unitary families (77.3%) and 55.7% were the products of a family of five or more members. The per capita income of 91.7% of the families was Rs. 150/-per month or below, 35.0% had educational level up to primary, and 68.4% were of 6 years or above in age. In terms of religion, 75.3% were Hindus. The majority of them were issues of high caste families and only 12.4% were children of "schedule castes." None of these variables was found to be statistically significant when an analysis of the total sample was carried out, only age was significant (p < 0.01). In other words, a greater number of sick children were in the age range of 6 years and above. In this particular study there was a remarkably low frequency of family history of psychiatric illness (7.2%).

Table 11

PHYSICAL ILLNESS AND CONGENITAL
DEFECT IN TOTAL AND SICK CHILDREN
(Total Sample = 272)

Illness	272	100.0
A. *Congenital*	B. *Nutritional Deficiency*	
Cleft lip and/or palate 3)	Anaemia	8)
Hydrocele 1)	Mersamus	6)
Increased web 2.2%		10.3%
space 2)	Vitamine A deficiency 3)	
Umbilical Hernia 1)	Ricket	11)
Sick 3 (43.0%)	12 (43.0%)	

In addition other congenital (2.2%) and physical (10.3%) ailments were oberved in these children (Table 11). Forty three percent of the cases of congenital defect and 43% of those suffering from malnutrition were suffering from active psychiatric ailments as well.

Further, in the same study (29) 35.8% of the healthy children and 19.6% of the sick children reported positive histories of neurotic traits until the age of 5 years.

Table 12

HISTORY OF NEUROTIC TRAITS UPTO 5 YEARS OF AGE

	Healthy children N=175		Sick children N=97	
	M	F	M	F
Grinding of teeth	3	-	1	1
Temper tantrum	6	3	3	-
Nail biting	5	2	3	1
Thumb sucking	16	6	2	1
Irritability	2	4	3	-
Night terrors/Night mares	6	1	-	-
Secondary enuresis	3	-	1	1
Talking in sleep	-	3	1	-
Disobedience	1	-	-	-
Quarrelsome	-	1	-	-
Somnambulism	-	-	-	1
Total	62 (35.8%)		19 (19.6%)	

We have estimated in our earlier studies that 2.2% of the children were mentally retarded in the urban population (60), whereas in rural areas it amounted to 2.5% (16). Similarly, on the basis of these studies we had estimated that 2 million children were suffering from mental subnormalities of various degrees in this largest state of India, i.e. Uttar Pradesh (13).

Our recent field study (29) aimed at finding out the psychiatric morbidity in children revealed that 21.2% of the children were mentally retarded (Table 10). There were 50 cases (18.4%) of borderline retardation, 4 cases (1.4%) of mild and 4 cases (1.4%) of moderate retardation (Table 13).

Table 13

*DEGREE OF MENTAL RETARDATION**
(N=58)

I.Q.	No. of cases
68 - 83 (Borderline retardation)	50
52 - 67 (Mild retardation)	4
36 - 51 (Moderate retardation)	4

* Classification of degree of retardation is based on D.S.M. II of A.P.A.

Evaluation of etiological factors in these children showed that only one case developed mental retardation as a result of intracranial infection; the rest of the cases were of idiopathic origin.

The I.Q. of non-retarded children (N = 132) of three years or above in the same study revealed that 23.6% male and 18.6% female had an I.Q. above 110. The majority of males (76.4%) and females (81.4%) had an I.Q. of 84 - 110 (Table 14).

Table 14

CLASSIFICATION OF I.Q. OF HEALTHY CHILDREN

I.Q.	Male (N=68)		Female (N=64)	
84 - 90	20	(29.4%)	16	(25.0%)
91 - 100	12	(17.6%)	14	(22.7%)
101 - 110	20	(29.4%)	22	(33.7%)
111 - 120	8	(11.8%)	6	(9.3%)
121 - 130	5	(7.4%)	2	(3.1%
131 - 140	3	(4.4%)	4	(6.2%)

Inspite of the fact that the treatment meted out to emotionally disturbed children has been a shabby one, conditions under which the professional personnel have had to operate were primitve ones, shortage of man power has been a severe one, and the awareness on the part of families who were harbouring these children a shallow one, yet the number of child guidance clinics operating at this time in this country is not an unrespectable one. Sixty five child guidance clinics with adequate or inadequate, complete or incomplete, personnel and/or facilities are available for extending help to the needy children.

A child guidance clinic with a clinical psychologist, a social worker, one stenograper and two attendants came into being in this hospital in 1956. For the years 1972 and 1973, a compilation of the data reveals that 722 new cases were registered in this clinic. Whereas the psychologist was conducting most of the therapeutic programmes until 1971, one lecturer in child psychiatry was added to the staff in late 1971. Children up to the age of 12 years formed 14.6% of the total

Table 15

DIAGNOSTIC AND SOCIODEMOGRAPHIC VARIABLES (CHILD GUIDANCE CLINIC) 1972-1973

		Age		Sex		Domicile		Religion				Education			Income					
		6 yrs.	Above 6 yrs.	Male	Female	Rural	Urban	Hindu	Muslim	Sikh	Christian	Illiterate	Primary	VI-X	Up to 100	101-200	201-300	301-400	401-500	500
Mental Retardation	N 394	84	310	305	89	152	242	346	43	2	3	332	45	17	210	116	49	7	3	9
	% 54.6	21.3	78.7	77.4	22.6	38.6	61.4	87.8	10.9	0.5	0.8	84.3	11.4	4.3	53.3	29.4	12.4	1.8	0.8	2.3
Mental Retardation with epilepsy	N 52	16	36	39	13	24	28	44	8	-	-	40	11	1	25	15	7	3	2	-
	% 7.2	30.8	69.2	75.0	25.0	46.2	53.8	84.6	15.4	-	-	76.9	21.2	1.9	48.1	28.8	13.5	5.8	3.8	-
Epilepsy	N 45	7	38	29	16	16	29	30	15	-	-	23	10	12	19	18	4	3	1	-
	% 6.2	15.6	84.4	64.4	35.6	35.6	64.4	66.7	33.3	-	-	51.1	22.2	26.7	42.2	40.0	8.9	6.7	2.2	-

Table 15

DIAGNOSTIC AND SOCIODEMOGRAPHIC VARIABLES
(CHILD GUIDANCE CLINIC) 1972-1973

			Age		Sex		Domicile		Religion				Education			Income					
			6 yrs.	Above 6 yrs.	Male	Female	Rural	Urban	Hindu	Muslim	Sikh	Christian	Illiterate	Primary	VI-X	Up to 100	101-200	201-300	301-400	401-500	500
Conversion Reaction	N	36	2	34	14	22	13	23	29	7	-	-	5	16	15	11	8	9	3	2	3
	%	5.0	5.6	94.4	38.9	61.1	36.1	63.9	80.6	19.4	-	-	13.9	44.4	41.7	30.6	22.2	25.0	8.3	5.6	8.3
Behavioral Disorder	N	25	3	22	17	8	5	20	12	13	-	-	7	18	-	7	8	4	2	3	1
	%	3.5	12.0	88.0	68.0	32.0	20.0	80.0	48.0	52.0	-	-	28.0	72.0	-	28.0	32.0	16.0	8.0	12.0	4.0
Organic Brain Syndrome	N	15	2	13	9	6	3	12	11	4	-	-	2	8	5	4	5	2	3	1	-
	%	2.1	13.3	86.7	60.0	40.0	20.0	80.0	73.3	26.7	-	-	13.3	53.4	33.3	26.7	33.3	13.3	20.0	6.7	-
Enuresis	N	12	-	12	4	8	-	12	10	2	-	-	-	12	-	4	3	3	2	-	-
	%	1.7	-	100.0	33.3	66.7	-	100.0	83.3	16.7	-	-	-	100.0	-	33.3	25.0	25.0	16.7	-	-

	Total																			
Speech Disorder N	8	-	8	6	2	1	7	6	2	-	-	2	6	-	1	2	3	1	1	-
%	1.1	-	100.0	75.0	25.0	12.5	87.5	75.0	25.0	-	-	25.0	75.0	-	12.5	25.0	37.5	12.5	12.5	-
Hyperkinetic Syndrome N	7	1	6	4	3	2	5	5	2	-	-	2	5	-	-	1	4	1	1	-
%	0.9	14.3	85.7	57.1	42.9	28.6	71.4	71.4	28.6	-	-	28.6	71.4	-	-	14.3	57.1	14.3	14.3	-
Schizophrenia N	7	1	6	5	2	2	5	6	1	-	-	1	4	2	2	4	1	-	-	-
%	0.9	14.3	85.7	71.4	28.6	28.6	71.4	85.7	14.3	-	-	14.3	57.1	28.6	28.6	57.1	14.3	-	-	-
Miscellaneous N	18	4	14	11	7	3	15	12	6	-	-	4	9	5	9	2	4	2	1	-
%	2.5	22.2	77.8	61.1	38.9	16.7	83.3	66.7	33.3	-	-	22.2	50.0	27.8	50.0	11.1	22.2	11.1	5.6	-
Not yet Diagnosed N	65	24	41	27	38	24	41	46	19	-	-	33	24	8	41	14	5	3	2	-
%	9.0	36.9	63.1	41.5	58.5	36.9	63.1	70.8	29.2	-	-	50.8	36.9	12.3	63.1	21.5	7.7	4.6	3.1	-
No psychiatric illness N	38	16	22	30	8	15	23	29	9	-	-	16	18	4	18	12	4	3	1	-
%	5.3	42.1	57.9	78.9	21.1	39.5	60.5	76.3	23.7	-	-	42.1	47.4	10.5	47.4	31.6	10.5	7.9	2.6	-
Total N	722	160	562	498	224	260	462	586	131	2	3	467	186	69	351	208	99	33	18	13
%	100	22.2	77.8	69.0	31.0	36.0	64.0	81.2	18.1	0.3	0.4	64.7	25.8	9.5	48.6	28.8	13.7	4.6	2.5	1.8

out-patient attendance during 1972 and 1973. The diagnostic break up of 722 children is given in Table 15.

It may be seen that mentally retarded children accounted for 61.8% of the children seen during 1972 and 1973 in this clinic (28); 52.3% of the cases had behavioral manifestations and only 9.5% of the cases came with initial complaints of low intellectual performance. There were only a few cases (6%) with borderline retardation and they were usually brought for some other symptoms. Subnormality was detected during evaluation of the case. It may further be observed that the other major illnessess seen were epilepsy with mental retardation (7.2%) and epilepsy (6.2%). Other disorders were very few. (Conversion reaction - 5.0%, behavioural disorder - 3.5%, enuresis - 1.7%, organic brain syndrome - 2.1%, hyperkinetic reaction and schizophrenia 0.9% each). Of the cases examined, 5.3% did not have any emotional problem; they mainly suffered from physical diseases only.

Sixty five cases (9.3%) did not return to the clinic after their initial visit, which made the task of assigning a firm label of diagnosis a difficult one. However, a category "Not yet diagnosed" is listed to account for these 65 cases.

It was also considered desirable to observe, evaluate and discuss the socio-economic variables relating to these children. Age, sex, religion, education, and income were the important variables taken into account for this purpose. In Table 15 data is provided for each diagnostic category. The following results were observed: predominance of male children (male : female = 69 : 31), older children past 6 years of age (77.8%), children from urban areas (64.0%), children from Hindu families (81.2%), and those coming from the lowest income groups of Rs. 200/-per month or less (77.4%). It is of interest to note that male children out numbered females in all diagnostic groups, except in neurotic disorders like conversion reaction and enuresis where a reverse trend is seen. Thus, the conversion reaction is not only more common in adult females but also in female children.

It would certainly be of some interest to review the presenting symptomatology of these children. All cases of conversion reaction were of typical hysterical fits. In addition other symptoms like headache, body aches and pains, and loss of appetite were associated features in all these cases.

Forty three cases of epilepsy and all those with a combined diagnoses of epilepsy and mental subnormality were suffering from major epilepsy, whereas only 2 cases of epilepsy were of a minor type. Out of 12 cases of enuresis, 10 had only nocturnal bed wetting, whereas 2 had a combination of night and day bed wetting. Speech disorders were delayed speech (1 case) and stammering (7 cases).

Another study (58) which was conducted during 1973 revealed 51 children with an I.Q. less than 70. It was aimed at (a) determining the cases with known genetically predisposed characteristics, (b) identifying cases with known environmental precipitating factors, and (c) determining cases of idiopathic etiology. Detailed clinical evaluation, pedigree analysis, buccal smears, biochemical screening tests, and dermatoglyphic impression techniques were employed for the study of genetic predisposition in these cases. The results are reproduced in Table 16.

Table 16

DISTRIBUTION OF SUBNORMALITY ACCORDING TO ETIOLOGICAL FACTORS*

Etiology		No. of cases	Percentage
(a) Patients with characteristics clinical picture		9	17.65
Mongolism	2		
Spastic deplegia	2		
Microcephaly	3		
Hydrocephalous	1		
Wilson disease	1		
(b) Patients with known environmental causes		7	13.73
Post Natal Head Injury	1		
Bacterial infections	2		
Viral encephalitis	4		
(c) Idiopathic		35	68.62

* Sethi, B.B.; Agarwal, S.S. and Gupta, A.K. - (58)

It was further observed in this study that sex chromatin analysis was compatable with the phenotypic sex of all children. Only one case was found suffering from an inborn error of metabolism, i.e. Wilson's disease. Only one of the two cases of mongolism was found to have dermatoglyphic features indicating Down's syndrome. In patients with spastic diplegia, microcephaly, hydrocephalous and Wilson's disease, there was a significant deviation in dermatoglyphic characteristics from the normal. Neither idiopathic cases nor those with known precipitating factors presented any significant difference in dermatoglyphic impressions from the normal. Even in the family history of consangunious marriage or where more than one sib was involved, there was no detectable abnormality in urinary screening and dermatoglyphic patterns. However, 4 patients had a very low ridge count and marked preponderance of arches.

Table 17

INTELLECTUAL LEVEL OF SUBNORMAL CASES*

Severely retarded	197	65.7%
Moderately retarded	69	23.0%
Mildly retarded	34	11.3%
Total	300	100.0%

* Gupta, S.C. (68)

Table 18

DEMOGRAPHIC AND SOCIO-ECONOMIC VARIABLES IN MENTAL RETARDATION*

		No.	Percentage
Sex	Male	206	68.7
	Female	94	31.3
Age in years	1 - 5	90	30.0
	6 - 10	132	44.0
	11 - 15	59	19.7
	above 16	19	6.3
Domicile	Rural	56	18.7
	Urban	244	81.3
Religion	Hindu	248	82.7
	Muslim	47	15.7
	Sikh	5	1.6
Family income	Below 100	71	23.7
(Monthly in Rs.)	100 - 400	140	46.7
	401 - 800	69	23.0
	above 800	20	6.6

* Gupta, S.C. (68).

In an analysis of 300 mentally retarded children registered between 1966 and 1968 in the child guidance clinic of K.G's. Medical College, Lucknow, Gupta (68) observed that the majority of cases were severely retarded (Table 17) and were less than 10 years of age (Table 18). The ratio of male to female children was 2:1, most of these cases were drawn from the lower socio-economic group (Table 18). Further, speech defects were one of the main reasons for psychiatric consultation (Table 19).

Table 19

MAIN COMPLAINTS IN MENTALLY
RETARDED CHILDREN*

Speech defect	194
Lower understanding	143
Temper tantrum and behaviour disorder	126
Physical ailment	76
Poor concentration and memory	68
Retarded milestones	54
Enuresis	40
School backwardness	37
Abnormal behaviour	35
Lack of socialization	32

* Gupta, S.C. (68)

Other commonly occurring problems in children in India have also received our attention from time to time, and we have tried to study the phenomenon in a limited manner. For example, enuresis was studied by us in clinical as well as in survey work. During a field survey of 850 families (14) conducted by three stage random sampling in the urban localities of Lucknow, the prevalence rate of enuresis was found to be 12.1/1000 (14). Similarly, in a study of 500 rural families, bed wetting was present in 1.9% of the cases (16). Further, in a clinical study during the years 1968 to 1969 at this child guidance clinic Mahendru et al. (69) reported a series of 37 (63.0%) children diagnosed for enuresis during a period of 14 months. Investigators in the same study also evaluated other behavioral symptoms (Table 20) and their socio-economic variables. The majority of these cases were Hindus (82.8%); 64% were found to have normal intellect, 36% were intellectually retarded, 55.2% were males and 44.8% were females. The symptom analysis revealed that the majority of children had multiple problems.

Table 20

PRESENTING SYMPTOMS*

Symptoms	No. of cases
Enuresis	37
Obstinacy and temper tantrum	30
Food fads	23
Wandering	20
Timidity and shyness	17
Stealing	12
Nail biting	11
Truancy	10
Nightmares	9

* Mahendru *et al.* (69)

In a study of migrated population, Sethi *et al.* (61) observed a higher occurrence of bed wetting in the migrated group (17.5%) than in the non-migrated group (6.8%).

In a report from our urban health centre, Thacore *et al.* (70) listed 20 cases (29.9%) of bed wetting. There was one case of bed wetting with mental retardation from a total clinical psychiatric evaluation of 67 cases. In the same study children up to the age of 15 years formed 39.0% of the total clinic sample.

In an extensive survey study on epidemiology (71) conducted in the years 1967 to 1968 from a section of urban population in Northern India, there were 37.3% emotionally disturbed children less than 15 years of age amongst all sick individuals. The diagnostic break up revealed that mental retardation was present in 30 patients, special symptoms included cases of bed wetting (38 cases) and speech disturbances (3 cases). In cases of mental retardation, males out numbered females.

A glance at Table 21 gives the extent of the problems of juvenile delinqents apprehended in India in the period 1958 to 1963 and the number of cases sent to the court for trial. The

Table 21

NUMBER OF DELINQUENTS APPREHENDED AND SENT TO COURTS FOR TRIAL*

Year	No. of cases apprehended	No. of cases sent to courts
1958	29,774	27,601
1959	47,925	45,779
1960	49,276	47,299
1961	53,776	47,825
1962	53,083	49,071
1963	51,349	48,370

* Marfatia, J.C. (72)

number disposed of before being brought to the court has always been less than 1.0% (72) of those apprehended. According to *Crime in India 1963* (72) the state of Maharashtra topped the list in reporting the highest number of delinquents (12081) followed by Madras (10646) and Gujrat (3508). Among the eight cities reviewed (72), Madras city (5189) had the maximum number of cases followed by Hyderabad (2638) and Bombay (2279).

The total number of juvenile delinquents brought before Bombay Juvenile Court during 1968 to 1969 was 3058, of which 2247 were boys and 811 were girls. The children, 2102 boys and 645 girls, were admitted to the "Remand House" for varying periods of detention (72).

Marfatia (72) has provided the data for the nature of offence committed by delinquents during 1964 to 1969 (Table 22).

Table 22

DISTRIBUTION OF DELINQUENTS ACCORDING TO NATURE OF OFFENCES*

Nature of offence	1964-65	1965-66	1966-67	1967-68	1968-69
Offences against property	25.72	30.68	32.40	30.00	29.77
offences against laws and controls	17.21	9.93	4.43	7.11	7.79
Offences against persons	1.42	1.72	1.26	1.89	1.64
Sex offences	0.03	0.35	0.33	-	0.27
Breach of probation supervision	0.30	0.42	0.06	0.39	0.33
Miscellaneous	0.82	2.40	5.53	5.36	7.89
Total	45.50	45.50	44.01	44.75	47.59

* Marfatia, J.C. (72).

Keeping in view the problem of delinquency as it exists in Indian children, we were inclined to investigate its psychodynamics and some of its genetic aspects as well.

During 1973, 140 male delinquents 6 to 18 years of age, were reported to be in the Government Approved School, Lucknow; 52 delinquents were in the age group of 11-18 (73). The offences committed by them were: assault - 21.2%; theft - 25.0%; wandering - 34.6%; and miscellaneous offences - 19.2%. The majority of these were Hindus (61.5%). The second largest group was Muslims (30.8%). Subjects from urban areas outnumbered rural ones by a ratio of 3 : 2. These delinquents were studied for "aggression" and intelligence on the basis of clinical interview, Rorschach test, and Bhatia performance battery of intelligence. Analysis revealed that a significantly greater number of aggressive delinquents (32 cases) were drawn from unitary families with poor economic status. Non-aggressives (20 cases) overwhelmingly belonged to rural domicile and came mostly from a joint family. Psychometric findings indicated higher levels of hostility responses as well as extrapunitive tendencies in the aggressive delinquents, whereas the non-aggressive ones had a significantly higher score on the intrapunitive scale. The two groups could not be differentiated in terms of their intellectual level. However, it was observed that delinquents in general had a somewhat low I.Q. (73). The mean I.Q. in the aggressive group was 88.6 (S.D. = 5.4) and in the non-aggressive group 90.5 (S.D. = 7.8).

Tandon (74) studied 50 male delinquents for his doctoral thesis and reported a mean age of 13.2 years (range 11-16 yrs.); the vast majority of subjects were drawn from the poor income groups of urban community and had an educational level up to primary or even less. Childhood bereavement before the age of 11 was observed in 46% of the cases. Three fourths of the subjects were drawn from unitary families; 66% of the fathers were either illiterate or had primary education; disturbed relationships between parents and siblings was observed in two thirds. More than 60% of the cases attained an I.Q. level of 70-83.

A paper on genetic aspects of 100 juvenile delinquents was presented by Sethi et al. (75) at The First Annual Conference of Indian Society of Human Genetics, Bombay, 1974.

The report was based on dermatoglyphic and buccal smear studies. The results revealed; a higher incidence of ulnar loops on the ring finger of the right hand: a higher incidence of tented arches in the index finger of both hands; a lower a-b-ridge count in both hands; a higher incidence of loops in the I_3 area of the palm of the right hand: a lower incidence of loops in the I_3 area of the feet: and a higher tab angle in the right hand. All these were statistically significant as compared with normal controls. However, quantitative characteristics like the total ridge count and atd angle, which are more specifically shown to be genetically determined, did not show any significant deviation in delinquents compared to normal controls. Buccal smears of all these subjects were negative for sex chromatin body, thus corresponding to their phenotype. Out of these 100 delinquents, 80 were Hindus, 19 Muslims and 1 Chinese. Offences were: assault 21.2%; theft 25.0%; wandering 34.6%; and travelling without ticket 19.2%.

So far we have been discussing several reports concerning relevant studies which have made their appearance from this center. It would be equally interesting to comment upon similar or other studies concerning children carried out by other well known investigators in this country.

Analysis of data from a private psychiatric nursing home at Lucknow during a four year period showed that new registrations for the children below 16 years of age was: 1962 - 12.8%, 1963 - 13.5%, 1964 - 14.2%, and 1965 - 13% (76).

Mental retardation has been one of the most commonly investigated disorders in this country. More than 100 reports concerning various aspects of the syndrome have made their appearance during the last two decades or so. The incidence and prevalence as reported for the disorder vary from investigator to investigator and from one center to the other. The reasons for such varied findings are mainly two-folds. Difficulty of exact categorization of the intellectual level of children utilizing I.Q. as a differentiating variable. After an excellent review of psychologic tests for use in India, Malin (77) points out that from the foregoing history and summary for diagnostic instruments for the mental assessment of our mentally deficient Indian children and the still narrowing influences of regional languages, we may conclude that in only 4 or 5 of the major language areas do we have any test at all. This would leave 30% of our children without any test. Due to the non-availability of standardized intelligence tests which may be applicable to the whole of India, the estimates or categorizations offer grave problems. We would require standard tests based on the availability of local dialects or else we would not be able to offer any reliable data. There are cultural and local factors which differ from one part to the other. Marfatia in a paper reat at the First All India Conference of Mental Retardation held at New Delhi (78), observed that reliable statistics were not available for the incidence of mental retardation in India. On the basis of impressions gathered during a number of years of psychiatric practice, he estimated that there were 13,000,000 mental defectives in this country in comparison to 5.5 million in the U.S.A. and 300,000 in England and Wales. The figures quoted by him in the same paper from the Child Guidance Clinic of the Tata Institute of Social Sciences, Bombay, for the period July 1950 to June 1957 is give in Table 23. About one fourth of the case load in that clinic contained mentally retarded children.

Table 23

*CHILD GUIDANCE CLINIC REFERRAL**

Total No. of referred cases   982
Cases of Mental Retardation   237 (24.13%)

* Marfatia, J.C. (78)

It has also been observed that the other two child guidance clinics of Bombay with which Marfatia was connected were also overloaded with mentally retarded children.

An intensive study of 100 cases of mental retardation was undertaken by Marfatia (17) and his associates. The sample was drawn from one of the oldest and largest schools in India for such children. This particular school admits mentally defective children, usually above an I.Q. of 40, in the age range of 7-20 years. One hundred unselected children from 240 day students and boarders, whose parents were cooperative, were admitted to this enquiry. Investigations included examination of urine and blood, X-ray, sex chromatin, urinary amino acid examination, phenyl pyruric acid excretion, EEG, glucose tolerance test, radio active iodine uptake, urinary sugar, chromatography, serum glucose-6-phosphate dehydrogenase estimation, serum copper oxidase estimation, dermatoglyphic studies, and angiography. A detailed clinical history and psychological assessment was also done. The cases were subdivided into 7 groups as shown in Table 24.

Table 24

ETIOLOGICAL CLASSIFICATION OF MENTALLY
RETARDED CHILDREN*

Etiological factors		Cases
A	Genetic or probably genetic	42%
B	Chromosomal Aberrations	16%
	Down's Syndrome 14%	
	Others 2%	
C	Resulting from Antenatal factors	9%
D	Resulting from Perinatal factors	15%
E	Resulting from Neonatal factors	4%
F	Subsequently Acquired	11%
H	Unclassifiable	17%

* Marfatia (17).

Marfatia (17) has reported associated behavioural manifestations as well. Table 25 indicates that personality disorders form the bulk (76%) of the behavioural disorders.

Nagaraja (79) reported statistics for a seven year period from the Department of Child Psychiatry, Niloufer Hospital, Hyderabad, and provided figures for yearly sex incidence (Table 26), diagnostic break up (Table 27); and result of therapy (Table 28).

TABLE 25

Emotional and Behavioral Problems in Mentally
Retarded Children (N = 100)

Antisocial Behavior	3%
Personality Disorders	76%
Habit Disorders	42%
Neurotic Features	15%
Hyperkinesis	29%
Psychotic Features	5%

*   Marfatia - (17).

Table 26

TOTAL NUMBER OF CASES WITH SEX INCIDENCE**

Year	Total No. of cases	Male	Female
1959	45	24	21
1960	163	103	60
1961	148	87	61
1962	97	61	36
1963	115	65	50
1964	117	64	53
1965	170	101	69

** Nagaraja - (79).

Table 27

DISEASE ENTITIES AND ITS INCIDENCE*

Year	Adjustment reaction of childhood				Psychoneurosis				Psychosis				Psychosomatic				Personality deviation				M. R.			
	Male		Female		Male		Female		Male		Female		Male		Female		Male		Female		Male		Female	
	O.P.	In.P.	O.P.	In.P.	O.P.	In.P.	O.P.	In.P.	O.P.	In.P.	O.P.	In.P.	O.P.	In.P.	O.P.	In.P.	O.P.	In.P.	O.P.	In.P.	O.P.	In.P.	O.P.	In.P.
1959	16	-	9	-	-	2	-	7	-	1	1	1	-	-	-	-	1	-	-	-	4	-	4	-
1960	26	1	22	3	6	4	6	9	6	2	1	-	5	1	2	1	-	2	-	-	51	-	16	-
1961	17	1	14	3	3	-	6	9	4	1	5	2	3	1	-	4	4	1	-	-	51	-	18	-
1962	8	2	-	1	1	3	6	5	4	-	1	-	1	2	3	4	-	-	-	-	34	1	22	1
1963	13	2	8	2	13	3	5	8	3	-	5	-	-	-	3	3	-	1	-	-	21	6	19	1
1964	13	2	8	5	2	6	7	9	-	1	1	-	2	2	-	2	2	1	-	-	30	-	15	4
1965	21	2	7	3	11	3	17	12	5	5	1	1	2	1	2	3	11	1	-	-	35	1	23	-

O. P. = Out-patient; In. P. = Indoor patient

* Nagaraja - (79).

Table 28

TREATMENT ANALYSIS

Year		Adjustment reaction of childhood			Psychoneurosis			Psychosis			Psychosomatic			Personality deviation			M. R.		
		Cured	Improved	Not Improved	Cured	Improved	Not cured	Cured	Improved	Not cured	Cured	Improved	Not cured	Cured	Improved	Not Improved	Cured	Improved	Not Improved
1959	Male	10	5	2	-	2	-	-	1	-	-	-	-	-	-	1	-	3	1
	Female	7	-	1	2	3	2	-	-	1	-	-	-	-	-	-	-	2	2
1960	Male	13	10	3	7	2	1	1	4	3	5	1	-	-	2	-	-	19	32
	Female	14	9	2	11	3	16	-	-	1	4	-	-	-	-	-	-	5	11

Year	Sex																			Total
1961	Male	18	-	3	-	3	-	-	3	-	2	-	4	-	2	1	2	-	11	40
	Female	17	-	-	-	-	-	-	3	3	1	1	3	1	-	-	-	-	5	13
1962	Male	3	4	2	-	2	1	-	4	-	-	3	-	-	-	-	-	-	11	24
	Female	-	1	-	2	4	5	2	1	-	-	3	1	-	-	-	-	4	4	13
1963	Male	3	11	1	5	9	5	1	2	-	1	-	-	-	1	-	1	-	3	25
	Female	1	3	6	3	7	3	3	2	2	1	3	3	-	-	-	-	-	2	9
1964	Male	10	3	2	2	5	2	1	1	-	-	-	1	1	-	2	1	-	6	35
	Female	8	1	2	2	11	2	3	-	1	1	2	-	-	-	-	1	-	9	11
1965	Male	20	3	-	2	12	2	-	7	3	-	3	-	-	8	4	-	2	1	33
	Female	8	2	-	1	28	1	-	1	-	1	4	1	-	-	-	-	5	-	18

The analysis reveals that a variety of disorders were observed, but there had always been predominance of mentally retarded children in the out-patient department with a very negligible number of these children hospitalized. The majority of children diagnosed as adjustment reaction of childhood also received treatment from the out-patient department. It is also of interest to note that indoor patients were predominantly females. The poorest result of therapy was evident in mentally retarded children (Table 28).

Nagaraja (80), in a review presented at The First All India Conference of Mental Retardation, New Delhi, offered comments on the etiology of mentally retarded children (Table 29).

Table 29

CAUSATIVE FACTORS IN MENTALLY RETARDED CHILDREN*

Causes	No. of cases
Infantile convulsion	85
Meningitis	40
Anoxia	24
Encephalitis	30
Prematurity	30
Cerebral palsy	8
Congenital	18
Unknown	55
Typhoid	1
Jaclia	2
Whooping cough	5
Measles	4
Icteritis	6
Head Injury	11
Toxemia	19
Syphilis	7
Marasmus	2
Small pox	3
Polio	2

*   Jaya Nagaraja - (80).

Jaya Nagaraja (80) observed that cases of mental retardation with idiopathic origin are in the minority, whereas cases with known causes form a larger series. The later may be prevented if detected in time. She emphasized at length the role of primary and secondary preventation in retarded children.

At the Department of Neurology, All India Institute of Medical Sciences, New Delhi, a study on mental retardation was carried out (81). One of the 286 cases studied, 66% were found to have primary mental retardation and in only 34% an etiology such as postencephalitis, birth anoxia and prematurity could be found. The male to female ratio was 2.5 :1. The age at which the parents noticed the child to be mentally defective was variable. In cases with unknown etiology, 82% had the defect at birth while in 91% of the postencephalitic cases the defect was evident between 4 months to 3 years of age. The most common symptom besides mental retardation was cerebral seizures (52%). Hyperkenesia was present in 18%, speech defects in 10%, and hemiparesis and quadripresis in 16%. Karyography revealed trisomy in 4 cases (monogolism), trisomy X with mental retardation in one case, and unequal total length at 1 and 3 positions in another. Twenty cases showed excessive aminoaciduria, which included two cases of Wilson's disease and one case of phenylketonuria. The hemagglutination test for toxoplasmosis was strongly positive in two cases.

Menon et al. (82) studied 255 mentally retarded children at the Government Mental Hospital, Madras, for neurometabolic disorders in order to find out the incidence and type of such disorders. They employed a set of screening cases were found to be excreting an excess of aminoacids and tests on random samples of urine. One hundred and forty two other abnormal substances in the urine. By paper chromatographic analysis, a definite association was found between generalised amino-aciduria and mental retardation. Phenylketonuria was found in three patients. Two cases of cerebral lipodosis as well as one case of gorgoylism were also detected during the course of this study.

Head injury and relevant brain damage and its effects on psychological performance at different age levels was studied at the Department of Neurology and Neurosurgery, Madras

Medical College, Madras (83). Of the 238 cases of head injury examined psychologically, 60 were examined repeatedly and studied for their level of psychological performance. The study included patients from different age groups. From the data analysed some tentative conclusions could be drawn to indicate that the psychological disturbance in organic brain damage of young individuals was more serious than in the older ones.

Another study on head injury at the same institution (83) revealed that the ratio of head injury in children and adults was approximately 1:2. Falls and road traffic accidents caused most of the head injuries in children, while in adults road traffic accidents predominated. Birth injuries were quite rare. Children with minimal or no loss of consciousness sometimes developed fatal complications. Apparently severe injuries in children seemed to carry a good prognosis. Fractures of the skull occurred more frequently and intracranial hematomatas less frequently in children than adults. In general, children required hospitalization for a shorter period and post-traumatic complications were relatively rare.

A study aimed at finding the psychiatric morbidity in school children at Ranchi (North India) was conducted at the Hospital for Mental Disease, Kanke, Ranchi, by Bhaskaran and Shukla (84) by utilising a random sampling of school children and adolescents (both boys and girls) in the age range of 11 to 18 years. A comprehensive questionaire and Mohsin's general intelligence test were used as tools. The study revealed that: (a) in general girls had more psychiatric problems than the boys by registering higher scores for neurotic features, phobias, obsessive-compulsive features, sleep disturbances, depressive features and scholastic problems; (b) problems relating to domestic adaptation, speech and sex were found to be nearly equal in incidence in boys and girls. Boys revealed higher scores than girls on intellectual tests.

Teja et al. (18) in a clinical study on "The Child with Speech Problems" conducted at the Child Guidance Clinic of the Post-graduate Institute of Medical Education and Research, Chandigarh, tried to study (a) the prevalence and type of speech disturbances in clinics, and (b) the role of psychological variables in relation to these problems. The study included cases between January 1967 and September 1970. Cases with the primary diagnosis of mental retardation were excluded. Speech disturbances as the main symptom appeared in 6.6% of the cases. The type of speech disturbances is shown in Table 30.

Table 30

*TYPE OF SPEECH DISORDERS**

Diagnosis	Number of cases
Delayed speech	5
Lalling	2
Hysterical aphonia	3
Stuttering	26

* Teja *et al.* (18)

Stuttering was the major diagnostic group. Ten cases of stuttering had other associated disturbances like borderline mental retardation, esonophelia, optic atrophy and behavioural disturbances. Other important observations of the study were (a) significantly more males than females in the sample, (b) the predominance of cases belonging to urban areas, (c) a comparatively higher incidence from the income group of Rs. 100-299 per month, (d) 67.7% of cases had the onset of the symptoms before the age of 5, and (e) the eldest sibling in either sex formed the bulk of "speech problems". The family history of emotional disorder and precipitating factors revealed about 50% of the cases had a positive family history of emotional illness (Table 31), and 58.3% of the cases had triggering events including psychological and physical illnesses and stress.

Further, faulty paternal and maternal attitudes, marital disharmony amongst the parents, sibling rivalry, neurotic traits and problems were found favoring disturbed interpersonal relationships. Such factors should be contributing towards the etiology of speech disturbances. A long list of neurotic problems and traits (Table 32), the chief being enuresis and situation fears, were observed in these children.

Table 31

FAMILY HISTORY OF PSYCHIATRIC ILLNESS*

Type of illness	Sibs.	Father	Mother	Other
Late speech	1	-	-	-
Schizophrenia	1	-	-	1
Mental retardation	1	-	-	-
Reactive depression	-	-	1	-
Epilepsy	-	-	-	1
Psychosomatic Asthma	-	-	1	-
Stuttering	5	3	1	4

* Teja *et al.* (18)

During 1964 to 1968, Jain *et al.* (19) studied functional speech defects (stammering, stuttering, and babbling) in children with various behavior problems at a child guidance cliniic in Amritsar utilizing Kanner's (86) definition for such disorders. The study included 90 children and was undertaken to evaluate some of the psychopathological and etiological factors. Patient age ranged between 9 and 14 years; none of these children had speech defects resulting from a physical lesion. The study revealed (a) the incidence of speech disorder as 11.2% of the whole clinical sample, stammering was six times more frequent than babbling, and both these speech disorders were six times more common in boys than in girls; (b) 31% were first born and 29% were youngest sibs; (c) 52% of these children belonged to III and IV grades of socio-economic status as against 65% ± 1

Table 32

NEUROTIC PROBLEMS AND TRAITS IN CHILDREN WITH SPEECH PROBLEM*

Traits	No. of cases
Nocturnal enuresis	9
Situational fears	6
Delinquent traits	2
Feeding difficulties	3
Sibling rivalry	3
Nail biting	3
Temper tantrum	3
Thumb sucking	2
Sleep talking	2
Pica	1
Sleeping with parent after 5 years of age	1
Grinding teeth during sleep	1
Night mare, night terror	3

* Teja *et al.* (18)

S.D. of the normal probability curve; (d) 70.7% of the children were drawn from urban areas; (e) stammering/stuttering started in 80.5% of the children after the age of 3 years in contrast to 69.2% of the babblers who started below 3 years of age; (f) 70% of the stammerers had an illness duration of three years or more while 39% of the babblers had a similar duration. In addition, the mode of onset (Table 33), psychological factors of etiological importance (Table 34) and associated behavioral problems were also investigated. Socio-economic status, place

Table 33

*SHOWING MODE OF ONSET OF STAMMERING/
STUTTERING AND BABBLING**

Mode of onset	Stammer-ing/ stutter-ing		Babbling	
	N	%	N	%
From the very beginning	5	7	9	69
Sudden appearance	4	5	0	0
Insidious	23	30	0	0
Painful emotional experi-ence	7	9	0	0
Birth of another baby	10	13	0	0
Imitation	1	1	0	0
Fever	17	22	2	15.5
Other physical illnesses	10	13	2	15.5
Total	77	100	13	100

*Jain, C.K.; Kishore, B. and Manchanda, S.S.-(19).

Table 34

*SHOWING PSYCHOLOGICAL FACTORS OF POSSIBLE
ETIOPATHOGENIC* SIGNIFICANCE*

Psychological factors	Stammering/stuttering		Babbling		Total
	N	%	N	%	N
Pampering & over protection	29	38	6	46	35
Parental discord	3	4	0	0	3
Frequent scolding & beating	5	6	0	0	5
Neglected child	1	1	1	8	2
Temperamental inconsistencies of the parents	9	12	1	8	10
Maternal deprivation	0	0	1	8	1
Painful emotional experience	1	1	0	0	1
Poor in studies	18	20	0	0	13
Imitation	3	4	0	0	3
Not known	18	23	4	31	22

Jain *et al.* (19)

TABLE 35

SEX, AGE, ECONOMIC-STATUS AND BIRTH ORDER
(N=100)*

Sex and age	0-1½	1½-3	3-6	6-3	9-4	Total
Male	-	1	18	9	38	66
Female	2	-	11	9	12	34

Economic Status				
1000-above	500-1000	200-500	100-200	Below 100
1	4	30	61	14

Birth Order								
Only	Eldest	Youngest	2	3	4	5	6	7
8	14	31	15	16	7	8	-	1

of residence, heredity and handedness had no significance in the causation of the disorder, while factors like birth order, age of onset, intellectual level, backwardness in studies, pampering, over protection, temperamental inconsistencies of the parents, their rigid attitude, strict discipline at home, scolding and beating, other painful experiences, jealousy and rivalry as a result of another sibling's arrival were noticed to be of etiological significance.

Table 36

INCIDENCE OF MAIN ETIOLOGICAL FACTORS*

A.	Organic cases	No. of patient	Incidence %
	Mental deficiency	4	4
	Epilepsy	18	18
	Encephalitis	16	16
	P.U.O.	1	1
B.	Psychogenic	61	61

* Manchanda, S.S.; Kishore, B.; C. Jain* C.K.; Gurmeet Singh; Kashyap, U.B. - (87).

One hundred consecutive children referred to the Child Guidance Clinic and Baby Welfare Clinic, V.J. Hospital, Amritsar were studied by Manchanda *et al.* (87). Table 35 shows the sex, age, economic status, and birth order of the saimple, while Table 36 shows the incidence of the main etiological factors. A detailed list of the incidence of behavior problems according to sex and place of residence is shown in Table 37. The analysis revealed a variety of behavioral abnormalities in

Table 37

SHOWING INCIDENCE OF BEHAVIOUR PROBLEMS.
MALE AND FEMALE AND RURAL URBAN
DISTRIBUTION*

Disorders	No.	M : F	U : R	Incidence %
A. Food intake:	35	26 : 9	22 : 13	
1. Pica	5	3 : 2	3 : 2	5
2. Food faddism	9	7 : 2	5 : 4	9
3. Refusal of food	6	6 : 0	4 : 2	6
Overeating	15	10 : 5	10 : 5	15
B. Sleep:	36	30 : 6	28 : 8	
1. Restlessness	5	3 : 2	4 : 1	5
2. Nightmares	8	6 : 2	6 : 2	8
3. Somniloquy	18	16 : 2	14 : 4	18
4. Somnambulism	5	5 : 0	4 : 1	5
C. Speech:	22	15 : 7	11 : 11	
1. Babbling	4	3 : 1	2 : 2	4
2. Stammering	9	8 : 1	5 : 4	9
3. Dysphonia	3	1 : 2	1 : 2	3
4. Mutism	4	1 : 3	2 : 2	4
5. Irrelevant speech	2	2 : 0	1 : 1	2
D. Motor Behaviour:	32	22 : 10	23 : 9	
1. Tics	4	4 : 0	4 : 0	4
2. Hyperkinesia	27	18 : 9	18 : 9	27
3. Hypokinesia	1	0 : 1	1 : 0	1

E. Body manipulation: 10   8 : 2   7 : 3
   1. Thumb sucking   1   0 : 1   1 : 0   1
   2. Nail biting   4   4 : 0   2 : 2   4
   3. Teeth grinding   5   4 : 1   4 : 1   5

F. Sex Behaviour: 2   1 : 1   2 : 0
   1. Masturbation   2   1 : 1   2 : 0   2

G. Emotional behaviour:117   78 : 39   74 : 43
   1. Jealousy   4   4 : 0   2 : 2   4
   2. Fear   6   4 : 2   4 : 2
   3. Temper tantrum   37   22 : 15   23 : 14   37
   4. Anger   38   26 : 12   24 : 14   38
   5. Obstinacy   30   20 : 10   20 : 10   30
   6. Irritability   2   2 : 0   1 : 1   2

H. School behaviour: 59   46 : 13   43 : 16
   1. Lying   5   3 : 2   4 : 1   5
   2. Disobedience   16   10 : 6   10 : 6   16
   3. Stealing   7   7 : 0   6 : 1   7
   4. Destructive   11   8 : 3   8 : 3   11
   5. Abusiveness   16   14 : 2   12 : 4   16
   6. Cruelty   1   1 : 0   1 : 0   1
   7. Truancy   3   3 : 0   2 : 1   3

I. Psychosomatic: 62   34 : 28   51 : 11
   1. Headache   8   4   4   6 : 2   8
   2. Vomiting   5   1 : 3   5 : 0   5
   3. Pain in abdomen 9   4 : 5   7 : 2   9
   4. Breath holding
      spells   1   1 : 0   1 : 0   1
   5. Tachycardia   1   1 : 0   1 : 0   1
   6. Enuresis   27   15 : 12   22 : 5   27
   7. Polyuria   10   6   4   8 : 2   10
   8. Hiccough   1   1 : 0   1 : 0   1

J. Hysterical behaviour: 7   4 : 3   6 : 1   7

---

* Manchanda *et al.* - (87).

Table 38

BEHAVIOURAL ABNORMALITY IN CHILDREN ADMITTED FOR PHYSICAL* AILMENTS (N=1000)

Behavioural disorder	Percentage
Sleep	27.7
Food intake	29.0
Speech	12.4
Motor Behaviour	8.7
Body manipulation	37.4
Sex behaviour	2.0
Emotional behaviour	47.3
Social behaviour	30.6
Psychosomatic	75.8
Neurotic behaviour	2.7

Manchanda *et al.* (87)

Table 39

DIAGNOSTIC BREAK UP*

Diagnosis	Percentage
Organic brain syndrome	39
Hysterical fits	5
Information not available	60
Behavioural disorders	50
Total	100

Kishore *et al.* (21)

these cases. The investigators in the same paper also commented that 1000 children were admitted for various physical
ailments. When interrogated, no child was free from one or
the other behavioral problem. A wide variety of associated
behavioral abnormalities (Table 38) like sleep disturbances,
food intake, speech disorder, etc. were observed in these children.

In a study of hysteria, Dutta Ray and Mathur (88)
reported 4 (5.5%) male cases and 22 (8.5%) female cases of
hysteria in the age range of 13 - 15 years, whereas only 7.9% of
the total sample was in this group. All the male children were
unmarried, whereas only one female in this age group was
married and the rest were unmarried. Amongst the male children, there were 3 cases of convulsive hysteria and 1 case of
conversion. Amongst the female children, 4 cases were of
convulsive hysteria and 18 cases of conversion hysteria. No
case of constitutional syndrome or dissociative hysteria was
reported in this age group.

Bassa (89) published case reports of 7 brain damaged
children and observed that physiotherapy seems to be the
treatment of choice for brain damaged children. He suggested
that attention should be paid to emotional factors of the
child and parents. Further, with the use of appropriate drugs
and psychotherapy including counselling for parents, rehabilitation can be considerably quickened in several cases of cerebral palsy.

Saroja Bai (90) reported an 8-year-old boy diagnosed as
Gulles da La Tourette's Disease. The boy displayed hundreds
of fits in a day only during the awakened period. The fits involved all four limbs, the head, and neck with vocal utterances
of barking and flickering of eyelids. The boy was of normal
intelligence.

Kishore *et al.* (21) studied 100 consecutive cases of
"Behaviour Problem Children" attending a child guidance clinic,
Amritsar, to (a) delineate the common behavior problems in an
attempt to classify them in proper groups, (b) to study whether
the character of these behavior deviations have a correlation
with social factors like sex, age, and birth order, and (c) to
delineate the etiopathogenic psychological factors. The
diagnostic break up of 100 cases is given in Table 39.

Further, a detailed study of 50 cases of behavioral disorders was carried out, and common behavioual problems were subclassified into 5 subgroups (Table 40) mainly on the basis of clusters (21).

Table 40

DIFFERENT BEHAVIOUR PATTERNS IN THE
PARTICULAR BEHAVIOUR PATTERN CLUSTERS*

(a) Monosymptomatic anxious reaction pattern (Total No. of cases 16).

Behaviour pattern	M	F	Total
Headache	2	3	5
Muscular aches & pains	-	1	1
Pain abdomen	2	4	6
Vomiting	1	2	3
Belching	1	0	1

(b) Unsocial aggressive reaction pattern (Total No. of cases 3)

Behaviour pattern	M	F	Total
Disobedience	3	-	3
Destructiveness	3	-	3
Lying	2	-	2
Abusiveness	3	-	3
Stealing	2	-	2
Masturbation	1	-	1
Suicidal	1	-	1

(c) Aggressive reaction pattern (Total No. of cases 8).

Behavior pattern	M	F	Total
Anger	8	-	8
Tantrums	5	-	5
Hyperactivity	3	-	3
Restlessness	3	-	3
Nail biting	3	-	3
Teeth grinding	2	-	2

(d) Regressive reaction patterns (Total No. of cases 15).

Behaviour pattern	M	F	Total
Refusal of food	1	-	1
Food fads	1	1	2
Stammering	3	-	3
Babbling	-	1	1
Thumb sucking	-	1	1
Enuresis	3	8	11
Frequent micturition	2	1	3

(e) Aggressive regressive reaction (Total No. of cases 8)

Behaviour pattern	M	F	Total
Anger	4	2	6
Tantrums	4	1	5
Hyperactivity	4	-	4
Restlessness	2	-	2
Teeth grinding	2	-	2
Nail biting	1	-	1
Refusal of food	1	-	1
Food faddism	1	-	1
Stammering	-	-	-
Babbling	-	1	1
Thumb sucking	-	1	1
Enuresis	4	2	6

* Kishore, B.; Jain, C.K. and Manchanda, S.S.-(21).

Table 41A

*BEHAVIOUR PATTERN CLUSTERS AND SEX,AGE AND BIRTH ORDER**

*Behaviour pattern clusters and their sex distribution**

Behaviour pattern clusters	M	F	Total
Monosymptomatic anxious R.	6	10	16
Unsocialised Agg. R.	3	-	3
Aggressive R.	8	-	8
Regressive R.	6	9	15
Aggressive Reg. R.	7	1	8
Total	30	20	50

* Kishore *et al.* (21)

Table 41B

Behaviour pattern clusters and the Age-Range of their onset*

Behaviour pattern clusters:	Age-Range of onset in years					
	1-3	3-6	6-9	9-12	12-15	total
Monosymptomatic anxious reaction	-	-	1	8	7	16
Unsocialised aggressive R	-	-	-	1	2	3
Aggressive R.	-	2	4	1	1	8
Regressive R.	-	5	8	1	1	15
Aggr. Reg. R.	-	-	6	1	1	8
Total	-	7	19	12	12	50
%	-	14	38	24	24	-

* Kishore *et al.* (21)

     Social factors like sex, age of onset of symptoms and birth order seemed to be significant major determinants (21).

Table 41C

Birth Order in the different behaviour pattern clusters*

Behaviour pattern clusters	Birth position in the family								
	Only	Eldest	Youngest	2nd	3rd	4th	5th	6th	Total
Monosymptomatic anxious reaction	2	4	4	2	1	1	1	1	16
Unsocialised Aggr. R.	-	-	-	-	3	-	-	-	3
Aggressive R.	1	3	3	1	-	-	-	-	8
Regressive R.	1	4	8	2	-	-	-	-	15
Aggr. Reggr. R.	1	1	4	-	1	1	-	-	8
Total	5	12	19	5	5	2	1	1	50
%	10	24	38	10	10	4	2	2	-

* Kishore *et al.* (21)

Table 42

THE PREDOMINANT ETIOPATHOGENIC PSYCHOLOGICAL FACTORS*

Etiopathogenic factors	Monosymp-tomatic axnous		Unsociali-sed Aggr.		Aggressive		Regressive		Aggr.		Reg.		Total		Grand total
	M	F	M	F	M	F	M	F	M	F	M	F	M	F	
Pampering and over protection	2	2	-	-	4	-	2	2	4	-	-	-	12	4	16
Rejection Loss of mother	-	-	1	-	-	-	-	1	-	1	-	-	1	2	3
Separated parents	-	-	1	-	-	-	-	-	-	-	-	-	1	-	1
Alcoholic father	-	-	1	-	-	-	-	-	-	-	-	-	1	-	1

Parental discord	-	-	-	-	2	2	1	2	-	6	1	7
Neglected child	2	-	-	-	1	1	3	-	-	2	5	7
Inconsistent parent discipline	-	-	-	-	1	-	1	-	-	-	1	1
Neurotic parent	1	-	1	0	-	-	-	1	-	1	0	1
Sib. rivalry	-	1	-	-	-	1	1	-	-	-	2	2
Fear of school because of inability to compete	2	5	-	-	-	-	-	-	-	2	5	7
Low financial condition & inability to compete with neighbours	1	-	-	1	1	-	-	1	-	4	-	4
Total	6	10	3	-	8	6	9	7	1	30	20	50

* Kishore, B.; Jain, C.K. and Manchanda, S.S. (21).

Table 41 shows that certain groups of reactions are common in male children. The explanaion offered is in term of differing upbringing of the male and female child in India. The onset of symptoms and a particular type of behavior is explained with the help of a psychodynamic theory in Indian children. Psychological factors like pampering, overprotection, rejection, etc. (Table 42) were found to be significantly etiopathogenic in development of these behavioral disorders (21).

Possession states or syndromes are typical culture bound phenomena occurring in India. Some interesting findings have been presented in an over-all review of these patients by investigators. Regarding its incidence in children, Verma et al. (91) observed that 2.5% (9 cases) of possession syndromes, studied by them at Ranchi during 1966, were between the ages of 10 to 15 years. No case of 10 years or under was observed by them; most were females although there were a few boys as well. The condition manifested in the form of being possessed by supernatural powers, Gods and Goddess. It occurred in endemic form, and has been described as an "infection" being passed on from one to the other.

Teja et al. (92), in a study of possession states in Indian patients, only found 2 cases between 10 and 15 years of age. One was a girl and the other was a boy. Both were unmarried and received a diagnostic label of "hysteria". The boy was possessed by God Hanuman.

A very rare type of case named "Idiot Savant", the first of its kind in India, was reported by Malhotra et al. (93) from the Child Guidance Clinic of the Post-Graduate Institute of Medical Education and Research, Chandigarh. These patients are neither idiots, nor savants, but the name has stuck. In these individuals some remarkable talent, well beyond the accomplishment of an average person, is associated with mental retardation. This particular case, a 15 year-old Hindu boy coming from a Northern hilly area, was suffering from Cretinism. He had an I.Q. of 55, and in addition had a remarkable ability of calendar calculation, which put him in the category of an "Idiot Savant".

De Souza et al. (94) analysed 63 cases of enuresis (nocturnal) seen at the Gujrat Research Society's Child Guidance Clinic, Bombay, during the period of January, 1957 to May,

1966. Enuresis formed 13.4% of the cases seen during this period at the clinic. Out of 63 cases, it was found to be primary in 51 cases and in 12 cases it was of acquired variety. Only 6 cases were referred to the clinic for enuresis alone. The study included 36 male and 27 female children. The age break up of the cases revealed that 14 cases were less than 5 years, 31 cases 6 to 10 years, and 8 cases 11 to 15 years. Family histories revealed neurosis or psychosis (12.7%) and enuresis in family members in the past (9.5%). Associated hypersomnia was detected in 5 children (8%). Eighteen children (29.4%) reported fear; they were too frightened to get up in the night and find their way to the toilet. Thirty six cases (57%) belonged to middle class families, 17 cases (27%) to lower class, and 10 cases (16%) to upper classes. Forty cases (63.5%) were residing in unitary families, whereas 23 cases (36.5%) were from joint families. In terms of causative factors, faulty parental attitudes (27 cases 42.9%), faulty trauma (2 cases 3.2%), aggresive outlet (25 cases 39.7%), insecurity (5 cases 8%), and environmental familial stress (16 cases 25.4%) were detected.

Nigam *et al.* (95) studied the phenomenon of bed wetting in a Government General Hospital for a period of 2 years. The study was aimed to evaluate the etiological factors and treatment of the disorder. It was observed that enuresis was more frequent in boys (64.3%), highest incidence was in the age group of 4-6 (47.6%), it occurred more frequently in middle (46.4%) and lower (33.3%) socio-economic classes. The sample was dominated by regular bed wetting (60.7%), the occassional bed wetters were 39.3%. There was greater prevalence of bed wetting among later born (12.8%) and of large family (11.6%) sibs. Enuretic children were found to have a smaller bladder. A slight higher percentage of recovery was noticed in regular bed wetters when put on psychotherapy and imipramine hydrochloride (30.9%) as compared to those receiving imipramine only (72.8%). The response to combined therapy in occasional bed wetters was also better (100%) as compared to imipramine only. Response was poorest in cases who received placebo and psychotherapy.

Recently 60 children referred to the Child Guidance Clinic at Maulana Azad Medical College and the Associated Irwin and G.B. Pant Hospital, New Delhi, for the complaint of enuresis were studied for "frustration reaction" (96). The findings were compared with 50 non-enuretic children. Thus, three groups of children, i.e. primary enuretics, secondary enuretics and normal children, were compared with each other for their frustration and reaction using the Indian adaptation of Rosenyweig's P.F. study (children form). These groups were matched for their age. The study revealed that: (1) neither of the three groups differed from each other in respect to the direction of aggression, (2) primary enuretics differed from secondary enuretics and also from normal children both with respect to the type of reaction and S-E patterns, (3) secondary enuretics were found to be closer to the normal children than to primary enuretics as far as their frustration reaction was concerned.

Behavioral disorders were studied in 98 children between 2 and 5 years of age from a rural area (31) in Northern India. The incidence observed was: thumb sucking, 5.98% (males = 5.88%, females = 6.06%); nail biting, 1.49% (F = 3.03%); night terrors, 16.42% (M = 20.57%, F = 12.12%); bed wetting, 31.33% (M = 32.35%, F = 30.30%); mud eating, 28.36% (M = 26.47%, F = 30.30%); grinding teeth, 13.44% (M = 11.78%, F = 15.16%); and others, 2.98% (M = 2.94%, F = 3.03%) which included mouth breathing and picking of eye lashes in one case each. Again, Koshi et al. (36) reported bed wetting in 2.4% of the boys and 4.1% of the girls and nail biting in 3.6% of the boys and 2.9% of the girls in 879 primary school children in urban areas in the age group of 3 to 15 years.

Malhotra (30), in a study of morbidity in children below 5 years of age in Delhi, found thumb sucking in 8.2%, nail biting in 0.4%, night terrors in 0.4%, bed wetting in 0.4%, food fads in 0.8%, and mud eating in 10.2% of the cases. The tendency to urinate when irritated was present in 0.4% of the cases. Only 2.7% of the children appeared to be dull, while 5.9% of the cases were bright. The rest could be classified as average.

Cases of mental retardation were studied at Bangalore (97) for metabolic defects. The analysis of urine sample from 1234 cases showed that there were 8 cases with phenylketonuria, 3 with homocystinuria, 2 with Hartnup's disease, and 7 with mucopolysacceharidosis of the Hurle's type. Other reports from India on such metabolic disorders show: phenylketonuria-3 cases from New Delhi and 2 from Vellore (98, 99), and one from Madras (100); homocystinuria 2 cases from New Delhi (101);

Hartnup's disease 1 case from Hyderabad (102) and 1 case from Trichur (103); and Hurler's disease 1 case shown by biopsy from Vellore (104).

A comparative study on specific therapy with the educable retarded was conducted by Jaya Nagaraja (105) at Hyderabad during 1964 to 1965. The plan of the study included division of the children with their parents into 4 groups with each group consisting of five children and their parents. Each child was assessed for his I.Q. simultaneously with the family work up. One group of children received a specific therapeutic program while their parents received counselling for their management for the same number of hours. In the second group, only the patients received therapy sessions and their parents did not receive any counselling. In the third group, the patients did not have any specific therapy sessions, but the parents received the counselling. Neither the patients nor the parents of the fourth group received any help except an initial and final assessment. The results revealed that counselling for parents and therapy for the child offered the maximum beneficial effects. Counselling to the parents alone in absence of therapy to the child was less beneficial for improving the lot of the retarded.

Suicide in younger age groups has been reported in Indian studies. Sathyavathi and Murti Rao (106) found that children below 10 years of age did not commit suicide; only a few subjects between 10 and 15 did so. Ganapathi and Venkoba Rao (107) reported that 3.7% of the cases below the age of 10 committed suicide. In another study, Venkoba Rao and Chinnian (108) found 3 students below 10 years and 6 students between 10 and 15 years of age from a group of 35 students studied for attempted suicide.

In a psychiatric and sociological study of children of mentally ill parents, 461 children in the age range of 2 to 17 years were screened. Data (clinical, psychological and sociological) were collected basically with reference to the child's environment and the influence of the latter upon the child's emotional life. The principal object of this study was to test the hypothesis that mental illness in a parent has a psychologically damaging effect upon the child. Two other groups included children of patients attending the antenatal department (control group), and parents of mentally ill children (counter study group). Psychological disturbances were noted in 43.5% of the children of mentally ill parents and 45.8% of the control cases. Mental morbidity was noted in 17.4% the parents of mentally ill out-patient children. In all the groups, enuresis and temper tantrum were found to be the prominent symptoms in children (85).

A study of 30 randomly selected delinquent children was undertaken at Pondicherry to evaluate and assess the family background and parental characteristics (109). Some interesting observations were made regarding the family of these children. Out of 30, ten children had lost their fathers and 9 had lost their mothers. One boy had an unmarried mother. Further, in 13 families the parents lived as couples without any valid contract of marriage. Seven fathers had a second wife, 2 mothers had run away from home, 2 mothers had extra-marital association for monetary gain, and the majority of fathers reported extra-marital relations. Thus, the family of these children lacked in warmth, affection, understanding, and identification; there was lack of a close, cohesive social unit. Most of these children belonged to the low economic group.

Further, 22 fathers and 4 mothers took liquor at one time or another, and 4 fathers had been arrested by the police for various offences. Most of the fathers were found imposing inadequate or inconsistent discipline and were physically beating the child. The majority of the mothers were careless in their supervision, quarrelsome, abusive and easily excitable (109).

Lastly, motivations for training in children have been studied in this country (110). Nearly 1,700 children on grade V of single teacher class rooms were surveyed at New Delhi, using tests developed to measure their adjustment towards the parents, school teachers, friends and others, the amount of their trust and dependence on the latter, their levels of initiative, intelligence and patterns of reaction to frustrating situations. The overall levels of the mental health of these children was quite high and tended to balance healthily between dependence and independence. The level of the children's trust of their teachers was also high; initiative and activity levels were slightly above average. A tendency was noted for ego defensive reactions (e.g. blaming the environment when faced with frustration). Interaction analysis of teachers showed that the experimental training of teachers (in which a feed back was given to them on class room behavior) induced the application of positive attitudes through praising, encouraging and asking questions.

PROBLEM OF CLASSIFICATION

Wig and Singh (111) observed in 1967 that no standard or commonly accepted classification exists for psychiatric disorders in India. They also pointed out that the Indian Psychiatric Society did not take any step in this direction. Since then a few workers have proposed classificating schemata to be followed, but none, till this date, has been universally accepted in this country. Indian psychiatrists are using an inconsistent way of classifying and labelling the disorders. They were guided by their own orientations as observed during their training years. At most of the large psychiatric hospitals, either the WHO classification or D.S.M.II of the American Psychiatric Association is employed for this purpose.

Wig and Singh (111) proposed a new classification which they felt was suitable for use in India. In this classification no separate category of childhood disorder was mentioned, but mental deficiency was classified as a separate group. The specific mention of childhood disorders could be seen in schizophrenia and in transient situational personality disorders. Mental deficiency was classified in this schemata on the basis of known and unknown etiologies labelled as primary and secondary retardation. In addition to organic causes, mental retardation arising as a result of social and environmental factors was also included under secondary mental retardation.

An exhaustive modification in classification schemata of ICD-8 of WHO and D.S.M.II of A.P.A. have been suggested for the categories of childhood disorders (21). These suggestions were offered on the basis of analysis of behavioral problems of Indian children. Kishore et al. (21) took into consideration several studies and felt that a large segment of behavior problems in Indian children can not be classified into the DSM-II of A.P.A. 308.0 to 308.5 categories, should be subclassified under 308.9 which stand for 'other reactions' of children. The larger segment of the behaviour problems seen in our setting revolves around 3 main areas (21): aggressive reaction, regressive reactions and psychosomatic or psychoneurotic symptoms. Kishore *et al.* (21), therefore, proposed the addition of the aggressive, regressive, aggressive-regressive, and monosymptomatic anxious reactions of childhood under the DSM-II 308 category. Thus, it appears that so far we have no satisfactory classification of our own, and Indian psychiatrists depend on the ICD-8 DSM-II and sometimes label a condition according to their own orientation.

EXISTING FACILITIES FOR MENTALLY RETARDED AND EMOTIONALLY DISTURBED CHILDREN

It has been mentioned earlier that existing facilities for psychiatric treatment, especially for emotionally disturbed and mentally retarded children, are most inadequate and growth in this direction had been a slow one. Kulkarni (112) in a review presented at the First All India Conference on Mental Retardation, New Delhi, observed that it could be safely presumed that the number of mentally retarded persons in India would be a hundred times or may be even a thousand more times than a mere 1500 and odd seats available in about 50 institutions existing through out the country. These institutions are special schools. Some of them funcion full time, while others offer part time facilities. Only a small number of them offer residential facilities. Table 43 indicates the number of such special institutions for the mentally retarded in different states of the Indian

Table 43

DISTRIBUTION OF SPECIAL INSTITUTIONS FOR MENTALLY RETARDED

State	No. of Institution
Andhra Pradesh	3
Bihar	2
Delhi	7
Gujarat	3
Kerala	1
Madhya Pradesh	1
Tamil Nadu	1
Maharashtra	18
Mysore	2
Punjab	1
Uttar Pradesh	5
West Bengal	6

* Boi (113).

Republic. About 10 states and union administrated territories do not have any such institutions or programmes for mentally handicapped children (113).

Most of these institutions for the mentally retarded are situated in metropolitan cities (Table 44).

Table 44

DISTRIBUTION OF INSTITUTIONS FOR MENTALLY RETARDED ACCORDING TO SIZE OF CITY*

Metropolitan cities	35
Large towns	7
Small towns	6
Villages	3

* Boi (113)

Table 45 and Table 46 indicate the type of these institutions and the type of facilities offered by them (113).

About 30% of such institutions are government aided, 20% are owned by the state or central government, the rest are being managed by private agencies. There are a limited number of seats available in these institutions, the fees charged by them are high, they are situated at distant places, and are mostly out of reach for a common man.

It has been observed that there are only four child guidance clinics up to 1950 (114), but during the last two decades there had been a rapid increase in the number of such clinics; approximately 65 such clinics are functioning at present. Almost all child guidance clinics are attached to medical colleges. Only about 40% of such clinics are running full time facilities for emotionally disturbed children, and still fewer are managed by trained psychiatrists and auxillary staff. Some of these child guidance clinics are providing domicillary services as well. The treatments given at such clinics are in the form of drugs, psychotherapy, play therapy, and guidance in vocational training.

CULTURALLY DETERMINED TREATMENTS

We have mentioned earlier that modern psychiatric understanding of emotional disorders in children is only of very recent origin in this country, consequently modern psychiatric

Table 45

CLASSIFICATION OF INSTITUTION ACCORDING TO NAME*

Homes	10
Hospitals	2
Medical Rehabilitation Institute	1
Occupational Therapy Centre	1
Special Schools	24
Special classes	2
Certified school	1
Vocational Training centres	2
Special Schools without specific indication	8
	51

Table 46

SHOWING THE KIND OF PROGRAMMES OFFERED BY INSTITUTIONS*

Types of programmes	No. of institutions
Clinical	10
Teacher training	3
Medical Rehabilitation	5
Education	39
Purely vocational training	1
Educational and vocational	11
Medical Rehabilitation and vocational	3
Educational and pre-vocational	16
Research	7
Psychotherapy	1
Care and medical treatment	2

* Boi (113).

facilities are located at very few centers, but still a vast majority of Indians are not aware of such facilities. However, such diseases always existed and have been handled by techniques which have established themselves as a part and parcel of this culture. In our culture emphasis is placed on "purification" and emotionally or physically ill patients were and are still being treated in *mandirs* (a) and *majars* (b) by Pandits (c), *ozha* (d) and *maulvi* (e) who can be categorised as "charm healers" and "faith healers." Somasundaram (115) has observed that some of the beliefs and customs prevailing amongst the modern men have their origins in the prehistoric times. Diseases were viewed as a result of malevolent influences exercised by a God or supernatural being, or by another human being, alive or dead. As such, the ill were proposed to be treated by those who are very "near" to God. Such methods of treatment were not only prevalent in India, but could be seen in Egypt and Greece. For example "Incubation" or "Temple sleep" was practised by ancient Egyptians, the temples were those of "Imphotep" the God of healing, the "Temple sleep" in the Asklepicia, the Greek God of healing.

In India among Hindus and Muslims, religion is very much alive and the place of worship continues to play an important role as the place of religious cure. Many such "temples" exist where fixed rituals are practised by Hindus for the cure of illnesses. Somasundaram (116) described such temples and rituals which are in the form of strenuous physical exercises, such as climbing, paradakshanams, etc., and are usually done on an empty stomach in Tamil Nadu in the South of India. It has been suggested that in addition to "faith" certain group factors such as interreaction between families with similar problems, also play an important role in clarifying doubts, strengthening the beliefs, and in the solution of emotional problems. Another important aspect of these temples is that they employ a method similar to the "total push", and patients are kept engaged almost continuously from morning until midnight. The rituals have been equated with modified insulin therapy by Somasundaram (115).

a = Temples   b = Muslim place of religious practice
c = Hindu priest   d = Faith healer   e = Muslim priest

Another such form of treatment is in the form of a "dip" or frequent baths in holy rivers, tanks or ponds spread through out the length and breadth of India. Each such tank or pond is "famous" for providing "cures" for a certain type of disorder. It has been thought that in addition to faith, and group reaction, such frequent baths had a physiological role in treatments like hydrotherapy (115).

A description of "Witch Doctors has been given by Singh (116). Such witch doctors can be found in almost all the "Indian tribes" although their methods of treatment may differ from each other. To free themselves from the diseases, tribal people propitiate the dieties and take the services of imposter-doctors, known as Gunia, Disari or Gurumai, who pretend to counteract the effects of black art. These witch doctors employ methods for diagnosis like going into a trance during which they are supposed to talk to God, by going through their book of *pangi* (a), by examining the fingers, and by examining the *kaudi* (b) brought by the patient. The method of treatment is that when ever a man, woman or a child falls ill, the village witch doctor will be consulted, who at first may administer some herbs to the sick. If the illness is not cured, he comes to the house of the patient, sits in a room, falls "unconscious" after a few minutes, and remains in a trance for some time. Later he sits up and behaves and speaks as if he is possessed. In the trance state he gives out the cause of illness and ascribes it to the existence of bones in a corner of the house, or to the failure to propitiate a certain God or to some devil or to some sorcery of an enemy of the patient. He proposes to remove the cause of some future day and orders the master of the family to have certain things for that day, a fowl being one of the items prescribed. On the appointed day, the witch-doctor visits the patient's house and recites some prayers in a tone and intonation deemed peculiarly suited to the occasion. If the illness is due to the devil, he ties a talisman around the neck or hand or the patient. If it is due to sorcery, he puts some red and yellow cooked rice in a bamboo dish with a light in the middle. The whole thing is taken out of the house and left where two roads cross.

a = Book of astrology   b = Special type of rice

The Gadaba witch-doctors have the following three methods for the treatment of the patient: (1) mantras and sueta (sacred thread); (2) herbal medicine, and (3) worship and sacrifices to the Gods and Goddesses. The Gadaba witch-doctors employ mantras for the treatment. Sometimes they write them on wood or leaf and tie it to the hand of the patient with the help of a thread. Along with these medical techniques, they also sacrifice pigs, hens, or goats to the Gods and Goddesses. Gadaba believes that by offering sacrifices and prayer they will please the dooma (witches), Gods and Goddesses.

As the sacrifices are made in front of the patient, the latter gets mental relief and assurance that by such acts the dooma will be pleased and will refrain from harming him in the future.

These methods seem to have some psychotherapeutic value to the patient. In most of the cases, the patients suffering from physical illness fail to get relief from these methods.

It is very interesting to note that in a well conducted and controlled study at one of such tribal villages, Singh (116) found that although Block hospitals have provided some of the modern medical facilities to the tribals, they were reluctant to avail of these facilities.

The method of *tantric* treatment, including *zhar-phuk* (reciting sacred words) and physically torturing mentally sick patients, needs some elaboration. This is done by the witch-doctor in certain groups of tribes to remove the evil spirit from the body of the patient. During the whole process, the witch doctor behaves with authority and the patient behaves as if he/she is possessed.

BIBLIOGRAPHY

1. Sethi, B. B. Future perspectives of Psychiatry in India. Unpublished, (1972).
2. Vaghbhata Ayurveda and Mental Health. All India Psychiatric Conference. Bangalore, (1974).
3. Ramachandra Rao, S. K. Mind in Distress. Bhela's View- All India Psychiatric Conference. Bangalore, (1974).
4. Venkoba Rao, A. *Indian J. Hist. Med. 11*, 2, (1966).
5. Subrahmanyam, H. S. Indian Philosophy and Psychiatry. All India Psychiatric Conference. Bangalore, (1974).
6. Kurup, P. N. V. Ayurveda and Mental Health - All India Psychiatric Conference. Bangalore, (1974).
7. Sethi, B. B. and Gupta, S. C. Psychiatry in India Unpublished, (1972).
8. Sethi, B. B., Thacore, V. R. and Gupta, S. C. *Amer. J. Psychother. 22*, 1, (1968).
9. Sethi, B. B., Sachdev, S. and Nag, D. *Amer. J. Psychother. 19*, 445, (1965).
10. Metrand, G. S. and Crouzet, F. *Studies in the Cultural History of India.* Shiva Lal Agarwal and Co, Agra, (1965).
11. Uttar Pradesh - a portrait of population. Census of India 1971. Govt. Press Aishbagh, Lucknow.
12. Srinivas, M.N. *Caste in Modern India.* Asia Publishing House, Bombay.
13. Gupta, S. C. and Sethi, B. B. *Indian J. Psychiat. 12*, 264, (1970).
14. Sethi, B. B., Gupta, S. C., Mahendru, R. K. and Kumari, P. *Brit. J. Psychiat. 124*, 243, (1974).
15. Sethi, B. B. and Gupta, S. C. *Amer. J. Psychother. 27*, 61, (1973).
16. Sethi, B. B., Gupta, S. C., Kumar, R., and Kumari, P. *Indian J. Psychiat. 14*, 183, (1972).
17. Marfatia, J. C. *Mentally Retarded Children - An Intensive Study of 100 Cases* Popular Prakashan, Bombay, (1972).

18. Teja, J. S., Malhotra, H. K. and Verma, S. K. *Indian J. Psychiat.* *14*, 207, (1972).
19. Jain, C. K., Kishore, B. and Manchanda, S. S. *Arch. Child Health 10*, 876, (1968).
20. Bassa, D. M. *Indian J. Psychiat.* *4*, 139, (1962).
21. Kishore, B., Jain, C. K. and Manchanda, S. S. *Indian J. Psychiat.* *14*, 213, (1972).
22. Bhaskaran, K. and Saxena B. M. *Indian J. Psychiat. 12*, 177, (1970).
23. Uday Shankar. *Problem Children.* Atma Ram and Sons, Delhi p. 22, (1958).
24. Ray Chauduri, A. K. *J. Nerv. Ment. Dis. 124*, 478, (1956).
25. Rao, S. *J. Nerv. Ment. Dis. 138*, 87, (1964).
26. Sundar Raj, M. and Rao, B. S. S. R. *Amer. J. Psychiat. 112*, 1127, (1966).
27. Teja, J. S. *Indian J. Psychiat.* *9*, 203, (1967).
28. Sethi, B. B. and Lal, N. Two years analysis of Child guidance clinic. Unpublished, (1974).
29. Sethi, B. B. and Lal, N. Psychiatric morbidity in children. Unpublished, (1974)
30. Malhotra, P. A Study of morbidity In Children Below 5 years in Delhi. Doctoral Thesis. K. G.'s. Medical College, Lucknow University, Lucknow. (1964).
31. Singhal, G. K. A Study of Morbidity In Children Under 5 years. Age Group In villages Around Experimental Teachings Health Sub-Centre Banthara, Lucknow. Doctoral Thesis. K. G.'s. Medical College, Lucknow University, Lucknow. (1971).
32. Mukherjee, S. and Mukherjee, S. N. *Indian J. Pediat. 38*, 389, (1971).
33. Millis, H. *Ann. Human Genet. 22*, 362, (1958).
34. Venkatacholam, P. S. *Bull. W. H. O. 26*, 193, (1962).
35. Sen, M. *Indian J. Pediat. 20*, 67, (1953).
36. Koshi, E. T., Prasad, B. G., Jain, V. C. and Bhushan, V. *Indian J. Med. Res. 58*, 1742, (1970).
37. Indian Council of Medical Research. Special Report Series No. 36= Review of Nutrition Survey carried out in India, Indian Council of Medical Research, New Delhi, (1964).

38. Khanna, K. K. *Indian J. Pediat.* *37*, 275, (1970).
39. Gopalan, C. *J. Pediat.* *57*, 89, (1960).
40. Gopalan, C., Balasubramanian, S. C., Ramasastri, B. V. and Rao, V. K. *Diet Atlas of India.* National Institute of Nutrition, Hyderabad, (1969).
41. Banik, N. D. D., Krishna, R., Mane, S. I. S. and Raj, L. *Indian J. Pediat.* *38*, 147, (1971).
42. Rao, S. K., Swaminathan, M. C., Swarup, S. and Patwardhan, V. N. Bull. W. H. O. *20*, 603, (1959).
43. Sharma, R. G. *Indian J. Psychiat.* *15*, 272, (1973).
44. Mac Gregor, E. F. *J. Amer. Med. Ass.* *210*, 17, (1969).
45. I. C. M. R. Growth and Physical development of Indian Infant and children. Part I-II Statistics Division. Indian Council of Medical Research, New Delhi, (1968).
46. Ghosh, L., Sen. M., and Chandrasekhar, S. *Indian J. Pediat.* *11*, 1, (1944).
47. Rao, M. N., and Bhattacharjee, B. *Indian J. Pediat.* *19*, 1, (1952).
48. Paul, S. S. and Ahluwalia, D. *Indian J. Child Health* *6*, 363, (1957).
49. Chopra, D. R. and Speetjens, A. *Burma Med. J.* *11*, 225, (1963).
50. Arora, S., Rajeshwara, Rao, N. and Radhakrishan Rao, M. V. *Indian J. Child Health* *12*, 612, (1963)
51. Singh, R. and Venkatachalam, P. S. *Indian J. Med. Res.* *50*, 494, (1962).
52. Kalra, K., Kishore, N. and Dayal, R. S. *Indian J. Pediat.* *34*, 73, (1967).
53. Achar, S. T. and Yankauer, A. *Indian J. child Health* *11*, 157, (1962).
54. Pathak, P. *Indian Pediat.* *6*, 18, (1969).
55. Kandoth, W. K., Sonnad, L. and Athavale, V. B. *Indian Pediat.* *8*, 176, (1971).
56. Patel, N. V. and Kaul, K. K. *Indian Pediat.* *8*, 443, (1971).
57. Das, V. K. and Sharma, N. L. *Indian J. Pediat.* *40*, (1973).
58. Sethi, B. B., Agarwal, S. S. and Gupta, A. K. Genetic aspects of mental retardation. Unpublished.
59. Teja, J. S., Shah, D. K. and Verma, S. K. *Indian J. Ment. Retardation* *3*, 75, (1970).

60. Sethi, B. B., Gupta, S. C. and Kumar, R. *Indian J. psychiat.* *9,* 280, (1967).

61. Sethi, B. B., Gupta, S. C., Mahendru, R. K. and Kumari, P. *Indian J. Psychiat.* *14,* 115, (1972).

62. Sethi, B. B. and Gupta, S. C. *Indian J. Psychiat.* *12,* 13, (1970).

63. Dube, K. C. *Acta Psychiat. Scand.* *46,* 327, (1970).

64. Elnager, M. N., Maitre, P. and Rao, M. N. *Brit. J. Psychiat.* *118,* 499, (1971).

65. Dube, K. C. *Soc. Psychiat.* *3,* 4, (1967).

66. Dube, K. C. *Indian J. Psychiat.* *4,* 11, (1964).

67. Verghese, A. and Beig, A. *Indian J. Psychiat. 16,* 1, (1974).

68. Gupta, S. C. *Indian J. Mental Retardation 3,* 69, (1970).

69. Mahendru, R. K., Gupta, S. C., Agarwal, A. K. and Sethi, B. B. *Indian J. Psychiat.* *12,* 238, (1970).

70. Thacore, V. R., Gupta, S. C. and Suraiya, M. *Indian J. Psychiat.* *13,* 253, (1971).

71. Thacore, V. R. *Mental Illness in An Urban Community 1973.* United Publishers, Allahabad.

72. Marfatia, J. C. Psychiatric Problems of Children. Third Edition Popular Prakashan, Bombay, (1974).

73. Sethi, B. B., Gupta, S. C. and Agarwal, S. S. A Psychosocial Study of Delinquents with Special Reference to Aggression Personal communication, (1973).

74. Tandon, A. K. A Psychosocial study of Juvenile Delinquency. Doctoral thesis. K. G.'s. Medical College, Lucknow University, Lucknow, (1973).

75. Sethi, N., Gupta, S. C., Sethi, B. B. and Agarwal, S. S. Genetic Studies In Juvenile Delinquency. Paper presented at Ist Annual Conference of Indian Society of Human Genetics, Bombay, (1974).

76. Statistics - Annual report 1965 Nur Manzil Psychiatric Centre, Lucknow. *Indian J. Psychiat.* *3,* 328.

77. Malin, S. *J. Rehabil. 1,* 32, (1968).

78. Marfatia, J. C. Mental Deficiency. Report of the First all India Conference on Mental Retardation. p. 12-28: Federation for welfare of the mentally retarded (India) C/0 Model School, Kasturba Niketan, Lajpat Nagar, New Delhi, (1966).

79. Jaya Nagaraja *Indian J. Psychiat.* *8*, 291, (1966).

80. Jaya Nagaraja The mentally retarded - A Review. Report of the first all India Conference on mental retardation. p-48-51, Federation for welfare of the mentally retarded (India) C/o Model School Kasturba Niketan, Lajpat Nagar, New Delhi, (1966).

81. Indian Council of Medical Research, Bulletin (1972) - Vol. No. 2 Mental Retardation Page 3. Ed. Dr. S. L. Bhatia: Research information Bulletin - Division of Publication & Information, Ansari, Nagar, New Delhi-16.

82. Sarda, Menon, M., Shamuga Sundaram, E. R. B. and Somasundaram, O. *Indian Council Med. Res. Bull.* *2*, 7, (1972).

83. Indian Council of Medical Research -(1972): Brain damage and Psychological Performance. Indian Council of Medical Research Bulletin. 2; 5.

84. Bhaskaran, K. and Shukla, T. R. *Indian Council Med. Res. Bull.* *2*, 8, (1972).

85. Venkoba Rao, A., Krishna Murthy, K. A. and Bhaskaran Rao, K., *Indian Council Med. Res. Bull.* *2*, 9, (1972).

86. Kanner, L. *Child Psychiatry.* Charles C. Thomas, Springfield, (1966).

87. Manchanda, S. S., Kishore, B., Jain, C. K., Singh, G. and Kashyap, U. B. *Indian Pediat.* *6*, 538, (1969).

88. Dutta Ray, S. and Mathur, S. B. *Indian J. Psychiat.* *8*, 82, (1966).

89. Bassa, D. M. *Indian J. Psychiat.* *8*, 114, (1966).

90. Saroja Bai, B. K. *Indian J. Psychiat.* *8*, 299, (1966).

91. Verma, L. P., Srivastava, D. K. and Sahay, R. N. *Indian J. Psychiat.* *12*, 58, (1970).

92. Teja, J. S., Khanna, B. C. and Subrahmaniam. *Indian J. Psychiat.* *12*, 71, (1970).

93. Malhotra, H. K., Khanna, B. C. and Verma, S. K. *Indian J. Psychiat.* *15*, 49, (1973).

94. DeSouza, A., Parekh, H. C. and Doongaji, D. R. *Indian J. Psychiat.* *9*, 1, (1967).

95. Nigam, P., Tandon, V. K., Lal, N. and Thacore, V. R. *Indian J. Pediat.* *40*, 180, (1973).

96. Singh, M. V., Saini, L. and Paliwal, T. R. *Indian J. Psychiat.* *16*, 131, (1974).

97. Sridhara Rama Rao, B. S., Narayanan, H. S., Channa-basavanna, S. M., Subhash, M. N. and Narayana Reddy G. N. *Indian J. Psychiat.* *16*, 136, (1974).
98. Centerwall, W. R. and Itteyerah, T. R. *Lancet* *2*, 193, (1966).
99. Joshua, G., John, E. and Jadar, M. *Indian Pediat.* *5*, 382, (1968).
100. Chandra, P., Trhirupuram, S. and Raju, B. V. *Indian Pediat.* *5*, 177, (1968).
101. Verma, I. C. and Sinclair, S. *Indian J. Pediat.* *37*, 265, (1970).
102. Srikantiah, S. G., Venkatachalam, P. S. and Reddy, V. *Lancet* *1*, 282, (1964).
103. Nair, K. P. B. and Rao, B. S. S. *Indian Pediat.* *38*, 375, (1971).
104. Abraham, J., Chakrapani, B., Singh, M., Kokrady, S. and Baccahawat, B. K. *Indian J. Med. Res.* *57*, 1761, (1969).
105. Jaya Nagaraja *Indian J. Psychiat.* *8*, 220, (1966).
106. Satyavathi, K. and Murti Rao, D. L. N. *Trans. All India Inst. Ment. Health* *2*, 1, (1961).
107. Ganapathi, M. N. and Venkoba Rao, A. *J. Indian Med. Ass.* *46*, 18, (1966).
108. Venkoba Rao, A. and Chinnian, R. R. *Indian J. Psychiat.* *4*, 389, (1972).
109. Jayashankarappa, B. S. and Prasada Rao, D. C. V. *Indian J. Psychiat.* *38*, 265, (1971).
110. Pareek, U. and Venkateswara Rao, T. Motivation training for mental health I. C. M. R. Bulletin p. 7 Ed. Bhatia, S.L. Division of Publication and Information, Ansari Nagar, New Delhi, (1972).
111. Wig, N. N. and Singh, G. *Indian J. Psychiat.* *9*, 158, (1967).
112. Kulkarni, V. M. Mental retardation: A General Review. Mental Retardation in India, Report of the first all India Conference on mental retardation. Federation for the welfare of Mentally Retarded; c/o Model School, Kasturba Niketan, Lajpat Nagar, New Delhi, (1966).
113. Boi, G. K. Institutions for the mentally retarded. Mental retardation In India. Report of the first all India Confer-

ence on Mental Retardation. Federation for welfare of the mentally retarded, Model School, Kasturba Niketan Lajpat Nagar, New Delhi, (1966).

114. Singh, M. V. *Indian J. Pediat.* *38*, 272, (1971).
115. Somasundaram, O. *Indian J. Psychiat.* *15*, 38, (1973).
116. Singh, V. K. *Indian J. Psychiat.* *15*, 358, (1973).

MENTAL HEALTH IN CHILDREN, Volume I
Edited By D. V. Siva Sankar
Copyright © 1975 by
PJD Publications Ltd., Westbury, N.Y.

CAN NEONATE SLEEP PATTERNING BE USED AS AN AID IN UNDERSTANDING AND PREVENTING SCHIZOPHRENIA OR OTHER CHILDHOOD PSYCHOPATHOLOGY?

James Minard

New Jersey Medical School
Newark, New Jersey

If childhood psychopathology is to be prevented and its origins are to be understood, the infant must be studied. In this study, the optimal time may be the neonate period, when both mother and infant are usually together under medical supervision. The most prominent neonate activity is sleep, but its study has often been avoided because of theoretical and methodological difficulties. However, a consideration of current, neurophysiologically based theory, methods of sleep research, and already obtained results indicate that these difficulties may be surmounted. Schizophrenia is of special interest, not only because children may develop obvious pathology or because Bleuler wrote of schizophrenic infants, but also because of increasing evidence that the adult psychosis has its roots in genetic characteristics of the infant interacting with characteristics of the childhood environment which prove pathological for the particular individual.

THE BASIS FOR SCHIZOPHRENIA IN NEURO-
PHYSIOLOGICAL PATTERNING

When the concept of schizophrenia was being formulated, Freud had already failed in attempting a neurophysiological theory of personality, and Bleuler wished for knowledge of the "primary symptoms" of the "cerebral disease" he named schozophrenia, but the physiology of their time was too simple and psychology separated structure from function. About ten years ago, a review of the literature on schizophrenia led me to the belief that a basis for schizophrenia was to be found in the neurophysiological basis for the perception and thought developed during childhood and early adolescence. Hebb and others have described neurophysiologically based psychological theories. Such a view does not discount double bind situations or other social causation. However, social variables might be regarded as more distal causes of distorted thought and perception when compared with the neurophysiological basis for these processes. Bio-chemistry might be regarded as an integral part of this basis.

Donald Hebb (1) described a basis for perception and thought in a psychological theory using widely known neurophysiological concepts. Essentially, Hebb stated that genetics and experience could create sequentially patterned linkages between neurons (that is to say, an increased readiness for one neuron to fire another) in an organized sequence of many neurons serving to represent external stimulus patterns, sequences of images or sequences of ideas. He called these "cell assemblies" and "phase sequences." Phase sequences consisted of temporally and spatially organized cell assemblies. They provided a basis for the process of attention. Since Hebb wrote during an era of learning theory and allowed for change with experience, texts describing his theory recognize that he described how experience might establish reverberating neuronal circuits but fail to recognize the role he gave to genetic influences (2).

Another deficiency in nearly all accounts of Hebb's theory was failure to recognize that motor neurons were an essential part of his hypothesized representative process, especially when these processes were new. Despite misunderstandings, Hebb's theory was extremely influential, more general than "special purpose" theories such as Hull's and saw elaboration in interesting work such as studies of stimulus novelty, emotion, and the original studies of sensory deprivation. The imagery of sensory deprivation and of dreams of rem sleep are phenomena well in accord with Hebb's concept of an active brain with experientially organized neuronal connections.

In the recent book, *Languages of the Brain,* Pribram (3) gives to the neuron's synaptic spaces, to what he calls the "junctional microstructure," the same intense theoretical attention Hebb gave to neurons themselves. Pribram uses this junctional microstructure to describe how the brain might create holograms, those remarkable representative processes able to create realistic three dimensional images even after parts of the hologram have been destroyed.

The emphasis Pribram and Hebb gave to neurons was given by Jacobsen to muscle fibers in his account of thinking (4) For Jacobsen, the body's millions of muscle fibers are instruments in a complex orchestra of imagery, thought and feeling, directed by the brain's representative process. Essentially, he holds that it is easier to comprehend the orchestra than the activities of its conductor. Using amplifiers more sensitive than those commercially available, he has gathered data clearly suggesting all central representative processes have peripheral representation.

Each of these three theories attempts to provide a complete account, yet they are not inconsistent with each other and may all be necessary to account completely for the facts of normal and abnormal mental function as its basis is present in neuronal organization, motor coordination or tension. After all, one theory deals with muscles, one with neurons controlling muscles and one with the spaces through which the neurons communicate. These theories, and other theories guided by neurophysiology, make it clear that if the brain is to provide an adequate basis for perception and thought, if it is to allow function without tensions and discontrol, it must be capable of producing a high degree of patterning. *Search for a neurophysiological basis of schizophrenic disorder of perception and thought must include a search for disorder of the brain's capacity to produce patterning.*

EVIDENCE FOR NEUROPHYSIOLOGICAL PATTERNING IN SLEEP

Unfortunately, conventional research methodology allows sleep to show relatively little patterning. The conventional approach is now exemplified in hundreds of studies and in the *Manual of Standardized Terminology, Techniques and Scoring System for Sleep Stages of Human Subjects* (5).

This methodology consists largely of classifying the data of a sleep study into five categories, usually five sleep stage percentages, after research which may require seven nights of continuous psychophysiological monitoring before even baseline data are obtained. Rarely have such elephantine research labors birthed such a tsetse fly of data.

Stage-to-stage changes do show some patterning. However, the emphasis on sleep stage percent arose in part because early investigators complained that subjects could not be individually identified on the basis of charts showing stage-to-stage shifts, whereas sleep stage percents were sometimes found to be associated with interesting clinical variables.

Despite a strong emphasis on stage rem associated with dreaming in the adult, and some evidence for its disruption in schizophrenia, the bulk of sleep work in schizophrenia indicated that this disorder was associated with disruption of the non-rem stages of sleep, particularly stage IV, characterized by at least 50% delta (high amplitude slow EEG). Stage III has 20-50% delta and is not always distinguished from IV in research or theory. These delta EEG sleep stages are also characterized by a lack of rapid eye movement activity, presence of general muscle tonus, and regular respiration. It is these stages which are absent in the depressed, the senile, and the decerebrate. They are undeveloped in the neonate. Some of the more interesting reports of stage IV lack in schizophrenics are to be found in the Lafayette Clinic reports showing correlation between delta EEG sleep deficiency and a biochemical abnormality associated with schizophrenia but affected by exercise. Other reports include those of Feinberg, Itil, Kunugi, Kupter, Larry, and others as reviewed by Broughton and others (6). Mirsky (7) used research with adult schizophrenics' sleep as part of his basis for inferring that the neurophysiological basis for schizophrenia was mesodiencephalic hyperactivity cortically damped during development.

Broughton (8) has summarized evidence showing that the more bizarre sleep phenomena such as sleep walking and intense night terror have their origin, not in psychological response to the imagery of dreaming rem sleep, but to simple arousal during non-rem sleep. This arousal may be triggered by a response to noise, which may have its basis in auditory hypersensitivity. In night terrors, the direct experiential consequences of arousal may become elaborated as rem sleep is stormed through on the way to wakefulness. Dream imagery and hypnopompic hallucinations may contribute to the experience and (when the muscular inhibition of rem sleep occurred prior to wakefulness) there may be misinterpretation of the normal physiological inhibition of all muscles which sometimes persists for a while after an arousal. Night terror is most frightening when it is an experience of the real world while in a state of partial arousal. Unlike simple drowsiness, the semi-aroused state is inappropriate and unfamiliar. The elaborate, truly terrifying quality of the experience of night terror and its psychological complexity when examined after the event are all in marked contrast to the simplicity of its origin. We have wondered if schizophrenia is also a complex semi-aroused state, one improved by tranquilizers partly because they convert it to drowsiness.

Simply standing some people on their feet during non-rem sleep will cause them to sleep walk. When I am asked to help with a problem of sleep walking or night terror, I have recommended that the sleeper be thoroughly tucked in in a way that shows respect but provides restraint and have suggested several techniques of noise control. Whatever the results of further exploration in this area, we do have enough evidence from the research at hand to conclude that non-rem delta EEG sleep is important, that its absence or disruption is related to clinically significant differences in behaviour and that, in particular, it is more likely than most sleep states to be disrupted or absent in adult schizophrenics.

In a film (9), in related papers, and in grant proposals, Dr. Donald Coleman, and other collaborators and I have proposed first, that sleep is not one thing (10, 11, 12) and certainly not the passive state it was once thought to be, but rather is an organized pattern of different states composed of disparate phenomena partially controlled by interacting pacemakers or centers of neuronal activity serving to time physiological activity and behavior during sleep. These pacemakers are assumed to control one another in initiating organized sequences of central and peripheral activity.

Jouvet, Dement and others have by now thoroughly demolished the once prevalent idea that sleep is one passive state. Even after most of their data were available, Hernandez Peon once clung to the parsimony of the concept that sleep was a single process, but even he and his followers agreed with data showing the rem state to be more different from the non-rem state than sleep is from wakefulness.

Our belief in pacemaking centers is also supported by data. Jouvet has combined elegant neurosurgery with a histo-fluorescent approach to the biochemistry of small regions of the brainstem and provided enough data on the raphe nuclei, locus coeruleus and other brainstem areas to make their functional specialization evident (13,14), although for us and other researchers he has not disproved the possibility of an ascending hierarchy of control similar to that known to exist for respiration. For non-rem sleep, Jouvet's own research indicates the cortex is important, but, in general, he has held that pacemakers such as the raphe nuclei are "the pianist" while higher centers are "the piano" (15). We differed from most by believing that the various sleep states were each composed of heterogeneous phenomena with differing psychological signi-ficance, but we do maintain that, in some research, it may even be unwise to assume all neonate rapid eye movements have the same significance (12, 16). Others have held a related view (17).

We were on the most uncertain ground when we said sleep was patterned. A high degree of individual patterning was not evident from adult records studied by conventional procedures, or for that matter from any records of any organism being studied around 1965. This may be due in part to the reluctance of researchers to directly observe sleeping adults. Fortunately, we shifted from studying adults to studying healthy, term newborn and they have tolerance of direct observation absent in adults. We found that, in a quiet room, behavior such as the spontaneous startle of quiet sleep would fire off with its own autonomous rhythm, a rhythm which was rather constant for each infant in our sample, although there were differences from infant to infant (9). Filmed at high speed, the startle proved beautifully organized, with all visible body parts abruptly and spontaneously snapping into a startle-like contraction fast enough to be missed during an eye blink, then snapping out in a Moro-like termination which produced a hand tremor at the end because of the vigor with which the hands were flung outward. We found that the sharp onset of movement artifact on our physiological records allowed rather accurate timing of this response.

Gregory Williams (18) participated in an analysis of infant quiet non-rem sleep recordings showing the evenly spaced bursts of relatively high amplitude, delta-containing EEG punctuating the lower-amplitude EEG about every 7-10 seconds in an EEG "tracé alternant". This EEG was disrupted by startles every 2-4 minutes. As we had anticipated, but had not told Mr. Williams, the startles of these well-organized term newborn often occurred when a burst of EEG would normally be expected. Both simple visual inspection (9) and objective statistics supported this impression of rhythmic coordination between an EEG phenomena and behavior.

Interestingly, the startle was not always autonomous since, if present, noise or jarring movement could elicit a startle similar to those occurring spontaneously. Quiet sleep of normal, term infants is also characterized by regular respiration and an almost complete absense of the many movements characterizing active, rem sleep. On the whole, in the normal term neonate, quiet non-rem sleep is an impressively controlled, regular state giving many evidences of centrally mediated patterning.

The quiet, non-rem sleep of the neonate, which contains some delta frequency EEG, seems likely to be showing a part of the capacity necessary for development of the delta stages of adult non-rem sleep. In both adult delta and infant quiet sleep, all spontaneous movement is reduced and respiration becomes regular. Neonate quiet sleep is sometimes called "regular sleep." Because of the impressive evidence of regularity, control and patterning provided by quiet sleep, and because of neurophysiologically based psychological theory such as that of Hebb, Pribram and Jacobsen, we were not surprised when the experienced pediatrician and sleep researcher, Arthur Parmalee(19) suggested quiet sleep also showed evidence of the neurophysiologic basis one would expect to be necessary for development of the process of attention.

The cell assemblies and phase sequences of Hebb are, fundamentally, timing mechanisms as well as a hypothesized basis for perception, thought and attention; quiet, non-rem sleep of the neonate obviously requires rhythmic timing. The capacity for rhythmic timing of brain activity in selected areas may serve as a sort of "scaffolding", a necessary precursor to the orderly development of organized neuronal activity accurately representing experience or providing a basis for thought. Incidentally, especially when one considers Hebb's inclusion of motor neurons and genetic influences, phase sequences are not unlike the "schema" (20) of Piaget. The theories of Hebb and Piaget mesh in a way which makes each more convincing. Piaget tells how behavior develops, Hebb tells why and each provides an abundance of measures related to important variables.

Without precise timing, Jacobsen's orchestra-like coordination of musculature would disintegrate into conflict and chaos; without timing of the sequencing of incoming information, input would be too disorderly to permit the accurate construction of Pribram's holograms.

In addition to showing a capacity which may be essential during the future development of attention, the regularity of quiet sleep may show a capacity important in keeping psychological disturbance at a reasonable level. It is well known that rhythmic stimulation calms. Rhythmic stimulation of course implies rhythmic brain activity in selected areas, and the statement that "rhythmic stimulation calms" is a statement implying that certain rhythmic brain activity calms. The selective, rhythmic organization shown during quiet sleep may be available to contribute to calmness during wakefulness. We assume that, in general, the same brain is present during sleep and wakefulness, like a partially hard-wired computer able to run at least two types of programs.

REM sleep is not characterized by so much regularity of EEG and behavior. It is characterized by abrupt, coordinated shifts of eye position (21). The EEG may be relatively lower in amplitude and always lacks the tracé alternant indicative of quiet non-rem sleep. Respiration is irregular. Periodically, movements and expressions over-ride a general inhibition of muscle tonus. We have timed the coordination of the eyes and find the typical neonate moving them within a millisecond of each other hundreds of times during each period of inter-feeding sleep. While developing a rem detector we found the intentional eye movements of waking adults were often unable to duplicate this remarkable display of inborn coordination by the sleeping neonate.

Theories equating rem sleep with dreaming are un-convincing when applied to the infant, so other attempts have been made to cenceptualize the functional significance of neonate rem sleep. On the basis of several considerations, Dewan hypothesized that rem sleep served a "programming" function, that it was especially well suited for setting up the general procedures for coping with new situations (22). Newborn obviously have more programming to do than mature organisms. The programming hypothesis fits with the fact that newborn generally have substantially more rem sleep than adults, and animals which must learn have more than instinctive,"fixed program" species. In one study supporting the programming hypothesis, wearing distorted lenses during wakefulness increased the rem sleep of normal college students during the period of adaption to distortion (22, 23). However, simply restricting eye movements during wakefulness, a necessary consequence of most arrangements for wearing distorting lenses, may change rem frequency. Berger (24) found that when monkeys were conditioned to *low* rates of waking eye movements they showed an abundance of rem during sleep. Conversely, higher rates during wakefulness were associated with lower rates during sleep. We found that in our normal term neonates, both total rem and the rem rate declined significantly day-by-day during the first five days (16, 25). Berger's experimental results indicate infants may have shown declining rem because their waking eye movement was increasing.

We hypothesized that, in the neonate, the multivariable rem sleep state may have a programming function, as in the adult, but that the eye movement itself has functional significance which changes with maturation. We hypothesized that rem is initially a demonstration of the inborn neuro-physiological and muscular basis for visual fixation, shift of fixation, and visual following necessary for subsequent orderly construction of central nervous system processes representing visual objects.

We believe that, as objects of the visual world are represented within the nervous system, the neurons responsible for spontaneous rem become a part of more stable neuronal organizations, reducing their spontaneous firing and replacing it with firing triggered by activation of the more stable, larger organization (10). (In terms of Hebb's theory and Jouvet's data, cell assemblies involving neurons in the pontine and geniculate regions might enter phase sequences allowing a greater role to visual cortex.) Research by Petre-Quadens indicates the development of inhibition, presumably cortical inhibition, has its greatest effect on those rem which are closely spaced into "bursts." With them, she has found evidence for rem reduction (17). We hypothesize that, at birth, rem shows a *capacity* for perceptual development; subsequently, at least some rem probably show the *consequences* of perceptual development. In the adult, but not in the neonate, rem may scan dream stimuli. However, even when perceptual representations are developed, the eyes would not usually be expected to sketch out either perceived or hallucinated objects.

The *perceptual-development interpretation of neonate rem*, proposed above, received further experimental support as a consequence of work designed to better reveal overall sleep patterning and to develop more practical measures.

As a way of depicting overall patterning we first proposed individual cumulative recording of rem (9, 16, 21). A cumulative record for a sleeping neonate originally consisted of a line moving to the right as time passed and upward with each rem. In this form it shows both rem periods and intervals between each pair of eye movements. However, this presented too much data for our use at that time and was impractical for hand counted rem, so we adopted the practice of cumulating rem at the end of each minute. These records showed the clear-cut patterning characterized neonate sleep. They indicated that much of the day-to-day rem reduction occurred in the initial rem period, a sleep onset period not found in adults under normal circumstances.

We also found that it was efficient and reliable to observe directly the earliest eye movements after lid closure, timing the period from initial lid closure to them (26, 27). We called this measure the latency of observed eye movement or "loem." In several different samples of newborn, each observed by a different person, we found, as our rem frequencies and cumulative records suggested that loem increased day by day. This, of course, is consistent with a decline in sleep onset rem and has the advantage that no recording apparatus is attached to the infant. One of those who observed day to day loem increase was Dr. Evelyn McElroy. She, Dr. Thomas Kinney and I worked out a downward extension of scales designed to measure object representation in the older infant, essentially measures of stimulus fixation, following, and fixation on the place where a visual stimulus had disappeared. In a pilot study for her dissertation McElroy found this scale correlated with loem in the expected positive direction (28). In her subsequent dissertation, using another observer to measure loem and prevent experimenter bias, McElroy again obtained this finding (29). The correlation between loem and waking eye movement was present even when either age or a neurological estimate of age was partialled out, although loem correlated with each measure.

The studies by McElroy are the first to demonstrate a relationship between day-to-day changes in rem and day-to-day changes in behavior which may be important to the task of developing perception. The relationship is *not* between perception and the percentage of the multivariable stage-rem sleep. We have been unable to find evidence that percent stage rem changes in the early days of life, although it does gradually reduce to the adult percentage in subsequent months.

THE RELATIONSHIP OF NEONATAL SLEEP TO SCHIZOPHRENIA AND OTHER PSYCHOPATHOLOGY

We hypothesized that neonates of schizophrenics would show deficiencies in the organized patterning evidenced by sleep. Bleuler made splitting of psychological functioning central to the diagnosis of schizophrenia. Neurophysiologically based theories of psychological function indicated such splitting may be evident in neonate coordination of muscular patterns and the maintenance of psychophysiological state. We thought this disruption of neonate organization might have three causes: First, in some cases, there might be a transmitted genetic basis for deficiencies in the process of perception and thought. This genetic basis is very probably much more common in the human population than is the socially and personally destructive phenotype of eventually diagnosed schizophrenic psychosis. Identical twin research, while adding to the evidence that genetic factors contribute to increased incidence of schizophrenia, proves conclusively that one can have the same genes as a schizophrenic but not have a diagnosable form of the psychosis.

A second possible cause of deficiencies in organized patterning would be abnormal, perhaps psychotomimetic, metabolites in the mother's bloodstream. So long as these could pass the placental barrier, they might affect the relatively tiny neonate nervous system even if they were not able to make the substantially larger mother actively psychotic.

A third cause would be a difference based on behavioral or perinatal factors. To cite one often ignored variable, we know relatively little about consequences of the amount, timing and coordination of maternal movement, but it seems reasonable to suppose it may have effects on development of the basis for neonate function.

Of the three causes described here, only the first would be expected in the infant of a normal mother and a schizophrenic father. The second should be related to some metabolite present on the cord blood and the third to controllable or at least observable perinatal variables. Sometimes these variables can even be manipulated.

Experimentally, results have already indicated that the patterning of the spontaneous startle is unusual in each baby of a group of six clearly, severely schizophrenic mothers (30). Such a sequence is, of course, statistically significant for the population the sample represents. Spontaneous startles in newborn of schizophrenics were fragmented, flaccid, and grouped, rather than regularly periodic.

For replication of these observations, premature infants should not be used and the startle should have the form shown in our film except for the described distortions. It should occur within quiet sleep and be related as we have described to the bursts of high amplitude waves of a tracé alternant if it is present. Fragments can involve any limb or even the head. Posture must be carefully reported. Observations which do not follow these criteria will include phenomena characteristic of the premature, or fine and gross movements which should not be called startles. Such movements usually occur during rem or during a premature infant's indeterminant sleep. They have a slower onset, often lack the adduction-abduction form of the startle and are not related to the trace. Well developed startles have a characteristic sound and can typically be validated by artifact on the polygraph records. Presently we are replicating these observations in Baltimore and Newark, locations chosen because we believe rather different populations of schizophrenics will be sampled. A part of this Baltimore-Newark study will be development of a more complete film definition of the various forms of startle.

Conventional procedures of sleep stage scoring must be modified when they are applied to unusual infants. When records from five newborn of schizophrenics were scored blindly by research assistants using our film, the infant sleep scoring manual, and the modifications we devised, we found about half the quiet sleep in the neonates of clearly, severely schizophrenic mothers as we did in those of a varied control group studied and scored in the same manner (30). Variation within the control group was unimpressive and overlap of the groups was slight, even though our control group included babies of nonschizophrenic psychiatric patients who had been medicated and treated as if they were schizophrenic. It also included typical neonates and natural childbirth infants. A significant difference was present on both the first and third nights after birth. The records were rescored by an experienced scorer concerned only with quiet sleep with finding all the quiet sleep he possibly could. This slightly increased the quiet sleep and slightly reduced the group differences, though not significantly.

The group difference lay in the initiation of quiet sleep periods since average duration of a given quiet sleep period did *not* differ between the two groups, when we considered only those periods of quiet sleep which did occur. We cannot attribute differences to total sleep time; total sleep time did not differ between the groups, somewhat to our surprise.

Rem frequency and rem rate are labile variables sensitive to medication, stress, unusual sleeping conditions and, very possibly, to hypothyroidism and certain other hormonal or biochemical abnormalities. Neither rem rate nor rem frequency showed a group difference.

Essentially, the reduced quiet non-rem sleep in neonates replicates results reported for adult schizophrenics, except that the reduction is in a precursor of non-rem,delta EEG sleep as found in neonates of schizophrenics rather than in the delta EEG sleep of the schizophrenics themselves. A research assistant on this project, Mr. Tony Ritz, observed a theta frequency sawtooth in the EEGs of blindly scored records. This proved significantly related to maternal schizophrenia (30) but, at present, we have no theoretical basis or experimental support for the finding.

During the course of the research described here, a number of observations have been made which are relevant to problems other than schizophrenia. Three times we have seen reversal of the usual day-to-day decline in rem of neonates whose mothers were maintained on high doses of phenothiazine type tranquilizers. In one case, the infant subsequently had jaundice severe enough to require retention in the hospital and treatment. In another case, studied by reliable observational techniques, the latency of observed eye movement was a remarkable 45 minutes, when observed 12 hours after birth (26, 27). This is the longest latency of observed eye movement we have ever seen in any infant, at least 10 times the duration one would expect. During subsequent days loem shortened to essentially zero. This infant was described by a pediatric neurologist as showing opisthotonus. Both opisthotonus and jaundice are known side effects of excessive doses of the medication used. Others have reported confirming findings (31).

Nearly any medication given in high dosage is very apt to have the initial effect of rem suppression, then, when medication is withdrawn, a "rebound" increase in rem over baseline levels will occur. Rem frequency is a more sensitive measure of rebound than the multi-variable stage-rem sleep. In the two cases in which rem could be counted, the "rebound" frequency was about three times that of the initial frequency. There is some reason to suspect that neonates who show rebound do not have genetic basis for future schizophrenia (6).

The overall patterning of the cumulative rem record has thus far *not* shown distinctive characteristics associated with maternal schizophrenia. However this may be due to the inadequacy of present methods for comparison of cumulative records. Maternal tranquilization has not proved related to reduced quiet sleep.

When infants sleep with and without normal nursery noise, most appear to show few consistent effects. One, however, showed virtual abolition of rem under the noisy conditions although observed sleep was not otherwise affected. At eight days, results were even more striking. At this time no abnormality was suspected, but at 3 months the infant was diagnosed hyperactive and the diagnosis was confirmed at one year.

In general, we believe an infant is suspect if it has an unusually low frequency of rem in comparison with the usual infant studied under a given set of conditions. Drug effects, hypothyroidism, and hypersensitivity to noise are among the detectable causes which might be considered. In each case, if suspicion is verified, benign measures are available which may serve to prevent future disorder.

CONTRIBUTIONS OF NEONATE SLEEP RESEARCH

Neonate sleep research has the advantage that results cannot be attributed so readily to psychological interpretation of the experimental situation by the subject. The adult psychotic undoubtedly experiences some changes in sleep because of a psychotic interpretation of a physiologically monitored sleep experiment. During wakefulness, the problem of situational effects is even more severe. The pre-psychotic teenager or even the pre-psychotic three-year-old may show an altered emotionality in an experimental situation. For example, he may make a pre-psychotic interpretation of a situation in which shock is used to elicit a GSR. Such situationally determined effects may not wholly explain specific data of interest in past research, but they cloud its meaning. Such clouding is reduced when the measure is sleep and the subject is a neonate inexperienced in making even the most simple inferences about situations. However, to obtain useful data from sleeping neonates, conventional sleep-stage scoring seems insufficient, since it does not display patterning or allow observation of phenomena like those reported here. Conventional procedures were designed for normal, term neonates, as available manuals state.

Figure 1

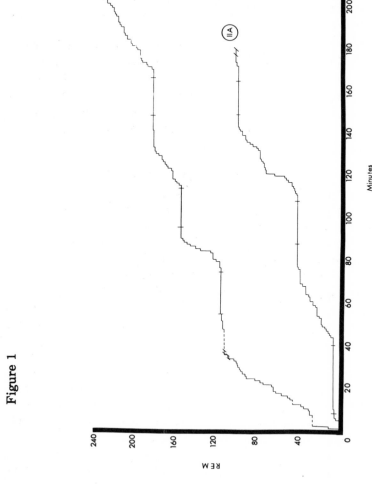

Figures 1, 2 and 3 show cumulative rem (sleeping rapid eye movements) for individual neonates one to four days post-partum. The number of rem is cumulated for each minute in such a way that 2 rem/min. would produce a 45° angle. Each record starts with sleep onset and ends with the termination of sleep. The first (I) and second (II) nights of recording from the inter-feeding period during the first (A) or second (B) half of the night are shown for each of the three infants. Fig. 1 shows normal day-to-day decline. It can be seen that this decline has a marked effect on the first 40 minutes of rem. Fig. 2 and 3 show dramatic reversal of the usual decline by "rebound" in two neonates born to mothers on phenothiazine medication during pregnancy.

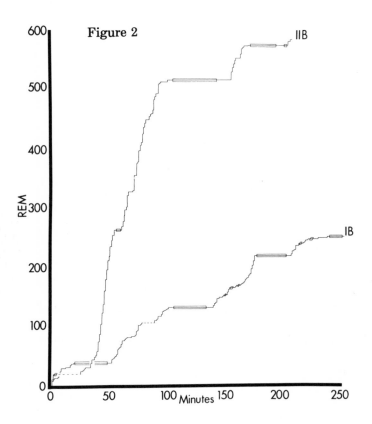

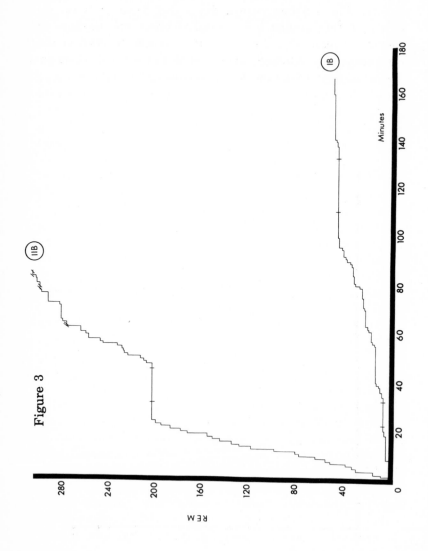

Figure 3

In our departures from conventional methodology, we have emphasized the direct observation of behavior, such as the spontaneous startle and loem; we have modified sleep stage scoring procedures to make them more suited to the subject, and used techniques such as cumulative recording to better reveal overall pattern. Cumulative rem recording emphasizes physiology. We also use films speeding behavior by a factor of 24 to provide a complementary approach emphasizing behavior and providing a surprisingly effective way of staging sleep of some neonates (32,33).

Whatever the implications of our particular findings, certain general conclusions are supported by the experience already described in this paper: Neonate sleep has repeatedly proved to have readily detected, highly organized individual patterning at both fine and gross levels. This patterning implies organization and timing like that implied by at least three neurophysiologically based theories of perception, attention and thought, as well as by Piaget's concept of "schema." Replicated studies have supported our belief that a neonate sleep characteristic, loem, is correlated with skill at tasks designed to measure a basis for developing waking object representation (28, 29). The tasks were obtained by extending a familiar Piaget-type scale downward. Disruption of this neurophysiological organization may be revealed in neonate sleep. There it may have implications for theories regarding the neurophysiological basis for schizophrenia, for the medication of pregnant psychotics and preventable consequences for subsequent childhood psychopathology.

Prevention can take many directions. Simply proposing neonate research to expectant parents and their doctors has desirable effects. In the case of expectant schizophrenics, it focuses attention on perinatal factors such as those increasing the probability of fetal or neonatal anoxia (34). Delivery anaesthesia has already been given attention, but what of maternal tranquilizers potentiating the effects of anaesthesia? The "rem rebound" phenomenon may aid in more precisely assessing how much the infant's nervous system is affected by maternal medication. Could vulnerability to perinatal factors be due in part to their reduction of the infant's tolerance to stresses such as normal noise during sleep? A loss of cumulative rem patterning or reduction of rem rate in the presence of noise would provide a clue to such a loss of tolerance.

In the face of psychology's preoccupation with waking social behavior and with the complexities of psychopathology, it would be presumptuous to suggest that some children have psychopathology simply because they did not have organized sleep during infancy and so were unable to achieve necessary parts of the development of a neurophysiological basis for perception, thought and attention. However, if we wish to understand and prevent childhood psychopathology we must test just such hypotheses. If lack of quiet sleep is a cause of future disorder, rather than simply an indicator of its basis, then it is useful to find that previous neonate sleep research shows ways in which neonate quiet sleep might be increased (35).

If disordered sleep is an indicator of a deficient neuro-physiological basis for developing social perception and interaction, then it is useful to find that neonate sleep research is one of the many sources of methods for aiding the development of early social interaction (36,37). By focusing attention on the behavior of the sleeping neonate, research has led to a concern with human ethology (behavioral mechanisms of the sort promoted in animal species by evolution). Whatever the implications of neonate sleep characteristics, they will be more meaningful and can be used more effectively in prevention of childhood psychopathology if we can achieve a better under-standing of the behavioral potential of our species.

ACKNOWLEDGMENTS

1. Preparation of this paper and research described were aided by the Schizophrenia Research Program of the Supreme Council 33 A.A. Scottish Rite, Northern Masonic Jurisdiction. Professional or collaborative assistance on our research and research thinking was received from Ibrahim Turek, M. D., Robert Mosser,M.D., Ronald Gutberlet,M.D., Paul Taylor, M.D., Donald Coleman,M.D. and their supervisors or chairmen. Nancy Minard, MLS edited and discussed the paper extensively. Useful comments were also made by those in the departments with which the author is affiliated.

REFERENCES

1. Hebb, D. O. In *The Organization of Behavior. A Neurophysiological Theory.* Wiley, New York, (1949).

2. Grossman, S. P. In *Essentials of Physiological Psychology.* Wiley, New York, p. 474, (1973).

3. Pribram, K.H. In *Languages of the Brain.* Prentice-Hall, New Jersey, (1971).

4. Jacobsen, E. Electrophysiology of mental activities and introduction to the psychological process of thinking. In *The Psychophysiology of Thinking.* Edited by McGuign, F. J. and Schoonover, R. A. Academic Press, New York, p. 3, (1973).

5. Rechtschaffer, A. and Kales, A. In *Manual of Standardized Terminology, Techniques and Scoring System for Sleep Stages of Human Subjects.* Public Health Service, U. S. Government Printing Office, Washington, D. C., (1968).

6. Broughton, R. Sleep and clinical pathological states. In *The Sleeping Brain: Perspectives in Brain Sciences.* Volume I. Brain Information Service/Brain Research Institute. Univ. Calif., Los Angeles, p. 363, (1972).

7. Mirsky, A. S. *Annu. Rev. Psychol. 20,* 321, (1969).

8. Broughton, R. J. *Science 159,* 1070, (1968).

9. Coleman, D. and Minard, J. In *The sleep of babies: Spontaneous cyclical phenomena during neonate sleep.* Pennsylvania State University, Psychological Cinema Register, (1970).

10. Minard, J. *Psychophysiol. 5,* 233, (1968).

11. Minard, J. *Psychophysiol. 6,* 331, (1969).

12. Minard, J., Quick, G. and Williams, G. A preliminary evaluation of alternative interpretations of neonatal REM: are REMs related? *Psychophysiol. 6*, 332, (1969).

13. Jouvet, M. Neurophysiological and biochemical mechanisms of sleep. In *Sleep: Physiology and Pathology.* Edited by Kales, H. Lippincott, Philadelphia, p. 89, (1969).

14. Jouvet, M. *Science, 3*, 32, (1969).

15. Jouvet, M. *Sleep.* Paper presented to NATO Advanced Studies Symposium on Basic Sleep Mechanisms. Castle Maele, Belgium, (1971), in press.

16. Minard, J. Williams, G., and Coleman, D. A change of possible neurological and psychological significance within the first week of neonate life: sleeping REM rate. American Psychological Association Proceedings, 271, (1969).

17. Petre-Quadens, O. *Acta Neurol. Belg. 69*, 769, (1969).

18. Williams, G. and Minard, J. *Psychophysiol. 6*, 264, (1969).

19. Parmalee, A. *Developmental Aspects of Sleep.* Conference Report #32, Brain Information Service/BRI Publications Office. Univ. Calif., Los Angeles, p. 37, (1973).

20. Piaget, J., In *The Mechanisms of Perception.* Basic Books, New York, (1969).

21. Minard, J. and Krausman, D. Electroencephalogr. *Clin. Neuro. 31*, 99, (1971).

22. Dewan, E. M. *Psychophysiol. 5*, 203, (1968).

23. Zimmerman, J., Stoyva, and Metcalf, *Psychophysiol. 7*, 298, (1970).

24. Berger, R. J. *J. Exp. Anal. Behav. 11,* 311, (1968).

25. Minard, J. and Williams, G. *Psychophysiol. 6,* 266, (1969).

26. Minard, J., Hayhurst, V. and Moore, L. Two studies of the incidence, latency, and correlates of rapid eye movements after the onset of neonate sleep. Paper presented at Eastern Psychological Association Convention, (1971).

27. Minard, J., Mosser, R., Morre, L. *et al. Psychophysiol. 9,* 98, (1972).

28. McElroy, E. The relationship of REM latency at sleep onset to the development of object permanence. Unpublished paper for Education in Human Development #222, University of Maryland, College Park, (1971).

29. McElroy, E. An investigation of the relationship between aspects of maturation and cognitive development among newborn infants. Ph.D. dissertation, University of Maryland, College Park, (1973).

30. Minard, J., Ritz, T. Minard, N. *et al.* Sleep in newborn of clearly, severely schizophrenic mothers: Interesting phenomena and REM rebound. In *Sleep Research* II. Brain Information Service/Brain Research Institute, Univ. Calif., Los Angeles, (1974).

31. Tamer, A., McKey, R., and Arias, D. *J. Pediatrics, 75,* 479, (1969).

32. Minard, J., Meltzer, S., McWilliams, Jun-ko, *et al.* Cumulative REM recording and staging of time-lapse film or polygraph records as complementary indicators of patterning during neonate sleep. In *The Nature of Sleep.* Edited by Jovanovic, J. Fischer-Verlag, Stuttgart, p. 104, (1973).

33. Minard, J., Mosser, R., Turek, I. *et al.* Neonate sleep as a source for possible indicators of effects of stress or of medications given to the mother during pregnancy. In *The Nature of Sleep.* Edited by Jovanovic, U. Fischer-Verlag, Stuttgart, p. 107, (1973).

34. Mednick, S.A., Mura, E., Schulsinger, F. *et al. Soc. Biol. 18,* 103, (1971).

35. Wolff, P.H. *Psychol. Issues 5,* 1, (1966).

36. Minard, J. and Minard, N. Variable social properties of neonate sleep smiles: A social survival hypothesis. In *Sleep Research* II. Brain Information Service/Brain Research Institute, Univ. Calif., Los Angeles, (1974).

37. Meltzer, S. W. The second environment: Sequential behaviors in neonate sleep, related maternal perception; effects of auditory stimulation on neonatal sleep behavior. In *Sleep Research* I. Brain Information Service/Brain Research Inst., Univ. Calif., Los Angeles, (1972).

Index

ABOUT THE OTHER VOLUMES IN THIS SERIES

This series of books on *"Mental Health in Children"* is divided into three monographs. Volume I deals with genetic, family and community aspects, as is highlighted in this monograph. Transcultural and societal systems are also considered.

Volume II deals with the psychological, physiological, neurological, and other aspects. Childhood autism is also included in this volume and Drs. Christozov, Wolman, Magaro and Ritvo have discussed the various aspects of autism in this volume. The other thirty papers include comprehensive papers on various aspects like psychophysiological indices of development, cerebral evoked responses, EEG studies, minimal brain dysfunction, hyperkinetic syndrome, sleep etc.

The contributing authors of Volume II include Drs. Adams, Barton, Bernstein, Blumberg, Christozov, Dudley, Dustman, Dykman, Greenberg, Hersh, Hutt, Johnson, Kohn, Karrer, Lansdown, Lipmann, Magaro, McConville, McKay, Minard, O'Malley, Ostrov, Ritvo, Sechzer, Seigel, Stern, Straumanis, Silverman, Tarter, White, Wolman and their colleagues.

Volume III deals with the psychiatric, diagnostic, basic biological, biochemical, therapeutic aspects, and also includes language disorders, behavior modification, longitudinal studies and program analysis. The contributing authors to this volume include Drs. Alderton, Bender, Braun, Brittin, Bruggen, Cheek, Christozov, Clausen, Coleman, Connolly, Cowen, Crow, Cytrynbaum, Friedhoff, Hansburgh, Hertzig, Hirt, Gottschalk, Klinge, Koch, Langenbeck, Manowitz, Marino, Melonascino, Narsimhachari, Olson, Piggot, Rapaport, Schiefelbush, Shapiro, Vom Saal, Wadeson, Windle, Wolpert and their associates.

The series is complemented with a companion volume on "Psychopharmacology of Childhood" which incorporates the various pharmacotherapeutic, psychopharmacologic and related studies. The contributing authors of this volume include Drs. Greenberg, Grinspoon, Koch, Kohn, Ludek, McCabe, Ommen, Schiefelbush, Shopsin, Simeon, Weiss and their associates.